W9-CPD-897

The Gospel of
Sri Ramakrishna

Originally recorded in Bengali
by M, a disciple of the Master

Sri Ramakrishna

The Gospel of
Sri Ramakrishna

*Translated into English
with an Introduction by*
SWAMI NIKHILANANDA

ABRIDGED EDITION

NEW YORK
RAMAKRISHNA-VIVEKANANDA CENTER

THE GOSPEL OF SRI RAMAKRISHNA
(ABRIDGED EDITION)
Copyright © 1942, 1948, 1958, by Swami Nikhilananda
Printed in the United States of America

All rights in this book are reserved.
No part of the book may be reproduced in any
manner whatsoever without written permission
except in the case of brief quotations embodied
in critical articles and reviews. For information
address Ramakrishna-Vivekananda
Center, 17 E. 94th Street,
New York, N.Y. 10028

Sixth Printing 1996

ISBN 0-911206-02-7

Library of Congress Catalog Card No. 58-8948

To the monastic members
of the Ramakrishna Order
and the devotees of Ramakrishna
in all parts of the world,
reflectors of his godliness,
bearers of his universal message,
and my unfailing inspiration

FOREWORD

By way of a Foreword two letters are given here. The first of these was written to M about sixty years ago by Sri Sarada Devi, the wife and companion in spiritual life of Sri Ramakrishna, now universally respected as the Holy Mother. She sent it to him after listening to a reading of Sri Ramakrishna's conversations as recorded in the original work, *Sri Ramakrishna Kathamrita*, in Bengali.

The second letter, which is from Swami Vivekananda, was written to M after the second part of his book was published.

My beloved child,

The words you heard from the Master are true. You need not be afraid to publish them. It was the Master who left these words in your keeping. Now he is bringing them out according to the needs of the time. You should know that people's spiritual consciousness will not be awakened unless these words see the light of day. His words which are in your keeping are true, every one of them. When you read them to me I felt as if he himself was speaking.

MOTHER

Dehra Dun
24th November, 1897

My dear M,

Many, many thanks for your second leaflet. It is indeed wonderful. The move is quite original, and never was the life of a great teacher brought before the public untarnished by the writer's mind as you are doing. The language also is beyond all praise—so fresh, so pointed, and withal so plain and easy. I cannot express in adequate terms how I have enjoyed it. I am really in a transport when I read these words. Strange, isn't it? Our teacher and Lord was so original, and each one of us will have to be original or nothing. I now understand why none of us attempted his life before. It has been reserved for you—this great work. He is with you, evidently.

With love and namaskar,

VIVEKANANDA

P. S. Socratic dialogues are Plato all over. You are entirely hidden. Moreover, the dramatic part is infinitely beautiful. Everybody likes it, here or in the West.

PREFACE

This book is a thoroughly revised edition of *Ramakrishna: Prophet of New India,* which was published in 1948. The standard edition of *The Gospel of Sri Ramakrishna,* published in 1942, is already familiar to students of religion and philosophy in India and the West, and especially to those who, in their practice of spiritual discipline, look to Hinduism for help and guidance.

The present edition is an abridgement of the original work. There are two main reasons for its publication. First, the unabridged edition contains many references to Hindu mythology and folklore with which the general Western reader is unfamiliar, as well as discussions of certain recondite aspects of Hinduism. These features create unnecessary difficulties. Second, this latter edition, being a complete translation of all the authentically recorded conversations of Sri Ramakrishna, contains repetitions which are largely responsible for its one thousand and sixty-three pages. It is not convenient to carry such a book around or to use it for daily devotional study. The abridged version removes the difficulties, yet without in any way minimizing the importance of the regular edition. On the contrary, it is hoped that the present volume may stimulate the reader's desire to read all the recorded words of Sri Ramakrishna. We are grateful to Mr. J. Wendell Parr for his generosity in helping to defray the expense of printing this edition.

Utmost care has been taken to present the abridged edition as a book complete in itself. The teachings have not been distorted in order to reduce the size. The over-all impression of the big book will be found in the small one. The lengthy Introduction has been retained with slight omissions. It gives a biographical sketch of Sri Ramakrishna and deals with the various aspects of Hindu religious thought discussed in the *Gospel*. Appendix A gives a short biography of Sri Chaitanya, another God-man of India often mentioned in the book. Appendix B contains a detailed discussion of Tantra, a system of religious philosophy intimately related to Sri Ramakrishna's teachings. The Glossary will be a help in understanding names and terms unfamiliar to Western readers. The diacritical marks are explained under Notes on Pronunciation.

The Gospel of Sri Ramakrishna is the literal translation of the *Sri Sri Ramakrishna Kathāmrita,* written in the Bengali language, which contains Sri Ramakrishna's conversations with his disciples, devotees, and visitors. It was recorded, under the pseudonym of "M," by Mahendranath Gupta, who committed the conversations to his diary, as he heard them, from day to day. They possess the authenticity and vividness of stenographic reports.

Sri Ramakrishna, whose name became a household word in India within fifty years of his death, is now becoming known to Europe and America through the writings of Swami Vivekananda and the activities of the monks of the Ramakrishna Order. Among the savants of the West, Max Müller and Romain Rolland have written about him. Both in India and in the outside world men have begun to recognize him as belonging in the line of such religious prophets as

Krishna, Buddha, and Christ. He represents the very core of the time-honoured spiritual wisdom of India. In this age of reason and scepticism he brings us a direct report from the realm of the Spirit. His utterances bear evidence of his communion with God. Sri Ramakrishna's body and senses, mind and ego, purified by spiritual disciplines, became instruments for the revelation of supersensuous truths. His words are direct and graphic. They silence all doubts. They have an impelling power to subdue the mind's restlessness and give it peace and certitude.

The malady of our age, as indeed of every age, is spiritual. The cause of humanity's sickness is attachment to lust and greed, or, to use Sri Ramakrishna's expressive words, "woman" and "gold." The undisciplined ego has aggravated this illness. The remedy lies in its control. Sri Ramakrishna's life is a demonstration of the triumph of Spirit over matter. He reached a depth in spiritual consciousness which transcends time and space and has a universal appeal. His life and teachings attract all sincere souls, no matter what their faith or creed.

NIKHILANANDA

New York
October 15, 1957

CONTENTS

NOTES ON THE PRONUNCIATION OF TRANSLITERATED SANSKRIT AND VERNACULAR WORDS

a	has the sound of				*o* in *come*.
ā	"	"	"	"	*a* in *far*.
e, ē	"	"	"	"	*a* in *evade*.[1]
i	"	"	"	"	*ee* in *feel*.
o	"	"	"	"	*o* in *note*.
u	"	"	"	"	*u* in *rule*.
ai, ay	has the sound of				*oy* in *boy*.
au	"	"	"	"	*o* pronounced deep in the throat.
ch	"	"	"	"	*ch* in *church*.
ḍ	"	"	"	"	hard *d* in English.
g	"	"	"	"	*g* in *god*.
jn	"	"	"	"	hard *gy* in English.[2]
ś	"	"	"	"	*sh* in *shut*.

sh may be pronounced as in English.
t and d are pronounced as in French.
th has the sound of *t-h* in *boat-house*.

Other consonants appearing in the transliterations are pronounced as in English.

Diacritical marks have generally not been used in proper names belonging to recent times or in modern and well-known geographical names.

Sri Ramakrishna is pronounced in Bengal as Śri Rāmkrishna.

---

[1] Final *e* in proper names is mute.
[2] Jnāna is pronounced as *gyāna*.

Introduction

INTRODUCTION

By Swami Nikhilananda

Sᴿɪ Rᴀᴍᴀᴋʀɪsʜɴᴀ was born at Kāmārpukur, a village in the Hooghly District which preserved during the last century the idyllic simplicity of the rural areas of Bengal. Situated far from the railway, it was untouched by the glamour of the city. It contained rice-fields, tall palms, royal banyans, a few lakes, and two cremation grounds. South of the village a stream took its leisurely course. A mango orchard dedicated by a neighbouring zemindar to the public use was frequented by the boys for their noonday sports. A highway passed through the village to the great temple of Jagannāth at Puri, and the villagers, most of whom were farmers and craftsmen, entertained many passing holy men and pilgrims. The dull round of the rural life was broken by lively festivals, the observance of sacred days, religious singing, and other innocent pleasures.

About his parents Sri Ramakrishna once said: "My mother was the personification of rectitude and gentleness. She did not know much about the ways of the world; innocent of the art of concealment, she would say what was in her mind. People loved her for her open-heartedness. My father, an orthodox brāhmin, never accepted gifts from the śudras. He spent much of his time in worship and meditation, and in repeating God's name and chanting His glories. Whenever in his daily prayers he invoked the Goddess Gāyatri, his chest flushed with emotion and tears rolled down his

1

cheeks. He spent his leisure hours making garlands
for the Family Deity, Raghuvir."

Khudiram Chattopadhyaya and Chandra Devi, the
parents of Sri Ramakrishna, were married in 1799. At
that time Khudiram was living in his ancestral village
of Dereypore, not far from Kāmārpukur. Their first
son, Ramkumar, was born in 1805, and their first
daughter, Katyayani, in 1810. In 1814 Khudiram
was ordered by his landlord to bear false witness in
court against a neighbour. When he refused to do so,
the landlord brought a false case against him and deprived him of his ancestral property. Thus dispossessed,
he arrived, at the invitation of another landlord, in the
quiet village of Kāmārpukur, where he was given a
dwelling and about an acre of fertile land. The crops
from this little property were enough to meet his
family's simple needs. Here he lived in simplicity,
dignity, and contentment.

Ten years after his coming to Kāmārpukur, Khudiram made a pilgrimage on foot to Rāmeśwar, at the
southern extremity of India. The image of Śiva worshipped there under the name of Rāmeśwara, the Lord
of Rāma, was said to have been installed by Rāma on
His way back to India after the destruction of Rāvana,
the monster-king of Ceylon. Two years later was born
his second son, whom he named Rameswar. Again in
1835, at the age of sixty, he made a pilgrimage, this
time to Gayā. Here, from ancient times, Hindus have
come from the four corners of India to offer food and
drink at the sacred footprint of the Lord Vishnu for
the satisfaction of the souls of their departed ancestors
and relatives. At this holy place Khudiram had a dream
in which the Lord Vishnu promised to be born as his
son. And Chandra Devi, too, in front of the Śiva temple

at Kāmārpukur, had a vision indicating the birth of a divine child. Upon his return the husband found that she had conceived.

It was on February 18, 1836, that the child, to be known afterwards as Ramakrishna and honoured as the God-man of modern India, was born. In memory of the dream at Gayā he was given the name of Gadadhar, the "Bearer of the Mace," an epithet of Vishnu. Three years later a little sister was born.

BOYHOOD

Gadadhar grew up into a healthy and restless boy, full of fun and sweet mischief. He was intelligent and precocious and endowed with a prodigious memory. On his father's lap he learnt by heart the names of his ancestors and the hymns to the gods and goddesses, and at the village school he was taught to read and write. But his greatest delight was to listen to recitals of stories from Hindu mythology and the epics. These he would afterwards recount from memory, to the great joy of the villagers. Painting he enjoyed; the art of moulding images of the gods and goddesses he learnt from the potters. But arithmetic was his great aversion.

At the age of six or seven Gadadhar had his first experience of spiritual ecstasy. One day in June or July, when he was walking along a narrow path between paddy-fields, eating the puffed rice that he carried in a basket, he looked up at the sky and saw a beautiful, dark thunder-cloud. As it spread, rapidly enveloping the whole sky, a flight of snow-white cranes passed in front of it. The beauty of the contrast overwhelmed the boy. He fell to the ground, unconscious, and the puffed rice went in all directions. Some villagers found him and carried him home in their arms. Gadadhar said later that in that state he had experienced an indescribable joy.

Gadadhar was seven years old when his father died. This incident profoundly affected him. For the first time the boy realized that life on earth was impermanent. Unobserved by others, he began to slip into the mango orchard or into one of the cremation grounds, and he spent hours absorbed in his own thoughts. He also became more helpful to his mother in the discharge of her household duties. He gave greater attention to reading and hearing the stories recorded in the Purānas. And he became interested in the wandering monks and pious pilgrims who would stop at Kāmārpukur on their way to Puri. These holy men, the custodians of India's spiritual heritage and the living witnesses of the ideal of renunciation of the world and all-absorbing love of God, entertained the little boy with stories from the Hindu epics, stories of saints and prophets, and also stories of their own adventures. He, on his part, fetched their water and fuel and served them in various ways. Meanwhile, he was observing their meditation and worship.

At the age of nine Gadadhar was invested with the sacred thread. This ceremony conferred upon him the privileges of his brāhmin lineage, including the worship of the Family Deity, Raghuvir, and imposed upon him the many strict disciplines of a brāhmin's life. During the ceremony of investiture he shocked his relatives by accepting a meal cooked by his nurse, a śudra woman. His father would never have dreamt of doing such a thing. But in a playful mood Gadadhar had once promised this woman that he would eat her food, and now he fulfilled his plighted word. The woman had piety and religious sincerity, and these were more important to the boy than mere social conventions.

Gadadhar was now permitted to worship Raghuvir. Thus began his first training in meditation. He devoted himself so wholeheartedly to the worship that the stone image very soon appeared to him as the living Lord of the Universe. His tendency to lose himself in contemplation was first noticed at this time. Behind his boyish light-heartedness was seen a deepening of his spiritual nature.

About this time, on the Śivarātri night, consecrated to the worship of Śiva, a dramatic performance was arranged. The principal actor, who was to play the part of Śiva, suddenly fell ill, and Gadadhar was persuaded to act in his place. While friends were dressing him for the role of Śiva—smearing his body with ashes, matting his locks, placing a trident in his hand and a string of rudrāksha beads around his neck—the boy appeared to become absent-minded. He approached the stage with slow and measured step, supported by his friends. He looked the living image of Śiva. The audience loudly applauded what it took to be his skill as an actor, but it was soon discovered that he was really lost in meditation. His countenance was radiant and tears flowed from his eyes. He was lost to the outer world. The effect of this scene on the audience was tremendous. The people felt blessed as by a vision of Śiva Himself. The performance had to be stopped, and the boy's mood lasted till the following morning.

Gadadhar himself now organized a dramatic company with his young friends. The stage was set in the mango orchard. The themes were selected from the stories of the *Rāmāyana* and the *Mahābhārata*. Gadadhar knew by heart almost all the roles, having heard them from professional actors. His favourite theme was the Vrindāvan episode of Krishna's life, depicting the exquisite love-stories of Krishna and the milkmaids and cowherd boys. Gadadhar would play the parts of Rādhā or Krishna and would often lose himself in the character he was portraying. His natural feminine grace heightened the dramatic effect. The mango orchard would ring with the loud kirtan of the boys. Lost in song and merry-making, Gadadhar became indifferent to the routine of school.

In 1849 Ramkumar, the eldest brother, went to Calcutta to improve the financial condition of the family.

Gadadhar was on the threshold of youth. He had become the pet of the women of the village. They loved to hear him talk, sing, or recite from the holy books. They enjoyed his knack of imitating voices. Their woman's instinct recognized the innate purity and guilelessness of this boy of clear skin, beaming eyes, smiling face, and inexhaustible fun. The pious elderly women looked upon him as Gopāla, the Baby Krishna, and the younger ones saw in him the youthful Krishna of Vrindāvan. He himself so idealized the love of the gopis for Krishna that he sometimes yearned to be born as a woman in order to be able to love Sri Krishna with all his heart. He would be born in a brāhmin family and become a widow soon after marriage. His sole occupation would be to meditate on Krishna, worship Him, and cook for Him, devoting spare moments to spinning. During the cow-dust hour, at sundown, so Sri Ramakrishna dreamt, the widow, with sweets made by her own hands, would await the arrival of her Beloved. The very thought filled his mind with great joy.

COMING TO CALCUTTA

At the age of sixteen Gadadhar was summoned to Calcutta by his elder brother Ramkumar, who wished assistance in his priestly duties. Ramkumar had opened a Sanskrit academy to supplement his income, and it was his intention gradually to turn his younger brother's mind to education. Gadadhar applied himself heart and soul to his new duty as family priest to a number of Calcutta families. His worship was very different from that of the professional priests. He spent hours decorating the images and singing hymns and devotional songs; he performed with love the other duties of his office. People were impressed with his ardour. But to his studies he paid scant attention.

Ramkumar did not at first oppose the ways of his temperamental brother. He wanted Gadadhar to become used to the conditions of city life. But one day he decided to warn the boy about his indifference to the world. After all, in the near future Gadadhar must, as a householder, earn his livelihood through the performance of his brāhminical duties; and these required a thorough knowledge of Hindu law, astrology, and kindred subjects. He gently admonished Gadadhar and asked him to pay more attention to his studies. But the boy replied spiritedly: "Brother, what shall I do with a mere bread-winning education? I would rather acquire that wisdom which will illumine my heart and give me satisfaction for ever."

The anguish of the inner soul of India found expression through these passionate words of the young Gadadhar. For what did his unsophisticated eye see around him in Calcutta, at that time the metropolis

of India and the centre of modern culture and learning?
Greed and lust held sway in the higher levels of society,
and the occasional religious practices were merely
outer forms from which the soul had long ago departed.
Gadadhar had never seen anything like this at Kāmārpukur among the simple and pious villagers. The sādhus
and wandering monks whom he had served in his boyhood had revealed to him an altogether different India.
He had been impressed by their devotion and purity,
their self-control and renunciation. He had learnt from
them and from his own intuition that the ideal of
life as taught by the ancient sages of India was the
realization of God.

Ramkumar could hardly understand the import of
his young brother's reply. He described in bright
colours the happy and easy life of scholars in Calcutta
society. But Gadadhar intuitively felt that scholars un-
inspired by knowledge of God were, to use one of his
own vivid illustrations, like so many vultures, soaring
high on the wings of intellect, but with their eyes fixed
on the charnel-pit of greed and lust. So he stood firm
and Ramkumar had to give way.

KĀLI TEMPLE AT DAKSHINESWAR

At that time there lived in Calcutta a rich widow
named Rāni Rasmani, belonging to the śudra caste,
who was known far and wide not only for her business
ability, courage, and intelligence, but also for her
largeness of heart, piety, and devotion to God. She was
assisted in the management of her vast property by
her son-in-law Mathuranath Biswas.

In 1847 the Rāni purchased twenty acres of land
at Dakshineswar, a village about four miles north of

Calcutta. Here she created a temple garden and constructed several temples. Her Ishta, or Chosen Ideal, was the Divine Mother, Kāli.

The temple garden stands directly on the east bank of the Ganges. The northern section of the land and a portion to the east contain an orchard, flower gardens, and two small reservoirs. The southern section is paved with brick and mortar. The visitor arriving by boat ascends the steps of an imposing bathing-ghāt which leads to the chāndni, a roofed terrace, on either side of which stand in a row six temples of Śiva. East of the terrace and the Śiva temples is a large court, paved, rectangular in shape, and running north and south. Two temples stand in the centre of this court, the larger one, to the south and facing south, being dedicated to Kāli, and the smaller one, facing the Ganges, to Rādhākānta, that is, Krishna, the Consort of Rādhā. Nine domes with spires surmount the temple of Kāli, and before it stands the spacious nātmandir, or music hall, the terrace of which is supported by stately pillars. At the northwest and southwest corners of the temple compound are two nahabats, or music towers, from which music flows at different times of day, especially at sunup, noon, and sundown, when the worship is performed in the temples. Three sides of the paved courtyard—all except the west—are lined with rooms set apart for kitchens, storerooms, dining rooms, and quarters for the temple staff and guests. The chamber in the northwest angle, just beyond the last of the Śiva temples, is of special interest to us; for here Sri Ramakrishna was to spend a considerable part of his life. To the west of this chamber is a semicircular porch overlooking the river. In front of the porch runs a footpath, north and south, and beyond the path is a large garden and, below the garden, the Ganges. The orchard to the north of the buildings contains the Panchavati, the banyan, and the bel-tree, associated with Sri Ramakrishna's spiritual practices. Outside and to the north of the temple compound proper is the kuthi, or bungalow, used by members of Rāni Rasmani's family visiting the garden. And north of the temple garden, separated from it by a high wall, is a powder-magazine belonging to the British Government.

ŚIVA

In the twelve Śiva temples are installed the emblems of the Great God of renunciation in His various aspects, which are worshipped daily with proper rites. Śiva requires few articles of worship. White flowers and bel-leaves and a little Ganges water offered with devotion are enough to satisfy the benign Deity and win from Him the boon of liberation.

RĀDHĀKĀNTA

The temple of Rādhākānta, also known as the temple of Vishnu, contains the images of Rādhā and Krishna, the symbol of union with God through ecstatic love. The two images stand on a pedestal facing the west. The floor is paved with marble. From the ceiling of the porch hang chandeliers protected from dust by coverings of red cloth. Canvas screens shield the images from the rays of the setting sun. Close to the threshold of the inner shrine is a small brass cup containing holy water. Pious visitors reverently drink a few drops from the vessel.

Kālī

The main temple is dedicated to Kālī, the Divine Mother, here worshipped as Bhavatārini, the Saviour of the Universe. The floor of this temple also is paved with marble. The basalt image of the Mother, dressed in gorgeous gold brocade, stands on a white marble image of the prostrate body of Her Divine Consort, Śiva, the symbol of the Absolute. On the feet of the Goddess are, among other ornaments, anklets of gold. Her arms are decked with jewelled ornaments of gold. She wears necklaces of gold and pearls, a golden garland of human heads, and a girdle of human arms. She wears a golden crown, golden earrings, and a golden nose-ring with a pearl-drop. She has four arms. The lower left hand holds a severed human head and the upper grips a bloodstained sabre. One right hand offers boons to Her children; the other allays their fear. The majesty of Her posture can hardly be described. It combines the terror of destruction with the reassurance of motherly tenderness. For She is the Cosmic Power, the totality of the universe, a glorious harmony of the pairs of opposites. She deals out death, as She creates and preserves. She has three eyes, the third being the eye of Divine Wisdom; they strike dismay into the wicked, yet pour out affection for Her devotees.

The whole symbolic world is represented in the temple garden—the Trinity of the Nature Mother (Kālī), the Absolute (Śiva), and Love (Rādhākānta), the Arch spanning heaven and earth. The terrific Goddess of Tantra, the soul-enthralling Flute-player of the *Bhāgavata*, and the Self-absorbed Absolute of the Vedas live together, creating the greatest synthesis of religions. All aspects of Reality are represented there. But of this divine household, Kāli is the pivot, the sovereign Mistress. She is Prakriti, the Procreatrix, Nature, the Destroyer, the Creator. Nay, She is something greater and deeper still for those who have eyes to see. She is the Universal Mother, "my Mother," as Ramakrishna would say, the All-powerful, who reveals Herself to Her children under different aspects and Divine Incarnations, the Visible God, who leads the elect to the Invisible Reality; and if it so pleases Her, She takes away the last trace of ego from created beings and merges it in the consciousness of the Absolute, the undifferentiated Godhead. Through Her grace the finite ego loses itself in the illimitable Ego—Ātman—Brahman.

Rāni Rasmani spent a fortune for the construction of the temple garden and another fortune for its dedication ceremony, which took place on May 31, 1855.

Sri Ramakrishna—henceforth we shall call Gadadhar by his familiar name[1]—came to the temple garden with his elder brother Ramkumar, who was appointed as a priest of the Kāli temple. Sri Ramakrishna did not at first approve of Ramkumar's working for the śudra Rasmani. The example of their orthodox father was still fresh in his mind. He objected also to eating the cooked offerings of the temple, since, according to orthodox Hindu custom, such food can be offered to the Deity only in the house of a brāhmin. But the holy atmosphere of the temple grounds, the solitude of the surrounding woods, the loving care of his brother,

---

[1] No definite information is available as to the origin of this name. Most probably it was given by Mathur Babu, as Ramlal, Sri Ramakrishna's nephew, has said, on the authority of his uncle himself.

the respect shown him by Rāni Rasmani and Mathur Babu, the living presence of the Goddess Kāli in the temple, and, above all, the proximity of the sacred Ganges, which Sri Ramakrishna always held in the highest respect, gradually overcame his disapproval, and he began to feel at home.

Within a very short time Sri Ramakrishna attracted the notice of Mathur Babu, who was impressed by the young man's religious fervour and wanted him to participate in the worship in the Kāli temple. But Sri Ramakrishna loved his freedom and was indifferent to any worldly career. The position of priest in a temple founded by a rich woman did not appeal to his mind. Further, he hesitated to take upon himself the responsibility for the costly ornaments and jewelry of the temple. Mathur had to wait for a suitable occasion.

At this time there came to Dakshineswar a youth of sixteen, destined to play an important role in Sri Ramakrishna's life. Hriday, a distant nephew[2] of Sri Ramakrishna, hailed from Sihore, a village not far from Kāmārpukur, and had been his boyhood friend. Clever, exceptionally energetic, and endowed with great presence of mind, he moved, as will be seen later, like a shadow about his uncle and was always ready to help him, even at the sacrifice of his personal comfort. He was destined to be a mute witness of many of the spiritual experiences of Sri Ramakrishna, and the caretaker of his body during the stormy days of his spiritual practice. Hriday came to Dakshineswar in search of a job, and Sri Ramakrishna was glad to see him.

[2] Hriday's mother was the daughter of Sri Ramakrishna's aunt (Khudiram's sister). Such a degree of relationship is termed in Bengal that of a "distant nephew."

Unable to resist the persuasion of Mathur Babu,
Sri Ramakrishna at last entered the temple service on
condition that Hriday should be asked to assist him.
His first duty was to dress and decorate the image of
Kālī.

One day the priest of the Rādhākānta temple accidentally dropped the image of Krishna on the floor,
breaking one of its legs. The pundits advised the Rāni
to install a new image, since the worship of an image
with a broken limb was against the scriptural injunctions. But the Rāni was fond of the image, and she
asked Sri Ramakrishna's opinion. In an abstracted mood
he said: "This solution is ridiculous. If a son-in-law
of the Rāni broke his leg, would she discard him and
put another in his place? Wouldn't she rather arrange
for his treatment? Why should she not do the same
thing in this case too? Let the image be repaired and
worshipped as before." It was a simple, straightforward
solution and was accepted by the Rāni. Sri Ramakrishna
himself mended the break. The priest was dismissed
for his carelessness, and at Mathur Babu's earnest request Sri Ramakrishna accepted the office of priest in
the Rādhākānta temple.

SRI RAMAKRISHNA AS A PRIEST

Born in an orthodox brāhmin family, Sri Ramakrishna knew the formalities of worship, its rites and
rituals. The innumerable gods and goddesses of the
Hindu religion are the human aspects of the indescribable and incomprehensible Spirit, projected by It for
the benefit of the finite human mind. They understand
and appreciate human love and emotion, help men to
realize their secular and spiritual ideals, and ultimately

enable men to attain liberation from the miseries of phenomenal life. The Source of light, intelligence, wisdom, and strength is the One alone from whom comes the fulfilment of desire. Yet, as long as a man is bound by his human limitations, he finds it easy to worship God through human forms. He must use human symbols. Therefore Hinduism asks its devotees to look on God as the ideal father, the ideal mother, the ideal husband, the ideal son, or the ideal friend. But the name ultimately leads to the Nameless, the form to the Formless, the word to the Silence, the emotion to the serene realization of Peace in Existence-Knowledge-Bliss Absolute. The gods gradually merge in the Godhead. But until that realization is achieved, the devotee cannot dissociate human factors from his worship. Therefore the Deity is bathed and clothed and decked with ornaments. He is fed and put to sleep. He is propitiated with hymns, songs, and prayers. And there are appropriate rites connected with all these functions. For instance, to secure for himself external purity, the priest bathes himself in holy water and puts on a holy cloth. He purifies the mind and the sense-organs by appropriate meditations. He fortifies the place of worship against evil forces by drawing around it circles of fire and water. He awakens the different spiritual centres of the body and invokes the Supreme Spirit in his heart. Then he transfers the Supreme Spirit to the image before him and worships the image, regarding it no longer as clay or stone, but as the embodiment of Spirit, throbbing with Life and Consciousness. After the worship the Supreme Spirit is recalled from the image to Its true sanctuary, the heart of the priest. The real devotee knows the absurdity of worshipping the Transcendental Reality with material articles—clothing That which pervades the whole universe and the beyond, putting on a pedestal That which cannot be limited by space, feeding That which is disembodied and incorporeal, singing before That whose glory the music of the spheres tries vainly to proclaim. But through these rites the devotee aspires to go ultimately beyond rites and rituals, forms and names, words and praise, and to realize God as the All-pervading Consciousness.

Hindu priests are thoroughly acquainted with the rites of worship, but few of them are aware of their underlying significance. Ignorant priests move their hands and limbs mechanically, in obedience to the letter of the scriptures, and repeat the holy mantras like parrots. But from the very beginning the inner meaning of these rites was revealed to Sri Ramakrishna. As he sat facing the image, a strange transformation came over his mind. While going through the prescribed ceremonies he would actually find himself encircled by a wall of fire protecting him and the place of worship from unspiritual vibrations, or he would feel the rising of the mystic Kundalini through the different centres of the body. The glow on his face, his deep absorption, and the intense atmosphere of the temple impressed everyone who saw him worship the Deity.

Ramkumar wanted Sri Ramakrishna to learn the intricate rituals of the worship of Kāli. To become a priest of Kāli one must undergo a special form of initiation from a qualified guru, and for Sri Ramakrishna a suitable brāhmin was found. But no sooner had the brāhmin initiated him by uttering the holy word in his ear than Sri Ramakrishna, overwhelmed with emotion, gave a loud cry and plunged into deep concentration.

Mathur begged Sri Ramakrishna to take charge of the worship in the Kāli temple. The young priest pleaded his incompetence and his ignorance of the scriptures. Mathur insisted that devotion and sincerity would more than compensate for any lack of formal knowledge and make the Divine Mother manifest Herself through the image. In the end Sri Ramakrishna had to yield to Mathur's request. He became the priest of Kāli.

In 1856 Ramkumar breathed his last. Sri Ramakrishna had already witnessed his father's death. Even then he had come to realize how impermanent is life on earth. The more he was convinced of the transitory nature of worldly things, the more eager he became to realize God, the Fountain of Immortality.

THE FIRST VISION OF KĀLI

And, indeed, he soon discovered what a strange Goddess he had chosen to serve. He became gradually enmeshed in the web of Her all-pervading presence. To the ignorant She is, to be sure, the image of destruction; but he found in Her the benign, all-loving Mother. Her neck is encircled with a garland of heads, and Her waist with a girdle of human arms, and two of Her hands hold weapons of death, and Her eyes dart a glance of fire, but, strangely enough, Ramakrishna felt in Her breath the soothing touch of tender love and saw in Her the Seed of Immortality. She stands on the bosom of Her Consort, Śiva; it is because She is the Śakti, the Power, inseparable from the Absolute. She is surrounded by jackals and other unholy creatures, the denizens of the cremation ground. But is not the Ultimate Reality above holiness and un-

holiness? She appears to be reeling under the spell of
wine. But who would create this inscrutable mad world
unless under the influence of a divine drunkenness?
Is not disorder the very foundation of our seemingly
ordered universe? The cosmos has evolved out of the
primeval chaos. Kāli is the highest symbol of all the
forces of Nature, the synthesis of their antinomies,
the Ultimate Divine in the form of Woman. She now
became to Sri Ramakrishna the only Reality, and the
world became an unsubstantial shadow. Into Her
worship he poured his soul. Before him She stood as
the transparent portal to the shrine of the ineffable
Brahman.

The worship in the temple intensified Sri Ramakrishna's yearning for a living vision of the Mother of
the Universe. He began to spend in meditation the
time not actually employed in the temple service; and
for this purpose he selected an extremely solitary place.
A deep jungle, thick with underbrush and prickly
plants, lay to the north of the temples. Used at one
time as a burial ground, it was shunned by people even
during the daytime for fear of evil spirits. There Sri
Ramakrishna began to spend the whole night in meditation, returning to his room only in the morning with
eyes swollen as though from much weeping. While
meditating he would lay aside his cloth and his brāhminical thread. Explaining this strange conduct, he
once said to Hriday: "Don't you know that when one
thinks of God one should be freed from all ties? From
our very birth we have the eight fetters of hatred,
shame, lineage, pride of good conduct, fear, secretiveness, caste, and grief. The sacred thread reminds me
that I am a brāhmin and therefore superior to all.
When calling on the Mother one has to set aside all

such ideas." Hriday thought his uncle was becoming insane.

As his love for God deepened, he began either to forget or to drop the formalities of worship. Sitting before the image, he would spend hours singing the devotional songs of great devotees of the Mother, like Kamalākānta and Rāmprasād. Those rhapsodical songs, describing the direct vision of God, only intensified Sri Ramakrishna's longing. He felt the pangs of a child separated from its mother. Sometimes, in agony, he would rub his face against the ground and weep so bitterly that people, thinking he had lost his earthly mother, would sympathize with him in his grief. Sometimes, in moments of scepticism, he would cry: "Art Thou real, Mother, or is it all fiction—mere poetry without any reality? If Thou dost exist, why do I not see Thee? Is religion a mere fantasy and art Thou only a figment of man's imagination?" Sometimes he would sit on the prayer carpet for two hours like an inert object. He began to behave in an abnormal manner, most of the time unconscious of the world. He almost gave up food; and sleep left him altogether.

But he did not have to wait very long. He has thus described his first vision of the Mother: "I felt as if my heart were being squeezed like a wet towel. I was overpowered with a great restlessness and a fear that it might not be my lot to realize Her in this life. I could not bear the separation from Her any longer. Life seemed to be not worth living. Suddenly my glance fell on the sword that was kept in the Mother's temple, and I determined to put an end to my life. I jumped up like a madman and seized it, when suddenly the blessed Mother revealed Herself. The buildings with their different parts, the temple, and everything else vanished from my sight, leaving no trace whatsoever, and in their stead I saw a limitless, infinite, effulgent Ocean of Bliss. As far as the eye could see, the shining billows were madly rushing at me from all sides with a terrific noise, to swallow me up. I was panting for breath. I was caught in the rush and collapsed, unconscious. What was happening in the outside world I did not know; but within me there was a steady flow of undiluted bliss, altogether new, and I felt the presence of the Divine Mother." On his lips when he regained consciousness of the world was the word "Mother."

GOD-INTOXICATED STATE

Yet this was only a foretaste of the intense experiences to come. The first glimpse of the Divine Mother made him the more eager for Her uninterrupted vision. He wanted to see Her both in meditation and with eyes open. But the Mother began to play a teasing game of hide-and-seek with him, intensifying both his joy and his suffering. Weeping bitterly during moments of separation from Her, he would pass into a trance and then find Her standing before him, smiling, talking, consoling, bidding him be of good cheer, and instructing him. During this period of spiritual practice he had many uncommon experiences. When he sat to meditate, he would hear strange clicking sounds in the joints of his legs, as if someone were locking them up, one after the other, to keep him motionless; and at the conclusion of his meditation he would again hear the same sounds, this time unlocking them and leaving him free to move about. He would see flashes like a swarm of fireflies floating before his eyes, or a sea of deep mist around him, with luminous waves of molten silver. Again, from a sea of translucent mist the Mother would appear to him: first Her feet, then Her waist, breast, face, and head, finally Her whole person; he would feel Her breath and hear Her voice. Worshipping in the temple, sometimes he would become exalted, sometimes he would remain motionless as stone, sometimes he would almost collapse from excessive emotion. Many of his actions, being contrary to all tradition, seemed sacrilegious to people. He would take a flower and touch it to his own head, body, and feet, and then offer it to the Goddess. Or, like a drunkard, he would reel to the throne of the Mother, touch Her chin by way of showing his affection for Her, and sing, talk, joke, laugh, and dance. Or he would take a morsel of food from the plate and hold it to Her mouth, begging Her to eat it, and would not be satisfied till he was convinced that She had really eaten. After the Mother had been put to sleep at night, from his own room he would hear Her ascending to the upper storey of the temple with the light steps of a happy girl, Her anklets jingling. Then he would discover Her standing with flowing hair, Her black form silhouetted against the sky of the night, looking at the Ganges or at the distant lights of Calcutta.

Naturally the temple officials took him for an insane person. His worldly well-wishers brought him to skilled physicians; but no medicine could cure his malady. Many a time he doubted his sanity himself; for he had been sailing across an uncharted sea with no earthly guide to direct him. His only haven of security was the Divine Mother Herself. To Her he would pray: "I do not know what these things are. I am ignorant of mantras and the scriptures. Teach me, Mother, how

to realize Thee. Who else can help me? Art Thou not
my only refuge and guide?" And the sustaining presence of the Mother never failed him in his distress or
doubt. Even those who criticized his conduct were
greatly impressed with his purity, guilelessness, truthfulness, self-control, and holiness. They felt an uplifting influence in his presence.

It is said that samādhi, or trance, no more than opens
the portal of the spiritual realm. Sri Ramakrishna felt
an unquenchable desire to enjoy God in various ways.
For his meditation he built a place in the northern
wooded section of the temple garden. With Hriday's
help he planted there five sacred trees. The spot, known
as the Panchavati, became the scene of many of his
visions.

As his spiritual mood deepened he more and more
felt himself to be a child of the Divine Mother. He
learnt to surrender himself completely to Her will
and let Her direct him.

"O Mother," he would constantly pray, "I have
taken refuge in Thee. Teach me what to do and what
to say. Thy will is paramount everywhere and is for
the good of Thy children. Merge my will in Thy will
and make me Thy instrument."

His visions became deeper and more intimate. He
no longer had to meditate to behold the Divine Mother.
Even while retaining consciousness of the outer world,
he would see Her as tangibly as the temples, the trees,
the river, and the men around him.

On a certain occasion Mathur Babu stealthily entered the temple to watch the worship. He was profoundly moved by the young priest's devotion and
fervour. He felt that Sri Ramakrishna had transformed
the stone image into the living Goddess.

Sri Ramakrishna one day fed a cat with the food that was to be offered to Kāli. This was too much for the manager of the temple garden, who considered himself responsible for the proper conduct of the worship. He reported Sri Ramakrishna's insane behaviour to Mathur Babu.

Sri Ramakrishna has described the incident thus: "The Divine Mother revealed to me in the Kāli temple that it was She who had become everything. She showed me that everything was full of Consciousness. The image was Consciousness, the altar was Consciousness, the water-vessels were Consciousness, the door-sill was Consciousness, the marble floor was Consciousness—all was Consciousness. I found everything inside the room soaked, as it were, in Bliss—the Bliss of God. I saw a wicked man in front of the Kāli temple; but in him also I saw the power of the Divine Mother vibrating. That was why I fed a cat with the food that was to be offered to the Divine Mother. I clearly perceived that all this was the Divine Mother—even the cat. The manager of the temple garden wrote to Mathur Babu saying that I was feeding the cat with the offering intended for the Divine Mother. But Mathur Babu had insight into the state of my mind. He wrote back to the manager: 'Let him do whatever he likes. You must not say anything to him.'"

One of the painful ailments from which Sri Ramakrishna suffered at this time was a burning sensation in his body, and he was cured by a strange vision. During worship in the temple, following the scriptural injunctions, he would imagine the presence of sin in himself and also its destruction. One day he was meditating in the Panchavati, when he saw come out of him a red-eyed man of black complexion, reeling like a drunkard. Soon there emerged from him another person, of serene countenance, wearing the ochre cloth of a sannyāsi and carrying in his hand a trident. The second person attacked the first and killed him with the trident. Thereafter Sri Ramakrishna was free of his pain.

About this time he began to worship God by assuming the attitude of a servant toward his master. He imitated Hanumān, the monkey chieftain of the *Rāmāyana,* the ideal servant of Rāma and traditional model for this form of self-effacing devotion. His movements began to resemble those of a monkey. His eyes became restless. He lived on fruits and roots. With his cloth tied around his waist, a portion of it hanging in the form of a tail, he jumped from place to place instead of walking. And after a short while he was blessed with a vision of Sitā, the divine consort of Rāma, who entered his body and disappeared with the words, "I bequeath to you my smile." From then on, that smile was always on his face, even in samādhi.

Mathur had faith in the sincerity of Sri Ramakrishna's spiritual zeal, but began now to doubt his sanity. He had watched him jumping about like a monkey. One day, when Rāni Rasmani was listening to Sri Ramakrishna's singing in the temple, the young priest abruptly turned and slapped her. Apparently listening to his song, she had actually been thinking of a lawsuit. She accepted the punishment as though the Divine Mother Herself had imposed it; but Mathur was distressed. He begged Sri Ramakrishna to keep his feelings under control and to heed the conventions of society. God Himself, he argued, followed laws. God never permitted, for instance, flowers of two colours to grow on the same stalk. The following day

Sri Ramakrishna presented Mathur Babu with two hibiscus flowers growing on the same stalk, one red and one white.

Mathur and Rāni Rasmani began to ascribe Sri Ramakrishna's mental ailment in part, at least, to his observance of rigid continence. Thinking that a natural life would relax the tension of his nerves, they engineered a plan with two women of ill fame. But as soon as the women entered his room, Sri Ramakrishna beheld in them the manifestation of the Divine Mother of the Universe and went into samādhi uttering Her name.

HALADHARI

In 1858 there came to Dakshineswar a cousin of Sri Ramakrishna, Haladhari by name, who was to remain there about eight years. On account of Sri Ramakrishna's indifferent health, Mathur appointed this man to the office of priest in the Kāli temple. He was a complex character, versed in the letter of the scriptures but hardly aware of their spirit. He loved to participate in hair-splitting theological discussions, and by the measure of his own erudition he proceeded to gauge Sri Ramakrishna. An orthodox brāhmin, he thoroughly disapproved of his cousin's unorthodox actions, but he was not unimpressed by Sri Ramakrishna's purity of life, ecstatic love of God, and yearning for realization.

One day Haladhari upset Sri Ramakrishna with the statement that God is incomprehensible to the human mind. Sri Ramakrishna has described the great moment of doubt when he wondered whether his visions had really misled him: "With sobs I prayed to the Mother, 'How canst Thou have the heart to deceive me like this because I am a fool?' A stream of tears flowed from my eyes. Shortly afterwards I saw a volume of mist rising from the floor and filling the space before me. In the midst of it there appeared a face with flowing beard, calm, highly expressive, and fair. Fixing its gaze steadily upon me, it said solemnly, 'Remain in bhāvamukha, on the borderline between absolute and relative consciousness.' This it repeated three times and then it slowly disappeared in the mist, which itself dissolved. This vision reassured me."

A garbled report of Sri Ramakrishna's failing health, indifference to worldly life, and various abnormal actions reached Kāmārpukur and filled his poor mother's heart with anguish. At her repeated request he returned to his village for a change of air. But his boyhood friends did not interest him any more. A divine fever was consuming him. He spent a great part of the day and night in one of the cremation grounds, in meditation. The place reminded him of the impermanence of the human body, of human hopes and achievements. It also reminded him of Kāli, the Goddess of destruction.

MARRIAGE AND AFTER

But in a few months his health showed an improvement and he recovered to some extent his natural buoyancy of spirit. His happy mother was encouraged to think it might be a good time to arrange his marriage. The boy was now twenty-three years old. A wife would bring him back to earth. And she was delighted when her son welcomed her suggestion. No doubt seeing in it the finger of God, Sri Ramakrishna himself indicated where the prospective bride was to be found.

Saradāmani, a little girl of five, lived in the neighbouring village of Jayrāmbāti. Even at this age she had been praying to God to make her character as stainless and fragrant as the white tuberose. Looking at the full moon, years later, she would say: "O God, there are dark spots even on the moon. But make my character spotless." It was she who was selected as the bride for Sri Ramakrishna.

The marriage ceremony was duly performed. Such early marriage in India is in the nature of a betrothal, the marriage being consummated when the girl attains puberty. But Sri Ramakrishna and Saradamani never lived the usual life of husband and wife. Sri Ramakrishna stayed at Kāmārpukur about a year and a half and then returned to Dakshineswar.

Hardly had he entered the compound of the Kāli temple when he found himself again in the whirlwind. His madness reappeared tenfold. The same meditation and prayer, the same ecstatic moods, the same burning sensation, the same weeping, the same sleeplessness, the same indifference to the body and the outside world, the same divine delirium. He subjected himself to fresh disciplines in order to eradicate greed and lust, the two great impediments to spiritual progress. With a rupee in one hand and some earth in the other, he would reflect on the comparative value of these two for the realization of God, and finding them equally worthless he would toss them, with equal indifference, into the Ganges. Women he regarded as manifestations of the Divine Mother. Never even in a dream did he think of them otherwise. And to root out of his mind the idea of caste superiority, he cleaned, at night, the dirty places in a pariah's house with his long and neglected hair. When he would sit in meditation, birds would perch on his head and peck in his hair for grains of food. Snakes would crawl over his body, and neither would be aware of the other. Sleep left him altogether. Day and night, spiritual visions flitted before him. He saw the sannyāsi who had previously killed sin in him again coming out of his body, threatening to strike him with his trident if he did not concentrate on God. Or the same sannyāsi would visit distant places, following a luminous path, and bring him reports of what was happening there. Sri Ramakrishna used to say later that in the case of an advanced devotee the mind itself becomes the guru, living and moving like an embodied being.

Rāni Rasmani, the foundress of the temple garden, passed away in 1861. After her death her son-in-law Mathur became the sole executor of the estate. He placed himself and his resources at Sri Ramakrishna's disposal and began to look after his physical comfort. Sri Ramakrishna later spoke of him as one of his five "suppliers of stores" appointed by the Divine Mother. Whenever a desire arose in his mind, Mathur fulfilled it without hesitation.

THE BRĀHMANI

There came to Dakshineswar at this time a brāhmin woman who was to play an important part in Sri Ramakrishna's spiritual unfoldment. Born in East Bengal, she was an adept in the Tāntric and Vaishnava methods of worship. She was slightly over fifty years of age, handsome, and garbed in the orange robe of a Hindu nun. Her sole possessions were a few books and two pieces of wearing-cloth.

Sri Ramakrishna welcomed the visitor with great respect, described to her his experiences and visions, and told her of people's belief that these were symptoms of madness. She listened to him intently and said: "My son, everyone in this world is mad. Some are mad for money, some for creature comforts, some for name and fame; and you are mad for God." She assured him that he was passing through the almost unknown spiritual experience described in the scriptures as mahābhāva, the most exalted rapture of divine love, which, she told him, manifests itself in a devotee through nineteen physical symptoms, such as the shedding of tears, tremor of the body, horripilation, perspiration, and a sensation of burning. The bhakti scriptures, she further told him, had recorded only two instances of the experience, namely, those of Sri Rādhā and Sri Chaitanya.

Very soon a tender relationship sprang up between Sri Ramakrishna and the Brāhmani, she looking upon him as the Baby Krishna, and he upon her as mother. Day after day she watched his ecstasy during the kirtan and meditation, his samādhi, his mad yearning; she also recognized in him a power to transmit spirituality to others. Finally she came to the conclusion that such spiritual manifestations were not possible for an ordinary devotee, not even for a highly developed soul; only an Incarnation of God was capable of them. She proclaimed openly that Sri Ramakrishna, like Sri Chaitanya, was an Incarnation of God.

When Sri Ramakrishna told Mathur what the Brāhmani said about him, Mathur shook his head in doubt. He was unwilling to accept him as an Incarnation of God, an Avatār, comparable to Rāma, Krishna, Buddha, and Chaitanya, though he admitted Sri Ramakrishna's extraordinary spirituality. Whereupon the Brāhmani asked Mathur to arrange a conference of scholars to discuss the matter with her. He agreed to the proposal

and a meeting was arranged in the nātmandir in front
of the Kāli temple.

Two famous pundits of the time were invited:
Vaishnavcharan, the leader of Vaishnava society, and
Gauri. The first to arrive was Vaishnavcharan, with
a distinguished company of scholars and devotees. The
Brāhmani, like a proud mother, proclaimed her view
before him and supported it with quotations from the
scriptures. As the pundits discussed the abstruse theological points, Sri Ramakrishna, perfectly indifferent to
everything happening around him, sat in their midst
like a child, immersed in his own thoughts, sometimes
smiling, sometimes chewing a pinch of spices from
a pouch, or again saying to Vaishnavcharan with a
nudge: "Look here. Sometimes I feel like this, too."
Presently Vaishnavcharan declared himself in total
agreement with the Brāhmani's view. He said that Sri
Ramakrishna had undoubtedly experienced mahābhāva
and that this was the certain sign of the rare manifestation of God in a man. The people assembled there,
especially the officers of the temple garden, were struck
dumb. Sri Ramakrishna said to Mathur, like a boy:
"Just fancy, he too says so! Well, I am glad to learn
that after all it is not a disease."

When, a few days later, Pundit Gauri arrived,
another meeting was held, and he agreed with the
view of the Brāhmani and Vaishnavcharan. To Sri
Ramakrishna's remark that Vaishnavcharan had declared him to be an Avatār, Gauri replied: "Is that all he
has to say about you? Then he has said very little. I
am fully convinced that you are that fountain of
spiritual power, only a small fraction of which descends on earth, from time to time, in the form of an
Incarnation."

"Ah!" said Sri Ramakrishna with a smile. "You seem to have quite outbid Vaishnavcharan in this matter. What have you found in me that makes you entertain such an idea?"

Gauri said: "I feel it in my heart and I have the scriptures on my side. I am ready to prove it to anyone who challenges me."

"Well," Sri Ramakrishna said, "it is you who say so; but, believe me, I know nothing about it."

Thus the insane priest was, by verdict of the great scholars of the day, proclaimed a Divine Incarnation. His visions were not the result of an overheated brain; they had precedents in spiritual history. And how did the proclamation affect Sri Ramakrishna himself? He remained the simple child of the Mother that he had been since the first day of his life. Years later, when two of his householder disciples openly spoke of him as a Divine Incarnation and the matter was reported to him, he said with a touch of sarcasm: "Do they think they will enhance my glory that way? One of them is an actor on the stage and the other a physician. What do they know about Incarnations? Why, years ago pundits like Gauri and Vaishnavcharan declared me to be an Avatār. They were great scholars and knew what they were saying. But that did not cause a ripple in my mind."

Sri Ramakrishna was a learner all his life. He often used to quote a proverb to his disciples: "Friend, the longer I live the more I learn." When the excitement created by the Brāhmani's declaration was over, he set himself to the task of practising spiritual disciplines according to the traditional methods laid down in the Tantra and Vaishnava scriptures. Hitherto he had pursued his spiritual ideal according to the promptings of his own mind and heart. Now he accepted the Brāhmani as his guru and set foot on the traditional highways.

TANTRA

According to Tantra,[3] the Ultimate Reality is Chit, or Consciousness, which is identical with Sat, or Being, and with Ānanda, or Bliss. This Ultimate Reality, Satchidānanda, Existence-Knowledge-Bliss Absolute, is the same as the Reality preached in the Vedas. And man is one with this Reality; but under the influence of māyā, or ignorance, he has forgotten his true nature. He takes to be real a merely apparent world of subject and object, and this error is the cause of his bondage and suffering. The goal of spiritual discipline is the re-discovery of his true identity with the Divine Reality.

For the achievement of this goal Vedānta prescribes an austere negative method of discrimination and re-nunciation, which can be followed by only a few individuals endowed with sharp intelligence and un-shakable will power. But Tantra takes into considera-tion the natural weakness of human beings, their lower appetites, and their love for the concrete. It combines philosophy with rituals, meditation with ceremonies, renunciation with enjoyment. The underlying purpose is gradually to train the aspirant to meditate on his oneness with the Ultimate.

The average man wishes to enjoy the material objects of the world. Tantra bids him enjoy these, but at the same time discover in them the presence of God. Mystical rites are prescribed by which, slowly, the sense-objects become spiritualized and sense at-

[3] For a fuller description of the subject see Appendix B.

traction is transformed into love of God. So the very "bonds" of man are turned into "releasers." The very poison that kills is transmuted into the elixir of life. Outward renunciation is not necessary. Thus the aim of Tantra is to sublimate bhoga, or enjoyment, into yoga, or union with Consciousness. For, according to this philosophy, the world with all its manifestations is nothing but the sport of Śiva and Śakti, the Absolute and Its inscrutable Power.

The disciplines of Tantra are graded to suit aspirants of all degrees. Exercises are prescribed for people with "animal," "heroic," and "divine" outlooks. Certain of the rites require the presence of members of the opposite sex. Here the aspirant learns to look on woman as the embodiment of the Goddess Kālī, the Mother of the Universe. The very basis of Tantra is the Motherhood of God and the glorification of woman. Every part of a woman's body is to be regarded as incarnate Divinity. But the rites are extremely dangerous. The help of a qualified guru is absolutely necessary. An unwary devotee may lose his foothold and fall into a pit of depravity.

According to Tantra, Śakti is the active creative force in the universe. Śiva, the Absolute, is a more or less passive principle. Further, Śakti is as inseparable from Śiva as fire's power to burn from fire itself. Śakti, the Creative Power, contains in Its womb the universe and therefore is the Divine Mother. All women are Her symbols. Kālī is one of Her several forms. Meditation on Kālī, the Creative Power, is the central discipline of Tantra. While meditating, the aspirant at first regards himself as one with the Absolute and then thinks that out of that Impersonal Consciousness emerge two entities, namely, his own self and the living form of the

Goddess. He then projects the Goddess into the tangible
image before him and worships it as the Divine Mother.

Sri Ramakrishna set himself to the task of practising
the disciplines of Tantra; at the bidding of the
Divine Mother Herself he accepted the Brāhmani
as his guru. The Goddess Kāli, one of the forms of
the Divine Śakti, was his chosen ideal. He performed
profound and delicate ceremonies in the Panchavati
and under the bel-tree at the northern extremity of
the temple compound. He practised all the disciplines
of the sixty-four principal Tantra books, and it took
him never more than three days to achieve the result
promised in any one of them. After the observance
of a few preliminary rites he would be overwhelmed
with a strange divine fervour and go into samādhi,
where his mind would dwell in Divine Consciousness.
Born with the "divine" disposition, he had no need
of the five ingredients of the Tantric worship in
their physical form. As he uttered the name of
Kāli, he would be filled with the joy of divine inebriation, and people saw him in that state actually
reeling or talking incoherently like a drunkard. Evil
ceased to exist for him. The word "carnal" lost its
meaning. He went into ecstasy at the sight of a prostitute, of drunkards revelling in a tavern, and of the
sexual union of a dog and a bitch. The whole world
and everything in it appeared as the lilā, the sport, of
Śiva and Śakti. He beheld everywhere manifest the
power and beauty of the Mother; the whole world,
animate and inanimate, appeared to him as pervaded
with Chit, Consciousness, and with Ānanda, Bliss. He
did not, like a Vedāntic scholar, repudiate the world
as māyā, but gave it a spiritual status, seeing in it the
manifestation of Chit and Ānanda. The barrier be-

tween matter and energy broke down for him, and he
saw even a grain of sand and a blade of grass vibrating
with energy. The universe appeared to him as a lake
of mercury or of silver.

He saw in a vision the Ultimate Cause of the universe
as a huge luminous triangle giving birth every moment
to an infinite number of worlds. He heard the Anāhata
Śabda, the great sound Om, of which the innumerable
sounds of the universe are only so many variations. He
acquired the eight supernatural powers of yoga, which
make a man almost omnipotent; and these he spurned
as of no value whatsoever to the Spirit. He had a vision
of the divine Māyā, the inscrutable Power of God, by
which the universe is created and sustained, and into
which it is finally absorbed. In this vision he saw a
woman of exquisite beauty, heavy with child. She
emerged from the Ganges, came to the land, and
presently gave birth to a child, which she began to
nurse tenderly. A moment later she assumed a terrible
aspect, seized the child between her grim jaws, and
crushed it. As she swallowed the child she re-entered
the waters of the Ganges.

But the most remarkable experience during this
period was the awakening of the Kundalini Śakti, the
"Serpent Power." He actually saw the Power, at first
lying asleep at the bottom of the spinal column, then
waking up and ascending along the Sushumnā canal
and through its six centres, or lotuses, to the Sahasrāra,
the thousand-petalled lotus in the top of the head. He
further saw that as the Kundalini went upward the
different lotuses bloomed. And this phenomenon was
accompanied by visions and trances. Later on he described to his disciples and devotees the various movements of the Kundalini: the fishlike, birdlike,

monkeylike, and so on. The awakening of the Kundalini is the beginning of spiritual consciousness, and its union with Śiva in the Sahasrāra, ending in samādhi, is the consummation of the Tantric disciplines.

One of the results of his practice of Tantra was the deepening of his respect for womanhood. To him every woman was the embodiment of the Divine Śakti, and he could not, even in a dream, regard a woman in any other way. His relationship with his own wife was entirely on the spiritual plane. He taught that the most effective way for a man to overcome carnal desire was to regard woman as the manifestation of the Divine Mother. He forbade his disciples, however, to practise the rituals prescribed for a sadhaka of "heroic" disposition.

About this time it was revealed to him that in a short while many devotees would seek his guidance.

VAISHNAVA DISCIPLINES

After completing the Tāntric sādhanā Sri Ramakrishna followed the Brāhmani in the disciplines of Vaishnavism. The Vaishnavas are worshippers of Vishnu, the "All-pervading," the Supreme God, who is also known as Hari and Nārāyana. Of Vishnu's various Incarnations, the two with the largest number of followers are Rāma and Krishna.

Vaishnavism is exclusively a religion of bhakti. Bhakti is intense love of God, attachment to Him alone; it is of the nature of bliss and bestows upon the lover immortality and liberation. God, according to Vaishnavism, cannot be realized through logic or reason; and without bhakti all penances, austerities, and rites are futile. Man cannot realize God by self-exertion alone;

for such realization His grace is necessary, and this grace is felt by the pure in heart. The mind is to be purified through bhakti. The pure mind then remains for ever immersed in the ecstasy of God-vision. It is the cultivation of this divine love that is the chief concern of the Vaishnava religion.

There are three kinds of devotion: tāmasic, rājasic, and sāttvic. If a person, in his devotion to God, is actuated by malevolence, arrogance, jealousy, or anger, then his devotion is tāmasic, since it is influenced by tamas, the quality of inertia and darkness. If he worships God from a desire for fame or wealth, or from any other worldly ambition, then his devotion is rājasic, since it is influenced by rajas, the quality of activity. But if a person loves God without any thought of material gain, if he performs his duties to please God alone and maintains toward all created beings the attitude of friendship, then his devotion is called sāttvic, since it is influenced by sattva, the quality of harmony. But the highest devotion transcends the three gunas, or qualities, being a spontaneous, uninterrupted inclination of the mind toward God, the Inner Soul of all beings. It wells up in the heart of a true devotee as soon as he hears the name of God or mention of God's attributes. A devotee possessed of this love would not accept even the joy of heaven if it were offered him. His one desire is to love God under all conditions—in pleasure and pain, life and death, honour and dishonour, prosperity and adversity.

There are two stages of bhakti. The first is known as vaidhi-bhakti, or love of God regulated by scriptural injunctions. For the devotees of this stage are prescribed formal worship, hymns, prayers, the repetition of God's name, and the chanting of His glories. This lower bhakti in course of time matures into parā-bhakti, or supreme devotion, known also as prema, the most intense form of divine love. Divine love is an end in itself. It exists potentially in all human hearts, but in the case of bound creatures it is misdirected to earthly objects.

To develop the devotee's love for God, Vaishnavism humanizes God. God is to be regarded as the devotee's Master, Friend, Child, or his Husband or Sweetheart, each succeeding relationship representing an intensification of love. These bhāvas, or attitudes toward God, are known as dāsya, sakhya, vātsalya, and madhur. Hanumān, the cowherd boys of Vrindāvan, Rāma's mother Kausalyā, and Rādhikā, Krishna's sweetheart, exhibit, respectively, the most perfect examples of these forms. Vaishnavism also speaks of a serene attitude toward God, called śānta. In it there is no intensity of love, and hence it is regarded as inferior to the other attitudes. In the ascending scale the glories of God are gradually forgotten and the devotee realizes more and more the intimacy of divine communion. Finally he regards himself as the mistress of his Beloved, and no barrier remains to separate him from his Ideal. No social or moral obligation can bind to the earth his soaring spirit. He experiences perfect union with the Godhead. A devotee of Vaishnavism wishes to retain both his own individuality and the personality of God. To him God is the Purushottama, the Supreme Person.

While practising the discipline of the madhur bhāva, the male devotee often regards himself as a woman in order to develop the most intense form of love for Sri Krishna, the only Purusha, or Man, in the universe. This assumption of the attitude of the opposite sex has a deep psychological significance. It is a matter of common experience that an idea may be cultivated to such an intense degree that every idea alien to it is driven from the mind. This peculiarity of the mind may be utilized for the subjugation of the lower desires and the development of the spiritual nature. Now, the idea which is the basis of all carnal desires in a man is the conviction of his indissoluble association with a male body. If he can inoculate himself thoroughly with the idea that he is a woman, he can get rid of the desires peculiar to his male body. Again, the idea that he is a woman can in turn be made to give way to another higher idea, namely, that he is neither man nor woman, but the Impersonal Spirit. The Impersonal Spirit alone can enjoy real communion with the Impersonal God. Hence the highest realization of the Vaishnava comes close to the transcendental experience of the Vedāntist.

A beautiful expression of the Vaishnava worship of God through love is to be found in the Vrindāvan episode of the *Bhāgavata*. The gopis, or milkmaids, of Vrindāvan regarded the six-year-old Krishna as their Beloved. They sought no personal gain or happiness from His love. They surrendered to Krishna their bodies, minds, and souls. Of all the gopis, Rādhikā, or Rādhā, because of her intense love for Him, was the closest to Krishna. She manifested mahābhāva and was united with her Beloved. This union, expressed through sensuous language, represents a supersensuous experience.

Sri Chaitanya, also known as Gaurānga, Gorā, or Nimāi, born in Bengal in 1485 and regarded as an Incarnation of God, is a great prophet of the Vaishnava religion. Chaitanya declared the chanting of God's name to be the most efficacious spiritual discipline for the Kaliyuga.

Sri Ramakrishna, assuming the attitude of the monkey Hanumān, had already worshipped God as his Master. Through his devotion to Kāli he had worshipped God as his Mother. He was now to take up the other relationships prescribed by the Vaishnava scriptures.

RĀMLĀLĀ

About the year 1864 there came to Dakshineswar a wandering Vaishnava monk, Jatadhari, whose Ideal Deity was Rāma. He always carried with him a small metal image of the Deity, which he called by the endearing name of Rāmlālā, the Boy Rāma. Toward this little image he displayed the tender affection of Kausalyā for her divine Son, Rāma. As a result of lifelong spiritual practice he had actually realized in the metal image the presence of his Ideal. Rāmlālā was no longer for him a metal image, but the living God. He devoted himself to nursing Rāma, feeding Rāma, playing with Rāma, taking Rāma for a walk, and bathing Rāma. He found that the image responded to his love.

Sri Ramakrishna, much impressed with his devotion, requested Jatadhari to spend a few days at Dakshineswar. Soon Rāmlālā became the favourite companion of Sri Ramakrishna too. Later on he described to the devotees how the little image would dance gracefully before him, jump on his back, insist on being taken in his arms, run to the fields in the sun, pluck flowers from the bushes, and play pranks like a naughty boy. A very sweet relationship sprang up between him and Rāmlālā, for whom he felt the love of a mother.

One day Jatadhari requested Sri Ramakrishna to keep the image and bade him adieu with tearful eyes. He declared that Rāmlālā had fulfilled his innermost prayer and that he now had no more need of formal worship. A few days later Sri Ramakrishna was blessed through Rāmlālā with a vision of Rāmachandra Himself, whereby he realized that the Rāma of the *Rāmāyana,* the son of Daśaratha, pervades the whole universe as Spirit and Consciousness; that He is its Creator, Sustainer, and Destroyer; that, in still another aspect, He is the transcendental Brahman, without form, attribute, or name.

While worshipping Rāmlālā as the Divine Child, Sri Ramakrishna's heart became filled with motherly tenderness and he began to regard himself as a woman. His speech and gestures changed. He began to move freely with the ladies of Mathur's family, who now looked upon him as one of their own sex. During this time he worshipped the Divine Mother as Her companion or handmaid.

In Communion with the Divine Beloved

Sri Ramakrishna now devoted himself to scaling the almost inaccessible heights of dualistic worship, namely, the complete union with Sri Krishna as the Beloved of the heart. He regarded himself as one of the gopis of Vrindāvan, mad with longing for her divine Sweetheart. At his request Mathur provided him with woman's dress and jewelry. In this love-pursuit, food and drink were forgotten. Day and night he wept bitterly for the vision of Sri Krishna. The yearning turned into a mad frenzy; for the divine Krishna began to play with him the old tricks He had played with the gopis. He would tease and taunt, now and then revealing Himself, but always keeping at a distance. Sri Ramakrishna's anguish brought on a return of the old physical symptoms: the burning sensation, an oozing of blood through the pores, a loosening of the joints, and the stopping of physiological functions.

The Vaishnava scriptures advise one to propitiate Rādhā and obtain her grace in order to realize Sri Krishna. So the tortured devotee now turned his prayer to her. Within a short time he enjoyed a blessed vision. He saw and felt the figure of Rādhā disappearing into his own body.

He said later on: "It is impossible to describe the heavenly beauty and sweetness of Rādhā. Her very appearance showed that she had completely forgotten herself in her passionate love for Krishna. Her complexion was a light yellow."

Now one with Rādhā, he manifested the great ecstatic love, the mahābhāva, which had found in her its fullest expression. Later Sri Ramakrishna said: "The manifestation in a man of the nineteen different kinds of emotion for God is called, in the books of bhakti, mahābhāva. An ordinary man takes a whole lifetime to express even a single one of these. But in this body [meaning himself] there has been a complete manifestation of all nineteen."

The love of Rādhā is the precursor of the resplendent vision of Sri Krishna. Sri Ramakrishna soon experienced that vision. The enchanting form of Krishna appeared to him and merged in his person. He became Krishna; he totally forgot his own individuality and the world; he saw Krishna in himself and in the universe. Thus he attained to the fulfilment of the worship of the Personal God. He drank from the fountain of Immortal Bliss. The agony of his heart vanished for ever. He realized Amrita, Immortality, beyond the shadow of death.

One day, listening to a recitation of the *Bhāgavata* on the verandah of the Rādhākānta temple, he fell into a divine mood and saw the soul-enthralling form of Krishna. He perceived luminous rays issuing from Krishna's Lotus Feet in the form of a stout rope; it touched first the *Bhāgavata* and then his own chest, connecting all three—God, the scripture, and the devotee. "After this vision," he used to say, "I came to realize that Bhagavān, Bhakta, and *Bhāgavata*— God, Devotee, and Scripture—are in reality one and the same."

VEDĀNTA

The Brāhmani was the enthusiastic teacher and astonished beholder of Sri Ramakrishna in his spiritual progress. She became proud of the achievements of her unique pupil. But the pupil himself was not permitted to rest; his destiny beckoned him forward. His Divine Mother would allow him no respite till he had left behind the entire realm of duality with its visions, emotions, and ecstatic dreams. But for the new ascent the old tender guide would not suffice. The Brāhmani, on whom he had depended for three years, saw her son escape from her to follow the command of a teacher with masculine strength, a sterner mien, a gnarled physique, and a virile voice. The new guru was a wandering monk, the sturdy Totapuri, whom Sri Ramakrishna learnt to address affectionately as Nangtā, the "Naked One," because of his total renunciation of all earthly attachments and objects, including even a piece of wearing-cloth.

Totapuri was the bearer of a philosophy new to Sri Ramakrishna, the Non-dualistic Vedānta, whose conclusions Totapuri had experienced in his own life. This ancient Hindu system designates the Ultimate Reality as Brahman, also described as Satchidānanda, Existence-Knowledge-Bliss Absolute. Brahman is the only Real Existence. In It there is no time, no space, no causality, no multiplicity. But through māyā— Its inscrutable Power—time, space, and causality are projected and the One appears to break into the many. The non-dual Spirit appears as multiple individuals endowed with forms and subject to the conditions of time. The Immortal becomes a victim of birth and death. The Changeless undergoes change. The sinless Pure Soul, hypnotized by Its own māyā, experiences the joys of heaven and the pains of hell. But these experiences based on the duality of the subject-object relationship are unreal. Even the vision of a Personal God is, ultimately speaking, as illusory as the experience of any other object. Man attains his liberation, therefore, by piercing the veil of māyā and rediscovering his total identity with Brahman. Knowing himself to be one with the Universal Spirit, he realizes ineffable Peace. Only then does he go beyond the fiction of birth and death; only then does he become immortal. And this is the ultimate goal of Vedānta—to dehypnotize the soul now hypnotized by its own ignorance.

The path of the Vedāntic discipline is the path of negation, "neti," in which, by stern determination, all that is unreal is renounced. It is the path of jnāna, knowledge, the direct method of realizing the Absolute. After the negation of everything relative, including the discriminating ego itself, the aspirant merges in the One without a second, in the bliss of nirvikalpa samādhi, where subject and object are alike dissolved. The soul goes beyond the realm of thought. The domain of duality is transcended. Māyā is left behind with all its changes and modifications. The Real Man towers above the delusions of creation, preservation, and destruction. An avalanche of indescribable Bliss sweeps away all relative ideas of pain and pleasure, good and evil. There shines in the heart the glory of the Eternal Brahman, Existence-Knowledge-Bliss Absolute. Knower, knowledge, and known are dissolved in the Ocean of one eternal Consciousness; love, lover, and beloved merge in the unbounded Sea of supreme Felicity; birth, growth, and death vanish in infinite Existence. All doubts and misgivings are quelled for ever; the oscillations of the mind are stopped; the momentum of past actions is exhausted. Breaking down the ridgepole of the tabernacle in which the soul has made its abode for untold ages, stilling the body, calming the mind, drowning the ego, the joy of Brahman wells up in that superconscious state. Space disappears into Pure Being, time is swallowed up in eternity, and causation becomes a dream of the past. Only Existence is. Who can describe what the soul then feels in its communion with the Self?

Even when a man descends from this dizzy height, he is devoid of ideas of "I" and "mine"; he looks on the body as a mere shadow, an outer sheath encasing the soul. He does not dwell on the past, takes no thought for the future, and looks with indifference on the present. He surveys everything in the world with an eye of equality; he is no longer touched by the infinite variety of phenomena; he no longer reacts to pleasure and pain. He remains unmoved whether he—that is to say, his body—is worshipped by the good or tormented by the wicked; for he realizes that it is the one Brahman that manifests Itself through everything. The impact of such an experience devastates the body and mind. Consciousness becomes blasted, as it were, with an excess of light. In the Vedāntic books it is said that after the experience of nirvikalpa samādhi the body drops off like a dry leaf. Only those who are born with a special mission for humanity can return from this height to the valleys of normal life. They live and move in the world for the welfare of mankind. They are invested with a supreme spiritual power. A divine glory shines through them.

TOTAPURI

Totapuri arrived at the Dakshineswar temple garden toward the end of 1864. Probably born in the Punjab, he was the head of a monastery in that province of India and claimed leadership of seven hundred sannyāsis. Trained from early youth in the disciplines of Advaita Vedānta, he looked upon the world as an illusion, and the gods and goddesses of the dualistic worship as mere fantasies. Prayers, ceremonies, rites, and rituals were meaningless to him; about these he was utterly indifferent. Exercising discrimination and unshakable will power, he had liberated himself from attachment to the sense-objects of the relative universe. For forty years he had practised austere discipline on the bank of the sacred Narmadā and had finally realized his identity with the Absolute. Thenceforward he roamed in the world as an unfettered soul, a lion free from the cage. Clad in a loincloth, he spent his days under the canopy of the sky alike in storm and sunshine, feeding his body on the slender pittance of what people offered of their own accord. He had been visiting the estuary of the Ganges. On his return journey along the bank of the sacred river, led by the inscrutable Divine Will, he stopped at Dakshineswar.

Totapuri, discovering at once that Sri Ramakrishna was qualified to be a student of Vedānta, asked to initiate him into its mysteries. With the permission of the Divine Mother, Sri Ramakrishna agreed to the proposal. But Totapuri explained that only a sannyāsi could receive the teaching of Vedānta. Sri Ramakrishna agreed to renounce the world, but with the stipulation that the ceremony of his initiation into the monastic order be performed in secret, to spare the feelings of his old mother, who had been living with him at Dakshineswar.

On the appointed day, in the small hours of the morning, a fire was lighted in the Panchavati. Totapuri and Sri Ramakrishna sat before it. The flames played on their faces. Beside the gentle Ramakrishna, Totapuri seemed like a rock. The monk was tall and robust, a sturdy and tough oak. His constitution and mind were of iron. He was a strong leader of men.

In the burning flame before him Sri Ramakrishna performed the rituals by which a candidate for monastic life destroys his attachment to relatives, friends, body, mind, sense-organs, ego, and the world. The leaping flames swallowed it all, making the initiate free and pure. The sacred thread and the tuft of hair were consigned to the fire, completing his severance from caste, sex, and society. Last of all he burnt in that fire, with all that is holy as his witness, his desire for enjoyment here and hereafter. He uttered

the sacred mantras giving assurance of safety and fear-
lessness to all beings, who were only manifestations of
his own Self. The rites completed, the disciple received from the guru the loincloth and ochre robe, the
emblems of his new life.

The teacher and the disciple repaired to the meditation room near by. Totapuri began to impart to Sri
Ramakrishna the great truths of Vedānta.

"Brahman," he said, "is the only Reality, ever pure,
ever illumined, ever free, beyond the limits of time,
space, and causation. Though apparently endowed
with names and forms through the inscrutable power
of māyā, that enchantress who makes the impossible
possible, Brahman is really One and undivided. When
a seeker merges in the beatitude of samādhi, he does
not perceive time and space or name and form, the
offspring of māyā. Whatever is within the domain
of māyā is unreal. Give it up. Destroy the prison-
house of name and form and rush out of it with the
strength of a lion. Dive deep in search of the Self and
realize It in samādhi. You will find the world of
name and form vanishing into void, and the puny ego
dissolving in Brahman-Consciousness. You will realize
your identity with Brahman, Existence-Knowledge-
Bliss Absolute." Quoting an Upanishad, Totapuri
said: "That knowledge is limited by which one sees
or hears or knows another. What is limited is worthless
and can never give real felicity. But the Knowledge by
which one sees no other or hears no other or knows
no other, which is beyond duality, is infinite and
great, and through such Knowledge one attains limitless Bliss. How can the mind and senses grasp That
which shines in the heart of all as the Eternal Subject?"

Totapuri asked the disciple to withdraw his mind

from all objects of the relative world, including the gods and goddesses, and to concentrate on the Absolute. But the task was not easy even for Sri Ramakrishna. He found it impossible to take his mind beyond Kāli, the Divine Mother of the Universe. "After the initiation," Sri Ramakrishna later said, describing the event, "Nangtā began to teach me the various conclusions of Advaita Vedānta and asked me to withdraw the mind completely from all objects and dive deep into Ātman. But in spite of all my attempts I could not altogether cross the realm of name and form and bring my mind to the unconditioned state. I had no difficulty in taking the mind from all the objects of the world. But the radiant and all too familiar figure of the Blissful Mother, the Embodiment of the essence of Pure Consciousness, appeared before me as a living reality. Her bewitching smile prevented me from passing into the Great Beyond. Again and again I tried, but She stood in my way every time. In despair I said to Nangtā: 'It is hopeless. I cannot raise my mind to the unconditioned state and come face to face with Ātman.' He grew excited and sharply said: 'What? You can't do it? But you have to.' He cast his eyes around. Finding a piece of glass he took it up and stuck it between my eyebrows. 'Concentrate the mind on this point!' he thundered. Then with stern determination I again sat to meditate. As soon as the gracious form of the Divine Mother appeared before me, I used my discrimination as a sword and with it clove Her in two. The last barrier fell. My spirit at once soared beyond the relative plane. I lost myself in samādhi."

Sri Ramakrishna remained completely absorbed in samādhi for three days. "Is it really true?" Totapuri cried out in astonishment. "Is it possible that he has attained in a single day what it took me forty years of strenuous practice to achieve? Great God! It is nothing short of a miracle!" With the help of Totapuri, Sri Ramakrishna's mind finally came down to the relative plane.

Totapuri, a monk of the most orthodox type, never stayed at a place more than three days, for fear of creating attachment. But he remained at Dakshineswar eleven months. He too had something to learn.

Totapuri had no idea of the struggles of ordinary men in the meshes of passion and desire. Having maintained all through life the guilelessness of a child, he laughed at the idea of a man's being led astray by the senses. He was convinced that the world was māyā and had only to be denounced to vanish for ever. A born Non-dualist, he had no faith in a Personal God. He did not believe in the terrible aspect of Kāli, much less in Her benign aspect. Music and the chanting of God's holy name were to him only so much nonsense. He ridiculed the spending of emotion on the worship of a Personal God.

KĀLI AND MĀYĀ

Sri Ramakrishna, on the other hand, though fully aware, like his guru, that the world is an illusory appearance, did not slight māyā, like an orthodox monist, but acknowledged its power in the relative life. He was all love and reverence for māyā, perceiving in it a mysterious and majestic expression of Divinity. To him māyā itself was God, for everything was God. It was one of the faces of Brahman. What he had realized on the heights of the transcendental plane, he also found here below, everywhere about him, under the mysterious garb of names and forms. And this garb was a perfectly transparent sheath, through which he recognized the glory of the Divine Immanence. Māyā, the mighty weaver of the garb, is none other than Kāli, the Divine Mother. She is the primordial Divine Energy, Śakti, and She can no more be distinguished from the Supreme Brahman than can the power of burning be distinguished from fire. She projects the world and again withdraws it. She spins it as the spider spins its web. She is the Mother of the Universe, identical with the Brahman of Vedānta and with the Ātman of Yoga. As eternal Lawgiver, She makes and unmakes laws; it is by Her imperious will that karma yields its fruit. She ensnares men with illusion and again releases them from bondage with a look of Her benign eyes. She is the supreme Mistress of the cosmic play; and all objects, animate and inanimate, dance by Her will. Even those who realize the Absolute in nirvikalpa samādhi are under Her jurisdiction as long as they live on the relative plane.

Thus, after nirvikalpa samādhi, Sri Ramakrishna realized māyā in an altogether new role. The binding aspect of Kāli vanished from before his vision. She no longer obscured his understanding. The world became the glorious manifestation of the Divine Mother. Māyā became Brahman. The Transcendental Itself broke through the Immanent. Sri Ramakrishna discovered that māyā operates in the relative world in two ways, and he termed these "avidyāmāyā" and "vidyāmāyā." Avidyāmāyā represents the dark forces of creation: sensuous desires, evil passions, greed, lust, cruelty, and so on. It sustains the world system on the lower planes. It is responsible for the round of man's birth and death. It must be fought and vanquished. But vidyāmāyā is the higher force of creation: the spiritual virtues, the enlightening qualities, kindness, purity, love, devotion. Vidyāmāyā elevates a man to the higher planes of consciousness. With the help of vidyāmāyā the devotee rids himself of avidyāmāyā; he then becomes māyātita, free of māyā. The two aspects of māyā are the two forces of creation, the two powers of Kāli; and She stands beyond them both. She is like the effulgent sun, bringing into existence clouds of different colours and shapes, shining through and standing behind them and thus conjuring up wonderful forms in the blue autumn heaven.

The Divine Mother asked Sri Ramakrishna not to be lost in the featureless Brahman but to remain in bhāvamukha, on the threshold of absolute consciousness, the border line between the Absolute and the Relative. He was to keep himself at the "sixth centre" of Tantra, from which he could see not only the glory of the seventh, but also the divine manifestations of the Kundalini in the lower centres. He gently oscillated back and forth across the dividing line. Ecstatic devotion to the Divine Mother alternated with serene absorption in the Ocean of Absolute Unity. He thus bridged the gulf between the Personal and the Impersonal, the immanent and the transcendent aspects of Reality. This is a unique experience in the recorded spiritual history of the world.

TOTAPURI'S LESSON

From Sri Ramakrishna Totapuri had to learn the significance of Kāli, the Great Fact of the relative world, and of māyā, Her indescribable Power.

One day, when the guru and the disciple were engaged in an animated discussion about Vedānta, a servant of the temple garden came there and took a live coal from the sacred fire that had been lighted by the great ascetic. He wanted it to light his tobacco. Totapuri flew into a rage at the apparently sacrilegious act and was about to beat the man. Sri Ramakrishna rocked with laughter. "What a shame!" he cried. "You are explaining to me the reality of Brahman and the illusoriness of the world; yet now you have so far forgotten yourself as to be about to beat a man in a fit of passion. The power of māyā is indeed inscrutable!" Totapuri was embarrassed.

About this time Totapuri was laid up with a severe attack of dysentery. On account of this miserable illness he found it impossible to meditate. One night the pain became excruciating. He could no longer concentrate on Brahman. The body stood in the way. He became incensed with its demands. A free soul, he did not at all care for the body. So he determined to drown it in the Ganges. Thereupon he walked into the river. But, lo! He walked to the other bank.[4] Was there not enough water in the Ganges? Standing dumbfounded on the other bank he looked back across the water. The trees, the temples, the houses, stood out against the sky. Suddenly, in one dazzling moment, he saw on all sides the presence of the Divine Mother. She is in everything; She is everything. She is in the water; She is on land. She is the body; She is the

[4] This version of the incident is taken from the biography of Sri Ramakrishna by Swami Saradananda, one of the Master's direct disciples. According to another version, there was a sand-bank in the middle of the river, which one could reach by wading out during the ebb tide, and it was this sand-bank that Totapuri reached.

mind. She is pain; She is comfort. She is knowledge; She is ignorance. She is life; She is death. She is everything that one sees, hears, or imagines. She turns "yea" into "nay," and "nay" into "yea." Without Her grace no embodied being can go beyond Her realm. Man has no free will. He is not even free to die. Yet, again, beyond the body and mind She is the Transcendental Absolute. She is the Brahman that Totapuri had been worshipping all his life.

Totapuri returned to Dakshineswar and spent the remaining hours of the night meditating on the Divine Mother. In the morning he went to the Kāli temple with Sri Ramakrishna and prostrated himself before the image of the Mother. He now realized why he had spent eleven months at Dakshineswar. Bidding farewell to the disciple, he continued on his way, enlightened.

Sri Ramakrishna later described the significance of Totapuri's lesson: "When I think of the Supreme Being as inactive—neither creating nor preserving nor destroying—I call Him Brahman or Purusha, the Impersonal God. When I think of Him as active—creating, preserving, and destroying—I call Him Śakti or Māyā or Prakriti, the Personal God. But the distinction between them does not mean a difference. The Personal and the Impersonal are the same thing, like milk and its whiteness, the diamond and its lustre, the snake and its wriggling motion. It is impossible to conceive of the one without the other. The Divine Mother and Brahman are one."

After Totapuri's departure Sri Ramakrishna remained for six months in a state of absolute identity with Brahman. "For six months at a stretch," he said, "I remained in that state from which ordinary men can never return; generally the body falls off, after three weeks, like a sere leaf. I was not conscious of day or night. Flies would enter my mouth and nostrils just as they do a dead body's, but I did not feel them. My hair became matted with dust."

His body would not have survived but for the kindly attention of a monk who happened to be at Dakshineswar at that time and who somehow realized that for the good of humanity Sri Ramakrishna's body must be preserved. He tried various means, even physical violence, to recall the fleeing soul to the prison-house of the body, and during the resultant fleeting moments of consciousness he would push a few morsels of food down Sri Ramakrishna's throat. Meanwhile Sri Ramakrishna received the command of the Divine Mother to remain on the threshold of absolute consciousness. Soon thereafter he was afflicted with a serious attack of dysentery. Day and night the pain tortured him, and his mind gradually came down to the physical plane.

COMPANY OF HOLY MEN AND DEVOTEES

From now on Sri Ramakrishna began to seek the company of devotees and holy men. He had gone through the storm and stress of spiritual disciplines and visions. Now he realized an inner calmness and appeared to others as a normal person. But he could not bear the company of worldly people or listen to their talk. Fortunately the holy atmosphere of Dakshineswar and the liberality of Mathur attracted monks and holy men from all parts of the country. Sādhus of all denominations—monists and dualists, Vaishnavas and Vedāntists, Śāktas and worshippers of Rāma—flocked there in ever increasing numbers. Ascetics and visionaries came to seek Sri Ramakrishna's advice. Vaishnavas had come during the period of his Vaishnava sādhanā, and Tāntrics when he had practised the disciplines of Tantra. Vedāntists began to arrive after Totapuri's departure. In the room of Sri Ramakrishna, who was then in bed with dysentery, the Vedāntists engaged in scriptural discussions, and, forgetting his own physical suffering, he solved their doubts by referring directly to his own experiences. Many of the visitors were genuine spiritual souls, the unseen pillars of Hinduism, and their spiritual lives were quickened in no small measure by the sage of Dakshineswar. Sri Ramakrishna in turn learnt from them anecdotes concerning the ways and the conduct of holy men, which he subsequently narrated to his devotees and disciples. At his request Mathur provided him with large stores of foodstuffs, clothes, and so forth, for distribution among the wandering monks.

Sri Ramakrishna had not read books, yet he possessed an encyclopedic knowledge of religions and religious philosophies. This he acquired from his contacts with innumerable holy men and scholars. He had a unique power of assimilation; through meditation he made this knowledge a part of his being. Once, when he was asked by a disciple about the source of his seemingly inexhaustible knowledge, he replied: "I did not read books; but I heard the learned. I made a garland of their knowledge, wearing it round my neck, and I gave it as an offering at the feet of the Mother."

Sri Ramakrishna used to say that when the flowers bloom the bees come to them for honey of their own accord. Now many souls were visiting Dakshineswar to satisfy their spiritual hunger. He, the devotee and aspirant, became the Master. Gauri, the great scholar who had been one of the first to proclaim Sri Ramakrishna an Incarnation of God, paid the Master a visit in 1870 and with his blessings renounced the world. Narayan Shastri, another great pundit, who had mastered the six systems of Hindu philosophy and had been offered a lucrative post by the Mahārājā of Jaipur, met the Master and recognized him as one who had realized in life those ideals which he himself had encountered merely in books. Sri Ramakrishna initiated Narayan Shastri, at his earnest request, into the life of sannyās. Pundit Padmalochan, the court pundit of the Mahārājā of Burdwān, well known for his scholarship in both the Vedānta and Nyāya systems of philosophy, accepted the Master as an Incarnation of God. Krishnakishore, a Vedāntist scholar, became devoted to the Master. And there arrived Viswanath Upadhyaya, who was to become a favourite devotee; Sri Ramakrishna addressed him as "Captain." He was a high officer of the King of Nepal and had received the title of Colonel in recognition of his merit. A scholar of the Gītā, the *Bhāgavata,* and Vedānta philosophy, he daily performed the worship of his Chosen Deity with great devotion. "I have read the Vedas and the other scriptures," he said. "I have also met a good many monks and devotees in different places. But it is in Sri Ramakrishna's presence that my spiritual yearning has been fulfilled. To me he seems to be the embodiment of the truths of the scriptures."

The Knowledge of Brahman in nirvikalpa samādhi had convinced Sri Ramakrishna that the gods of the different religions are but so many manifestations of the Absolute on the relative plane, and that the Ultimate Reality could never be expressed by human tongue.

He understood that all religions lead their devotees by differing paths to one and the same goal. Now he became eager to explore some of the alien religions; for with him understanding meant actual experience.

ISLĀM

Toward the end of 1866 the Master began to practise the disciplines of Islām. Under the direction of his Mussalmān guru he abandoned himself to his new sādhanā. He dressed as a Mussalmān and repeated the name of Āllāh. His prayers took the form of the Islāmic devotions. He forgot the Hindu gods and goddesses—even Kālī—and gave up visiting the temples. He took up his residence outside the temple precincts. After three days he saw the vision of a radiant figure, perhaps Mohammed. This figure gently approached him and finally lost himself in Sri Rama krishna. Thus he realized the Mussalmān God. Thence he passed into communion with Brahman. The mighty river of Islām also led him back to the Ocean of the Absolute.

CHRISTIANITY

Eight years later, some time in November 1874, Sri Ramakrishna was seized with an irresistible desire to learn the truth of the Christian religion. He began to listen to readings from the Bible by Sambhu Charan Mallick, a gentleman of Calcutta and a devotee of the Master. Sri Ramakrishna became fascinated by the life and teachings of Jesus. One day he was seated in the parlour of Jadu Mallick's garden house[5]

[5] This expression is used throughout to translate the Bengali word denoting a rich man's country house set in a garden.

at Dakshineswar, when his eyes became fixed on a painting of the Madonna and Child. Intently watching it, he became gradually overwhelmed with divine emotion. The figures in the picture took on life, and the rays of light emanating from them entered his soul. The effect of this experience was stronger than that of the vision of Mohammed. In dismay he cried out, "O Mother! What are You doing to me?" And, breaking through the barriers of creed and religion, he entered a new realm of ecstasy. Christ possessed his soul. For three days he did not set foot in the Kāli temple. On the fourth day, in the afternoon, as he was walking in the Panchavati, he saw coming toward him a person with beautiful large eyes, serene countenance, and fair skin. As the two faced each other, a voice rang out in the depths of Sri Ramakrishna's soul: "Behold the Christ, who shed His heart's blood for the redemption of the world, who suffered a sea of anguish for love of men. It is He, the Master Yogi, who is in eternal union with God. It is Jesus, Love Incarnate." The Son of Man embraced the Son of the Divine Mother and merged in him. Sri Ramakrishna realized his identity with Christ, as he had already realized his identity with Kāli, Rāma, Hanumān, Rādhā, Krishna, Brahman, and Mohammed. The Master went into samādhi and communed with the Brahman with attributes. Thus he experienced the truth that Christianity, too, was a path leading to God-Consciousness. Till the last moment of his life he believed that Christ was an Incarnation of God. But Christ, for him, was not the only Incarnation; there were others—Buddha, for instance, and Krishna.

ATTITUDE TOWARD DIFFERENT RELIGIONS

Sri Ramakrishna accepted the divinity of Buddha and used to point out the similarity of his teachings to those of the Upanishads. He also showed great respect for the Tirthankaras, who founded Jainism, and for the ten Gurus of Śikhism. But he did not speak of them as Divine Incarnations. He was heard to say that the Gurus of Śikhism were the reincarnations of King Janaka of ancient India. He kept in his room at Dakshineswar a small statue of Tirthankara Mahāvira and a picture of Christ, before which incense was burnt morning and evening.

Without being formally initiated into their doctrines, Sri Ramakrishna thus realized the ideals of religions other than Hinduism. He did not need to follow any doctrine. All barriers were removed by his overwhelming love of God. So he became an adept who could speak with authority regarding the ideas and ideals of the various religions of the world. "I have practised," said he, "all religions—Hinduism, Islām, Christianity—and I have also followed the paths of the different Hindu sects. I have found that it is the same God toward whom all are directing their steps, though along different paths. You must try all beliefs and traverse all the different ways once. Wherever I look, I see men quarrelling in the name of religion —Hindus, Mohammedans, Brāhmos, Vaishnavas, and the rest. But they never reflect that He who is called Krishna is also called Śiva, and bears the name of the Primal Energy, Jesus, and Āllāh as well—the same Rāma with a thousand names. A lake has several ghāts. At one the Hindus take water in pitchers and call it 'jal'; at another the Mussalmāns take water in leather bags and call it 'pāni.' At a third the Christians call it 'water.' Can we imagine that it is not 'jal,' but only 'pāni' or 'water'? How ridiculous! The substance is one under different names, and everyone is seeking the same substance; only climate, temperament, and name create differences. Let each man follow his own path. If he sincerely and ardently wishes to know God, peace be unto him! He will surely realize Him."

It is interesting to note that when Sri Ramakrishna meditated on the way of Christianity and of Islām he completely gave up the Hindu religious observances, such as his daily visits to the temples, repetition of the names of the Hindu deities, and other acts of devotion. He even removed from his room the pictures of the Hindu gods and goddesses. He thus demonstrated that a pious Mussalmān or Christian, by loyalty to his own spiritual disciplines, can attain God-Consciousness.

In 1867 Sri Ramakrishna returned to Kāmārpukur to recuperate from the effect of his austerities. The peaceful countryside, the simple and artless companions of his boyhood, and the pure air did him much good. The villagers were happy to have their playful, witty, kind-hearted, and truthful Gadadhar back again, though they did not fail to notice the great change that had come over him during his years in Calcutta. His wife, Sarada Devi, now fourteen years old, soon arrived at Kāmārpukur. Her spiritual development was much beyond her age and she was able to understand immediately her husband's state of mind. She became eager to learn from him about God and to live with him as his attendant. The Master accepted her cheerfully both as his disciple and as his spiritual companion. Referring to the experiences of these few days, she once said: "I felt always as if a pitcher full of bliss were placed in my heart. The joy was indescribable."

PILGRIMAGE

On January 27, 1868, Mathur Babu with a party of some one hundred and twenty-five persons set out on a pilgrimage to the sacred places of northern India. At Vaidyanāth in Behar, when the Master saw the inhabitants of a village reduced by disease and starvation to mere skeletons, he requested his rich patron to feed the people and give each a piece of cloth. Mathur demurred at the added expense. The Master declared bitterly that he would not go on to Benares, but would live with the poor and share their miseries. He actually left Mathur and sat down with the villagers. Whereupon Mathur had to yield. On another occasion, two years later, Sri Ramakrishna showed a similar sentiment for the poor and needy. He accompanied Mathur on a tour to one of the latter's estates at the time of the collection of rents. For two years the harvests had failed and the tenants were in a state of extreme poverty. The Master asked Mathur to remit their rents, distribute help to them, and in addition give the hungry people a sumptuous feast. When Mathur grumbled, the Master said: "You are only the steward of the Divine Mother. They are the Mother's tenants. You must spend the Mother's money. When they are suffering, how can you refuse? You must help them." Again Mathur had to give in. Sri Ramakrishna's sympathy for the poor sprang from his perception of God in all created beings. His sentiment was not that of the humanist or philanthropist. To him the service of man was the same as the worship of God.

The party entered holy Benares by boat along the Ganges. When Sri Ramakrishna's eyes fell on this city of Śiva, where had accumulated for ages the devotion and piety of countless worshippers, he saw it to be made of gold, as the scriptures declare. He was visibly moved. During his stay in the city he treated every particle of its earth with utmost respect. At the Manikarnikā Ghāt, the great cremation ground of the city, he actually saw Śiva, with ash-covered body and tawny matted hair, serenely approaching each funeral pyre and breathing into the ears of the corpses the mantra of liberation, and then the Divine Mother removing from the dead their bonds. Thus he realized the significance of the scriptural statement that anyone dying in Benares attains salvation through Śiva's grace. He paid a visit to Trailanga Swami, the celebrated monk, whom he later declared to be a real paramahamsa, a veritable image of Śiva.

Sri Ramakrishna visited Allāhābād, at the confluence of the Ganges and the Jamunā, and then proceeded to Vrindāvan and Mathurā, hallowed by the legends, songs, and dramas about Krishna and the gopis. Here he had numerous visions and his heart overflowed with divine emotion. He wept and said: "O Krishna! Everything here is as it was in the olden days. You alone are absent." He visited the great woman saint Gangāmāyi, regarded by Vaishnava devotees as the reincarnation of an intimate attendant of Rādhā. She was sixty years old and had frequent trances. She spoke of Sri Ramakrishna as an incarnation of Rādhā. With great difficulty he was persuaded to leave her.

On the return journey Mathur wanted to visit Gayā,

but Sri Ramakrishna declined to go. He recalled his
father's vision at Gayā before his own birth and felt
that in the temple of Vishnu he would become
permanently absorbed in God. Mathur, honouring the
Master's wish, returned with his party to Calcutta.

From Vrindāvan the Master had brought a handful
of dust. Part of this he scattered in the Panchavati; the
rest he buried in the little hut where he had practised
meditation. "Now this place," he said, "is as sacred as
Vrindāvan."

In 1870 the Master went on a pilgrimage to
Nadiā, the birthplace of Sri Chaitanya. As the boat
by which he travelled approached the sand-bank close
to Nadiā, Sri Ramakrishna had a vision of the "two
brothers," Sri Chaitanya and his companion Nityānanda, "bright as molten gold" and with haloes,
rushing to greet him with uplifted hands. "There they
come! There they come!" he cried. They entered his
body and he went into a deep trance.

RELATION WITH HIS WIFE

In 1872 Sarada Devi paid her first visit to her husband at Dakshineswar. Four years earlier she had seen
him at Kāmārpukur and had tasted the bliss of his divine company. Since then she had become even more
gentle, tender, introspective, serious, and unselfish. She
had heard many rumours about her husband's insanity.
People had shown her pity in her misfortune. The
more she thought, the more she felt that her duty was to
be with him, giving him, in whatever measure she
could, a wife's devoted service. She was now eighteen
years old. Accompanied by her father, she arrived at
Dakshineswar, having come on foot the distance of
eighty miles. She had had an attack of fever on the

way. When she arrived at the temple garden the Master said sorrowfully: "Ah! You have come too late. My Mathur is no longer here to look after you." Mathur had passed away the previous year.

The Master took up the duty of instructing his young wife, and this included everything from house-keeping to the Knowledge of Brahman. He taught her how to trim a lamp, how to behave toward people according to their differing temperaments, and how to conduct herself before visitors. He instructed her in the mysteries of spiritual life—prayer, meditation, japa, deep contemplation, and samādhi. The first lesson that Sarada Devi received was: "God is every-body's Beloved, just as the moon is dear to every child. Everyone has the same right to pray to Him. Out of His grace He reveals Himself to all who call upon Him. You too will see Him if you but pray to Him."

Totapuri, coming to know of the Master's marriage, had once remarked: "What does it matter? He alone is firmly established in the Knowledge of Brahman who can adhere to his spirit of discrimination and re-nunciation even while living with his wife. He alone has attained the supreme illumination who can look on man and woman alike as Brahman. A man who dis-criminates about sex may be a good aspirant, but he is still far from the goal." Sri Ramakrishna and his wife lived together at Dakshineswar, but their minds al-ways soared above the worldly plane. A few months after Sarada Devi's arrival Sri Ramakrishna arranged, on an auspicious day, a special ritualistic worship of Kāli. Instead of an image of the Deity, he placed on the seat the living image, Sarada Devi herself. The worshipper and the worshipped went into deep samādhi and in the transcendental plane their souls were united.

After several hours Sri Ramakrishna came down again to the relative plane, sang a hymn to the Great Goddess, and surrendered, at the feet of the living image, himself, his rosary, and the fruit of his life-long sādhanā. This is known in Tantra as the Shoraśi Pujā, the "Adoration of Woman." Sri Ramakrishna realized the significance of the great statement of the Upanishad: "O Lord, Thou art the woman, Thou art the man; Thou art the boy, Thou art the girl; Thou art the old, tottering on their crutches. Thou pervadest the universe in its multiple forms."

By his marriage Sri Ramakrishna admitted the great value of marriage in man's spiritual evolution, and by adhering to his monastic vows he demonstrated the imperative necessity of self-control, purity, and continence, for the realization of God. By his unique spiritual relationship with his wife he proved that husband and wife can live together as spiritual companions. Thus his life is a synthesis of the ways of life of the householder and the monk.

The "Ego" of the Master

In the nirvikalpa samādhi Sri Ramakrishna had realized that Brahman alone is real and the world is illusory. By keeping his mind six months on the plane of the non-dual Brahman, he had attained to the state of the vijnāni, the knower of Truth in a special and very rich sense, who sees Brahman not only in himself and in the transcendental Absolute, but in everything of the world. In this state of vijnāna, sometimes, bereft of body-consciousness, he would regard himself as one with Brahman; sometimes, conscious of the dual world, he would regard himself as God's devotee, servant, or child. In order to enable the Master to work

for the welfare of humanity, the Divine Mother had
kept in him a trace of ego, which he described—according to his mood—as the "ego of Knowledge," the
"ego of Devotion," the "ego of a child," or the "ego
of a servant." In any case this ego of the Master, consumed by the fire of the Knowledge of Brahman, was
an appearance only, like a burnt string. He often referred to this ego as the "ripe ego" in contrast with the
ego of the bound soul, which he described as the
"unripe" or "green" ego. The ego of the bound soul
identifies itself with the body, relatives, possessions,
and the world; but the "ripe ego," illumined by Divine
Knowledge, knows the body, relatives, possessions, and
the world to be unreal and establishes a relationship of
love with God alone. Through this "ripe ego" Sri
Ramakrishna dealt with the world and his wife. One
day, while stroking his feet, Sarada Devi asked the
Master, "What do you think of me?" Quick came the
answer: "The Mother who is worshipped in the
temple is the mother who has given birth to my body
and is now living in the nahabat, and it is She again
who is stroking my feet at this moment. Indeed, I
always look on you as the personification of the Blissful
Mother Kāli."

Sarada Devi, in the company of her husband, had
rare spiritual experiences. She said: "I have no words
to describe my wonderful exaltation of spirit as I
watched him in his different moods. Under the influence of divine emotion he would sometimes talk on
abstruse subjects, sometimes laugh, sometimes weep,
and sometimes become perfectly motionless in samādhi.
This would continue throughout the night. There was
such an extraordinary divine presence in him that now
and then I would shake with fear, and wonder how

the night would pass. Months went by in this way. Then one day he discovered that I had to keep awake the whole night lest, during my sleep, he should go into samādhi—for it might happen at any moment—and so he asked me to sleep in the nahabat."

SUMMARY OF THE MASTER'S SPIRITUAL EXPERIENCES

We have now come to the end of Sri Ramakrishna's sādhanā, the period of his spiritual discipline. As a result of his supersensuous experiences he reached certain conclusions regarding himself and spirituality in general. His conclusions about himself may be summarized as follows:

First, he was an Incarnation of God, a specially commissioned person, whose spiritual experiences were for the benefit of humanity. Whereas it takes an ordinary man a whole life's struggle to realize one or two aspects of God, he had in a few years realized God in His diverse aspects.

Second, he knew that he had always been a free soul, that the various disciplines through which he had passed were really not necessary for his own liberation but were solely for the benefit of others. Thus the terms liberation and bondage were not applicable to him. As long as there are beings who consider themselves bound, God must come down to earth as an Incarnation to free them from bondage, just as a magistrate must visit any part of his district in which there is trouble.

Third, he came to foresee the time of his death. His words with respect to this matter were literally fulfilled.

About spirituality in general the following were his conclusions:

First, he was firmly convinced that all religions are true, that every doctrinal system represents a path to God. He had followed all the main paths and all had led him to the same goal. He was the first religious prophet recorded in history to preach the harmony of religions.

Second, the three great systems of thought known as Dualism, Qualified Non-dualism, and Absolute Non-dualism—Dvaita, Viśishtādvaita, and Advaita—he perceived to represent three stages in man's progress toward the Ultimate Reality. They were not contradictory but complementary and suited to different temperaments. For the ordinary man with strong attachment to the senses, a dualistic form of religion, prescribing a certain amount of material support, such as music and other symbols, is useful. A man of God-realization transcends the idea of worldly duties, but the ordinary mortal must perform his duties, striving to be unattached and to surrender the results to God. The mind can comprehend and describe the range of thought and experience up to the Viśishtādvaita, and no farther. The Advaita, the last word in spiritual experience, is something to be felt in samādhi, for it transcends mind and speech. From the highest standpoint, the Absolute and Its manifestation are equally real—the Lord's Name, His Abode, and the Lord Himself are of the same spiritual essence. Everything is Spirit, the difference being only in form.

Third, Sri Ramakrishna realized the wish of the Divine Mother that through him She should found a new Order, consisting of those who would uphold the universal doctrines illustrated in his life.

Fourth, his spiritual insight told him that those who were having their last birth on this earth and those who had sincerely called on the Lord even once in their lives must come to him.

During this period Sri Ramakrishna suffered several bereavements. The first was the death of a nephew named Akshay. After the young man's death Sri Ramakrishna said: "Akshay died before my very eyes. But it did not affect me in the least. I stood by and watched how the soul left the body. It was like a sword being drawn from its scabbard. I enjoyed the scene and laughed and sang and danced over it. They removed the body and cremated it. But the next day as I stood there (*pointing to the southeast verandah of his room*), I felt a racking pain for the loss of Akshay, as if somebody were squeezing my heart like a wet towel. I wondered at it and thought that the Mother was teaching me a lesson: I was not much concerned even with my own body—much less with a relative; but if such was my pain at the loss of a nephew, how much more must be the grief of householders at the loss of their near and dear ones!" In 1871 Mathur died, and some five years later Sambhu Mallick, who, after Mathur's passing away, had taken care of the Master's comforts. In 1873 died his elder brother Rameswar, and in 1876, his beloved mother. These bereavements left their imprint on the tender human heart of Sri Ramakrishna, albeit he had realized the immortality of the soul and the illusoriness of birth and death.

In March 1875, about a year before the death of his mother, the Master met Keshab Chandra Sen. The meeting was a momentous event for both Sri Ramakrishna and Keshab. Here the Master for the first time came into actual contact with a worthy representative of modern India.

Brāhmo Samāj

Keshab was the leader of the Brāhmo Samāj, one of the two great movements that, during the later part of the nineteenth century, played an important role in shaping the course of the renascence of India. The founder of the Brāhmo movement had been the great Rājā Rammohan Roy (1774-1833). Though born in an orthodox brāhmin family, Rammohan Roy had shown great sympathy for Islām and Christianity. He had gone to Tibet in search of the Buddhist mysteries. He had extracted from Christianity its ethical system but had rejected the divinity of Christ, as he had denied the Hindu Incarnations. The religion of Islām influenced him, to a great extent, in the formulation of his monotheistic doctrines. But he always went back to the Vedas for his spiritual inspiration. The Brāhmo Samāj, which he founded in 1828, was dedicated to the "worship and adoration of the Eternal, the Unsearchable, the Immutable Being, who is the Author and Preserver of the Universe." The Samāj was open to all without distinction of colour, creed, caste, nation, or religion.

The real organizer of the Samāj was Devendranath Tagore (1817-1905), the father of the poet Rabindranath. His physical and spiritual beauty, aristocratic aloofness, penetrating intellect, and poetic sensibility made him the foremost leader of the educated Bengalis. These addressed him by the respectful epithet of Maharshi, the "Great Seer." The Maharshi was a Sanskrit scholar and, unlike Rājā Rammohan Roy, drew his inspiration entirely from the Upanishads. He was an implacable enemy of image worship and also fought to stop the infiltration of Christian ideas into the Samāj. He gave the movement its faith and ritual. Under his influence the Brāhmo Samāj professed One Self-existent Supreme Being who had created the universe out of nothing, the God of Truth, Infinite Wisdom, Goodness, and Power, the Eternal and Omnipotent, the One without a second, whom men should love and obey, believe in and worship, to merit salvation in the world to come.

By far the ablest leader of the Brāhmo movement was Keshab Chandra Sen (1838-1884). Unlike Rājā Rammohan Roy and Devendranath Tagore, Keshab was born in a middle-class Bengali family and educated in an English school. He did not know Sanskrit and very soon broke away from the popular Hindu religion. Even at an early age he came under the spell of Christ and professed to have received the special favour of John the Baptist, Christ, and St. Paul. When he strove to introduce Christ to the Brāhmo Samāj, a rupture with Devendranath became inevitable. In 1868 Keshab broke with the older leader and founded the Brāhmo Samāj of India, Devendra retaining leadership of the first Brāhmo Samāj, now called the Ādi Samāj.

Keshab possessed a complex nature. When passing through a great moral crisis, he spent much of his time in solitude and felt that he heard the voice of God. When a devotional form of worship was introduced into the Brāhmo Samāj, he spent hours in singing kirtan with his followers. He visited England in 1870 and impressed the English people with his musical voice, his simple English, and his spiritual fervour. He was entertained by Queen Victoria. Returning to India, he founded centres of the Brāhmo Samāj in various parts of the country. Not unlike a professor of comparative religion in a European university, he began to discover, about the time of his first contact with Sri Ramakrishna, the harmony of religions. He became sympathetic toward the Hindu gods and goddesses, explaining them in a liberal fashion. Further, he believed that he was called by God to dictate to the world God's newly revealed law, the New Dispensation, the Navavidhān.

In 1878 a schism divided Keshab's Samāj. Some of his influential followers accused him of infringing the Brāhmo principles by marrying one of his daughters to a wealthy man before she had attained the marriageable age approved by the Samāj. This group seceded and established the Sādhāran Brāhmo Samāj, Keshab remaining the leader of the Navavidhān. Keshab now began to be drawn more and more toward the Christ ideal, though under the influence of Sri Ramakrishna his devotion to the Divine Mother also deepened. His mental oscillation between Christ and the Divine Mother of Hinduism found no position of rest. In Bengal and some other parts of India the Brāhmo movement took the form of unitarian Christianity, scoffed at Hindu rituals, and preached a crusade against image worship. Influenced by Western culture, it declared the supremacy of reason, advocated the ideals of the French Revolution, abolished the caste-system among its own members, stood for the emancipation of women, agitated for the abolition of early marriage, sanctioned the remarriage of widows, and encouraged various educational and social-reform movements. The immediate effect of the Brāhmo movement in Bengal was the checking of the proselytizing activities of the Christian missionaries. It also raised the culture of India in the estimation of her English masters. But it was an intellectual and eclectic religious ferment born of the necessity of the time. Unlike Hinduism, it was not founded on the deep inner experience of sages and prophets. Its influence was confined to a comparatively few educated men and women of the country, and the vast masses of the Hindus remained outside it. It sounded monotonously only one of the notes in the rich gamut of the Eternal Religion of the Hindus.

Ārya Samāj

The other movement playing an important part in the nineteenth-century religious revival of India was the Ārya Samāj. The Brāhmo Samāj, essentially a movement of compromise with European culture, tacitly admitted the superiority of the West. But the founder of the Ārya Samāj was a pugnacious Hindu sannyāsi who accepted the challenge of Islām and Christianity and was resolved to combat all foreign influence in India. Swami Dayananda (1824-1883) launched this movement in Bombay in 1875, and soon its influence was felt throughout western India. The Swami was a great scholar of the Vedas, which he explained as being strictly monotheistic. He preached against the worship of images and re-established the ancient Vedic sacrificial rites. According to him the Vedas were the ultimate authority on religion, and he accepted every word of them as literally true. The Ārya Samāj became a bulwark against the encroachments of Islām and Christianity, and its orthodox flavour appealed to many Hindu minds. It also assumed leadership in many movements of social reform. The caste-system became a target of its attack. Women it liberated from many of their social disabilities. The cause of education received from it a strong impetus. It started agitation against early marriage and advocated the remarriage of Hindu widows. Its influence was strongest in the Punjab, the battleground of the Hindu and Islāmic cultures. A new fighting attitude was introduced into the slumbering Hindu society. Unlike the Brāhmo Samāj, the influence of the Ārya Samāj was not confined to the intellectuals. It was a force that spread to the masses. It was a dogmatic movement intolerant of those who disagreed with its views, and it emphasized only one way, the Ārya Samāj way, to the realization of Truth. Sri Ramakrishna met Swami Dayananda when the latter visited Bengal.

KESHAB CHANDRA SEN

Keshab Chandra Sen and Sri Ramakrishna met for the first time in the garden house of Jaygopal Sen at Belghariā, a few miles from Dakshineswar, where the great Brāhmo leader was staying with some of his disciples. In many respects the two were poles apart, though an irresistible inner attraction was to make them intimate friends. The Master had realized God as Pure Spirit and Consciousness, but he believed in the various forms of God as well. Keshab, on the other hand, regarded image worship as idolatry and gave allegorical explanations of the Hindu deities. Keshab was an orator and a writer of books and magazine articles; Sri Ramakrishna had a horror of lecturing and hardly knew how to write his own name. Keshab's fame spread far and wide, even reaching the distant shores of England; the Master still led a secluded life in the village of Dakshineswar. Keshab emphasized social reforms for India's regeneration; to Sri Ramakrishna God-realization was the only goal of life. Keshab considered himself a disciple of Christ and accepted in a diluted form the Christian sacraments and Trinity; Sri Ramakrishna was the simple child of Kāli, the Divine Mother, though he too, in a different way, acknowledged Christ's divinity. Keshab was a householder and took a real interest in the welfare of his children, whereas Sri Ramakrishna was a paramahamsa and completely indifferent to the life of the world. Yet, as their acquaintance ripened into friendship, Sri Ramakrishna and Keshab held each other in great love and respect. Years later, at the news of Keshab's death, the Master felt as if half his body had become paralysed. Keshab's concepts of the harmony of religions and the Motherhood of God were deepened and enriched by his contact with Sri Ramakrishna.

Sri Ramakrishna, dressed in a red-bordered dhoti, one end of which was carelessly thrown over his left shoulder, came to Jaygopal's garden house accompanied by Hriday. No one took notice of the unostentatious visitor. Finally the Master said to Keshab, "People tell me you have seen God; so I have come to hear from you about God." A magnificent conversation followed. The Master sang a thrilling song about Kāli and forthwith went into samādhi. When Hriday uttered the sacred "Om" in his ears, he gradually came back to consciousness of the world, his face still radiating a divine brilliance. Keshab and his followers were charmed. The contrast between Sri Ramakrishna and the Brāhmo devotees was very interesting. There sat this small man, thin and extremely delicate. His eyes were illumined with an inner light. Good humour gleamed in his eyes and lurked in the corners of his mouth. His speech was Bengali of a homely kind with a slight, delightful stammer; and he held men enthralled by his wealth of spiritual experience, his inexhaustible store of simile and metaphor, his power of observation, his bright and subtle humour, his wonderful catholicity, his ceaseless flow of wisdom. And around him now were the sophisticated men of Bengal, the best products of Western education, with Keshab, the idol of young Bengal, as their leader.

Keshab's sincerity was enough for Sri Ramakrishna. Henceforth the two saw each other frequently, either at Dakshineswar or at the temple of the Brāhmo Samāj. Whenever the Master was in the temple at the time of divine service, Keshab would request him to speak to the congregation. And Keshab would visit the saint, in his turn, with offerings of flowers and fruits.

Gradually other Brāhmo leaders began to feel Sri Ramakrishna's influence. But they were by no means uncritical admirers of the Master. They particularly disapproved of his ascetic renunciation and condemnation of "woman" and "gold." They measured him according to their own ideals of the householder's life. Some could not understand his samādhi and described it as a nervous malady. Yet they could not resist his magnetic personality.

The Brāhmo leaders received much inspiration from their contact with Sri Ramakrishna. It broadened their religious views and kindled in their hearts the yearning for God-realization; it made them understand and appreciate the rituals and symbols of the Hindu religion, convinced them of the manifestation of God in diverse forms, and deepened their thoughts about the harmony of religions. The Master, too, was impressed by the sincerity of many of the Brāhmo devotees. He told them about his own realizations and explained to them the essence of his teachings, such as the necessity of renunciation, sincerity in the pursuit of one's own course of discipline, faith in God, the performance of one's duties without thought of results, and discrimination between the Real and the unreal.

This contact with the educated and progressive Bengalis opened Sri Ramakrishna's eyes to a new realm of thought. Born and brought up in a simple village, without any formal education, and taught by the orthodox holy men of India in religious life, he had had no opportunity to study the influence of modernism on the thoughts and lives of the Hindus. He could not properly estimate the result of the impact of Western education on Indian culture. He was a Hindu of the Hindus, renunciation being to him the only means to the realization of God. From the Brāhmos he learnt that the new generation of India made a compromise between God and the world. Educated young men were influenced more by the Western philosophers than by their own prophets. But Sri Ramakrishna was not dismayed, for he saw in this, too, the hand of God. And though he expounded to the Brāhmos all his ideas about God and austere religious disciplines, yet he bade them accept from his teachings only as much as suited their tastes and temperaments.

Among the Brāhmo leaders who knew the Master closely, besides Keshab Chandra Sen, were Pratap Chandra Mazumdar, Vijaykrishna Goswāmi, Trailokyanath Sannyal, and Shivanath Shastri.

THE MASTER'S YEARNING FOR HIS OWN DEVOTEES

Contact with the Brāhmos increased Sri Ramakrishna's longing to meet aspirants who would be able to follow his teachings in their purest form. "There was no limit," he once declared, "to the longing I felt at that time. During the daytime I somehow managed to control it. The secular talk of the worldly-minded was galling to me, and I would look wistfully to the day when my own beloved companions would come. I hoped to find solace in conversing with them and relating to them my own realizations. Every little incident would remind me of them, and thoughts of them wholly engrossed me. I was already arranging in my mind what I should say to one and explain to another, and so on. But when the day would come to a close I would not be able to curb my feelings. The thought that another day had gone by and yet they had not come oppressed me. When, during the evening service, the temples rang with the sound of bells and conch-shells, I would climb to the roof of the kuthi in the garden and, writhing in anguish of heart, cry at the top of my voice: 'Come, my children! Oh, where are you all? I cannot bear to live without you.' A mother never longed so intensely for the sight of her child, nor a friend for his companion, nor a lover for his sweetheart, as I longed for them. Oh, it was indescribable! Shortly after this period of yearning the devotees[6] began to arrive."

In the year 1879 occasional writings about Sri Ramakrishna by the Brāhmos, in the Brāhmo magazines, began to attract his future disciples from the

[6] The word is generally used in the text to denote one devoted to God, a worshipper of the Personal God, or a follower of the path of love. A devotee of Sri Ramakrishna is one who is devoted to Sri Ramakrishna and follows his teachings. The word "disciple," when used in connexion with Sri Ramakrishna, refers to one who had been initiated into spiritual life by Sri Ramakrishna and who regarded him as his guru.

educated middle-class Bengalis, and they continued to come till 1884. But others, too, came, feeling the subtle power of his attraction. They were an ever shifting crowd of people of all castes and creeds: Hindus and Brāhmos, Vaishnavas and Śāktas, the educated with university degrees and the illiterate, old and young, titled aristocrats and beggars, journalists and artists, pundits and devotees, philosophers and the worldly-minded, jnānis and yogis, men of action and men of faith, virtuous women and prostitutes, officeholders and vagabonds, philanthropists and self-seekers, drama-tists and drunkards, builders-up and pullers-down. He gave to them all, without stint, from his illimitable store of realization. No one went away empty-handed. He taught them the lofty knowledge of the Vedānta and the soul-melting love of the Purāna. Twenty hours out of twenty-four he would speak without rest or respite. He gave to all his sympathy and enlighten-ment, and he touched them with that strange power of the soul which could not but melt even the most hardened. And people understood him according to their powers of comprehension.

It is fascinating to visualize the Master as he sat on his bed talking to the devotees. "Ramakrishna was a small brown man with a short beard and beautiful eyes, long dark eyes, full of light, obliquely set and slightly veiled, never very wide open, but seeing half-closed a great distance both outwardly and inwardly. His mouth was open over his white teeth in a be-witching smile, at once affectionate and mischievous. Of medium height, he was thin to emaciation and extremely delicate. His temperament was high-strung, for he was supersensitive to all the winds of joy and sorrow, both moral and physical. He was indeed a living reflection of all that happened before the mirror of his eyes, a two-sided mirror, turned both out and in."[7]

The Master's Method of Teaching

Sri Ramakrishna remained as ever the willing instrument in the hand of God, the child of the Divine Mother, untouched by the idea of being a teacher. He used to say that three words—guru, father, and master—pricked his flesh like thorns. Yet he was an extraordinary teacher. He stirred his disciples' hearts more by a subtle influence than by actions or words. He never claimed to be the founder of a religion or the organizer of a sect. Yet he was a religious dynamo. He was the verifier of all religions and creeds. He was like an expert gardener, who, after preparing the soil and removing the weeds, plants his seeds, knowing that the plants will grow because of the inherent power of the seeds, producing each its appropriate flowers and fruits. He never thrust his ideas on anybody. He understood people's limitations and worked on the principle that what is good for one may be bad for another. He had the unusual power of knowing the devotees' minds, even their inmost souls, at the first sight. He accepted disciples with the full knowledge of their past tendencies and future possibilities. The life of evil did not frighten him, nor did religious squeamishness raise anybody in his estimation. He saw in everything the unerring finger of the Divine Mother. Even the light that leads astray was to him the light from God.

To those who became his intimate disciples the

[7] Romain Rolland, *The Life of Ramakrishna*, p. 64.

Master was a friend, companion, and playmate. Even the chores of religious discipline would be lightened in his presence. The devotees would be so inebriated with pure joy in his company that they would have no time to ask themselves whether he was an Incarnation, a perfect soul, or a yogi. His very presence was a great teaching; words were superfluous. In later years his disciples remarked that while they were with him they would regard him as a comrade, but afterwards would tremble to think of their frivolities in the presence of such a great person. They had convincing proof that the Master could, by his mere wish, kindle in their hearts the love of God and give them His vision.

Through all this fun and frolic, this merriment and frivolity, he always kept before them the shining ideal of God-Consciousness and the path of renunciation. He prescribed ascents steep or graded according to the powers of the climber. He permitted no compromise with the basic principles of purity. An aspirant had to keep his body, mind, senses, and soul unspotted; had to have a sincere love for God and an ever mounting spirit of yearning. The rest would be done by the Mother.

His disciples were of two kinds: the householders, and the young men, some of whom were later to become monks. There was also a small group of women devotees.

HOUSEHOLDER DEVOTEES

For the householders Sri Ramakrishna did not prescribe the hard path of total renunciation. He wanted them to discharge their obligations to their families. Their renunciation was to be mental. Spiritual life could not be acquired by flying away from responsibilities. A married couple should live like brother and sister after the birth of one or two children, devoting their time to spiritual talk and contemplation. He encouraged the householders, saying that their life was, in a way, easier than that of the monk, since it was more advantageous to fight the enemy from inside a fortress than in an open field. He insisted, however, on their repairing into solitude every now and then to strengthen their devotion and faith in God through prayer, japa, and meditation. He prescribed for them the companionship of sādhus. He asked them to perform their worldly duties with one hand, while holding to God with the other, and to pray to God to make their duties fewer and fewer so that in the end they might cling to Him with both hands. He would discourage in both the householders and the celibate youths any lukewarmness in their spiritual struggles. He would not ask them to follow indiscriminately the ideal of non-resistance, which ultimately makes a coward of the unwary.

Below are brief accounts of a few of Sri Ramakrishna's householder devotees.

SURENDRA

Suresh Mitra, a beloved disciple whom the Master often addressed as Surendra, had received an English education and held an important post in an English firm. With many other educated young men of the time, he prided himself on his atheism and led a Bohemian life. He was addicted to drinking. He cherished an exaggerated notion about man's free will. Like most gay people a victim of mental depression, he was brought to Sri Ramakrishna by Ramchandra Dutta, one of the Master's disciples. When he heard the Master

asking a devotee to practise the virtue of self-surrender
to God, he was impressed. But though he tried thenceforth to do so, he was unable to give up his old associates and his drinking. One day the Master said in
his presence, "Well, when a man goes to an undesir-
able place, why doesn't he take the Divine Mother with
him?" And to Surendra Sri Ramakrishna said: "Why
should you drink wine as wine? Offer it to Kāli and
then take it as Her prasād, as consecrated drink. But
see that you don't become intoxicated; you must not
reel and your thoughts must not wander. At first you
will feel ordinary excitement, but soon after you will
experience spiritual exaltation." Gradually Surendra's
entire life was changed. The Master designated him
as one of those commissioned by the Divine Mother
to defray a great part of his expenses. Surendra's purse
was always open for the Master's comfort.

Mahendra or M

Mahendranath Gupta, better known as "M," arrived
at Dakshineswar in February 1882. He belonged to the
Brāhmo Samāj and was headmaster of the Vidyāsāgar
High School at Śyāmbāzār, Calcutta. At the very first
sight the Master recognized him as one of his "marked"
disciples. Mahendra recorded in his diary Sri Ramakrishna's conversations with his devotees. These are the
first directly recorded words, in the spiritual history
of the world, of a man recognized as belonging in the
class of Buddha and Christ. The present volume is a
translation of this diary. Mahendra was instrumental,
through his personal contacts, in spreading the Master's
message among many young and aspiring souls.

NAG MAHĀSHAY

Durgacharan Nag, also known as Nag Mahāshay, was the model householder among the lay disciples of Sri Ramakrishna. He was the embodiment of the Master's ideal of life in the world, unstained by worldliness. In spite of his intense desire to become a sannyāsi, Sri Ramakrishna asked him to live in the world in the spirit of a monk, and the disciple truly carried out this injunction. A man of the medical profession, he was born of a poor family and even during his boyhood often sacrificed everything to lessen the sufferings of the needy. He had married at an early age and after his wife's death had married a second time to obey his father's command. But he once said to his wife: "Love on the physical level never lasts. He is indeed blessed who can give his love to God with his whole heart. Even a little attachment to the body endures for several births. So do not be attached to this cage of bone and flesh. Take shelter at the feet of the Mother and think of Her alone. Thus your life here and hereafter will be ennobled." The Master spoke of him as a "blazing light." He received every word of Sri Ramakrishna in dead earnest. One day he heard the Master saying that it was difficult for doctors, lawyers, and brokers to make much progress in spirituality. Of doctors he said, "If the mind clings to the tiny drops of medicine, how can it conceive of the Infinite?" That was the end of Durgacharan's medical practice and he threw his chest of homoeopathic medicines into the Ganges. Sri Ramakrishna assured him that he would not lack simple food and clothing. He bade him serve holy men. On being asked where he would find real holy men, the Master said that the sādhus themselves would seek his company. No sannyāsi could have lived a more austere life than Durgacharan.

GIRISH GHOSH

Girish Chandra Ghosh was a born rebel against God, a sceptic, a Bohemian, a drunkard. He was the greatest Bengali actor and dramatist of his time, the father of the modern Bengali stage. Like other young men he had imbibed all the vices of the West. He had plunged into a life of dissipation and had become convinced that religion was only a fraud. Materialistic philosophy he justified as enabling one to get at least a little fun out of life. But a series of reverses shocked him and he became eager to solve the riddle of life. He had heard people say that in spiritual life the help of a guru was imperative and that the guru was to be regarded as God Himself. But Girish was too well acquainted with human nature to see perfection in a man. His first meeting with Sri Ramakrishna did not impress him at all. He returned home feeling as if he had seen a freak at a circus; for the Master, in a semi-conscious mood, had inquired whether it was evening, though the lamps were burning in the room. But their paths often crossed and Girish could not avoid further encounters. The Master attended a performance in Girish's Star Theatre. On this occasion, too, Girish found nothing impressive about him. One day, however, Girish happened to see the Master dancing and singing with the devotees. He felt the contagion and wanted to join them but restrained himself for fear of ridicule. Another day Sri Ramakrishna was about to give him spiritual instruction, when Girish said: "I don't want to listen to instructions. I have myself written many instructions. They are of no use to me. Please help me in a more direct way if you can." This pleased the Master and he asked Girish to cultivate faith.

As time passed, Girish began to learn that the guru is the one who silently unfolds the disciple's inner life. He became a steadfast devotee of the Master. He often loaded the Master with insults, drank in his presence, and took liberties which astounded the other devotees. But the Master knew that at heart Girish was tender, faithful, and sincere. He would not allow Girish to give up the theatre. And when a devotee asked him to tell Girish to give up drinking, he sternly replied: "That is none of your business. He who has taken charge of him will look after him. Girish is a devotee of heroic type. I tell you, drinking will not hurt him." The Master knew that mere words could not induce a man to break deep-rooted habits, but that the silent influence of love worked miracles. Therefore he never asked him to give up alcohol, with the result that Girish himself eventually broke the habit. Sri Ramakrishna had strengthened Girish's resolution by allowing him to feel that he was absolutely free.

One day Girish felt depressed because he was unable to submit to any routine of spiritual discipline. In an exalted mood the Master said to him: "All right, give me your power of attorney. Henceforth I assume responsibility for you. You need not do anything." Girish heaved a sigh of relief. He felt happy to think that Sri Ramakrishna had assumed his spiritual responsibilities. But poor Girish could not then realize that he, on his part, also had to give up his ego and make himself an instrument in Sri Ramakrishna's hands. The Master began to discipline him according to this new attitude. One day Girish said about a trifling matter, "Yes, I shall do this." "Oh, no!" the Master corrected him. "You must not speak in that egotistic manner. You should say, 'God willing, I shall do it.'" Girish understood. Thenceforth he tried to give up all idea of personal initiative and surrender himself to the Divine Will. His mind began to dwell constantly on Sri Ramakrishna. This unconscious meditation in time chastened his turbulent spirit.

The householder devotees generally visited Sri Ramakrishna on Sunday afternoons and other holidays. Thus a brotherhood was gradually formed, and the Master encouraged their fraternal feeling. Now and then he would accept an invitation to a devotee's home, where other devotees would also be invited. Kirtan would be arranged and they would spend hours in dance and devotional music. The Master would go into trances or open his heart in religious discourses and in the narration of his own spiritual experiences. Many people who could not go to Dakshineswar participated in these meetings and felt blessed. Such an occasion would be concluded with a sumptuous feast.

Sri Ramakrishna also became acquainted with a number of people whose scholarship or wealth entitled them everywhere to respect. But he was not the man to be dazzled by outward show, glory, or erudition. A pundit without discrimination he regarded as a mere straw. He would search people's hearts for the light of God, and if that was missing he would have nothing to do with them. The Europeanized Kristodas Pal did not approve of the Master's emphasis on renunciation and said: "Sir, this cant of renunciation has almost ruined the country. It is for this reason that the

Indians are a subject nation today. Doing good to others, bringing education to the door of the ignorant, and above all, improving the material conditions of the country—these should be our duty now. The cry of religion and renunciation will, on the contrary, only weaken us. You should advise the young men of Bengal to act only in such a way as will uplift the country." Sri Ramakrishna gave him a searching look and found no divine light within. "You man of poor understanding!" he said sharply. "You dare to slight in these terms renunciation and piety, which our scriptures describe as the greatest of all virtues! After reading two pages of English you think you have come to know the world! You appear to think you are omniscient. Well, have you seen those tiny crabs that are born in the Ganges just when the rains set in? In this big universe you are even less significant than one of those small creatures. How dare you talk of *helping* the world? The Lord will look to that. You haven't the power in you to do it." After a pause the Master continued: "Can you explain to me how you can work for others? I know what you mean by helping them. To feed a number of persons, to treat them when they are sick, to construct a road or dig a well—isn't that all? These are good deeds, no doubt, but how trifling in comparison with the vastness of the universe! How far can a man advance in this line? How many people can you save from famine? Malaria has ruined a whole province; what could you do to stop its onslaught? God alone looks after the world. Let a man first realize Him. Let a man get the authority from God and be endowed with His power; then, and then alone, may he think of doing good to others. A man should first be purged of all egotism. Then alone will the Blissful

Mother ask him to work for the world." Sri Ramakrishna mistrusted philanthropy that presumed to pose
as charity. He warned people against it. He saw in most
acts of philanthropy nothing but egotism, vanity, a
desire for glory, a barren excitement to kill the boredom
of life, or an attempt to soothe a guilty conscience.
True charity, he taught, is the result of love of God—
service to man in a spirit of worship.

FUTURE MONKS

To the young men destined to be monks the Master
pointed out the steep path of renunciation, both external and internal. They must take the vow of absolute
continence and eschew all thought of greed and lust.
By the practice of continence, aspirants develop a subtle
power through which they understand the deeper mysteries of God. For them self-control is final, imperative,
and absolute. The sannyāsis are teachers of men and
their lives should be totally free from blemish. They
must not even look at a picture which may awaken
their carnal passions. The Master selected his future
monks from young men untouched by "woman" and
"gold" and plastic enough to be cast in his spiritual
mould. When teaching them the path of renunciation
and discrimination, he would not allow the householders to be anywhere near them. Among these the
two outstanding disciples were Narendra and Rakhal.

RAKHAL

Even before Rakhal's coming to Dakshineswar the
Master had had visions of him as his spiritual son and
as a playmate of Krishna at Vrindāvan. Rakhal was

born of wealthy parents. During his childhood he developed wonderful spiritual traits and used to play at worshipping gods and goddesses. In his teens he was married to a sister of Manomohan Mitra, a devotee from whom he first heard of the Master. His father objected to his association with Sri Ramakrishna but afterwards was reassured to find that many celebrated people were visitors at Dakshineswar. The relationship between the Master and this beloved disciple was that of mother and child. Sri Ramakrishna allowed Rakhal many liberties denied to others. But he would not hesitate to chastise the boy for improper actions. At one time Rakhal felt a childlike jealousy because he found that other boys were receiving the Master's affection. He soon got over it and realized that his guru was the Guru of the whole universe. The Master was worried to hear of his marriage but was relieved to find that his wife was a spiritual soul who would not be a hindrance to his progress.

NARENDRA

To spread his message to the four corners of the earth Sri Ramakrishna needed a strong instrument. With his frail body and delicate limbs he could not make great journeys across wide spaces. And such an instrument was found in Narendranath Dutta, his beloved Naren, later known to the world as Swami Vivekananda. Even before meeting Narendranath the Master had seen him, in a vision, as a sage immersed in the meditation of the Absolute. Describing this remarkable experience Sri Ramakrishna said that one day, as he was absorbed in meditation, his mind left the body and soared above the earth. It soon passed the many celestial regions, leaving behind the gods and goddesses who inhabited those lofty heavens. He then transcended the entire relative universe and entered the realm of the Absolute, where he saw seven holy men lost in contemplation of Brahman. The Master realized that these great souls must have surpassed even the gods and goddesses in holiness. As he watched them, a portion of the Absolute became, as it were, condensed and took the shape of a lovely child who clambered on the lap of one of the sages. At his tender touch the holy man opened his eyes and regarded the child with great affection. The child said that he would soon assume a human body on earth and asked if the holy man would not come down to assist him in his work for the redemption of mankind. The holy man agreed. Sri Ramakrishna said that Narendra was that holy man and also declared, in answer to an inquiry, that he himself was the divine child.

Narendra was born in Calcutta on January 12, 1863, of an aristocratic kāyastha family. His mother was steeped in the great Hindu epics, and his father, a distinguished attorney of the Calcutta High Court, was an agnostic about religion, a friend of the poor, and a mocker at social conventions. In his boyhood and youth Narendra possessed great physical courage and presence of mind, a vivid imagination, deep power of thought, keen intelligence, an extraordinary memory, a love of truth, a passion for purity, a spirit of independence, and a tender heart. An expert musician, he also acquired proficiency in physics, astronomy, mathematics, philosophy, history, and literature. He grew up into an extremely handsome young man. Even as a child he practised meditation and showed great power of concentration. Though free and passionate in word and action, he took the vow of austere religious chastity and never allowed the fire of purity to be extinguished by the slightest defilement of body or soul.

As he read in college the rationalistic Western philosophers of the nineteenth century, his boyhood faith in God and religion was unsettled. He would not accept religion on mere faith; he wanted demonstration of God. But very soon his passionate nature discovered that mere Universal Reason was cold and bloodless. His emotional nature, dissatisfied with a mere abstraction, required a concrete support to help him in the hours of temptation. He wanted an external power, a guru who, by embodying perfection in the flesh, would still the commotion of his soul. Attracted by the magnetic personality of Keshab, he joined the Brāhmo Samāj and became a singer in its choir. But in the Samāj he did not find the guru who could say that he had seen God.

In a state of mental conflict and torture of soul Narendra came to Sri Ramakrishna at Dakshineswar. He was then eighteen years of age and had been in college two years. He entered the Master's room accompanied by some light-hearted friends. At Sri Ramakrishna's request he sang a few songs, pouring his whole soul into them, and the Master went into samādhi. A few minutes later Sri Ramakrishna suddenly left his seat, took Narendra by the hand, and led him to the screened verandah north of his room. They were alone. Addressing Narendra most tenderly, as if he were a friend of long acquaintance, the Master said: "Ah! You have come very late. Why have you been so unkind as to make me wait all these days? My ears are tired of hearing the futile words of worldly men. Oh, how I have longed to pour my spirit into the heart of someone fitted to receive my message!" He talked thus, sobbing all the time. Then, standing before Narendra with folded hands, he addressed him as Nārāyana, God born on earth to remove the misery of humanity. Grasping Narendra's hand, he asked him to come again, alone, and very soon. Narendra was startled. "What is this I have come to see?" he said to himself. "He must be stark mad. Why, I am the son of Viswanath Dutta. How dare he speak this way to me?"

When they returned to the room and Narendra heard the Master speaking to others, he was surprised to find in his words an inner logic, a striking sincerity, and a convincing proof of his spiritual nature. In answer to Narendra's question, "Sir, have you seen God?" the Master said: "Yes, I have seen God. I have seen Him more tangibly than I see you. I have talked to Him more intimately than I am talking to you." Continuing, the Master said: "But, my child, who wants to see God? People shed jugs of tears for money, wife, and children. But if they would weep for God for only one day they would surely see Him." Narendra was amazed. These words he could not doubt. This was the first time he had ever heard a man saying that he had seen God. But he could not reconcile these words of the Master with the scene that had taken place on the verandah only a few minutes before. He concluded that Sri Ramakrishna was a monomaniac and returned home rather puzzled in mind.

During his second visit, about a month later, suddenly, at the touch of the Master, Narendra felt overwhelmed and saw the walls of the room and everything around him whirling and vanishing. "What are you doing to me?" he cried in terror. "I have my father and mother at home." He saw his own ego and the whole universe almost swallowed up in a nameless void. With a laugh the Master easily restored him. Narendra thought he might have been hypnotized, but he could not understand how a monomaniac could cast a spell over the mind of a strong person like himself. He returned home more confused than ever, resolved to be henceforth on his guard before this strange man.

But during his third visit Narendra fared no better. This time, at the Master's touch, he lost consciousness entirely. While he was still in that state, Sri Ramakrishna questioned him concerning his spiritual antecedents and whereabouts, his mission in this world, and the duration of his mortal life. The answers confirmed what the Master himself had intuitively known and inferred. Among other things, he came to know that Narendra was a sage who had already attained perfection, and that the day he learnt his real nature he would give up his body in yoga, by an act of will.

A few more meetings completely removed from Narendra's mind the last traces of the notion that Sri Ramakrishna might be a monomaniac or wily hypnotist. His integrity, purity, renunciation, and unselfishness were beyond question. But Narendra could not accept a man, an imperfect and erring mortal, as his guru. As a member of the Brāhmo Samāj, he could not believe that a human intermediary was necessary between man and God. Moreover, he openly laughed at Sri Ramakrishna's visions as hallucinations. Yet in the secret chamber of his heart he bore a great love for the Master.

Sri Ramakrishna was grateful to the Divine Mother for sending him one who doubted his realizations. Often he asked Narendra to test him as the moneychangers tested their coins. He laughed at Narendra's biting criticism of his spiritual experiences and samādhi. When at times Narendra's sharp words distressed him, the Divine Mother Herself would console him, saying: "Why do you listen to him? In a few days he will believe your every word." He could hardly bear Narendra's absences. Often he would weep bitterly for the sight of him. Sometimes Narendra would find the Master's love embarrassing; and one day he sharply scolded him, warning him that such infatuation would soon draw him down to the level of its object. The Master was distressed and prayed to the Divine Mother. Then he said to Narendra: "You rogue, I won't listen to you any more. Mother says that I love you because I see God in you, and the day I no longer see God in you I shall not be able to bear even the sight of you."

The Master wanted to train Narendra in the teachings of the Non-dualistic Vedānta philosophy. But Narendra, because of his Brāhmo upbringing, considered it wholly blasphemous to look on man as one with his Creator. One day at the temple garden he laughingly said to a friend: "How silly! This jug is God! This cup is God! Whatever we see is God! And we too are God! Nothing could be more absurd." Sri Ramakrishna came out of his room and gently touched him. Spellbound, he immediately perceived that everything was indeed God. A new universe opened around him. Returning home in a dazed state, he found there too that the food, the plate, the eater himself, the people around him, were all God. When he walked in the street, he saw that the cabs, the horses, the streams of people, the buildings, were all Brahman. He could hardly go about his day's business. His parents became anxious about him and thought he was ill. And when the intensity of the experience abated a little, he saw the world as a dream. Walking in the public square, he would strike his head against the iron fences to know whether they were real. It took him a number of days to recover his normal self. He had a foretaste of the great experiences yet to come and felt that the words of Vedānta were true.

At the beginning of 1884 Narendra's father suddenly died of heart failure, leaving the family in a state of utmost poverty. There were six or seven mouths to feed at home. Creditors were knocking at the door. Relatives who had accepted his father's unstinted kindness now became enemies, some even bringing suit to deprive Narendra of his ancestral home. Actually starving and barefoot, Narendra searched for a job, but without success. He began to doubt whether anywhere in the world there was such a thing as unselfish sympathy. Two rich women made evil proposals to him and promised to put an end to his distress; but he refused them with contempt.

Narendra began to talk of his doubt about the very existence of God. His friends thought he had become an atheist and piously circulated gossip adducing unmentionable motives for his unbelief. His moral character was maligned. Even some of the Master's disciples partly believed the gossip, and Narendra told these to their faces that only a coward believed in God through fear of suffering or hell. But he was distressed to think that Sri Ramakrishna, too, might believe these false reports. His pride revolted. He said to himself: "What does it matter? If a man's good name rests on such slender foundations, I don't care." But later on he was amazed to learn that the Master had never lost faith in him. To a disciple who complained about Narendra's degradation, Sri Ramakrishna replied sharply: "Hush, you fool! The Mother has told me it can never be so. I won't look at you if you speak that way again."

The moment came when Narendra's distress reached its climax. He had gone the whole day without food. As he was returning home in the evening he could hardly lift his tired limbs. He sat down in front of a house in sheer exhaustion, too weak even to think. His mind began to wander. Then, suddenly, a divine power lifted the veil over his soul. He found the solution of the problem of the coexistence of divine grace and misery, the presence of suffering in the creation of a blissful Providence. He felt bodily refreshed, his soul was bathed in peace, and he slept serenely.

Narendra now felt that he had a spiritual mission to fulfil. He resolved to renounce the world, as his grandfather had renounced it, and came to Sri Ramakrishna for his blessing. But even before he had opened his mouth, the Master knew what was in his mind and wept at the thought of separation. "I know you cannot lead a worldly life," he said, "but for my sake live in the world as long as I live."

One day, soon after, Narendra requested Sri Ramakrishna to pray to the Divine Mother to remove his poverty. Sri Ramakrishna bade him pray to Her himself, for She would certainly listen to his prayer. Narendra entered the shrine of Kāli. As he stood before the image of the Mother, he beheld Her as a living Goddess, ready to give wisdom and liberation. But he thought it was foolish to ask Her for petty worldly things, and prayed only for knowledge and renunciation, love and liberation. The Master rebuked him for his failure to ask the Divine Mother to remove his poverty and sent him back to the temple. But Narendra, standing in Her presence, again forgot the purpose of his coming. Thrice he went to the temple at the bidding of the Master, and thrice he returned, having forgotten in Her presence why he had come. He was wondering about it, when it suddenly flashed in his mind that this was all the work of Sri Ramakrishna; so now he asked the Master himself to remove his poverty, and was assured that his family would not lack simple food and clothing.

This was a very rich and significant experience for Narendra. It taught him that Śakti, the Divine Power, cannot be ignored in the world and that in the relative plane the need of worshipping a Personal God for protection from misery and distress is imperative. Sri Ramakrishna was overjoyed with the conversion. The next day, sitting almost on Narendra's lap, he said to a devotee, pointing first to himself, then to Narendra: "I see I am this, and again that. Really I feel no difference. A stick floating in the Ganges seems to divide the water; but in reality the water is one. Do you see my point? Well, whatever is, is the Mother—isn't that so?" In later years Narendra would say: "Sri Ramakrishna was the only person who, from the time he met me, believed in me uniformly throughout. Even my mother and brothers did not. It was his unwavering trust and love for me that bound me to him for ever. He alone knew how to love. Worldly people only make a show of love for selfish ends."

With the exception of the elder Gopal, all of the Master's monastic disciples were in their teens or slightly over. They came from middle-class Bengali families, and most of them were students in school or college. Their parents and relatives had envisaged for them bright worldly careers. They came to Sri Rama-krishna with pure bodies, vigorous minds, and uncon-taminated souls. All were born with unusual spiritual attributes. Sri Ramakrishna accepted them, even at first sight, as his children, relatives, friends, and com-panions. His magic touch unfolded them. And later each according to his measure reflected the life of the Master, becoming a torch-bearer of his message far and near.

WOMEN DEVOTEES

With his women devotees Sri Ramakrishna estab-lished a very sweet relationship. He himself embodied the tender traits of a woman; he had dwelt on the highest plane of Truth, where there is not even the slightest trace of sex; and his innate purity evoked only the noblest emotions in men and women alike. His women devotees often said: "We seldom looked on Sri Ramakrishna as a member of the male sex. We re-garded him as one of us. We never felt any constraint before him. He was our best confidant." They loved him as their child, their friend, and their teacher. In spiritual discipline he advised them to renounce lust and greed and especially warned them not to fall into the snares of men.

GOPĀL MĀ

Unsurpassed among the women devotees of the Mas-ter in the richness of her devotion and spiritual experi-ences was Aghoremani Devi, an orthodox brāhmin woman. Widowed at an early age, she had dedicated herself completely to spiritual pursuits. Gopāla, the

Baby Krishna, was her Ideal Deity, whom she worshipped following the vātsalya attitude of the Vaishnava religion, regarding Him as her own child. Through Him she satisfied her unassuaged maternal love, cooking for Him, feeding Him, bathing Him, and putting Him to bed. This sweet intimacy with Gopāla won her the sobriquet of Gopāl Mā, or Gopāla's Mother. For forty years she had lived on the bank of the Ganges in a small, bare room, her only companions being a threadbare copy of the *Rāmāyana* and a bag containing her rosary. At the age of sixty, in 1884, she visited Sri Ramakrishna at Dakshineswar. During the second visit, as soon as the Master saw her, he said: "Oh, you have come! Give me something to eat." With great hesitation she gave him some ordinary sweets that she had purchased for him on the way. The Master ate them with relish and asked her to bring him simple curries or sweets prepared by her own hands. Gopāl Mā thought he was a queer kind of monk, for, instead of talking of God, he only asked for food. She did not want to visit him again, but an irresistible attraction brought her back to the temple garden. She carried with her some simple curries that she had cooked herself.

Soon after, one early morning Gopāl Mā was meditating when she had a remarkable experience. Gopāla, her Ideal Deity, appeared before her, sat on her lap, and presently began to move all about the room. Every now and then she found Gopāla assuming Sri Ramakrishna's form. At daybreak she hastened to Dakshineswar, still carrying the Divine Child in her arms. She found the Master absorbed in deep samādhi and Gopāla frequently entering his body and coming out of it. She was steeped in bliss and returned to her hut in a dazed condition.

Gopāl Mā spent about two months in uninterrupted communion with God, the Baby Gopāla never leaving her for a moment. Then the intensity of her vision was lessened; had it not been, her body would have perished. The Master spoke highly of her exalted spiritual condition and said that such vision of God was a rare thing for ordinary mortals. The fun-loving Master one day confronted the critical Narendranath with this simple-minded woman. No two could have presented a more striking contrast. The Master knew of Narendra's lofty contempt for all visions; he asked the old lady to narrate her experiences to Narendra. With great hesitation she told him her story. Now and then she interrupted her maternal chatter to ask Narendra: "My son, I am a poor ignorant woman. I don't understand anything. You are so learned. Now tell me if these visions of Gopāla are true." As Narendra listened to the story he was profoundly moved. He said, "Yes, mother, they are quite true." Behind his cynical exterior Narendra, too, possessed a heart full of love and tenderness.

THE MARCH OF EVENTS

In 1881 Hriday was dismissed from service in the Kāli temple for an act of indiscretion, and was ordered by the authorities never again to enter the temple garden. In a way the hand of the Divine Mother may be seen even in this. Having taken care of Sri Rama-krishna during the stormy days of his spiritual discipline, Hriday had come naturally to consider himself the sole guardian of his uncle. None could approach the Master without his knowledge, and he would be extremely jealous if Sri Ramakrishna paid attention to anyone else. Hriday's removal made it possible for the real devotees of the Master to approach him freely and live with him in the temple garden.

During the week-ends the householders, enjoying a respite from their office duties, visited the Master. The meetings on Sunday afternoons were of the nature of little festivals. Refreshments were often served. Professional musicians now and then sang devotional songs. The Master and the devotees sang and danced, Sri Ramakrishna frequently going into ecstatic moods. The happy memory of such a Sunday would linger long in the minds of the devotees. Those whom the Master wanted for special instruction he would ask to visit him on Tuesdays and Saturdays. These days were particularly auspicious for the worship of Kāli.

The young disciples destined to be monks, Sri Ramakrishna invited on week-days, when the householders were not present. The training of the householders and of the future monks had to proceed along entirely different lines. Since M generally visited the Master on week-ends, the *Gospel of Sri Ramakrishna* does not contain much mention of the future monastic disciples.

Finally, there was a handful of fortunate disciples, householders as well as youngsters, who were privileged to spend nights with the Master in his room. They would see him get up early in the morning and walk up and down the room, singing of God's glories in his sweet voice and tenderly communing with the Mother.

Injury to the Master's Arm

One day in January 1884 the Master was going toward the pine-grove, when he went into a trance. He was alone. There was no one to support him or guide his footsteps. He fell to the ground and dislocated a bone in his left arm. This accident had a significant influence on his mind, the natural inclination of which was to soar above the consciousness of the body. The acute pain in the arm forced his mind to dwell on the body and on the world outside. But he saw even in this a divine purpose; for, with his mind compelled to dwell on the physical plane, he realized more than ever that he was an instrument in the hand of the Divine Mother, who had a mission to fulfil through his human body and mind. He also distinctly found that in the phenomenal world God manifests Himself, in an inscrutable way, through diverse human beings, both good and evil. Thus he would speak of God in the guise of the wicked, God in the guise of the pious, God in the guise of the hypocrite, God in the guise of the lewd. He began to take a special delight in watching the divine play in the relative world. Sometimes the sweet human relationship with God would appear to him more appealing than the all-effacing Knowledge of Brahman. Many a time he would pray: "Mother, don't make me unconscious through the Knowledge of Brahman. Don't give me Brahmajnāna, Mother. Am I not Your child, and naturally timid? I must have my mother. A million salutations to the Knowledge of Brahman! Give it to those who want it." Again he prayed: "O Mother, let me remain in contact with men! Don't make me a dried-up ascetic. I want to enjoy Your sport in the world." Often he said that though he had seen God manifested through many different forms, he liked best His manifestation as man. He was able to taste this very rich experience and enjoy the love of God and the company of His devotees because his mind, on account of the injury to his arm, was forced to come down to the consciousness of the body. Again, he would make fun of people who proclaimed him as a Divine Incarnation, by pointing to his broken arm. He would say, "Have you ever heard of God's breaking His arm?" It took about five months for the arm to heal.

BEGINNING OF HIS ILLNESS

In April 1885 it was noticed that Sri Ramakrishna had an inflammation of the throat. Prolonged conversation or absorption in samādhi, making the blood flow into the throat, would aggravate the pain. Yet when the annual Vaishnava festival was celebrated at Pānihāti, Sri Ramakrishna attended it against the doctor's advice. With a group of disciples he spent himself in music, dance, and ecstasy. The illness took a turn for the worse and was diagnosed as "clergyman's sore throat." The patient was cautioned against conversation and ecstasies. Though he followed the physician's directions regarding medicine and diet, he could neither control his trances nor withhold from seekers the solace of his advice. Sometimes, like a sulky child, he would complain to the Mother about the crowds, who gave him no rest day or night. He was overheard to say to Her: "Why do You bring here all these worthless people, who are like milk diluted with five times its quantity of water? My eyes are almost blinded with blowing the fire to dry up the water. My health is gone. It is beyond my strength. Do it Yourself, if You want it done. This (*pointing to his own body*) is but a perforated drum, and if You go on beating it day in and day out, how long will it last?"

But his large heart never turned anyone away. He

said, "Let me be condemned to be born over and over again, even in the form of a dog, if I can be of help to a single soul." And he bore the pain, singing cheerfully, "Let the body and the illness understand each other, but do you, O mind, dwell for ever in God's Bliss."

One night he had a hemorrhage of the throat. The doctor now diagnosed the illness as cancer. Narendra was the first to break this heart-rending news to the disciples. Within three days the Master was removed to Calcutta for better treatment. At Balaram's house he remained a week until a suitable place could be found at Śyāmpukur, in the northern section of Calcutta. During this week he dedicated himself practically without respite to the instruction of those beloved devotees who had been unable to visit him oftener at Dakshineswar. Discourses incessantly flowed from his tongue, and he often went into samādhi. Dr. Mahendra Sarkar, the celebrated homoeopath of Calcutta, was invited to undertake his treatment.

ŚYĀMPUKUR

In the beginning of September 1885 Sri Ramakrishna was moved to Śyāmpukur. Here Narendra organized the young disciples to attend the Master day and night. At first they concealed the Master's illness from their guardians; but when it became more serious they remained with him almost constantly, sweeping aside the objections of their relatives and devoting themselves wholeheartedly to the nursing of their beloved guru. These young men, under the watchful eyes of the Master and the leadership of Narendra, became the antaranga bhaktas, the members of Sri Rama-

krishna's intimate circle of devotees. They were privileged to witness many manifestations of the Master's
divine powers. Narendra received instructions regarding the propagation of his message after his death.

The Holy Mother—so Sarada Devi had come to be
affectionately known to Sri Ramakrishna's devotees—
was brought from Dakshineswar to look after the
general cooking and to prepare the special diet of the
patient. The dwelling space being extremely limited,
she had to adapt herself to cramped conditions. At
three o'clock in the morning she would take her bath
in the Ganges and then enter a small covered place on
the roof, where she spent the whole day cooking and
praying. After eleven at night, when the visitors went
away, she would come down to her small bedroom on
the first floor to enjoy a few hours' sleep. Thus she
spent three months, working hard, sleeping little, and
praying constantly for the Master's recovery.

At Syāmpukur the devotees led an intense life.
Their attendance on the Master was in itself a form
of spiritual discipline. His mind was constantly soaring
to an exalted plane of consciousness. Now and then
they would catch the contagion of his spiritual fervour.
They sought to divine the meaning of this illness of
the Master, whom most of them had accepted as an
Incarnation of God. One group, headed by Girish with
his robust optimism and great power of imagination,
believed that the illness was a mere pretext to serve a
deeper purpose. The Master had willed his illness in
order to bring the devotees together and promote
solidarity among them. As soon as this purpose was
served, he would himself get rid of the disease. A
second group thought that the Divine Mother, in
whose hand the Master was an instrument, had brought

about this illness to serve Her own mysterious ends. But the young rationalists, led by Narendra, refused to ascribe a supernatural cause to a natural phenomenon. They believed that the Master's body, a material thing, was subject, like all other material things, to physical laws. Birth, growth, maturity, decay, and death were laws of nature to which the Master's body could not but respond. But though holding differing views, they all believed that it was to him alone that they must look for the attainment of their spiritual goal.

In spite of the physician's efforts and the prayers and nursing of the devotees, the illness rapidly progressed. The pain sometimes appeared to be unbearable. The Master lived only on liquid food; his frail body was becoming a mere skeleton. Yet his face always radiated joy and he continued to welcome the visitors pouring in to receive his blessing. When certain zealous devotees tried to keep the visitors away, they were told by Girish, "You cannot succeed in it; he has been born for this very purpose—to sacrifice himself for the redemption of others."

The more the body was devastated by illness, the more it revealed the presence of the Divine Spirit. Through its transparency the gods and goddesses began to shine with ever increasing luminosity. On the day of the Kāli Pujā the devotees clearly saw in him the manifestation of the Divine Mother.

LAST DAYS AT COSSIPORE

When Sri Ramakrishna's illness showed signs of aggravation, the devotees, following the advice of Dr. Sarkar, rented a spacious garden house at Cossipore, in the northern suburbs of Calcutta. The Master was removed to this place on December 11, 1885.

It was at Cossipore that the curtain fell on the varied activities of the Master's life on the physical plane. His soul lingered in the body eight months more. It was the period of his great Passion, a constant crucifixion of the body and the triumphant revelation of the Soul. Here one sees the humanity and divinity of the Master passing and repassing across a thin border line. Every minute of those eight months was suffused with touching tenderness of heart and breath-taking elevation of spirit. Every word he uttered was full of pathos and sublimity.

It took the group only a few days to become adjusted to the new environment. The Holy Mother, assisted by Sri Ramakrishna's niece, Lakshmi Devi, and a few women devotees, took charge of the cooking for the Master and his attendants. Surendra willingly bore the major portion of the expenses, other householders contributing according to their means. Twelve disciples were constant attendants of the Master: Narendra, Rakhal, Baburam, Niranjan, Jogin, Latu, Tarak, the elder Gopal, Kali, Sashi, Sarat, and the younger Gopal. Sarada, Harish, Hari, and Gangadhar visited the Master from time to time and practised sādhanā at home. Narendra, preparing for his law examination, brought his books to the garden house in order to continue his studies during the infrequent spare moments. He encouraged his brother disciples to intensify their meditation, scriptural studies, and other spiritual disciplines. They all forgot their relatives and their worldly duties.

Among the attendants Sashi was the embodiment of service. He did not practise meditation, japa, or any

other disciplines, like his brother disciples. He was
convinced that service to the guru was the only religion
for him. He forgot food and rest and was ever ready at
the Master's bedside.

Pundit Shashadhar one day suggested to the Master
that the latter could remove the illness by concentrating
his mind on the throat, the scriptures having declared
that yogis had power to cure themselves in that way.
The Master rebuked the pundit. "For a scholar like you
to make such a proposal! What a shame!" he said.
"How can I withdraw the mind from the Lotus Feet of
God and turn it to this worthless cage of flesh and
blood?" "For our sake at least," begged Narendra and
the other disciples. "But," replied Sri Ramakrishna,
"do you think I enjoy this suffering? I want to be well,
but my recovery depends on the Mother."

NARENDRA: "Then please pray to Her. She must
listen to you."

MASTER: "But I cannot pray for my body."

NARENDRA: "You must do it, for our sake at least."

MASTER: "Very well, I shall try."

A few hours later the Master said to Narendra: "I
said to Her: 'Mother, I cannot swallow food because
of my pain. Make it possible for me to eat a little.'
She pointed you all out to me and said: 'What? You are
eating enough through all these mouths. Isn't that so?'
I was ashamed and could not utter another word." This
dashed all the hopes of the devotees for the Master's
recovery.

"I shall make the whole thing public before I go,"
the Master had said some time before. On January 1,
1886, he felt better and came down to the garden
for a little stroll. It was about three o'clock in the
afternoon. Some thirty lay disciples were in the hall

or sitting about under the trees. Sri Ramakrishna said to Girish, "Well, Girish, what have you seen in me, that you proclaim me before everybody as an Incarnation of God?" Girish was not the man to be taken by surprise. He knelt before the Master and said with folded hands, "What can an insignificant person like myself say about the One whose glory even sages like Vyāsa and Vālmiki could not adequately measure?" The Master was profoundly moved. He said: "What more shall I say? I bless you all. Be illumined!" He fell into a spiritual mood. Hearing these words the devotees, one and all, became overwhelmed with emotion. They rushed to him and fell at his feet. He touched them all, and each received an appropriate benediction. Each of them, at the touch of the Master, experienced ineffable bliss. Some laughed, some wept, some sat down to meditate, some began to pray. Some saw light, some had visions of their Chosen Ideals, and some felt within their bodies the rush of spiritual power.

Narendra, consumed with a terrific fever for realization, complained to the Master that all the others had attained peace and that he alone was unsatisfied. The Master asked what he wanted. Narendra begged for samādhi, so that he might altogether forget the world for three or four days at a time. "You are a fool," the Master rebuked him. "There is a state even higher than that. Isn't it you who sing, 'All that exists art Thou'? First of all settle your family affairs and then come to me. You will experience a state even higher than samādhi."

The Master did not hide the fact that he wished to make Narendra his spiritual heir. Narendra was to continue the work after Sri Ramakrishna's passing.

Sri Ramakrishna said to him: "I leave these young men in your charge. See that they develop their spirituality and do not return home." One day he asked the boys, in preparation for a monastic life, to beg their food from door to door without thought of caste. They hailed the Master's order and went out with begging-bowls. A few days later he gave the ochre cloth of the sannyāsi to each of them, including Girish, who was now second to none in his spirit of renunciation. Thus the Master himself laid the foundation of the future Ramakrishna Order of monks.

Sri Ramakrishna was sinking day by day. His diet was reduced to a minimum and he found it almost impossible to swallow anything. He whispered to M: "I am bearing all this cheerfully, for otherwise you would be weeping. If you all say that it is better that the body should go rather than suffer this torture, I am willing." The next morning he said to his depressed disciples seated near the bed: "Do you know what I see? I see that God alone has become everything. Men and animals are only frameworks covered with skin, and it is He who is moving through their heads and limbs. I see that it is God Himself who has become the block, the executioner, and the victim for the sacrifice." He fainted with emotion. Regaining partial consciousness, he said: "Now I have no pain. I am very well." Looking at Latu he said: "There sits Latu resting his head on the palm of his hand. To me it is the Lord who is seated in that posture."

The words were tender and touching. Like a mother he caressed Narendra and Rakhal, gently stroking their faces. He said in a half whisper to M, "Had this body been allowed to last a little longer, many more souls would have been illumined." He paused a moment

and then said: "But Mother has ordained otherwise. She will take me away lest, finding me guileless
and foolish, people should take advantage of me and
persuade me to bestow on them the rare gifts of
spirituality." A few minutes later he touched his chest
and said: "Here are two beings. One is She and the
other is Her devotee. It is the latter who broke his
arm, and it is he again who is now ill. Do you understand me?" After a pause he added: "Alas! To whom
shall I tell all this? Who will understand me?" "Pain,"
he consoled them again, "is unavoidable as long as there
is a body. The Lord takes on the body for His devotees'
sake."

Yet one is not sure whether or not the Master's
soul actually was tortured by this agonizing disease.
At least during his moments of spiritual exaltation—
which became almost constant during the closing days
of his life on earth—he lost all consciousness of the
body, of illness and suffering. One of his attendants[8]
said later on: "While Sri Ramakrishna lay sick he
never actually suffered pain. He would often say, 'O
mind! Forget the body, forget the sickness, and remain
merged in Bliss.' No, he did not really suffer. At times
he would be in such a state that the thrill of joy was
clearly manifested in his body. Even when he could
not speak he would let us know in some way that
there was no suffering, and this fact was clearly evident
to all who watched him. People who did not understand him thought that his suffering was very great.
What spiritual joy he transmitted to us at that time!
Could such a thing have been possible if he himself
had been suffering physically? It was during this
period that he taught us these truths: 'Brahman is

[8] Latu, later known as Swami Adbhutananda.

always unattached. The three gunas are in It, but It is unaffected by them, just as the wind carries odour yet remains odourless.' 'Brahman is Infinite Being, Infinite Wisdom, Infinite Bliss. In It there is no delusion, no misery, no disease, no death, no growth, no decay.' 'The Transcendental Being and the being within are one and the same. There is only one indivisible Absolute Existence.' "

The Holy Mother secretly went to a Śiva temple across the Ganges to intercede with the Deity for the Master's recovery. In a revelation she was asked to prepare herself for the inevitable end.

One day when Narendra was on the ground floor, meditating, the Master was lying awake in his bed upstairs. In the depths of his meditation Narendra felt as though a lamp were burning at the back of his head. Suddenly he lost consciousness. It was the yearned-for, all-effacing experience of nirvikalpa samādhi, when the embodied soul realizes its unity with the Absolute. After a very long time he regained partial consciousness but was unable to find his body. He could see only his head. "Where is my body?" he cried. The elder Gopal entered the room and said, "Why, it is here, Naren!" But Narendra could not find it. Gopal, frightened, ran upstairs to the Master. Sri Ramakrishna only said: "Let him stay that way for a time. He has worried me long enough."

After another long period Narendra regained full consciousness. Bathed in peace, he went to the Master, who said: "Now the Mother has shown you everything. But this revelation will remain under lock and key, and I shall keep the key. When you have accomplished the Mother's work you will find the treasure again."

Some days later, Narendra being alone with the

Master, Sri Ramakrishna looked at him and went into samādhi. Narendra felt the penetration of a subtle power and lost all outer consciousness. Regaining presently the normal mood, he found the Master weeping.

Sri Ramakrishna said to him: "Today I have given you my all and I am now only a poor fakir, possessing nothing. By this power you will do immense good in the world, and not until it is accomplished will you return." Henceforth the Master lived in the disciple.

Doubt, however, dies hard. After one or two days Narendra said to himself, "If in the midst of this racking physical pain he declares himself to be the Godhead, then only shall I accept him as an Incarnation of God." He was alone by the bedside of the Master. It was merely a passing thought, but the Master smiled. Gathering his remaining strength, he distinctly said, "He who was Rāma and Krishna is now, in this body, Ramakrishna—but not in your Vedāntic sense."[9] Narendra was stricken with shame.

MAHĀSAMĀDHI

It was Sunday, August 15, 1886. The Master's pulse became irregular. The devotees stood by the bedside. Toward dusk Sri Ramakrishna had difficulty in breathing. A short time afterwards he complained of hunger. A little liquid food was put into his mouth; some of it he swallowed, and the rest ran over his chin. Two attendants began to fan him. All at once he went into samādhi of a rather unusual type. The body became stiff. Sashi burst into tears. But after

[9] Both Rāma and Krishna are regarded by Hindu dualists as Divine Incarnations, God Himself. Non-dualistic Vedānta, however, does not accept an Incarnation as the Ultimate Reality.

midnight the Master revived. He was now very hungry and helped himself to a bowl of farina pudding. He said he was strong again. He sat up against five or six pillows, which were supported by the body of Sashi, who was fanning him. Narendra took his feet on his lap and began to rub them. Again and again the Master repeated to him, "Take care of these boys." Then he asked to lie down. Three times in ringing tones he cried the name of Kāli, his life's Beloved, and lay back. At two minutes past one there was a low sound in his throat and his head fell a little to one side. A thrill passed over his body. His hair stood on end. His eyes became fixed on the tip of his nose. His face was lighted with a smile. The final ecstasy began. It was mahāsamādhi, total absorption, from which his mind never returned. Narendra, unable to bear it, ran downstairs.

Dr. Sarkar arrived the following noon and pronounced that life had departed not more than half an hour before. At five o'clock the Master's body was brought downstairs, laid on a cot, dressed in ochre clothes, and decorated with sandal-paste and flowers. A procession was formed. The passers-by wept as the body was taken to the cremation ground at the Barānagore Ghāt on the Ganges.

While the devotees were returning to the garden house, carrying the sacred ashes, a calm resignation came to their souls and they cried, "Victory unto the Guru!"

The Holy Mother was weeping in her room, not for her husband, but because she felt that Mother Kāli had left her. As she was about to put on the marks of a Hindu widow, in a moment of revelation she heard the words of faith: "I have only passed from one room to another."

The Gospel of
Sri Ramakrishna

MASTER AND DISCIPLE

February 1882

IT WAS ON A SUNDAY in the spring of 1882, a few days after Sri Ramakrishna's birthday, that M met him the first time. Sri Ramakrishna lived at the Kālibāri, the abode of Mother Kāli, on the bank of the Ganges at Dakshineswar.

M, being at leisure on Sundays, had gone with his friend Sidhu to visit several gardens at Barānagore. As they were walking in Prasanna Bannerji's garden, Sidhu said: "There is a charming place on the bank of the Ganges where a paramahamsa lives. Would you like to go there?" M assented and they started immediately for the Dakshineswar temple garden. They arrived at the main gate at dusk and went straight to Sri Ramakrishna's room. And there they found him seated on a wooden couch, facing the east. With a smile on his face he was talking of God. The room was full of people, all seated on the floor, drinking in his words in deep silence.

M stood there speechless and looked on. It was as if he were standing where all the holy places met and as if Śukadeva himself were speaking the word of God, or as if Sri Chaitanya were singing the names and glories of the Lord in Puri with his devotees.

Sri Ramakrishna said: "When, hearing the name of Hari or Rāma once, you shed tears and your hair

stands on end, then you may know for certain that
you do not have to perform such devotions as the
sandhyā any more. Only then will you have the right
to renounce rituals; or rather, rituals will drop away
of themselves. Then it will be enough if you repeat
only the name of Rāma or Hari, or even simply Om."

M looked around him with wonder and said to himself: "What a beautiful place! What a charming man!
How beautiful his words are! I have no wish to move
from this spot." After a few minutes he thought, "Let
me see the place first; then I'll come back here and sit
down."

As he left the room with Sidhu, he heard the sweet
music of the evening service arising in the temple
from gongs, bells, drums, and cymbals. He could hear
music from the nahabat, too, at the south end of the
garden. The sounds travelled over the Ganges, floating
away and losing themselves in the distance. A soft
spring wind was blowing, laden with the fragrance of
flowers; the moon had just appeared. It was as if nature
and man together were preparing for the evening worship. M and Sidhu visited the twelve Śiva temples,
the Rādhākānta temple, and the temple of Bhavatārini.
And as M watched the services before the images his
heart was filled with joy.

On the way back to Sri Ramakrishna's room the
two friends talked. Sidhu told M that the temple garden had been built by Rāni Rasmani. He said that
God was worshipped there daily as Kāli, Krishna, and
Śiva, and that within the gates many sādhus and
beggars were fed. When they reached Sri Ramakrishna's door again, they found it shut, and Brindē,
the maid, standing outside. M, who had been trained
in English manners and would not enter a room unan-

nounced, asked her, "Is the holy man in?" Brindē replied, "Yes, he's in the room."

M: "How long has he lived here?"

BRINDĒ: "Oh, he has been here a long time."

M: "Does he read many books?"

BRINDĒ: "Books? Oh, dear no! They're all on his tongue."

M had just finished his studies in college. It amazed him to hear that Sri Ramakrishna read no books.

M: "Perhaps it is time for his evening devotions. May we go into the room? Will you tell him we are eager to see him?"

BRINDĒ: "Go right in, children. Go in and sit down."

Entering the room, they found Sri Ramakrishna alone, seated on the wooden couch. Incense had just been burnt and all the doors were shut. As he entered, M with folded hands saluted the Master. Then, at the Master's bidding, he and Sidhu sat on the floor. Sri Ramakrishna asked them: "Where do you live? What is your occupation? Why have you come to Barānagore?" M answered the questions, but he noticed that now and then the Master seemed to become absent-minded. Later he learnt that this mood is called bhāva, ecstasy. It is like the way an angler acts when sitting with his rod: the fish comes and swallows the bait, and the float begins to tremble; the angler is on the alert; he grips the rod and watches the float steadily and eagerly; he will not speak to anyone. Such was the state of Sri Ramakrishna's mind. Later M heard, and himself noticed, that Sri Ramakrishna would often go into this mood after dusk, sometimes becoming totally unconscious of the outer world.

M: "Perhaps you want to perform your evening devotions. In that case may we take our leave?"

SRI RAMAKRISHNA (*still in ecstasy*): "No. Evening devotions? No, it is not exactly that."

After a little conversation M saluted the Master and took his leave. "Come again," Sri Ramakrishna said.

On his way home M began to wonder: "Who is this serene-looking man who is drawing me back to him? Is it possible for a man to be great without being a scholar? How wonderful it is! I should like to see him again. He himself said, 'Come again.' I shall go tomorrow or the day after."

M's second visit to Sri Ramakrishna took place on the southeast verandah at eight o'clock in the morning. The Master was about to be shaved, the barber having just arrived. As the cold season still lingered he had wrapped himself in a red-bordered moleskin shawl. Seeing M, the Master said: "So you have come. That's good. Sit down here." He was smiling. He stammered a little when he spoke.

SRI RAMAKRISHNA (*to M*): "Where do you live?"

M: "In Calcutta, sir."

SRI RAMAKRISHNA: "Where are you staying here?"

M: "I am at Barānagore at my elder sister's—Ishan Kavirāj's house."

SRI RAMAKRISHNA: "Oh, at Ishan's? Well, how is Keshab now? He was very ill."

M: "Indeed, I have heard so too. But I believe he is well now."

SRI RAMAKRISHNA: "I made a vow to worship the Mother with green coconut and sugar on Keshab's recovery. Sometimes, in the early hours of the morning, I would wake up and pray to Her: 'Mother, please make Keshab well again. If Keshab doesn't

live, whom shall I talk with when I go to Calcutta?'
And so it was that I resolved to offer Her the green
coconut and sugar.

"Tell me, do you know of a certain Mr. Cook who
has come to Calcutta? Is it true that he is giving
lectures? Once Keshab took me on a steamer, and this
Mr. Cook, too, was in the party."

M: "Yes, sir, I have heard something like that; but
I have never been to his lectures. I don't know much
about him."

SRI RAMAKRISHNA: "Pratap's brother came here.
He stayed a few days. He had nothing to do and said
he wanted to live here. I came to know that he had
left his wife and children with his father-in-law. He
has a whole brood of them! So I took him to task.
Just fancy! He is the father of so many children! Will
people from the neighbourhood feed them and bring
them up? He isn't even ashamed that someone else is
feeding his wife and children, and that they have been
left at his father-in-law's house. I scolded him very
hard and asked him to look for a job. Then he was
willing to leave here.

"Are you married?"

M: "Yes, sir."

SRI RAMAKRISHNA (*with a shudder*): "Oh, Ramlal![1]
Alas, he is married!"

Like one guilty of a terrible offence, M sat motionless, his eyes fixed on the ground. He said to himself,
"Is it such a wicked thing to marry?"

The Master continued, "Have you any children?"

This time M could hear the beating of his own heart.

[1] A nephew of Sri Ramakrishna, and a priest in the
Kāli temple.

He whispered in a trembling voice, "Yes, sir, I have children."

Very sadly Sri Ramakrishna said, "Ah me! He even has children!"

Thus rebuked M sat speechless. His pride had received a blow. After a few minutes Sri Ramakrishna looked at him kindly and said: "You see, you have certain good signs. I know them by looking at a person's forehead, his eyes, and so on. Tell me, now, what kind of person is your wife? Is she a jnāni, a wise person, or is she ignorant?"

M: "She is all right. But I am afraid she is ignorant."

MASTER (with evident displeasure): "And you are a jnāni!"

M had yet to learn the distinction between knowledge and ignorance. Up to this time he had thought one got knowledge from books and schools. Later on he gave up this false idea. He was taught that to know God is knowledge, and not to know Him, ignorance. When Sri Ramakrishna exclaimed, "And you are a jnāni!", M's ego was again badly shocked.

MASTER: "Well, do you believe in God with form or without form?"

M, rather surprised, said to himself: "How can one believe in God without form when one believes in God with form? And if one believes in God without form, how can one believe that God has a form? Can these two contradictory ideas be true at the same time? Can a white liquid like milk be black?"

M: "Sir, I like to think of God as formless."

MASTER: "Very good. It is enough to have faith in either aspect. You believe in God without form; that is quite all right. But never for a moment think that this alone is true and all else false. Remember that God with form is just as true as God without form. But hold fast to your own conviction."

The assertion that both are equally true amazed M; he had never learnt this from his books. Thus his ego received a third blow; but since it was not yet completely crushed, he came forward to argue with the Master a little more.

M: "Sir, suppose one believes in God with form. Certainly He is not the clay image!"

MASTER (*interrupting*): "But why clay? It is an image of Spirit."

M could not quite understand the meaning of this "image of Spirit." "But, sir," he said to the Master, "one should explain to those who worship the clay image that it is *not* God, and that, while worshipping it, they should have God in view and not the clay image. One should not worship clay."

MASTER (*sharply*): "That's the one hobby of you Calcutta people—giving lectures and bringing others to the light! Nobody ever stops to consider how to get the light himself. Who are you to teach others?

"He who is the Lord of the Universe will teach everyone. He alone will teach us, who has created this universe; who has made the sun and moon, men and beasts, and all other beings; who has provided means for their sustenance; who has given children parents and endowed them with love to bring them up. The Lord has done so many things—will He not show people the way to worship Him? If they need teaching, then He will be the Teacher. He is our Inner Guide.

"Suppose there is an error in worshipping the clay image; doesn't God know that through it He alone is being invoked? He will be pleased with that very worship. Why should you get a headache over it? You had better try for knowledge and devotion yourself."

This time M felt that his ego was completely crushed. He now said to himself: "Yes, he has spoken the truth. What need is there for me to teach others? Have I known God? Do I really love Him? How true the proverb is: I haven't room enough for myself in my bed, and I am inviting a friend to share it with me! I know nothing about God, yet I am trying to teach others. What a shame! How foolish I am! This is not mathematics or history or literature, that one can teach it to others. No, this is the deep mystery of God. What he says appeals to me."

This was M's first argument with the Master, and happily his last.

MASTER: "You were talking of worshipping the clay image. Even if the image *is* made of clay, there is need for that kind of worship. God Himself has provided different forms of worship. He who is the Lord of the Universe has arranged all these forms to suit different men in different stages of knowledge.

"The mother cooks different dishes to suit the stomachs of her different children. Suppose she has five children. If there is a fish to cook, she prepares various dishes from it—pilau, pickled fish, fried fish, and so on—to suit their different tastes and powers of digestion.

"Do you understand me?"

M (*humbly*): "Yes, sir. How, sir, may I fix my mind on God?"

MASTER: "Repeat God's name and sing His glories, and now and then visit God's devotees and holy men. The mind cannot dwell on God if it is immersed day and night in worldliness, in worldly duties and responsibilities; it is most necessary to go into solitude now and then and think of God. To fix the mind on God is very difficult, in the beginning, unless one practises meditation in solitude. When a tree is young it should be fenced all around; otherwise it may be destroyed by cattle.

"There are three ways of meditating: think of God while doing your duties, or meditate on Him in a secluded corner of your house, or contemplate Him in a wood. And you should always discriminate between the Real and the unreal: God alone is real, the Eternal Substance; all else is unreal, that is, impermanent. By discriminating thus, one should shake off impermanent objects from the mind."

M (*humbly*): "How ought we to live in the world?"

MASTER: "Do all your duties, but keep your mind on God. Live with all—with wife and children, father and mother—and serve them. Treat them as if they were very dear to you, but know in your heart of hearts that they do not belong to you.

"A maidservant in the house of a rich man performs all the household duties, but her thoughts are fixed on her own home in her native village. She brings up her master's children as if they were her own. She even speaks of them as 'my Rāma' or 'my Hari.' But in her own mind she knows very well that they do not belong to her at all.

"The tortoise moves about in the water. But can you guess where her thoughts are? There on the bank, where her eggs are lying. Do all your duties in the world, but keep your mind on God.

"If you enter the world without first cultivating love for God, you will be entangled more and more. You will be overwhelmed with its danger, its grief, its sorrows. And the more you think of worldly things, the more you will be attached to them.

"First rub your hands with oil and then break open the jack-fruit; otherwise they will be smeared with its sticky milk. First secure the oil of divine love and then set your hands to the duties of the world.

"But one must go into solitude to attain this divine love. To get butter from milk you must let it set into curd in a secluded spot: if it is too much disturbed, milk won't turn into curd. Next, you must put aside all other duties, sit in a quiet spot, and churn the curd. Only then do you get butter.

"Further, by meditating on God in solitude the mind acquires knowledge, dispassion, and devotion. But the very same mind goes downward if it dwells in the world. In the world one only thinks of 'woman' and 'gold.'[2]

[2] The words "woman" and "gold" occur again and again in the teachings of Sri Ramakrishna to designate the chief impediments to spiritual progress. This favourite expression of the Master, "kāminikānchan," has often been misconstrued. By it he meant only "lust" and "greed," the baneful influence of which retards the aspirant's spiritual growth. He used the word "kāmini," or "woman," as a concrete term for the sex instinct when addressing his men devotees. He advised women, on the other hand, to shun "man." "Kānchan," or "gold," symbolizes greed, which is the other obstacle to spiritual life. Sri Ramakrishna never taught his disciples to hate any woman, or womankind in general. This can be seen clearly by going through all his teachings on this subject and judging them collectively. The Master looked on all women as so many images of the Divine Mother of the Universe. He paid the highest homage to womankind by accepting a woman as his guide while practising the very profound spiritual disciplines of Tantra. His wife, known and revered as the Holy Mother, was his constant companion and first disciple. At the end of

"The world is water and the mind, milk. If you pour milk into water they become one; you cannot find the pure milk any more. But turn the milk into curd and churn it into butter. Then, when that butter is placed in water, it will float. So, practise spiritual discipline in solitude and obtain the butter of knowledge and love. Even if you keep that butter in the water of the world the two will not mix. The butter will float.

"Together with this you must practise discrimination. 'Woman' and 'gold' are impermanent. God is the only Eternal Substance. What does a man get with money? Food, clothes, and a dwelling-place—nothing more. You cannot realize God with its help. Therefore money can never be the goal of life. That is the process of discrimination. Do you understand?"

M: "Yes, sir."

MASTER: "Consider: what is there in money or in a beautiful body? Discriminate and you will find that even the body of the most beautiful woman consists of bones, flesh, fat, and other disagreeable things. Why should a man give up God and direct his attention to such things? Why should he forget God for their sake?"

M: "Is it possible to *see* God?"

MASTER: "Yes, certainly. Living in solitude now and then, repeating God's name and singing His glories, and discriminating between the Real and the unreal —these are the means to employ to see Him."

M: "Under what conditions does one see God?"

MASTER: "Cry to the Lord with an intensely yearn-

---

his spiritual practice he literally worshipped her as the embodiment of the Goddess Kāli, the Divine Mother. After his passing away the Holy Mother became the spiritual guide not only of a large number of householders, but also of many monastic members of the Ramakrishna Order.

ing heart and you will certainly see Him. People shed a whole jug of tears for wife and children. They swim in tears for money. But who weeps for God? Cry to Him with a real cry.

"Longing is like the rosy dawn. After the dawn out comes the sun. Longing is followed by the vision of God.

"God reveals Himself to a devotee who feels drawn to Him by the combined force of these three attractions: the attraction of worldly possessions for the worldly man, the child's attraction for its mother, and the husband's attraction for the chaste wife. If one feels drawn to Him by the combined force of these three attractions, then one can attain Him.

"The point is, to love God even as the mother loves her child, the chaste wife her husband, and the worldly man his wealth. Join together these three forces of love, these three powers of attraction, and direct them all to God. Then you will certainly see Him.

"It is necessary to pray to Him with a longing heart. The kitten knows only how to call its mother, crying, 'Mew, mew!' It remains satisfied wherever its mother puts it. And the mother cat puts the kitten sometimes in the kitchen, sometimes on the floor, and sometimes on the bed. When it suffers it cries only, 'Mew, mew!' That's all it knows. But as soon as the mother hears this cry, wherever she may be, she comes to the kitten."

It was Sunday afternoon when M came on his third visit to the Master. He had been profoundly impressed by his first two visits to this wonderful man. He had been thinking of the Master constantly, and of the utterly simple way he explained the deep truths of the spiritual life. Never before had he met such a man.

Sri Ramakrishna was sitting on the small couch. The room was filled with devotees, who had taken advantage of the holiday to come to see the Master. M had not yet become acquainted with any of them; so he took his seat in a corner. The Master smiled as he talked with the devotees.

He addressed his words particularly to a young man of nineteen named Narendranath,[3] who was a college student and frequented the Brāhmo Samāj. His eyes were bright, his words were full of spirit, and he had the look of a lover of God.

M guessed that the conversation was about worldly men, who looked down on those who aspired to spiritual things. The Master was talking about the great number of such people in the world and about how to deal with them.

MASTER (to Narendra): "How do you feel about it? Worldly people say all kinds of things about the spiritually minded. But look here. When an elephant moves along the street, any number of curs and other small animals may bark and make a noise, but the elephant doesn't even look back at them. If people speak ill of you, what will you think of them?"

NARENDRA: "I shall think that dogs are barking at me."

MASTER (smiling): "Oh, no! You mustn't go that far, my child! (Laughter.) God dwells in all beings. But you may be intimate only with good people; you must keep away from the evil-minded. God is even in the tiger; but you cannot embrace the tiger on that account. (Laughter.) You may say, 'Why run away

[3] Subsequently world-famous as Swami Vivekananda.

from a tiger, which is also a manifestation of God?'
The answer to that is: Those who tell you to run away
are also manifestations of God; why shouldn't you
listen to them?

"Let me tell you a story. In a forest there lived a
holy man who had many disciples. One day he taught
them to see God in all beings and therefore to bow
low before them all. A disciple went to the forest to
gather wood for the sacrificial fire. Suddenly he heard
an outcry: 'Get out of the way! A mad elephant is
coming!' All but the disciple of the holy man took to
their heels. He reasoned that the elephant was also
God in another form. Then why should he run away
from it? He stood still, bowed before the animal, and
began to sing its praises. The māhut of the elephant
shouted: 'Run away! Run away!' But the disciple didn't
move. The animal seized him with its trunk, cast him
to one side, and went on its way. Hurt and bruised, the
disciple lay unconscious on the ground. Hearing what
had happened, his teacher and his brother disciples
came to him and carried him to the hermitage. With the
help of some medicine he soon regained consciousness.
Someone asked him, 'You knew the elephant was
coming; why didn't you leave the place?' 'But,' he said,
'our teacher told us that God Himself has taken all
these forms, of animals as well as men. Therefore,
thinking it was only the elephant God that was coming,
I didn't run away.' At this the teacher said: 'Yes, my
child, it is true that the elephant God was coming; but
the māhut God forbade you to stay there. Since all
are manifestations of God, why didn't you trust the
māhut's words? You should have heeded the words of
the māhut God.' (Laughter.)

"It is said in the scriptures that water is a form of

God. But some water is fit to be used for worship, some water for washing the face, and some only for washing plates or dirty linen. This last sort cannot be used for drinking or for worship. In like manner, God undoubtedly dwells in the hearts of all—holy and unholy, righteous and unrighteous; but a man should not have dealings with the unholy, the wicked, the impure. He must not be intimate with them. With some of them he may exchange words, but with others he shouldn't go even that far. He should keep aloof from such people."

A DEVOTEE: "Sir, if a wicked person is about to do harm, or actually does so, should we keep quiet then?"

MASTER: "A man living in society should make a show of anger to protect himself from evil-minded people. But he should not harm anybody in anticipation of harm likely to be done him.

"Listen to a story. Some cowherd boys used to tend their cows in a meadow where a terrible poisonous snake lived. Everyone was on the alert for fear of it. One day a brahmachāri was going along the meadow. The boys ran to him and said: 'Revered sir, please don't go that way. A venomous snake lives over there.' 'What of it, my good children?' said the brahmachāri. 'I am not afraid of the snake. I know some mantras.' So saying, he continued on his way along the meadow. But the cowherd boys, being afraid, did not accompany him. In the mean time the snake moved swiftly toward him with upraised hood. As soon as it came near, he recited a mantra, and the snake lay at his feet like an earthworm. The brahmachāri said: 'Look here. Why do you go about doing harm? Come, I will teach you a holy word. By repeating it you will learn to love God. In this way you will get rid of your violent nature and ultimately realize Him.' Saying this, he taught the snake a holy word and initiated him into spiritual life. The snake bowed before the teacher and said, 'Revered sir, how shall I practise spiritual discipline?' 'Repeat that sacred word,' said the teacher, 'and do not harm anybody.' As he was about to depart the brahma-chāri said, 'I shall see you again.'

"Some days passed and the cowherd boys noticed that the snake did not bite. They threw stones at it. Still it showed no anger; it behaved as if it were an earthworm. One day one of the boys came close to it, caught it by the tail, and, whirling it round and round, dashed it again and again on the ground and threw it away. The snake vomited blood and became unconscious. It was stunned. It could not move. So, thinking it dead, the boys went their way.

"Late at night the snake regained consciousness. Slowly and with great difficulty it dragged itself into its hole; its bones were broken and it could scarcely move. Many days passed. The snake became a mere skeleton covered with skin. Now and then, at night, it would come out in search of food. For fear of the boys it would not leave its hole during the daytime. Since receiving the sacred word from the teacher, it had given up injuring others. It lived on dirt, leaves, or the fruit that dropped from the trees.

"About a year later the brahmachāri came that way again and asked after the snake. The cowherd boys told him that it was dead. But he couldn't believe them. He knew that the snake would not die before attaining the fruit of the holy word with which it had been initiated. He found his way to the place and, searching here and there, called it by the name he had given it.

Hearing the teacher's voice, it came out of its hole and bowed before him with great reverence. 'How are you?' asked the brahmachari. 'I am all right, sir,' replied the snake. 'But,' the teacher asked, 'why are you so thin?' The snake replied: 'Revered sir, you ordered me not to harm anybody. So I have been living only on leaves and fruit. Perhaps that has made me thinner.'

"The snake had become righteous; it could not be angry with anyone. It had totally forgotten that the cowherd boys had almost killed it.

"The brahmachari said: 'It can't be mere want of food that has reduced you to this state. There must be some other reason. Think a little.' Then the snake remembered that the boys had dashed it against the ground. It said: 'Yes, revered sir, now I remember. The boys one day dashed me violently against the ground. They are ignorant, after all. They didn't realize what a great change had come over my mind. How could they know I wouldn't bite or harm anyone?' The brahmachari exclaimed: 'What a shame! You are such a fool! You don't know how to protect yourself. I asked you not to bite, but I didn't forbid you to hiss. Why didn't you scare them by hissing?'

"So you must hiss at wicked people. You must frighten them lest they should do you harm. But never inject your venom into them. One must not injure others.

"In this creation of God there is a variety of things: men, animals, trees, plants. Among the animals some are good, some bad. There are ferocious animals like the tiger. Some trees bear fruit sweet as nectar, and others bear fruit that is poisonous. Likewise, among human beings there are the good and the wicked, the holy and the unholy. There are some who are devoted to God, and others who are attached to the world.

"Men may be divided into four classes: those bound by the fetters of the world, the seekers after liberation, the liberated, and the ever-free.

"Among the ever-free we may count sages like Nārada. They live in the world for the good of others, to teach men spiritual truths.

"Those in bondage are sunk in worldliness and forgetful of God. Not even by mistake do they think of God.

"The seekers after liberation want to free themselves from attachment to the world. Some of them succeed and some do not.

"The liberated souls, such as the sādhus and mahātmās, are not entangled in the world, in 'woman' and 'gold.' Their minds are free from worldliness. Besides, they always meditate on the Lotus Feet of God.

"Suppose a net has been cast into a lake to catch fish. Some fish are so clever that they are never caught. They are like the ever-free. But most of the fish are entangled in the net. Some of them try to free themselves from it; they are like those who seek liberation. But not all the fish that struggle succeed. A very few do jump out of the net, making a big splash in the water. Then the fishermen shout, 'Look! There goes a big one!' But most of the fish caught in the net cannot escape, nor do they make any effort to get out. On the contrary, they burrow into the mud, net and all, and lie there quietly, thinking, 'We need not fear any more; we are quite safe here.' But the poor things do not know that the fishermen will drag them out with the net. These are like the men bound to the world.

"The bound souls are tied to the world by the fetters of lust and greed. They are bound hand and foot. They think that 'woman' and 'gold' will make them happy and give them security; they do not realize that these will lead them to annihilation. When a man thus bound to the world is about to die, his wife asks, 'You are about to go; but what have you done for me?' Again, such is his attachment to the things of the world that, when he sees the lamp burning brightly, he says: 'Dim the light. Too much oil is burning.' And he is on his death-bed!

"The bound souls never think of God. If they get any leisure they indulge in idle gossip and foolish talk, or they engage in fruitless work. If you ask one of them the reason, he answers, 'Oh, I cannot keep still; so I am making a fence.' When time hangs heavy on their hands they perhaps start playing cards."

There was deep silence in the room.

A DEVOTEE: "Sir, is there no help, then, for such a worldly person?"

MASTER: "Certainly there is. From time to time he should live in the company of holy men, and also go into solitude to meditate on God. Furthermore, he should practise discrimination and pray to God for faith and devotion. When a person has faith he has achieved everything. There is nothing greater than faith.

(*To Kedar*) "You must have heard about the tremendous power of faith. It is said in the Purāna that Rāma, who was God Himself—the embodiment of the Absolute Brahman—had to build a bridge to cross the sea to Ceylon. But Hanumān, His devotee, trusting in

Rāma's name, cleared the sea in one jump and reached the other side. He had no need of a bridge. (*All laugh.*)

"Once a man was about to cross the sea. Bibhishana wrote Rāma's name on a leaf, tied it in a corner of the man's wearing-cloth, and said to him: 'Don't be afraid. Have faith and walk on the water. But look here: the moment you lose faith you will be drowned.' The man was walking easily on the water. Suddenly he had an intense desire to see what was tied in his cloth. He opened it and found only a leaf with Rāma's name written on it. 'What is this?' he said to himself. 'Just the name of Rāma!' As soon as doubt entered his mind he sank under the water.

"If a man has faith in God, then even if he has committed the most heinous sins—such as killing a cow, a brāhmin, or a woman—he will certainly be saved through his faith. Let him only say to God, 'O Lord, I will not repeat such an action,' and he need not be afraid of anything."

When he had said this, the Master sang:

If only I can pass away repeating Durgā's name,
How canst Thou then, O Blessed One,
Withhold deliverance from me,
Wretched though I am?
I may have stolen a drink of wine, or killed an unborn
    child,
Or slain a woman or a cow,
Or even caused a brāhmin's death;
But, though it all be true,
Nothing of this can rouse in me the slightest trace of
    fear,
For through the power of Thy sweet name
My wretched soul may still aspire
Even to Brahman's realm.

Pointing to Narendra, the Master said: "You all see this boy. He behaves that way here. But he is quite another person when he plays in the chāndni. A naughty boy seems very gentle when with his father. Narendra and people of his type belong to the class of the ever-free. They are never entangled in the world. When they grow a little older they feel the awakening of inner consciousness and go directly toward God. They come to the world only to teach others. They never care for anything of the world. They are never attached to 'woman' and 'gold.'

"The Vedas speak of the homā bird. It lives high up in the sky and there it lays its egg. As soon as the egg is laid it begins to fall; but it is so high up that it continues to fall for many days. As it falls it hatches, and the chick falls. As the chick falls its eyes open; it grows wings. As soon as its eyes open, it realizes that it is falling and will be dashed to pieces on touching the earth. Then it at once shoots up toward the mother bird high in the sky."

At this point Narendra left the room. Kedar, Pran-krishna, M, and many others remained.

MASTER: "You see, Narendra excels in singing, playing on instruments, study—in everything. The other day he had a discussion with Kedar and tore his arguments to shreds. (All laugh.)

(To M) "Is there any book in English on reasoning?"

M: "Yes, sir, there is. It is called Logic."

MASTER: "Tell me what it says."

M was a little embarrassed. He said: "One part of the book deals with deduction from the general to the particular. For example: All men are mortal. Scholars are men. Therefore scholars are mortal. Another part deals with the method of reasoning from the particular

to the general. For example: This crow is black. That
crow is black. The crows we see everywhere are black.
Therefore all crows are black. But there may be a
fallacy in a conclusion reached that way; for on inquiry
one may find a white crow in some country. There is
another illustration: If there is rain, there is or has
been a cloud. Therefore rain comes from a cloud. Still
another example: This man has thirty-two teeth.
That man has thirty-two teeth. All the men we see have
thirty-two teeth. Therefore men have thirty-two teeth.
English logic deals with such inductions and de-
ductions."

Sri Ramakrishna barely heard these words. While
listening he became absent-minded. So the conversation did not proceed far.

When the meeting broke up, the devotees sauntered
in the temple garden. M went in the direction of the
Panchavati. It was about five o'clock in the afternoon.
After a while he returned to the Master's room. There,
on the small north verandah, he witnessed an amazing
sight.

Sri Ramakrishna was standing still, surrounded by
a few devotees. Narendra was singing. M had never
heard anyone except the Master sing so sweetly. When
he looked at Sri Ramakrishna he was struck with
wonder; for the Master stood motionless, with eyes
transfixed. He seemed not even to breathe. A devotee
told M that the Master was in samādhi. M had never
before seen or heard of such a thing. Silent with
wonder, he thought: "Is it possible for a man to be so
oblivious of the outer world in the consciousness of
God? How deep must be his faith and devotion to
bring about such a state!"

Narendra was singing:

Meditate, O my mind, on the Lord Hari,
The Stainless One, Pure Spirit through and
    through.
How peerless is the Light that shines in Him!
How soul-bewitching is His wondrous form!
How dear is He to all His devotees!

Ever more beauteous in fresh-blossoming love
That shames the splendour of a million moons,
Like lightning gleams the glory of His form,
Raising erect the hair for very joy.

The Master shuddered when this last line was sung.
His hair stood on end and tears of joy streamed down
his cheeks. Now and then his lips parted in a smile.
Was he seeing the peerless beauty of God, "that shames
the splendour of a million moons"? Was this the vision
of God, the Essence of Spirit? How much austerity and
discipline, how much faith and devotion, must be
necessary for such a vision!

The song went on:

Worship His feet in the lotus of your heart;
With mind serene and eyes made radiant
With heavenly love, behold that matchless sight.

Again that bewitching smile. The body motionless
as before, the eyes half shut, as if beholding a wonderful inner vision.

The song drew to a close. Narendra sang the last
lines:

Caught in the spell of His love's ecstasy,
Immerse yourself for evermore, O mind,
In Him who is Pure Knowledge and Pure Bliss.

The sight of the samādhi, and the divine bliss he had
witnessed, left an indelible impression on M's mind.
He returned home deeply moved. Now and then he

could hear within himself the echo of those soul-intoxicating lines:

Immerse yourself for evermore, O mind,
In Him who is Pure Knowledge and Pure Bliss.

The next day, too, was a holiday for M. He arrived at Dakshineswar at three o'clock in the afternoon. Sri Ramakrishna was in his room; Narendra, Bhavanath, and a few other devotees were sitting on a mat spread on the floor. They were all young men of nineteen or twenty. Seated on the small couch, Sri Ramakrishna was smilingly talking with them.

No sooner had M entered the room than the Master laughed aloud and said to the boys, "There he comes again!" They all joined in the laughter. M bowed low before him and took a seat. Before this he had saluted the Master with folded hands, like one with an English education. But that day he learnt to fall down at his feet in orthodox Hindu fashion.

Presently the Master explained the cause of his laughter to the devotees. He said: "A man once fed a peacock with a pill of opium at four o'clock in the afternoon. The next day, exactly at that time, the peacock came back. It had felt the intoxication of the drug and returned just in time to have another dose." (All laugh.)

M considered this an apt illustration. Even at home he had been unable to banish the thought of Sri Ramakrishna for a moment. His mind was constantly at Dakshineswar and he had counted the minutes until he should go there again.

In the mean time the Master was having great fun with the boys, treating them as if they were his most intimate friends. Peals of side-splitting laughter filled the room, as if it were a mart of joy. The whole thing was a revelation to M. He thought: "Didn't I see him only yesterday intoxicated with God? Wasn't he swimming then in the Ocean of Divine Love—a sight I had never seen before? And today the same person is behaving like an ordinary man! Wasn't it he who scolded me on the first day of my coming here? Didn't he admonish me, saying, 'And you are a jnāni!'? Wasn't it he who said to me that God with form is as true as God without form? Didn't he tell me that God alone is real, and all else illusory? Wasn't it he who advised me to live in the world unattached, like a maidservant in a rich man's house?"

Sri Ramakrishna was enjoying the company of the young devotees; now and then he glanced at M. He noticed that M sat in silence. The Master said to Ramlal: "You see, he is a little advanced in years and therefore somewhat serious. He sits quiet while the youngsters are making merry." M was then about twenty-eight years old.

The Master said to Narendra and M, "I should like to hear you speak and argue in English." They both laughed. But they continued to talk in their mother tongue. It was impossible for M to argue any more before the Master. Though Sri Ramakrishna insisted, they did not talk in English.

At five o'clock in the afternoon all the devotees except Narendra and M took leave of the Master. As M was walking in the temple garden, he suddenly came upon the Master talking to Narendra on the bank of the goose pond. Sri Ramakrishna said to Narendra: "Look here. Come a little oftener. You are a new-comer. On first acquaintance people visit each other quite often, as is the case with a lover and his sweetheart. (*Narendra and M laugh.*) So please come, won't you?"

Narendra, a member of the Brāhmo Samāj, was very particular about his promises. He said with a smile, "I shall try."

As they were returning to the Master's room, Sri Ramakrishna said to M: "When peasants go to market to buy bullocks for their ploughs, they can easily tell the good from the bad by touching their tails. On being touched there, some meekly lie down on the ground. The peasants at once recognize that these are without mettle and so reject them. They select only those bullocks that frisk about and show spirit when their tails are touched. Narendra is like a bullock of this latter class. He is full of inner spirit."

The Master smiled as he said this, and continued: "There are some people who have no grit whatever. They are like flattened rice soaked in milk—soft and mushy. No inner strength!"

It was dusk. The Master was meditating on God. He said to M: "Go and talk to Narendra. Then tell me what you think of him."

Evening worship was over in the temples. M met Narendra on the bank of the Ganges and they began to converse. Narendra told M about his studying in college, his being a member of the Brāhmo Samāj, and so on.

It was now late in the evening and time for M's departure; but he felt reluctant to go and instead went in search of Sri Ramakrishna. He had been fascinated by the Master's singing and wanted to hear more. At last he found the Master pacing alone in the nātmandir in front of the Kāli temple. Lamps were burning in the shrine-room on either side of the image of the

Divine Mother. A single lamp in the spacious nāt-mandir blended light and darkness into a kind of mystic twilight, in which the figure of the Master could be dimly seen.

M had been enchanted by the Master's sweet music. With some hesitation he asked him whether there would be any more singing that evening. "No, not tonight," said Sri Ramakrishna after a little reflection. Then, as if remembering something, he added: "But I'm going soon to Balaram Bose's house in Calcutta. Come there and you'll hear me sing." M agreed to go.

MASTER: "Do you know Balaram Bose?"

M: "No, sir. I don't."

MASTER: "He lives in Bosepārā."

M: "Well, sir, I shall find him."

As Sri Ramakrishna walked up and down the hall with M, he said to him: "Let me ask you something. What do you think of me?"

M remained silent. Again Sri Ramakrishna asked: "What do you think of me? What percentage of the Knowledge of God do I possess?"

M: "I don't know exactly what you mean by 'percentage.' But of this I am sure: Never before have I seen such knowledge, such ecstatic love, such faith in God, such renunciation, and such liberality anywhere."

The Master laughed.

M bowed low before him and took his leave. He had gone as far as the main gate of the temple garden when he suddenly remembered something and came back to Sri Ramakrishna, who was still in the nātmandir. In the dim light the Master, all alone, was pacing the hall, rejoicing in the Self—as the lion lives and roams alone in the forest.

In silent wonder M surveyed that great soul.

MASTER (*to M*): "What makes you come back?"

M: "Perhaps the house you asked me to go to belongs to a rich man. They may not let me in. I think I had better not go. I would rather meet you here."

MASTER: "Oh, no! Why should you feel like that? Just mention my name. Say that you want to see me; then someone will take you to me."

M nodded his assent and, after saluting the Master, took his leave.

2

VISIT TO VIDYĀSĀGAR

Saturday, August 5, 1882

Pundit Iswar Chandra Vidyāsāgar was born in
the village of Beersingh, not far from Kāmārpukur,
Sri Ramakrishna's birthplace. He was known as a
great scholar, educator, writer, and philanthropist.
One of the creators of modern Bengali, he was also
well versed in Sanskrit grammar and poetry. His
generosity made his name a household word with his
countrymen, most of his income being given in charity
to widows, orphans, indigent students, and other
needy people. Nor was his compassion limited to
human beings: he stopped drinking milk for years so
that the calves should not be deprived of it, and he
would not drive in a carriage for fear of causing discomfort to the horses. He was a man of indomitable
spirit, which he showed when he gave up the lucrative
position of principal of the Sanskrit College of Calcutta because of a disagreement with the authorities.
His affection for his mother was especially deep. One
day, in the absence of a ferryboat, he swam a raging
river at the risk of his life to fulfil her wish that he
should be present at his brother's wedding. His whole
life was one of utter simplicity. The title Vidyāsāgar,
meaning "Ocean of Learning," was given him in
recognition of his vast erudition.

Sri Ramakrishna had long wanted to visit Iswar

Chandra Vidyāsāgar. Learning from M that he was a teacher at Vidyāsāgar's school, the Master asked: "Can you take me to Vidyāsāgar? I should like very much to see him." M told Iswar Chandra of Sri Ramakrishna's wish, and the pundit gladly agreed; he asked M to bring the Master some Saturday afternoon at four o'clock. He only wanted to know what kind of paramahamsa the Master was, saying, "Does he wear an ochre cloth?" M answered: "No, sir. He is an unusual person. He wears a red-bordered cloth and polished slippers. He lives in a room in Rāni Rasmani's temple garden. In his room there is a couch with a mattress and mosquito net. He has no outer indication of holiness. But he doesn't know anything except God. Day and night he thinks of God alone."

On the afternoon of August 5 the Master left Dakshineswar in a hackney carriage, accompanied by Bhavanath, M, and Hazra. Vidyāsāgar lived in Bādurbāgān, in central Calcutta, about six miles from Dakshineswar. On the way Sri Ramakrishna talked with his companions; but as the carriage neared Vidyāsāgar's house his mood suddenly changed. He was overpowered with divine ecstasy. Not noticing this, M pointed out the garden house where Rājā Rammohan Roy had lived. The Master was annoyed and said, "I don't care about those things now." He was going into an ecstatic state.

The carriage stopped in front of Vidyāsāgar's house. The Master alighted, supported by M, who then led the way. In the courtyard there were many flowering plants. As the Master walked to the house he said to M, like a child, pointing to his shirt-buttons: "My shirt is unbuttoned. Will that offend Vidyāsāgar?" "Oh, no!" said M. "Don't be anxious about it. Nothing about you will be offensive. You don't have to button your shirt." He accepted the assurance simply, like a child.

Vidyāsāgar was about sixty-two years old, sixteen or seventeen years older than the Master. He lived in a two-storey house built in the English fashion, with lawns on all sides and surrounded by a high wall. After climbing the stairs to the second floor, Sri Ramakrishna and his devotees entered a room at the far end of which Vidyāsāgar was seated facing them, with a table in front of him. To the right of the table was a bench. Some friends occupied chairs on the other two sides.

Vidyāsāgar rose to receive the Master. Sri Ramakrishna stood in front of the bench, with one hand resting on the table. He gazed at Vidyāsāgar, as if they had known each other before, and smiled in an ecstatic mood. In that mood he remained standing a few minutes. Now and then, to bring his mind back to normal consciousness, he said, "I will have a drink of water."

In the mean time the young members of the household and a few friends and relatives of Vidyāsāgar had gathered around. Sri Ramakrishna, still in an ecstatic mood, sat on the bench. A young man, seventeen or eighteen years old, who had come to Vidyāsāgar to seek financial help for his education, was seated there. The Master sat down at a little distance from the boy, saying in an abstracted mood: "Mother, this boy is very much attached to the world. He belongs to Thy realm of ignorance."

Vidyāsāgar told someone to bring water and asked M whether the Master would like some sweetmeats also. Since M did not object, Vidyāsāgar himself went eagerly to the inner apartments and brought the sweets. They were placed before the Master. Bhavanath and

Hazra received their share. When they were offered to M, Vidyāsāgar said: "Oh, he is like one of the family. We needn't worry about him." Referring to a young devotee, the Master said to Vidyāsāgar: "He is a nice young man and is sound at the core. He is like the river Phalgu: the surface is covered with sand, but if you dig a little you will find water flowing underneath."

After taking some of the sweets, the Master, with a smile, began to speak to Vidyāsāgar. Meanwhile the room had become filled with people; some were standing and others were seated.

MASTER: "Ah! Today, at last, I have come to the 'ocean.'[1] Up till now I have seen only canals, marshes, or a river at the most. But today I am face to face with the sāgar, the ocean." (All laugh.)

VIDYĀSĀGAR (smiling): "Then please take home some salt water." (Laughter.)

MASTER: "Oh, no! Why salt water? You aren't the ocean of ignorance. You are the ocean of vidyā, knowledge. You are the ocean of condensed milk." (All laugh.)

VIDYĀSĀGAR: "Well, you may put it that way."

The pundit became silent. Sri Ramakrishna said: "Your activities are inspired by sattva. Though they are rājasic, they are influenced by sattva. Compassion springs from sattva. Though work for the good of others belongs to rajas, yet this rajas has sattva for its basis and is not harmful. Śuka and other sages cherished compassion in their minds to give people religious instruction, to teach them about God. You are distributing food and learning. That is good too. If

[1] This is an allusion to the title of the host; "Vidyāsāgar" means "Ocean of Learning."

these activities are done in a selfless spirit they lead
to God. But most people work for fame or to acquire
merit. Their activities are not selfless.

"Mere pundits are like a diseased fruit that becomes
hard and puckered and will not ripen at all. Such
a fruit has neither the freshness of a green fruit nor
the flavour of a ripe one. Vultures soar very high
in the sky, but their eyes are fixed on rotten carrion on
the ground. The book-learned are reputed to be wise,
but they are attached to 'woman' and 'gold.' Like the
vultures, they are in search of carrion. They are attached to the world of ignorance. Compassion, love of
God, and renunciation are the glories of true knowledge."

Vidyāsāgar listened to these words in silence. The
others, too, gazed at the Master and were attentive
to every word he said.

Vidyāsāgar, though a student of Hindu philosophy,
was reticent about giving spiritual instruction. Once,
when M asked him his opinion of it, Vidyāsāgar
said, "I think the philosophers have failed to explain
what was in their minds." But in his daily life he
followed all the rituals of Hindu religion and wore the
sacred thread of a brāhmin. About God he had once
declared: "It is indeed impossible to know Him. What,
then, should be our duty? It seems to me that we
should live in such a way that, if others followed our
example, this very earth would be heaven. Everyone
should try to do good to the world."

Sri Ramakrishna's conversation now turned to the
Knowledge of Brahman.

MASTER: "Brahman is beyond vidyā and avidyā,
knowledge and ignorance. It is beyond māyā, the
illusion of duality.

"The world consists of the illusory duality of knowledge and ignorance. It contains knowledge and devotion, and also attachment to 'woman' and 'gold'; righteousness and unrighteousness; good and evil. But Brahman is unattached to these. Good and evil apply to the jiva, the individual soul, as do righteousness and unrighteousness; but Brahman is not at all affected by them.

"One man may read the *Bhāgavata* by the light of a lamp, and another may commit a forgery by that very light; but the lamp is unaffected. The sun sheds its light on the wicked as well as on the virtuous.

"You may ask, 'How, then, can one explain misery and sin and unhappiness?' The answer is that these apply only to the jiva. Brahman is unaffected by them. There is poison in a snake; but though others may die if bitten by it, the snake itself is not affected by the poison.

"What Brahman is cannot be described. All things in the world—the Vedas, the Purānas, the Tantras, the six systems of philosophy—have been defiled, like food that has been touched by the tongue, for they have been read or uttered by the tongue. Only one thing has not been defiled in this way, and that is Brahman. No one has ever been able to say what Brahman is."

VIDYĀSĀGAR (*to his friends*): "Oh! That is a remarkable statement. I have learnt something new today."

MASTER: "A man had two sons. The father sent them to a preceptor to learn the Knowledge of Brahman. After a few years they returned from their preceptor's house and bowed low before their father. Wanting to measure the depth of their knowledge of

Brahman, he first questioned the older of the two boys. 'My child,' he said, 'you have studied all the scriptures. Now tell me, what is the nature of Brahman?' The boy began to explain Brahman by reciting various texts from the Vedas. The father did not say anything. Then he asked the younger son the same question. But the boy remained silent and stood with eyes cast down. No word escaped his lips. The father was pleased and said to him: 'My child, you have understood a little of Brahman. What It is cannot be expressed in words.'

"Men often think they have understood Brahman fully. Once an ant went to a hill of sugar. One grain filled its stomach. Taking another grain in its mouth it started homeward. On its way it thought, 'Next time I shall carry home the whole hill.' That is the way shallow minds think. They don't know that Brahman is beyond one's words and thought. However great a man may be, how much can he know of Brahman? Śukadeva and sages like him may have been big ants; but even they could carry at the utmost eight or ten grains of sugar!

"As for what has been said in the Vedas and the Purānas, do you know what it is like? Suppose a man has seen the ocean, and somebody asks him, 'Well, what is the ocean like?' The first man opens his mouth as wide as he can and says: 'What a sight! What tremendous waves and sounds!' The description of Brahman in the sacred books is like that. It is said in the Vedas that Brahman is of the nature of Bliss; It is Satchidānanda.

"Śuka and other sages stood on the shore of this Ocean of Brahman and saw and touched the water. According to one school of thought they never plunged into it. Those who do cannot come back to the world again.

"In samādhi one attains the Knowledge of Brahman —one realizes Brahman. In that state reasoning stops altogether and man becomes mute. He has no power to describe the nature of Brahman.

"Once a salt doll went to measure the depth of the ocean. (*All laugh.*) It wanted to tell others how deep the water was. But this it could never do, for no sooner had it got into the water than it melted. Now who was there to speak about the depth?"

A DEVOTEE: "Suppose a man has obtained the Knowledge of Brahman in samādhi. Doesn't he speak any more?"

MASTER: "Śankarāchārya[2] retained the 'ego of Knowledge' in order to teach others. After the vision of Brahman a man becomes silent. He reasons about It as long as he has not realized It. If you heat butter in a pan on the stove, it makes a sizzling sound as long as the water it contains has not dried up. But when no trace of water is left the clarified butter makes no sound. If you put an uncooked cake of flour in that butter it sizzles again. But after the cake is cooked all sound stops. Just so, a man established in samādhi comes down to the relative plane of consciousness in order to teach others, and then he talks about God.

"The bee buzzes as long as it is not sitting on a flower. It becomes silent when it begins to sip the honey. But sometimes, intoxicated with the honey, it buzzes again.

"An empty pitcher makes a gurgling sound when it is dipped in water. When it fills up it becomes silent. (*All laugh.*) But if the water is poured from it into

[2] One of the greatest philosophers of India.

another empty pitcher, then you will hear the sound
again.

"The rishis of old attained the Knowledge of Brahman. One cannot have this Knowledge so long as
there is the slightest trace of worldliness. How hard
the rishis laboured! Early in the morning they would
go away from the hermitage and spend the whole day
in solitude, meditating on Brahman. At night they
would return to the hermitage and eat a little fruit
or roots. They kept their minds aloof from the objects
of sight, hearing, touch, and other things of a worldly
nature. Only thus did they realize Brahman as their
own inmost Consciousness.

"But in the Kaliyuga, man, being totally dependent
on food for life, cannot altogether shake off the idea
that he is the body. In this state of mind it is not
proper for him to say, 'I am He.' When a man does
all sorts of worldly things, he should not say, 'I am
Brahman.' Those who cannot give up attachment to
worldly things and who find no means to shake off the
feeling of 'I,' should rather cherish the idea, 'I am
God's servant; I am His devotee.' One can also realize
God by following the path of devotion.

"The jnāni gives up his identification with worldly
things, discriminating, 'Not this, not this.' Only then
can he realize Brahman. It is like reaching the roof
of a house by leaving the steps behind, one by one.
But the vijnāni, who is more intimately acquainted
with Brahman, realizes something more. He realizes
that the steps are made of the same materials as the
roof: bricks, lime, and brick-dust. That which is realized
intuitively as Brahman, through the eliminating process
of 'Not this, not this,' is then found to have become
the universe and all its living beings. The vijnāni sees

that the Reality which is nirguna, without attributes, is also saguna, with attributes.

"A man cannot live on the roof a long time. He comes down again. Those who realize Brahman in samādhi come down also and find that it is Brahman that has become the universe and its living beings. In the musical scale there are the notes sā, rē, gā, mā, pā, dhā, and ni; but one cannot keep one's voice on 'ni' a long time. The ego does not vanish altogether. The man coming down from samādhi perceives that it is Brahman that has become the ego, the universe, and all living beings. This is known as vijnāna.

"The path of knowledge leads to Truth, as does the path that combines knowledge and love. The path of love, too, leads to this goal. The way of love is as good as the way of knowledge. All paths ultimately lead to the same Truth. But as long as God keeps the feeling of ego in us, it is easier to follow the path of love.

"The vijnāni sees that Brahman is immovable and actionless, like Mount Sumeru. This universe consists of the three gunas: sattva, rajas, and tamas. They are in Brahman. But Brahman is unattached.

"The vijnāni further sees that what is Brahman is the Bhagavān, the Personal God. He who is beyond the three gunas is the Bhagavān, with His six supernatural powers. Living beings, the universe, mind, intelligence, love, renunciation, knowledge—all these are the manifestations of His power. (*With a laugh*) If an aristocrat has neither house nor property, or if he has been forced to sell them, one doesn't call him an aristocrat any more. (*All laugh.*) God is endowed with the six supernatural powers. If He were not, who would obey Him? (*All laugh.*)

"Just see how picturesque this universe is! How many things there are! The sun, moon, and stars. And how many varieties of living beings! Big and small, good and bad, strong and weak—some endowed with more power, some with less."

VIDYĀSĀGAR: "Has God endowed some with more power and others with less?"

MASTER: "As the All-pervading Spirit, God exists in all beings, even in an ant. But the manifestations of His power are different in different beings; otherwise, how can one person put ten to flight, while another can't face even one? And why do all people respect you? Have you grown a pair of horns? (*Laughter.*) You have more compassion and learning. Therefore people honour you and come to pay you their respects. Don't you agree with me?"

Vidyāsāgar smiled.

The Master continued: "There is nothing in mere scholarship. The object of study is to find means of knowing God and realizing Him. A holy man treasured a book. When asked what it contained, he opened it and showed that on all the pages were written the words 'Om Rāma,' and nothing else.

"What is the significance of the Gītā? It is what you find by repeating the word ten times. It is then reversed into 'tāgi,' which means a person who has renounced everything for God. And the lesson of the Gītā is: 'O man, renounce everything and seek God alone.' Whether a man is a monk or a householder, he has to shake off all attachment from his mind.

"Chaitanyadeva set out on a pilgrimage to southern India. One day he saw a man reading the Gītā. Another man, seated at a distance, was listening and weeping. His eyes were swimming in tears. Chaitanya-

deva asked him, 'Do you understand all this?' The
man said, 'No, revered sir, I don't understand a word
of the text.' 'Then why are you crying?' asked Chaitanya. The devotee said: 'As I listen to the book, I see
Arjuna's chariot before me. I see Lord Krishna and
Arjuna seated in it, talking. I see all this and I weep.'

"Why does a vijnāni keep an attitude of love toward
God? The answer is that 'I-consciousness' persists. It
disappears in the state of samādhi, no doubt, but it
comes back. In the case of ordinary people the 'I' never
disappears. You may cut down the aśvattha tree, but
the next day new sprouts shoot up. (All laugh.)

"Even after the attainment of Knowledge this 'I-
consciousness' comes up, nobody knows from where.
You dream of a tiger. Then you awake. But your
heart keeps on palpitating! All our suffering is due
to this 'I.'

"Once Rāma asked Hanumān, 'How do you look
on Me?' Hanumān replied: 'O Rāma, as long as I have
the feeling of "I," I see that Thou art the whole and
I am a part; Thou art the Master and I am Thy servant.
But when, O Rāma, I have the knowledge of Truth,
then I realize that Thou art I, and I am Thou.'

"The relationship of master and servant is the proper
one. Since this 'I' must remain, let the rascal be God's
servant.

" 'I' and 'mine'—these constitute ignorance. 'My
house,' 'my wealth,' 'my learning,' 'my possessions'—
the attitude that prompts one to say such things comes
of ignorance. On the contrary, the attitude born of
Knowledge is: 'O God, Thou art the Master, and all
these things belong to Thee. House, family, children,
attendants, friends, are Thine.'

"One should constantly remember death. Nothing will survive death. We are born into this world to perform certain duties, like the people who come from the countryside to Calcutta on business. If a visitor goes to a rich man's garden, the superintendent says to him, 'This is our garden,' 'This is our lake,' and so forth. But if the superintendent is dismissed for some misdeed, he can't openly carry away even his worthless mangowood chest. He sends it secretly by the gate-keeper. (*Laughter.*)

"Can one know God through reasoning? Be His servant, surrender yourself to Him, and then pray to Him.

(*To Vidyāsāgar, with a smile*) "Well, what is your attitude?"

VIDYĀSĀGAR (*smiling*): "Some day I shall confide it to you." (*All laugh.*)

MASTER (*laughing*): "God cannot be realized through mere scholarly reasoning."

Intoxicated with divine love, the Master sang:

Has anyone truly understood what Mother Kāli is?
Even the six darśanas are powerless to reveal Her.
It is She, the scriptures say, that is the Inner Self
Of the yogi, who from the Self alone obtains his joy;
She that, of Her own sweet will, inhabits every living
    thing. . . .

Continuing, the Master said: "Did you notice that line? 'Even the six darśanas are powerless to reveal Her.' She cannot be realized by means of mere scholarship. One must have faith and love. If a man has faith in God, then he need not be afraid though he may have committed sin—nay, the vilest sin.

"Faith and devotion. One realizes God easily through devotion. He is grasped through ecstasy of love."

With these words the Master sang again:

How are you trying, O my mind, to know the nature of God?
You are groping like a madman locked in a dark room.
He is grasped through ecstatic love; how can you fathom Him without it?
Only through affirmation, never negation, can you know Him;
Neither through Veda nor through Tantra nor the six darśanas.

It is in love's elixir only that He delights, O mind;
He dwells in the body's inmost depths, in everlasting joy.
And, for that love, the mighty yogis practise yoga from age to age;
When love awakes, the Lord, like a magnet, draws to Him the soul.

He it is, says Rāmprasād, that I approach as Mother;
But shall I give away the secret here in the market-place?
From these hints I have given, O mind, guess what that Being is.

While singing, the Master went into samādhi. He was seated on the bench, facing west, the palms of his hands joined together, his body erect and motionless. Everyone watched him expectantly. Vidyāsāgar, too, was speechless and could not take his eyes away from the Master.

After a time Sri Ramakrishna showed signs of regaining the normal state. He drew a deep breath and said with a smile: "The means of realizing God are ecstasy of love and devotion—that is to say, one must love God. He who is Brahman is addressed as the Mother.

He it is, says Rāmprasād, that I approach as Mother;
But must I give away the secret here in the market-
    place?
From these hints I have given, O mind, guess what
    that Being is.

"Rāmprasād asks the mind only to guess the nature of God. He wishes it to understand that what is called Brahman in the Vedas is addressed by him as the Mother. He who is attributeless also has attributes. He who is Brahman is also Śakti. When thought of as inactive, He is called Brahman, and when thought of as the Creator, Preserver, and Destroyer, He is called the Primordial Energy, Kālī.

"Brahman and Śakti are identical, like fire and its power to burn. When we talk of fire we automatically mean also its power to burn. Again, the fire's power to burn implies the fire itself. If you accept the one you must accept the other.

"Brahman alone is addressed as the Mother. This is because a mother is an object of great love. One is able to realize God just through love. Ecstasy of feeling, devotion, love, and faith—these are the means. Listen to a song:

As is a man's meditation, so is the depth of his love;
As is the depth of his love, so is his gain;
And faith is the root of all.
If in the Nectar Lake of Mother Kālī's feet
My mind remains immersed,
Of little use are worship, oblations, or sacrifice.

"What is needed is absorption in God—loving Him

intensely. The 'Nectar Lake' is the Lake of Immortality. A man sinking in it does not die, but becomes immortal.

(*To Vidyāsāgar*) "The activities that you are engaged in are good. It is very good if you can perform them in a selfless spirit, renouncing egotism, giving up the idea that you are the doer. Through such action one develops love and devotion to God, and ultimately realizes Him.

"The more you come to love God, the less you will be inclined to perform action. When a daughter-in-law is with child, her mother-in-law gives her less work to do. As time goes by she is given less and less work. When the time of delivery nears, she is not allowed to do any work at all, lest it should hurt the child or cause difficulty at the time of birth.

"By these philanthropic activities you are really doing good to yourself. If you can do them disinterestedly, your mind will become pure and you will develop love of God. As soon as you have that love you will realize Him.

"Man cannot really help the world. God alone does that—He who has created the sun and the moon, who has put love for their children in parents' hearts, who has endowed noble souls with compassion, and holy men and devotees with divine love. The man who works for others, without any selfish motive, really does good to himself.

"There is gold buried in your heart, but you are not yet aware of it. It is covered with a thin layer of earth. Once you are aware of it, all these activities of yours will lessen. After the birth of her child, the daughter-in-law in the family busies herself with it alone. Everything she does is only for the child. Her mother-in-law doesn't let her do any household duties.

"Through selfless work, love of God grows in the heart. Then, through His grace, one realizes Him in course of time. God can be seen. One can talk to Him as I am talking to you."

In silent wonder all sat listening to the Master's words. It seemed to them that the Goddess of Wisdom Herself, seated on Sri Ramakrishna's tongue, was addressing these words not merely to Vidyāsāgar, but to all humanity for its good.

It was nearly nine o'clock in the evening. The Master was about to leave.

MASTER (*to Vidyāsāgar, with a smile*): "The words I have spoken are really superfluous. You know all this; you simply aren't conscious of it. There are countless gems in the coffers of Varuna. But he himself isn't aware of them."

VIDYĀSĀGAR (*with a smile*): "You may say as you like."

MASTER (*smiling*): "Oh, yes. There are many wealthy people who don't know the names of all their servants and are even unaware of many of the precious things in their houses." (*All laugh.*)

Everybody was delighted with the Master's conversation. Again addressing Vidyāsāgar, he said with a smile: "Please visit the temple garden some time—I mean the garden of Rasmani. It's a charming place."

VIDYĀSĀGAR: "Oh, of course I shall go. You have so kindly come here to see me, and shall I not return your visit?"

MASTER: "Visit me? Oh, never think of such a thing!"

VIDYĀSĀGAR: "Why, sir? Why do you say that? May I ask you to explain?"

MASTER (*smiling*): "You see, we are like small

fishing-boats. (*All smile.*) We can ply in small canals and shallow waters and also in big rivers. But you are a ship. You may run aground on the way!" (*All laugh.*)

Vidyāsāgar remained silent. Sri Ramakrishna said with a laugh, "But even a ship can go there at this season."

VIDYĀSĀGAR (*smiling*): "Yes, this is the monsoon season." (*All laugh.*)

M said to himself: "This is indeed the monsoon season of newly awakened love. At such times one doesn't care for prestige or formalities."

Sri Ramakrishna then took leave of Vidyāsāgar, who with his friends escorted the Master to the main gate, leading the way with a lighted candle in his hand. Before leaving the room, the Master prayed for the family's welfare, going into an ecstatic mood as he did so.

As soon as the Master and the devotees reached the gate, they saw an unexpected sight and stood still. In front of them was a bearded gentleman of fair complexion, aged about thirty-six. He wore his clothes like a Bengali, but on his head was a white turban tied after the fashion of the Śikhs. No sooner had he seen the Master than he fell prostrate before him, turban and all.

When he stood up the Master said: "Who is this? Balaram? Why are you here so late in the evening?"

BALARAM: "I have been waiting here a long time, sir."

MASTER: "Why didn't you come in?"

BALARAM: "All were listening to you. I didn't like to disturb you."

The Master got into the carriage with his companions.

VIDYĀSĀGAR (*to M, softly*): "Shall I pay the carriage hire?"

M: "Oh, don't bother, please. It's taken care of."

Vidyāsāgar and his friends bowed to Sri Ramakrishna, and the carriage started for Dakshineswar. But the little group, with the venerable Vidyāsāgar at their head holding the lighted candle, stood at the gate and gazed after the Master until he was out of sight.

3

ADVICE TO HOUSEHOLDERS

Thursday, August 24, 1882

SRI RAMAKRISHNA was talking to Hazra on the long
northeast verandah of his room, when M arrived.
He saluted the Master reverently.

MASTER: "I should like to visit Iswar Chandra
Vidyāsāgar a few times more. The painter first draws
the general outlines and then puts in the details and
colours at his leisure. The moulder first makes the
image out of clay, then plasters it, then gives it a coat
of whitewash, and last of all paints it with a brush. All
these steps must be taken successively. Vidyāsāgar is
fully ready, but his inner stuff is covered with a thin
layer. He is now engaged in doing good works; but he
doesn't know what is within himself. Gold is hidden
within him. God dwells within us. If one knows that,
one feels like giving up all activities and praying to God
with a yearning heart."

So the Master talked with M—now standing, now
pacing up and down the long verandah.

MASTER: "A little spiritual discipline is necessary
in order to know what lies within."

M: "Is it necessary to practise discipline all through
life?"

MASTER: "No. But one must be up and doing in
the beginning. After that one need not work hard.

The helmsman stands up and clutches the rudder firmly as long as the boat is passing through waves, storms, high wind, or around the curves of a river; but he relaxes after steering through them. As soon as the boat passes the curves and the helmsman feels a favourable wind, he sits comfortably and just touches the rudder. Next he prepares to unfurl the sail and gets ready for a smoke. Likewise, the aspirant enjoys peace and calm after passing the waves and storms of 'woman' and 'gold.'

"Some are born with the characteristics of the yogi; but they too should be careful. 'Woman' and 'gold' alone are the obstacles which make men deviate from the path of yoga and drag them into worldliness. Perhaps they have some desire for enjoyment. After fulfilling their desire they again direct their minds to God and thus recover their former state of mind, fit for the practice of yoga.

"Unless the mind becomes steady there cannot be yoga. It is the wind of worldliness that always disturbs the mind, which may be likened to a candle flame. If that flame doesn't flicker at all, then one is said to have attained yoga.

"Sometimes I used to assume a rājasic mood in order to practise renunciation. Once I had the desire to put on a gold-embroidered robe, wear a ring on my finger, and smoke a hubble-bubble with a long pipe. Mathur Babu procured all these things for me. I wore the gold-embroidered robe and said to myself after a while, 'Mind! This is what is called a gold-embroidered robe.' Then I took it off and threw it away. I couldn't stand the robe any more. Again I said to myself, 'Mind! This is called a shawl; and this, a ring; and this, smoking a hubble-bubble with a long pipe.' I threw those things away once for all; the desire to enjoy them never arose in my mind again."

It was almost dusk. The Master and M stood talking alone near the door on the southeast verandah.

MASTER (*to M*): "The mind of the yogi is always fixed on God, always absorbed in the Self. You can recognize such a man by merely looking at him. His eyes are wide open, with an aimless look, like the eyes of the mother bird hatching her eggs. Her entire mind is fixed on the eggs, and there is a vacant look in her eyes. Can you show me such a picture?"

M: "I shall try to get one."

As evening came on, the temples were lighted up. Sri Ramakrishna was seated on his small couch, meditating on the Divine Mother. Then he chanted the names of God. Incense was burnt in the room, where an oil lamp had been lighted. Sounds of conch-shells and gongs came floating on the air as the evening worship began in the temple of Kāli. The light of the moon flooded all the quarters. The Master again spoke to M.

MASTER: "Perform your duties in an unselfish spirit. The work that Vidyāsāgar is engaged in is very good. Always try to perform your duties without desiring any result."

M: "Yes, sir. But may I know if one can realize God while performing one's duties?"

MASTER: "All, without exception, perform work. Even to chant God's name and glories is work, as is the meditation of the Non-dualist on 'I am He.' Breathing is also an activity. There is no way of renouncing work altogether. So do your work but surrender the result to God."

M: "Sir, may I make an effort to earn more money?"

MASTER: "It is permissible to do so to support a religious family. You may try to increase your income, but in an honest way. The goal of life is not the earning of money, but the service of God. Money is not harmful if it is devoted to the service of God."

M: "How long should a man feel obliged to do his duty toward his wife and children?"

MASTER: "As long as they feel pinched for food and clothing. But one need not take the responsibility of a son when he is able to support himself. When the young fledgling learns to pick its own food, its mother pecks it if it comes to her for food."

M: "How long must one do one's duty?"

MASTER: "The blossom drops off when the fruit appears. One doesn't have to do one's duties after attaining God, nor does one feel like doing them then.

"If a drunkard takes too much liquor he cannot retain consciousness. If he takes only two or three glasses, he can go on with his work. As you advance nearer and nearer to God, He will reduce your activities little by little. Have no fear.

"Finish the few duties you have in hand, and then you will have peace. When the mistress of the house goes to bathe after finishing her cooking and other household duties, she won't come back, however you may shout after her."

M: "Sir, what is the meaning of the realization of God? What do you mean by God-vision? How does one attain it?"

MASTER: "According to the Vaishnavas, the aspirants and the seers of God may be divided into different classes: the beginners, those struggling to see God, the perfected ones, and the supremely perfect. He who has just set foot on the path may be called a beginner. He who has for some time been practising spiritual disciplines, such as worship, japa, meditation, and the chanting of God's name and glories, is called a struggling soul. He is a perfected soul who has known from his inner experience that God exists. An analogy is given in Vedānta to explain this. The master of the house is asleep in a dark room. Someone is groping in the darkness to find him. He touches the couch and says, 'No, it is not he.' He touches the window and says, 'No, it is not he.' He touches the door and says, 'No, it is not he.' This is known in Vedānta as the process of 'Neti, neti,' 'Not this, not this.' At last his hand touches the master's body and he exclaims, 'Here he is!' In other words, he is now conscious of the 'existence' of the master. He has found him, but he doesn't yet know him intimately.

"There is yet another type, known as the supremely perfect. It is quite a different thing when one talks to the master intimately, when one knows God very intimately through love and devotion. A perfected soul has undoubtedly attained God, but the supremely perfect has known God very intimately."

M: "When one sees God does one see Him with these eyes?"

MASTER: "God cannot be seen with these physical eyes. In the course of spiritual discipline one gets a 'love body,' endowed with 'love eyes,' 'love ears,' and so on. One sees God with those 'love eyes.' One hears the voice of God with those 'love ears.'

"But this is not possible without intense love of God. One sees God alone everywhere when one loves Him with great intensity. It is like a person with jaundice, who sees everything yellow. Then one feels, 'I am verily He.'

"One who thinks of God day and night beholds Him everywhere. It is like a man's seeing flames on all sides after he has gazed fixedly at one flame for some time."

"But that isn't the real flame," flashed through M's mind.

Sri Ramakrishna, who could read a man's inmost thought, said: "One doesn't lose consciousness by thinking of Him who is all Spirit, all Consciousness. Shivanath once remarked that too much thinking about God confounds the brain. Thereupon I said to him, 'How can one become unconscious by thinking of Consciousness?'"

M: "Yes, sir, I realize that. It isn't like thinking of an unreal object. How can a man lose his intelligence if he always fixes his mind on Him whose very nature is eternal Intelligence?"

MASTER (*with pleasure*): "It is through God's grace that you have understood that. The doubts of the mind will not disappear without His grace. Doubts do not disappear without Self-realization.

"But one need not fear anything if one has received God's grace. It is rather easy for a child to stumble if he holds his father's hand; but there can be no such fear if the father holds the child's hand. A man does not have to suffer any more if God, in His grace, removes his doubts and reveals Himself to him. But this grace descends upon him only after he has prayed to God with intense yearning of heart and practised spiritual discipline. The mother feels compassion for her child when she sees him running about breathlessly.

She has been hiding herself; now she appears before the child."

"But why should God make us run about?" thought M.

Immediately Sri Ramakrishna said: "It is His will that we should run about a little. It is great fun. God has created the world in play, as it were. This is called Mahāmāyā, the Great Illusion. Therefore one must take refuge in the Divine Mother, the Cosmic Power Itself. It is She who has bound us with the shackles of illusion. The realization of God is possible only when those shackles are severed."

October 16, 1882

It was Monday, a few days before the Durgā Pujā, the worship of the Divine Mother. Sri Ramakrishna was in a very happy state of mind, for Narendra was with him. Narendra had brought two or three young members of the Brāhmo Samāj to the temple garden. Besides them, Rakhal, Ramlal, Hazra, and M were with the Master.

Narendra had his midday meal with Sri Ramakrishna. Afterwards a temporary bed was made on the floor of the Master's room so that the disciples might rest awhile. A mat was spread, over which was placed a quilt covered with a white sheet. A few cushions and pillows completed the simple bed. Like a child, the Master sat near Narendranath on the bed. He talked with the devotees in great delight. With a radiant smile lighting his face, and his eyes fixed on Narendra, he was giving them various spiritual teachings, interspersing these with incidents from his own life.

MASTER: "After I had experienced samādhi my

mind craved intensely to hear only about God. I always searched for places where they were reciting or explaining the sacred books. I used to go to Krishnakishore to hear him read the *Adhyātma Rāmāyana*.

"What tremendous faith Krishnakishore had! Once, while at Vrindāvan, he felt thirsty and went to a well. Near it he saw a man standing. On being asked to draw a little water for him, the man said: 'I belong to a low caste, sir. You are a brāhmin. How can I draw water for you?' Krishnakishore said: 'Take the name of Śiva. By repeating His holy name you will make yourself pure.' The low-caste man did as he was told, and Krishnakishore, orthodox brāhmin that he was, drank that water. What tremendous faith!

"Once a holy man came to the bank of the Ganges and lived near the bathing-ghat at Āriādaha, not far from Dakshineswar. We thought of paying him a visit. I said to Haladhari: 'Krishnakishore and I are going to see a holy man. Will you come with us?' Haladhari replied, 'What is the use of seeing a mere human body, which is no better than a cage of clay?' Haladhari was a student of the Gitā and Vedānta philosophy, and therefore referred to the holy man as a mere 'cage of clay.' I repeated this to Krishnakishore. With great anger he said: 'How impudent of Haladhari to make such a remark! How can he ridicule as a "cage of clay" the body of a man who constantly thinks of God, who meditates on Rāma and has renounced all for the sake of the Lord? Doesn't he know that such a man is the embodiment of Spirit?' He was so upset by Haladhari's remarks that he would turn his face away from him whenever he met him in the temple garden; he stopped speaking to him.

"Once Krishnakishore asked me, 'Why have you

cast off the sacred thread?' In those days of God-vision I felt as if I were passing through a great storm; everything was blown away from me. No trace of my old self was left. I lost all consciousness of the world. I could hardly keep my cloth on my body, not to speak of the sacred thread! I said to Krishnakishore, 'Ah, you will understand if you ever happen to be as intoxicated with God as I am.'

"And it actually came to pass. He too passed through a God-intoxicated state, when he would repeat only the word 'Om' and shut himself up alone in his room. His relatives thought he was actually mad and called in a physician. Krishnakishore said to the physician, 'Cure me, sir, by all means, of my malady, but not of my Om.' (*All laugh.*)

"One day I went to see him and found him in a pensive mood. When I asked him about it, he said: 'The tax-collector was here. He threatened to dispose of my brass pots, my cups, and my few utensils if I didn't pay the tax; so I am worried.' I said: 'But why should that bother you? Let him take away your pots and pans. Let him even arrest your body. How will that affect you? For your nature is that of Kha!' (*Narendra and the others laugh.*) He used to say to me that he was Kha, the Spirit, all-pervading as the sky. He had got that idea from the *Adhyātma Rāmāyana*. I used to tease him now and then, addressing him as 'Kha.' Therefore I said to him that day, with a smile: 'You are Kha. Taxes should not move you!'

"In that state of God-intoxication I used to speak out my mind to all. I was no respecter of persons. Even to men of position I was not afraid to speak the truth.

"One day, in that state of divine intoxication, I went to the bathing-ghāt on the Ganges at Barānagore. There I saw Jaya Mukherji repeating God's name; but his mind was on something else. I went up and slapped him twice on the cheeks.

"At one time Rāni Rasmani was staying in the temple garden. She came to the shrine of the Divine Mother, as she frequently did when I worshipped Kāli, and asked me to sing. While I was singing, I noticed she was absent-minded. At once I slapped her on the cheeks. She became quite embarrassed and sat there with folded hands.

"Alarmed at my state of mind, I said to my cousin Haladhari: 'Just see my nature! How can I get rid of it?' After praying to the Divine Mother for some time with great yearning, I was able to shake off this habit.

"When one gets into such a state of mind, one doesn't enjoy any conversation but that about God. I used to weep when I heard people talk about worldly matters. When I accompanied Mathur Babu on a pilgrimage, we spent a few days in Benares at Raja Babu's house. One day I was seated in the drawing-room with Mathur Babu, Raja Babu, and others. Hearing them talk about various worldly things, such as their business losses and so forth, I wept bitterly and said to the Divine Mother: 'Mother, where have You brought me? I was much better off in the temple garden at Dakshineswar. Here I am in a place where I must hear about "woman" and "gold." But at Dakshineswar I could avoid it.'"

The Master asked the devotees, especially Narendra, to rest awhile, and he himself lay down on the smaller couch.

Late in the afternoon Narendra sang. Rakhal, Latu,

M, Hazra, and Priya, Narendra's Brāhmo friend, were present. The singing was accompanied by the drum:

With a joyful face chant the sweet name of God,
Till, like a wind, it churns the nectar sea;
Drink of that nectar ceaselessly
(Drink it yourself and share it with all).
If ever your heart goes dry, repeat God's name
(If it goes dry in the desert of this world,
Love of God will make it flow again).

Be watchful, that you may never forget to chant
His mighty name: when danger stares in your face,
Pray to your Father Compassionate.
Snap sin's bonds with a shout of joy
(Crying, "To God, to God be the victory!").
Come, let us be mad in the bliss of God,
Fulfilling all our hearts' desires,
And quench our thirst with the yoga of love.

When the music was over, Sri Ramakrishna held Narendra in his arms a long time and said, "You have made us so happy today!" The floodgate of the Master's heart was open so wide that night that he could hardly contain himself for joy. It was eight o'clock in the evening. Intoxicated with divine love, he paced the long verandah north of his room. Now and then he could be heard talking to the Divine Mother.

Narendra, M, and Priya were going to spend the night at the temple garden. This pleased the Master highly, especially since Narendra would be with him. The Holy Mother,[1] who was living in the nahabat, had prepared the supper. Surendra[2] bore the greater

---

[1] By this name Sri Ramakrishna's wife was known among his devotees.

[2] The name by which Sri Ramakrishna addressed Suresh Mitra, a beloved householder disciple.

part of the Master's expenses. The plates were set out on the southeast verandah of the Master's room.

While the devotees were enjoying their meal, Sri Ramakrishna stood by and watched them with intense delight. That night the Master's joy was very great.

After supper the devotees rested on the mat spread on the floor of the Master's room. They began to talk with him. It was indeed a feast of joy. The Master asked Narendra to sing the song beginning with the line: "In wisdom's firmament the moon of love is rising full."

Narendra sang, and other devotees played the drums and cymbals:

In wisdom's firmament the moon of love is rising full,
And love's flood tide, in surging waves, is flowing everywhere.
O Lord, how full of bliss Thou art! Victory unto Thee!

On every side shine devotees, like stars around the moon;
Their Friend, the Lord All-merciful, joyously plays with them.
Behold! the gates of paradise today are open wide.

The soft spring wind of the New Day raises fresh waves of joy;
Gently it carries towards the earth the fragrance of God's love,
Till all the yogis, drunk with bliss, are lost in ecstasy.

Upon the sea of the world unfolds the lotus of the New Day,
And there the Mother sits enshrined in blissful majesty.
See how the bees are mad with joy, sipping the nectar there.

Behold the Mother's radiant face, which so enchants
the heart
And captivates the universe. About Her Lotus Feet
Bands of ecstatic holy men are dancing in delight.

What matchless loveliness is Hers! What infinite
content
Pervades the heart when She appears! O brothers, says
Premdās,
I humbly beg you, one and all, to sing the Mother's
praise.

Sri Ramakrishna sang and danced, and the devotees
danced around him.

Shortly before midnight Narendra and the other
devotees lay down on a bed made on the floor of the
Master's room.

At dawn some of the devotees were up. They saw
the Master, naked as a child, walking up and down
the room repeating the names of the various gods and
goddesses. His voice was sweet as nectar. Now he would
look at the Ganges, now stop in front of the pictures
hanging on the walls and bow down before them,
chanting all the while the holy names in his sweet
voice. Now and then he said: "O Mother, Thou art
verily Brahman and Thou art verily Śakti. Thou art
Purusha and Thou art Prakriti. Thou art Virāt, Thou
art the Absolute and Thou dost manifest Thyself as
the Relative. Thou art verily the twenty-four cosmic
principles."

In the mean time the morning service had begun
in the temples of Kāli and Rādhākānta. Sounds of
conch-shells and cymbals were carried on the air. The
devotees came outside the room and saw the priests
and servants gathering flowers in the garden for the

divine service in the temples. From the nahabat floated the sweet melody of musical instruments, befitting the morning hours.

Narendra and the other devotees finished their morning duties and came to the Master. With a sweet smile on his lips Sri Ramakrishna was standing on the northeast verandah, close to his own room.

NARENDRA: "We noticed several sannyāsis belonging to the sect of Nānak in the Panchavati."

MASTER: "Yes, they arrived yesterday. (*To Narendra*) I'd like to see you all sitting together on the mat."

As they sat there the Master looked at them with evident delight. He then began to talk with them. Narendra asked about spiritual discipline.

MASTER: "Bhakti, love of God, is the essence of all spiritual discipline. Through love one acquires renunciation and discrimination naturally."

The sannyāsis belonging to Nānak's sect entered the room and greeted the Master, saying, "Namo Nārāyanāya."[3] Sri Ramakrishna asked them to sit down.

MASTER: "Nothing is impossible with God. Nobody can describe His nature in words. Everything is possible with Him. There lived at a certain place two yogis who were practising spiritual discipline. The sage Nārada was passing that way one day. Realizing who he was, one of the yogis said: 'You have just come from God Himself. What is He doing now?' Nārada replied, 'Why, I saw Him making camels and elephants pass and repass through the eye of a needle.' At this the yogi said: 'Is that anything to wonder at? Everything is possible with God.' But the other yogi said: 'What? Making elephants pass through the eye of a

[3] "Salutations to God." This is the way sādhus greet one another.

needle! Is that ever possible? You have never been to the Lord's dwelling-place.' "

When Narendra and his friends had finished bathing in the Ganges, the Master said to them earnestly: "Go to the Panchavati and meditate there under the banyan-tree. Shall I give you something to sit on?"

About half past ten Narendra and his Brāhmo friends were meditating in the Panchavati. After a while Sri Ramakrishna came to them. M, too, was present.

The Master said to the Brāhmo devotees: "In meditation one must be absorbed in God. By merely floating on the surface can you reach the gems lying at the bottom of the sea?"

Then he sang:

Taking the name of Kāli, dive deep down, O mind,
Into the soul's fathomless sea;
But never believe the bed of the ocean bare of pearls
If in the first few dives you fail.
With firm resolve and self-control
Dive deep and make your way to Mother Kāli's realm.

Deep in the sea, O mind, of the knowledge of Mother
    Kāli
Lie the lustrous pearls of peace;
If you but cherish love and follow the scriptures' rule,
You can possess them for yourself.

But in those silent ocean depths
Six alligators lurk—lust, anger, and the rest[4]—
Swimming about in search of prey.
Smear your body well with the turmeric of viveka;
The pungent smell of it will shield you from their
    touch.

[4] The six passions: lust, anger, avarice, delusion, pride, and envy.

Unnumbered precious pearls are strewn on the ocean
    bed:
Plunge in, says Rāmprasād, and gather handfuls there.

Narendra and his friends came down from their
seats on the cement platform of the Panchavati and stood
near the Master. He returned to his room with them.
The Master continued: "When you plunge in the water
of the ocean you may be attacked by alligators. But
they won't touch you if your body is smeared with
turmeric. There are no doubt six alligators—lust, anger,
avarice, and so on—within you, in the 'soul's fathomless depths.' But protect yourself with the turmeric of
discrimination and renunciation, and they won't touch
you.

"What can you achieve by mere lecturing and
scholarship if you have no discrimination and dispassion? God alone is real, and all else is unreal. God alone
is substance, and all else is nonentity. That is discrimination.

"First of all set up God in the shrine of your heart,
and afterwards deliver lectures as much as you like.
How will the mere repetition of 'Brahma' profit you if
you are not imbued with discrimination and dispassion?
It is the empty sound of a conch-shell.

"There lived in a village a young man named Padmalochan. People used to call him 'Podo' for short. In
this village there was a temple in a very dilapidated condition. It contained no image of God. Aśvattha and
other trees sprang up on the ruins of its walls. Bats
lived inside, and the floor was covered with dust and
the droppings of the bats. The people of the village
had stopped visiting the temple. One day after dusk the
villagers heard the sound of a conch-shell from the

direction of the temple. They thought perhaps someone had installed an image in the shrine and was performing the evening worship. One of them softly
opened the door and saw Padmalochan standing in a
corner, blowing the conch. No image had been set up.
The temple hadn't been swept or washed. Filth and
dirt lay everywhere. Then he shouted to Podo:

> You have set up no image here,
> Inside the shrine, you fool!
> Blowing the conch, you simply make
> Confusion worse confounded.
> Day and night eleven bats
> Scream here incessantly.

"There is no use in merely making a noise if you
want to establish the Deity in the shrine of your heart,
if you want to realize God. First of all purify the mind.
In the pure heart God takes His seat. One cannot
bring the holy image into the temple if the droppings
of bats are all around. The eleven bats are our eleven
organs: five of action, five of perception, and the mind.

"First of all invoke the Deity, and then give lectures
to your heart's content. First of all dive deep. Plunge
to the bottom and gather up the gems. Then you may
do other things. But nobody wants to plunge. People
are without spiritual discipline and prayer, without
renunciation and dispassion. They learn a few words
and immediately start to deliver lectures. It is difficult
to teach others. Only if a man gets a command from
God, after realizing Him, is he entitled to teach."

Thus conversing, the Master came to the west end
of the verandah. M stood by his side. Sri Ramakrishna
had repeated again and again that God cannot be
realized without discrimination and renunciation. This

made M extremely worried. He was then a young man of twenty-eight, educated in college in the Western way and was married. Having a sense of duty, he asked himself, "Do discrimination and dispassion mean giving up 'woman' and 'gold'?" He was really at a loss to know what to do.

M (to the Master): "What should one do if one's wife says: 'You are neglecting me. I shall commit suicide'?"

MASTER (in a serious tone): "Give up such a wife if she proves an obstacle to spiritual life. Let her commit suicide or anything else she likes. The wife that hampers her husband's spiritual life is an ungodly wife."

Immersed in deep thought, M stood leaning against the wall. Narendra and the other devotees remained silent a few minutes. The Master exchanged several words with them; then, suddenly going to M, he whispered in his ear: "But if a man has sincere love for God, then all come under his control—the king, wicked persons, and his wife. Sincere love of God on the husband's part may eventually help the wife to lead a spiritual life. If the husband is good, then through God's grace the wife may also follow his example."

These words had a most soothing effect on M's worried mind. All the while he had been thinking: "Let her commit suicide if she wants to. What can I do?"

M (to the Master): "This world is a terrible place indeed."

MASTER (to the devotees): "That is why Chaitanya said to his companion Nityānanda, 'Listen, brother, there is no hope of salvation for the worldly-minded.' "

On another occasion the Master had said to M privately: "Yes, there is no hope for a worldly man if he is not sincerely devoted to God. But he has nothing to fear if he remains in the world after realizing God. Nor need a man have any fear whatever of the world if he attains sincere devotion by practising spiritual discipline now and then in solitude. Chaitanya had several householders among his devotees; but they were householders in name only, for they lived unattached to the world."

It was noon. The worship was over and food offerings had been made in the temple. The doors of the temple were shut. Sri Ramakrishna sat down for his meal, and Narendra and the other devotees partook of the food offerings from the temple.

Sunday, October 22, 1882

It was the day of Vijayā, the last day of the celebration of the worship of Durgā, when the clay image is immersed in the water of a lake or river.

About nine o'clock in the morning M was seated on the floor of the Master's room at Dakshineswar, near Sri Ramakrishna, who was reclining on the small couch. Rakhal was then living with the Master, and Narendra and Bhavanath visited him frequently. Baburam had seen him only once or twice.

MASTER (*to M*): "How are you getting along with your meditation nowadays? What aspect of God appeals to your mind—with form or without form?"

M: "Sir, at present I can't fix my mind on God with form. On the other hand, I can't concentrate steadily on God without form."

MASTER: "Now you see that the mind cannot be fixed, all of a sudden, on the formless aspect of God. It is wise to think of God with form at the beginning."

M: "Do you mean to suggest that one should meditate on clay images?"

MASTER: "Why clay? These images are the embodiments of Consciousness."

M: "Even so, one must think of hands, feet, and the other parts of the body. But again, I realize that the mind cannot be concentrated unless one meditates, in the beginning, on God with form. You have told me so. Well, God can easily assume different forms. May one meditate on the form of one's own mother?"

MASTER: "Yes, the mother should be adored. She is indeed an embodiment of Brahman."

M sat in silence. After a few minutes he asked the Master: "What does one feel while thinking of God without form? Isn't it possible to describe it?" After some reflection the Master said, "Do you know what it is like?" He remained silent a moment and then said a few words to M about one's experiences when one realizes God with and without form.

MASTER: "You see, one must practise spiritual discipline to understand this correctly. Suppose there are treasures in a room. If you want to see them and lay hold of them, you must take the trouble to get the key and unlock the door. After that you must take the treasures out. But suppose the room is locked, and standing outside the door you merely say to yourself: 'Here I have opened the door. Now I have broken the lock of the chest. Now I have taken out the treasure.' Such brooding near the door will not enable you to achieve anything.

"You must practise discipline.

"The jnānis think of God without form. They don't accept the Divine Incarnation. Praising Sri Krishna, Arjuna said, 'Thou art Brahman Absolute.' Sri Krishna replied, 'Follow Me, and you will know whether or not I am Brahman Absolute.' So saying, Sri Krishna led Arjuna to a certain place and asked him what he saw there. 'I see a huge tree,' said Arjuna, 'and on it I notice fruits hanging like clusters of blackberries.' Then Krishna said to Arjuna, 'Go nearer and you will find that these are not clusters of blackberries, but clusters of innumerable Krishnas like Me, hanging from the tree.' In other words, Divine Incarnations without number appear and disappear on the Tree of the Absolute Brahman.

"I accept God with form when I am in the company of people who believe in that ideal, and I also agree with those who believe in the formless God."

M (smiling): "You are as infinite as He of whom we have been talking. Truly, no one can fathom your depths."

MASTER (smiling): "Ah! I see you have found it out. Let me tell you something. One should follow various paths. One should practise each creed for a time.

"There are two classes of yogis. Some roam about visiting various holy places and have not yet found peace of mind. But some, having visited all the sacred places, have quieted their minds. Feeling serene and peaceful, they settle down in one place and no longer move about. In that one place they are happy; they don't feel the need of going to any sacred place. If one of them ever visits a place of pilgrimage, it is only for the purpose of new inspiration.

"One undoubtedly finds inspiration in a holy place. I accompanied Mathur Babu to Vrindavan. Hriday and the ladies of Mathur's family were in our party. No sooner did I see the Kāliyadaman Ghāt than a divine emotion surged up within me. I was completely overwhelmed. Hriday used to bathe me there as if I were a small child.

"At dusk, the 'cow-dust hour,' I would walk on the bank of the Jamunā when the cattle returned along the sandy banks from their pastures. At the very sight of those cows the thought of Krishna would be kindled in my mind. I would run along like a madman, crying: 'Oh, where is Krishna? Where is my Krishna?'

"I went to Śyāmakunda and Rādhākunda[5] in a palanquin and got out to visit the holy Mount Govardhan. At the very sight of the mount I was overpowered with divine emotion and ran to the top. I lost all consciousness of the world around me. The residents of the place helped me to come down. On my way to the sacred pools of Śyāmakunda and Rādhākunda, when I saw the meadows, the trees, the shrubs, the birds, and the deer, I was overcome with ecstasy. My clothes became wet with tears. I said: 'O Krishna! everything here I see as it was in the olden days. You alone are absent.' Seated inside the palanquin I lost all power of speech. Hriday followed the palanquin. He had warned the bearers to be careful about me.

"Gangāmāyi became very fond of me in Vrindāvan. She was an old woman who lived all alone in a hut near the Nidhuvan. Referring to my spiritual condition and ecstasy, she said, 'He is the very embodiment of Rādhā.' She addressed me as 'Dulāli,' 'Darling.' When with her, I forgot my food and drink, my bath, and all thought of going home. On some days Hriday used to bring food from home and feed me. Gangāmāyi also served me with food prepared by her own hands.

[5] Places near Mathurā associated with the episode of Krishna and Rādhā.

"Gangāmāyi used to experience trances. At such times a great crowd would come to see her. One day, in a state of ecstasy, she climbed on Hriday's shoulders.

"I didn't want to leave her and return to Calcutta. Everything was arranged for me to stay with her. I was to eat double-boiled rice and we were to have our beds on either side of the cottage. All the arrangements had been made, when Hriday said: 'You have such a weak stomach. Who will look after you?' 'Why,' said Gangāmāyi, 'I shall look after him. I'll nurse him.' Hriday was dragging me by one hand and she by the other, when I remembered my mother, who was then living alone here in the nahabat of the temple garden. I found it impossible to stay away from her and said to Gangāmāyi, 'No, I must go.' I loved the atmosphere of Vrindāvan."

About eleven o'clock the Master took his meal, the offerings from the temple of Kālī. After taking his noonday rest he resumed his conversation with the devotees. Every now and then he uttered the holy word "Om" or repeated the sacred names of the deities.

After sunset the evening worship was performed in the temples. Since it was the day of Vijayā, the devotees first saluted the Divine Mother and then took the dust[6] of the Master's feet.

[6] A form of reverent salutation in which one touches the feet of a superior with one's forehead.

⫸ 4 ⫷

THE MASTER AND KESHAB

October 27, 1882

IT WAS FRIDAY, the day of the Lakshmi Pujā. Keshab Chandra Sen had arranged a boat trip on the Ganges for Sri Ramakrishna.

About four o'clock in the afternoon the steamboat with Keshab and his Brāhmo followers cast anchor in the Ganges alongside the Kāli temple at Dakshineswar. The passengers saw in front of them the bathing-ghāt and the chāndni. To their left, in the temple compound, stood six temples of Śiva, and to their right another group of six Śiva temples. The white steeple of the Kāli temple, the treetops of the Panchavati, and the silhouette of pine-trees stood high against the blue autumn sky. The gardens between the two nahabats were filled with fragrant flowers; along the bank of the Ganges were rows of flowering plants. The blue sky was reflected in the brown water of the river, the sacred Ganges, associated with the most ancient traditions of Indo-Āryan civilization. The outer world appeared soft and serene, and the hearts of the Brāhmo devotees were filled with peace.

Sri Ramakrishna was in his room talking with Vijay and Haralal. Several disciples of Keshab entered. Bowing before the Master, they said to him: "Sir, the steamer has arrived. Keshab Babu has asked us to take you there." A small boat was to carry the Master to the steamer. No sooner had he got into the boat

than he lost outer consciousness in samādhi. Vijay
was with him.

M was among the passengers. As the boat came
alongside the steamer, all rushed to the railing to
have a view of Sri Ramakrishna. Keshab became
anxious to get him safely on board. With great difficulty the Master was brought back to consciousness of
the world and taken to a cabin in the steamer. Still in an
abstracted mood, he walked mechanically, leaning on
a devotee for support. Keshab and the others bowed
before him, but he was not aware of them. Inside the
cabin there were a few chairs and a table. He was
made to sit on one of the chairs, Keshab and Vijay
occupying two others. Some devotees were also seated,
most of them on the floor, while many others had to
stand outside. They peered eagerly through the door
and windows. Sri Ramakrishna again went into deep
samādhi and became totally unconscious of the outer
world.

As the air in the room became stuffy because of the
crowd of people, Keshab opened the windows. He was
embarrassed to meet Vijay, since they had disagreed on
certain principles of the Brāhmo Samāj and Vijay had
separated himself from Keshab's organization, joining
another society.

The Brāhmo devotees looked wistfully at the Master.
He was gradually coming back to normal consciousness;
but the divine intoxication still lingered. He said to himself in a whisper: "Mother, why have You brought me
here? They are hedged around and not free. Can I
free them?" Did the Master find that the people
assembled there were locked within the prison walls of
the world? Did their helplessness make the Master
address these words to the Divine Mother?

Sri Ramakrishna became conscious of the outside world. Nilmadhav of Ghāzipur and a Brāhmo devotee were talking about Pāvhāri Bābā. Another Brāhmo devotee said to the Master: "Sir, these gentlemen visited Pāvhāri Bābā. He lives in Ghāzipur. He is a holy man like yourself." The Master could hardly talk; he only smiled. The devotee continued, "Sir, Pāvhāri Bābā keeps your photograph in his room." Pointing to his body the Master said with a smile, "Just a pillow-case."

The Master continued: "But you should remember that the heart of the devotee is the abode of God. He dwells, no doubt, in all beings, but He especially manifests Himself in the heart of the devotee. A land-lord may at one time or another visit all parts of his estate, but people say he is generally to be found in a particular drawing-room. The heart of the devotee is God's drawing-room.

"He who is called Brahman by the jnānis is known as Ātman by the yogis and as Bhagavān by the bhaktas. The same brāhmin is called priest, when worshipping in the temple, and cook, when preparing a meal in the kitchen. The jnāni, following the path of knowledge, always reasons about the Reality, saying, 'Not this, not this.' Brahman is neither 'this' nor 'that'; It is neither the universe nor its living beings. Reasoning in this way, the mind becomes steady. Finally it disappears and the aspirant goes into samādhi. This is the Knowledge of Brahman. It is the unwavering conviction of the jnāni that Brahman alone is real and the world illusory. All these names and forms are illusory, like a dream. What Brahman is cannot be described. One cannot even say that Brahman is a Person. This is the opinion of the jnānis, the followers of Vedānta philosophy.

"But the bhaktas accept all the states of consciousness. They take the waking state to be real also. They don't think the world to be illusory, like a dream. They say that the universe is a manifestation of God's power and glory. God has created all these—sky, stars, moon, sun, mountains, ocean, men, animals. They constitute His glory. He is within us, in our hearts. Again, He is outside. The most advanced devotees say that He Himself has become all this—the twenty-four cosmic principles, the universe, and all living beings. The devotee of God wants to eat sugar, and not to become sugar. (*All laugh.*)

"Do you know how a lover of God feels? His attitude is: 'O God, Thou art the Master, and I am Thy servant. Thou art the Mother, and I am Thy child.' Or again: 'Thou art my Father and Mother. Thou art the whole, and I am a part.' He doesn't like to say, 'I am Brahman.'

"The yogi seeks to realize the Paramātman, the Supreme Soul. His ideal is the union of the embodied soul and the Supreme Soul. He withdraws his mind from sense-objects and tries to concentrate on the Paramātman. Therefore, during the first stage of his spiritual discipline, he retires into solitude and with undivided attention practises meditation in a fixed posture.

"But the Reality is one and the same; the difference is only in name. He who is Brahman is verily Ātman, and again, He is the Bhagavān. He is Brahman to the followers of the path of knowledge, Paramātman to the yogis, and Bhagavān to the lovers of God."

The steamer had been going toward Calcutta; but the passengers, with their eyes fixed on the Master and their ears given to his nectar-like words, were oblivious of its motion. Dakshineswar, with its temples and gardens, was left behind. The paddles of the boat churned the waters of the Ganges with a murmuring sound. But the devotees were indifferent to all this. Spellbound, they looked on a great yogi, his face lighted with a divine smile, his countenance radiating love, his eyes sparkling with joy—a man who had renounced all for God and who knew nothing but God. Unceasing words of wisdom flowed from his lips.

MASTER: "The jnānis, who adhere to Non-dualistic Vedānta, say that the acts of creation, preservation, and destruction, the universe itself and all its living beings, are the manifestations of Śakti, the Divine Power.[1] If you reason it out, you will realize that all these are as illusory as a dream. Brahman alone is the Reality, and all else is unreal. Even this very Śakti is unsubstantial, like a dream.

"But though you reason all your life, unless you are established in samādhi you cannot go beyond the jurisdiction of Śakti. Even when you say, 'I am meditating,' or 'I am contemplating,' still you are moving in the realm of Śakti, within Its power.

"The Primordial Power is ever at play. She is creating, preserving, and destroying in play, as it were. This Power is called Kālī. Kālī is verily Brahman, and Brahman is verily Kālī. It is one and the same Reality. When we think of It as inactive, that is to say, not engaged in the acts of creation, preservation, and destruction, then we call It Brahman. But when It engages in these activities, then we call It Kālī or Śakti. The Reality is one and the same; the difference is in name and form.

[1] Known as māyā in the Vedānta philosophy.

"After the destruction of the universe, at the end of a great cycle, the Divine Mother garners the seeds for the next creation. She is like the elderly mistress of a house, who has a hotchpotch-pot in which she keeps different articles for household use. (*All laugh.*)

"Oh, yes! Housewives have pots like that, where they keep 'sea foam,'[2] blue pills, small bundles of seeds of cucumber, pumpkin, and gourd, and so on. They take them out when they want them. In the same way, after the destruction of the universe, my Divine Mother, the Embodiment of Brahman, gathers together the seeds for the next creation. After the creation the Primal Power dwells in the universe itself. She brings forth this phenomenal world and then pervades it. In the Vedas creation is likened to the spider's web. The spider brings the web out of itself and then remains in it. God is the container of the universe and also what is contained in it.

"Is Kāli, my Divine Mother, really black? She appears black because She is viewed from a distance; but when intimately known She is no longer so. The sky appears blue at a distance; but look at it close by and you will find that it has no colour. The water of the ocean, too, looks blue at a distance, but when you go near and take it in your hand, you find that it is colourless.

"Bondage and liberation are both of Her making. By her māyā worldly people become entangled in 'woman' and 'gold,' and again, through Her grace they attain liberation. She is called the Saviour, and the Remover of the bondage that binds one to the world.

[2] The Master perhaps referred to the cuttlefish bone found on the seashore. The popular belief is that it is hardened sea foam.

"The Divine Mother is always playful and sportive. This universe is Her play. She is self-willed and must always have Her own way. She is full of bliss. She gives freedom to one out of a hundred thousand."

A Brāhmo devotee: "But sir, if She likes She can give freedom to all. Why, then, has She kept us bound to the world?"

Master: "That is Her will. She wants to continue playing with Her created beings. In a game of hide-and-seek[3] the running about soon stops if in the beginning all the players touch the 'granny.' If all touch her, then how can the game go on? That displeases her. Her pleasure is in continuing the game."

Brāhmo devotee: "Sir, can't we realize God without complete renunciation?"

Master (with a laugh): "Of course you can! Why should you renounce everything? You are all right as you are, following the middle path.

"Let me tell you the truth: there is nothing wrong in your being in the world. But you must direct your mind toward God; otherwise you will not succeed. Do your duty with one hand and with the other hold to God. After the duty is over, you will hold to God with both hands.

"It is all a question of the mind. Bondage and liberation are of the mind alone. The mind will take the colour you dye it with. It is like white clothes just returned from the laundry. If you dip them in red dye, they will be red. If you dip them in blue or

[3] The allusion is to the Indian game of hide-and-seek, in which the leader, known as the "granny," bandages the eyes of the players and hides herself. The players are supposed to find her. If any player can touch her, the bandage is removed from his eyes and he is released from the game.

green, they will be blue or green. They will take only the colour you dip them in, whatever it may be. Haven't you noticed that, if you read a little English, you at once begin to utter English words? Then you put on boots and whistle a tune, and so on. It all goes together. Or if a scholar studies Sanskrit, he will at once rattle off Sanskrit verses. If you are in bad company, then you will talk and think like your companions. On the other hand, when you are in the company of devotees, you will think and talk only of God.

"The mind is everything. A man has his wife on one side and his daughter on the other. He shows his affection to them in different ways. But his mind is one and the same.

"Bondage is of the mind, and freedom is also of the mind. A man is free if he constantly thinks: 'I am a free soul. How can I be bound, whether I live in the world or in the forest? I am a child of God, the King of kings. Who can bind me?' If bitten by a snake, a man may get rid of its venom by saying emphatically, 'There is no poison in me.' In the same way, by repeating with grit and determination, 'I am not bound, I am free,' one really becomes so; one really becomes free.

"Once someone gave me a book of the Christians. I asked him to read it to me. It talked about nothing but sin. (*To Keshab*) Sin is the one thing people hear of at your Brāhmo Samāj, too. The wretch who constantly says, 'I am bound, I am bound' only succeeds in being bound. He who says day and night, 'I am a sinner, I am a sinner' verily becomes a sinner.

"One must have such burning faith in God that one can say: 'What? I have repeated God's name and can sin still cling to me? How can I be a sinner any more? How can I be in bondage any more?'

"If a man repeats God's name, his body, mind, and everything become pure. Why should one talk only about sin and hell, and such things? Say but once, 'O Lord, I have undoubtedly done wicked things, but I won't repeat them.' And have faith in His name.

"To my Divine Mother I prayed only for pure love. I offered flowers at Her Lotus Feet and prayed: 'Mother, here is Thy virtue, here is Thy vice. Take them both and grant me only pure love for Thee. Here is Thy knowledge, here is Thy ignorance. Take them both and grant me only pure love for Thee. Here is Thy purity, here is Thy impurity. Take them both, Mother, and grant me only pure love for Thee. Here is Thy dharma, here is Thy adharma. Take them both, Mother, and grant me only pure love for Thee.'

"Why shouldn't one be able to realize God in this world? But if one lives in the world, one must go into solitude now and then. It will be of great help to a man if he goes away from his family, lives alone, and weeps for God even for three days. Even if he thinks of God for one day in solitude, when he has the leisure, that too will do him good.

"The disease of worldliness is like typhoid. And there are a huge jug of water and a jar of savoury pickles in the typhoid patient's room. If you want to cure him of his illness, you must remove him from that room. The worldly man is like the typhoid patient. The various objects of enjoyment are the huge jug of water, and the craving for their enjoyment is his thirst. The very thought of pickles makes the mouth water; you don't have to bring them near. And he is surrounded with them. The companionship of a woman

is the pickles. Hence treatment in solitude is necessary.
One may enter the world after attaining discrimination
and dispassion."

Gradually the ebb tide set in. The steamboat was
speeding toward Calcutta. It passed under the Howrah
Bridge and came within sight of the Botanical Garden.
The captain was asked to go a little farther down the
river. The passengers were enchanted with the Master's
words, and most of them had no idea of time or of
how far they had come.

Keshab began to serve some puffed rice and grated
coconut. The guests held these in the folds of their
wearing-cloths and presently started to eat. Everyone
was joyful. The Master noticed, however, that Keshab
and Vijay rather shrank from each other; he was
anxious to reconcile them.

MASTER (to Keshab): "Look here. There is Vijay.
Your quarrel seems like the fight between Śiva and
Rāma. Śiva was Rāma's guru. Though they fought
with each other, yet they soon came to terms. But the
grimaces of the ghosts, the followers of Śiva, and the
gibberish of the monkeys, the followers of Rāma,
would not come to an end! (Loud laughter.) Such
quarrels take place even among one's own kith and
kin. Rāmānuja upheld the doctrine of Qualified Non-
dualism. But his guru was a pure Non-dualist. They
disagreed with each other and refuted each other's
arguments. That always happens. Still, to the teacher
the disciple is his own."

All rejoiced in the Master's company and his words.

MASTER (to Keshab): "You don't look into people's
natures before you make them your disciples, and so
they break away from you.

"All men look alike, to be sure, but they have different natures. Some have an excess of sattva, others an excess of rajas, and still others an excess of tamas. You must have noticed that the pastries known as puli all look alike. But their contents are very different. Some have condensed milk inside, some coconut kernel, and others mere boiled lentil paste. (*All laugh.*)

"Do you know my attitude? As for myself, I eat, drink, and live happily. The rest the Divine Mother knows. Indeed, there are three words that prick my flesh: 'guru,' 'master,' and 'father.'

"There is only one Guru, and that is Satchidānanda. He alone is the Teacher. My attitude toward God is that of a child toward its mother. One can get human gurus by the million. All want to be teachers. But who cares to be a disciple?

"It is extremely difficult to teach others. A man can teach only if God reveals Himself to him and gives the command. Unless you have a command from God, who will listen to your words?

"Don't you know how easily the people of Calcutta get excited? The milk in the pot puffs up and boils as long as the fire burns underneath. Take away the fuel and everything is quiet. The people of Calcutta love sensations. You may see them digging a well at a certain place. They say they want water. But if they strike a stone they give up that place; they begin at another place. And there, perchance, they find sand; they give up the second place too. Next they begin at a third. And so it goes. But it won't do if a man only imagines he has God's command.

"God does reveal Himself to a man and He does speak. Only then does one receive His command. How forceful are the words of such a teacher! They can move mountains. But mere lectures? People will listen to them for a few days and then forget them. They will never act upon mere words.

"At Kāmārpukur there is a small lake called the Hāldārpukur. Certain people used to befoul its banks. Others who came there to bathe would abuse the offenders loudly. But next morning they would find the same thing. The nuisance didn't stop. (*All laugh.*) The villagers finally informed the authorities about it. A constable was sent, who put up a notice there which read: 'Commit no nuisance.' This stopped the miscreants at once. (*All laugh.*)

"To teach others one must have a badge of authority; otherwise teaching becomes a mockery. A man who is himself ignorant starts out to teach others—like the blind leading the blind! Instead of doing good, such teaching does harm. After realizing God one obtains an inner vision. Only then can one diagnose a person's spiritual malady and give instruction.

"Without the commission from God a man becomes vain. He says to himself, 'I am teaching people.' This vanity comes from ignorance, for only an ignorant person feels that he is the doer. A man verily becomes liberated in life if he feels: 'God is the Doer. He alone is doing everything. I am doing nothing.' Man's sufferings and worries spring only from his persistent thought that he is the doer.

"You people speak of doing good to the world. Is the world such a small thing? And who are you, pray, to do good to the world? First realize God, see Him by means of spiritual discipline. If He imparts power, then you can do good to others; otherwise not."

A BRĀHMO DEVOTEE: "Then, sir, must we give up our activities until we realize God?"

MASTER: "No. Why should you? You must engage

in such activities as contemplation, singing His praises, and other daily devotions."

BRĀHMO: "But what about our worldly duties—duties associated with earning money, and so on?"

MASTER: "Yes, you may perform them too, but only as much as you need for your livelihood. At the same time, you must pray to God in solitude, with tears in your eyes, that you may be able to perform those duties in an unselfish manner. You should say to Him: 'O God, make my worldly duties fewer and fewer; otherwise, O Lord, I find that I forget Thee when I am involved in too many activities. I may think I am doing unselfish work, but it turns out to be selfish.' People who carry to excess the giving of alms or the distributing of food among the poor, fall victims to the desire of acquiring name and fame.

"Sambhu Mallick once talked about establishing hospitals, dispensaries, and schools, making roads, digging public reservoirs, and so forth. I said to him: 'Don't go out of your way to look for such works. Undertake only those works that present themselves to you and are of pressing necessity; and perform them in a spirit of detachment.' It is not good to become involved in many activities. That makes one forget God. Coming to the Kālighāt temple, some, perhaps, spend their whole time in giving alms to the poor. They have no time to see the Mother in the inner shrine! (*Laughter.*) First of all manage somehow to see the image of the Divine Mother, even by pushing through the crowd. Then you may or may not give alms, as you wish. You may give to the poor to your heart's content, if you feel that way. Work is only a means to the realization of God. A lover of God says: 'O Lord, give me a place at

Thy Lotus Feet. Keep me always in Thy company. Give me sincere and pure love for Thee.'

"Karmayoga is very hard indeed. In the Kaliyuga it is extremely difficult to perform the rites enjoined in the scriptures. Nowadays a man's life is centred on food alone. He has no time to perform many scriptural rites. Suppose a man is laid up with fever. If you attempt a slow cure with the old-fashioned indigenous remedies, before long his life may be snuffed out. He can't stand much delay. Nowadays the drastic 'D. Gupta'[4] mixture is appropriate. In the Kaliyuga the best way is bhaktiyoga, the path of devotion—singing the praises of the Lord, and prayer. The path of devotion alone is the religion for this age. (*To the Brāhmo devotees*) Yours also is the path of devotion. Blessed you are indeed that you chant Hari's name and sing the Divine Mother's glories. I like your attitude. You don't call the world a dream, like the Non-dualists. You are not Brahmajnānis like them; you are bhaktas, lovers of God. That you speak of Him as a Person is also good. You are devotees. You will certainly realize Him if you call on Him with sincerity and earnestness."

The boat cast anchor at Kayalāghāt and the passengers prepared to disembark. On coming outside they noticed that the full moon was up. The trees, the buildings, and the boats on the Ganges were bathed in its white light. A carriage was hailed for the Master, and M and a few devotees got in with him. The Master asked for Keshab. Presently the latter arrived and inquired about the arrangements

[4] A patent fever medicine containing a strong dose of quinine.

made for the Master's return to Dakshineswar. Then
he bowed low and took leave of Sri Ramakrishna.

The carriage drove through the European quarter
of the city. The Master enjoyed the sight of the
beautiful mansions on both sides of the well-lighted
streets. Suddenly he said: "I am thirsty. What's to
be done?" Nandalal, Keshab's nephew, stopped the
carriage before the India Club and went upstairs to
get some water. The Master inquired if the glass had
been well washed. On being assured that it had been,
he drank the water.

As the carriage went along, the Master put his head
out of the window and looked with childlike enjoyment at the people, the vehicles, the horses, and the
streets, all flooded with moonlight. Now and then he
heard European ladies singing at the piano. He was in
a very happy mood.

October 28, 1882

It was Saturday. The semi-annual Brāhmo festival,
observed each autumn and spring, was being celebrated in Benimadhav Pal's beautiful garden house
at Sinthi, about three miles north of Calcutta. The
house stood in a secluded place suited for contemplation. Trees laden with flowers, artificial lakes with
grassy banks, and green arbours enhanced the beauty
of the grounds. Just as the fleecy clouds were turning
gold in the light of the setting sun, the Master arrived.

Many devotees had attended the morning devotions,
and in the afternoon people from Calcutta and the
neighbouring villages joined them. Shivanath, the
great Brāhmo devotee whom the Master loved dearly,
was one of the large gathering of members of the

Brāhmo Samāj who had been eagerly awaiting Sri
Ramakrishna's arrival.

When the carriage bringing the Master and a few
devotees reached the garden house, the assembly
stood up respectfully to receive him. There was a
sudden silence, like that which comes when the curtain
in a theatre is rung up. People who had been conversing with one another now fixed their attention
on the Master's serene face, eager not to lose one word
that might fall from his lips.

At the sight of Shivanath the Master cried out
joyously: "Ah! Here is Shivanath! You see, you are a
devotee of God. The very sight of you gladdens my
heart. One hemp smoker feels very happy to meet
another. Very often they embrace each other in an
exuberance of joy."

The devotees burst out laughing.

MASTER: "Many people visit the temple garden at
Dakshineswar. If I see some among the visitors indifferent to God, I say to them, 'You had better sit
over there.' Or sometimes I say, 'Go and see the
beautiful buildings.' (Laughter.)

"Sometimes I find that the devotees of God are
accompanied by worthless people. Their companions
are immersed in gross worldliness and don't enjoy
spiritual talk at all. Since the devotees keep on, for a
long time, talking with me about God, the others
become restless. Finding it impossible to sit there
any longer, they whisper to their devotee friends:
'When shall we be going? How long will you stay
here?' The devotees say: 'Wait a bit. We shall go
after a little while.' Then the worldly people say in a
disgusted tone: 'Well then, you can talk. We shall
wait for you in the boat.' (All laugh.) Worldly people

will never listen to you if you ask them to renounce
everything and devote themselves wholeheartedly to
God. As worldly people are endowed with sattva,
rajas, and tamas, so also is bhakti characterized by
the three gunas.

"Do you know what a worldly person endowed with
sattva is like? Perhaps his house is in a dilapidated
condition here and there. He doesn't care to repair it.
The worship hall may be strewn with pigeon droppings
and the courtyard covered with moss, but he pays no
attention to these things. The furniture of the house
may be old; he doesn't think of polishing it and
making it look neat. He doesn't care for dress at all;
anything is good enough for him. But the man himself
is very gentle, quiet, kind, and humble; he doesn't
injure anyone.

"Again, among the worldly there are people with
the traits of rajas. Such a man has a watch and chain,
and two or three rings on his fingers. The furniture
of his house is all spick and span. On the walls hang
portraits of the Queen, the Prince of Wales, and other
prominent people; the building is whitewashed and
spotlessly clean. His wardrobe is filled with a large
assortment of clothes; even the servants have their
livery and all that.

"The traits of a worldly man endowed with tamas
are sleep, lust, anger, egotism, and the like.

"Similarly, bhakti, devotion, may be sattvic. A devotee who possesses it meditates on God in absolute
secret, perhaps inside his mosquito net. Others think
he is asleep. Since he is late in getting up, they think
perhaps he has not slept well during the night. His
love for the body goes only as far as appeasing his
hunger, and that also by means of rice and simple

greens. There is no elaborate arrangement about his meals, no luxury in clothes, and no display of furniture. Besides, such a devotee never flatters anybody for money.

"An aspirant possessed of rājasic bhakti puts a tilak[5] on his forehead and a necklace of holy rudrāksha beads, interspersed with gold ones, around his neck. (*All laugh.*) At worship he wears a silk cloth. He likes outer display.

"A man endowed with tāmasic bhakti has burning faith. Such a devotee literally extorts boons from God, even as a robber falls upon a man and plunders his money. 'Bind! Beat! Kill!'—that is his way, the way of the dacoits."

Saying this, the Master began to sing in a voice sweet with rapturous love, his eyes turned upward:

Why should I go to Gayā or Gangā, to Kāśi, Kānchi, or Prabhās,[6]
So long as I can breathe my last with Kāli's name upon my lips?
What need of worship has a man, what need of rituals any more,
If he repeats the Mother's name during the three holy hours?[7]
Rituals may pursue him close, but they can never overtake him.

Charity, vows, and giving of gifts have no appeal for Madan's[8] mind;

---

[5] A mark of sandal-paste or other material to denote one's religious affiliation.

[6] Five well-known places of pilgrimage.

[7] Dawn, noon, and dusk.

[8] The author of the song.

The blissful Mother's Lotus Feet are his prayer and
   sacrifice.
Who could ever have conceived the power Her holy
   name possesses?
Śiva Himself, the God of gods, sings Her praise with
   his five mouths.

The Master was beside himself with love for the
Divine Mother. He said, "One must take the firm
attitude: 'What? I have chanted the Mother's name.
How can I be a sinner any more? I am Her child, heir
to Her powers and glories.'

"If you can give a spiritual turn to your tamas, you
can realize God with its help. Force your demands
on God. He is by no means a stranger to you. He is
indeed your very own.

"Furthermore, you see, the quality of tamas can be
used for the welfare of others. There are three classes
of physicians: superior, mediocre, and inferior. The
physician who feels the patient's pulse and just says to
him, 'Take the medicine regularly' belongs to the
inferior class. He doesn't care to inquire whether or
not the patient has actually taken the medicine. The
mediocre physician is he who in various ways per-
suades the patient to take the medicine and says to
him sweetly: 'My good man, how will you be cured
unless you use the medicine? Take this medicine. I
have prepared it for you myself.' But he who, finding
the patient stubbornly refusing to take the medicine,
forces it down his throat, going so far as to put his knee
on the patient's chest, is the best physician. This is the
manifestation of tamas in the physician. It doesn't
injure the patient; on the contrary, it does him good.

"Like the physicians, there are three types of religious teachers. The inferior teacher only gives in-

struction to the student but makes no inquiries about his progress. The mediocre teacher, for the good of the student, makes repeated efforts to bring the instruction home to him, begs him to assimilate it, and shows his fondness for him in many other ways. But there is a type of teacher who goes to the length of using force when he finds the student persistently unyielding; I call him the best teacher."

A BRĀHMO DEVOTEE: "Sir, has God forms or has He none?"

MASTER: "No one can say with finality that God is only 'this' and nothing else. He is formless, and again He has forms. For the bhakta He assumes forms. But He is formless for the jnāni, that is, for him who looks on the world as a mere dream. The bhakta feels that he is one entity and the world another. Therefore God reveals Himself to him as a Person. But the jnāni —the Vedāntist, for instance—always reasons, applying the process of 'Not this, not this.' Through this discrimination he realizes, by his inner perception, that the ego and the universe are both illusory, like a dream. Then the jnāni realizes Brahman in his own consciousness. He cannot describe what Brahman is.

"Do you know what I mean? Think of Brahman, Existence-Knowledge-Bliss Absolute, as a shoreless ocean. Through the cooling influence, as it were, of the bhakta's love, the water is frozen at places into blocks of ice. In other words, God now and then assumes various forms for His lovers and reveals Himself to them as a Person. But with the rising of the Sun of Knowledge, the blocks of ice melt. Then one doesn't feel any more that God is a Person, nor does one see God's forms. What He is cannot be de-

scribed. Who will describe Him? He who would do
so disappears. He cannot find his 'I' any more.

"If one analyses oneself, one doesn't find any such
thing as 'I.' Take an onion, for instance. First of all
you peel off the red outer skin; then you find thick
white skins. Peel these off one after the other and you
won't find anything inside.

"In that state a man no longer feels the existence
of his ego. And who is there left to seek it? Who can
describe how he feels in that state—in his own Pure
Consciousness—about the real nature of Brahman?

"There is a sign of Perfect Knowledge. A man becomes silent when it is attained. Then the 'I,' which
may be likened to a salt doll, melts in the Ocean of
Existence-Knowledge-Bliss Absolute and becomes one
with It. Not the slightest trace of distinction is left.

"As long as his self-analysis is not complete, a man
argues with much ado. But he becomes silent when he
completes it. When the empty pitcher has been filled
with water, when the water inside the pitcher becomes
one with the water of the lake outside, no more sound
is heard. Sound comes from the pitcher as long as the
pitcher is not filled with water.

"All trouble and botheration come to an end when
the 'I' dies. You may indulge in thousands of reasonings,
but still the 'I' doesn't disappear. For people like you
and me it is good to have the feeling, 'I am a lover
of God.'

"The Saguna Brahman is meant for the bhaktas.
In other words, a bhakta believes that God has attributes and reveals Himself to men as a Person, assuming
forms. It is He who listens to our prayers. The prayers
that you utter are directed to Him alone. It doesn't
matter whether you accept God with form or not.

It is enough to feel that God is a Person who listens to our prayers, who creates, preserves, and destroys the universe, and who is endowed with infinite power.

"It is easier to attain God by following the path of devotion."

BRĀHMO DEVOTEE: "Sir, is it possible for one to see God? If so, why can't we see Him?"

MASTER: "Yes, He can surely be seen. One can see His forms, and His formless aspect too. How can I explain that to you?"

BRĀHMO DEVOTEE: "What are the means by which one can see God?"

MASTER: "Can you weep for Him with intense longing of heart? Men shed a jugful of tears for the sake of their children, for their wives, or for money. But who weeps for God? So long as the child remains engrossed with its toys, the mother looks after her cooking and other household duties. But when the child no longer relishes the toys, it throws them aside and yells for its mother. Then the mother puts the rice pot down from the hearth, runs in haste, and takes the child in her arms."

BRĀHMO DEVOTEE: "Sir, why are there so many different opinions about God's nature? Some say that God has form, while others say that He is formless. Again, those who speak of God with form tell us about His different forms. Why all this controversy?"

MASTER: "A devotee thinks of God as he sees Him. In reality there is no confusion about God. God explains all this to the devotee if the devotee only somehow realizes Him. You haven't set your foot in that direction. How can you expect to know all about God?

"Listen to a story. Once a man entered a jungle and saw a small animal on a tree. He came back and told another man that he had seen a creature of a beautiful red colour on a certain tree. The second man replied: 'When I went into the jungle I too saw that animal. But why do you call it red? It is green.' Another man who was present contradicted them both and insisted that it was yellow. Presently others arrived and contended that it was grey, violet, blue, and so forth and so on. At last they started quarrelling among themselves. To settle the dispute they all went to the tree. They saw a man sitting under it. On being asked, he replied: 'Yes, I live under this tree and I know the animal very well. All your descriptions are true. Sometimes it appears red, sometimes yellow, and at other times blue, violet, grey, and so forth. It is a chameleon. And sometimes it has no colour at all. Now it has a colour, and now it has none.'

"In like manner, one who constantly thinks of God can know His real nature; he alone knows that God reveals Himself to seekers in various forms and aspects. God has attributes; then again He has none. Only the man who lives under the tree knows that the chameleon can appear in various colours, and he knows, further, that at times it has no colour at all. It is the others who suffer from the agony of futile argument.

"Kabir used to say, 'The formless Absolute is my Father, and God with form is my Mother.' God reveals Himself in the form which His devotee loves most. His love for the devotee knows no bounds.

"Yours is the path of bhakti. That is very good; it is an easy path. Who can fully know the infinite God? And what need is there of knowing the Infinite? Having attained this rare human birth, my supreme need is to develop love for God's Lotus Feet.

"If a jug of water is enough to remove my thirst,

why should I measure the quantity of water in a lake? Suppose a man gets drunk on half a bottle of wine: what is the use of his calculating the quantity of wine in the tavern? What need is there of knowing the Infinite?

"The various states of the Brahmajnāni's mind are described in the Vedas. The path of knowledge is extremely difficult. One cannot obtain jnāna if one has the least trace of worldliness and the slightest attachment to 'woman' and 'gold.' This is not the path for the Kaliyuga.

"The Vedas speak of seven planes where the mind can dwell. When the mind is immersed in worldliness it dwells in the three lower planes—at the navel, the organ of generation, and the organ of evacuation. In that state the mind loses all its higher visions—it broods only on 'woman' and 'gold.' The fourth plane of the mind is at the heart. When the mind dwells there, one has the first glimpse of spiritual consciousness. One sees light all around. Such a man, perceiving the divine light, becomes speechless with wonder and says: 'Ah! What is this? What is this?' His mind does not go downward to the objects of the world.

"The fifth plane of the mind is at the throat. When the mind reaches this, the aspirant becomes free from all ignorance and illusion. He does not enjoy talking or hearing about anything but God. If people talk about worldly things he leaves the place at once.

"The sixth plane is at the forehead. When the mind dwells there, the aspirant sees the form of God day and night. But even then a little trace of ego remains. At the sight of that incomparable beauty of God's form, one becomes intoxicated and rushes forth to touch and embrace it. But one doesn't succeed. It is like the light inside a lantern. One feels as if one could touch the light; but one cannot on account of the glass.

"In the top of the head is the seventh plane. When the mind rises there, one goes into samādhi. Then the Brahmajnāni directly perceives Brahman. But in that state his body does not last many days. He remains unconscious of the outer world. If milk is poured into his mouth, it runs out. Dwelling on this plane of consciousness, he gives up his body in twenty-one days. That is the condition of the Brahmajnāni. But yours is the path of devotion. That is a very good and easy path.

"Once a man said to me, 'Sir, can you teach me quickly the thing you call samādhi?' (*All laugh.*)

"After a man has attained samādhi all his actions drop away. All devotional activities, such as worship, japa, and the like, as well as all worldly duties, cease to exist for such a person. At the beginning there is much ado about work. As a man makes progress toward God the outer display of his work diminishes, so much so that he cannot even sing God's name and glories. (*To Shivanath*) As long as you were not here at the meeting, people talked a great deal about you and your virtues. But no sooner had you arrived than all that stopped. Now the very sight of you makes everyone happy. They now simply say, 'Ah! Here is Shivanath Babu.' All other talk about you has stopped.

"Therefore I say, at the beginning of religious life a man makes much ado about work, but as his mind dives deeper into God he becomes less active. Last of all comes the renunciation of work, followed by samādhi.

"Generally the body does not remain alive after the attainment of samādhi. The only exceptions are sages

like Nārada, who live in order to bring spiritual light
to others; the same thing is true of Divine Incarnations,
like Chaitanya. After the well is dug one generally
throws away the spade and the basket. But some keep
them in order to help their neighbours. The great souls
who retain their bodies after samādhi feel compassion
for the suffering of others. They are not so selfish as to
be satisfied with their own illumination.

(*To Shivanath and the other Brāhmo devotees*)
"Can you tell me why you dwell so much on the
powers and glories of God? I asked the same thing of
Keshab Sen. One day Keshab and his party came to
the temple garden at Dakshineswar. I wanted to hear
how they lectured. A meeting was arranged in the
paved courtyard above the bathing-ghāt on the Ganges,
where Keshab gave a talk. He spoke very well. I went
into a trance. After the lecture I said to Keshab:
'Why do you so often say such things as: "O God,
what beautiful flowers Thou hast made! O God, Thou
hast created the heavens, the stars, and the ocean!"
and so on?' Those who love splendour themselves are
fond of dwelling on God's splendour.

"Once a thief stole the jewels from the images in
the temple of Rādhākānta. Mathur Babu entered the
temple and said to the Deity: 'What a shame, O God!
You couldn't save Your own ornaments.' 'The idea!'
I said to Mathur. 'Does He who has Lakshmi, the
Goddess of Wealth, for His handmaid and attendant
ever lack splendour? Those jewels may be precious
to you, but to God they are no better than lumps of
clay. Shame on you! You shouldn't have spoken so
meanly. What riches can you give to God to magnify
His glory?'

"Therefore I say, a man seeks the person in whom

he finds joy. What need has he to ask where that person lives, or the number of his houses, gardens, relatives, and servants, or the amount of his wealth? I forget everything when I see Narendra.

"Dive deep in the sweetness of God's Bliss. What need have we of His infinite creation and unlimited glory?"

The Master sang:

Dive deep, O mind, dive deep in the ocean of God's beauty;
If you can plunge to the uttermost depths,
There you will find the gem of love.

Seek out, O mind, seek out and find Vrindāvan in your heart.

Light up, O mind, light up true wisdom's shining lamp,
And it will burn with a steady flame
Unceasingly within your heart.

MASTER (to Shivanath): "I like to see you. How can I live unless I see pure-souled devotees? I feel as if they had been my friends in a former incarnation."

A BRĀHMO DEVOTEE: "Sir, do you believe in the reincarnation of the soul?"

MASTER: "Yes, they say there is something like that. How can we understand God's ways through our finite minds? Many people have spoken about reincarnation; therefore I cannot disbelieve it."

It was about half past eight when the evening worship began in the prayer hall. Afterwards the devotees began to sing. Sri Ramakrishna was dancing, intoxicated with love of God. The Brāhmo devotees danced around him to the accompaniment of drums and cymbals. All appeared to be in a very joyous mood. The place echoed and re-echoed with God's holy name.

Then the Master and the devotees enjoyed a supper of delicious dishes, which Benimadhav, their host, had provided.

December 1882

In the afternoon Sri Ramakrishna was seated on the west porch of his room in the temple garden at Dakshineswar. Among others, Baburam, Ramdayal, and M were present. These three were going to spend the night with the Master. M intended to spend the following day there, also, for he was having his Christmas holidays. Baburam had only recently begun to visit the Master.

MASTER (*to the devotees*): "A man becomes liberated even in this life when he knows that God is the Doer of all things. Once Keshab came here with Sambhu Mallick. I said to him, 'Not even a leaf moves except by God's will.' Where is man's free will? All are under God's will. Therefore I say: 'O Mother, I am the machine and Thou art the Operator; I am the chariot and Thou art the Driver. I move as Thou movest me; I do as Thou makest me do.' "

The devotees sang kirtan in the Master's room:

Sing, O bird that nestles deep within my heart,
Sing, O bird that sits on the Kalpa-tree of Brahman,
Sing God's everlasting praise.
Taste, O bird, of the four fruits of the Kalpa-tree:
Dharma, artha, kāma, moksha.
Sing, O bird, "He alone is the Comfort of my soul."
Sing, O bird, "He alone is my life's enduring Joy."
O thou wondrous bird of my life,
Sing aloud in my heart. Unceasingly sing, O bird.
Sing for evermore, even as the thirsty chātak
Sings for raindrops from the clouds.

The evening worship began in the temples. The Master was seated on the small couch in his room, absorbed in meditation. He went into an ecstatic mood and said a little later: "Mother, please draw him to Thee. He is so modest and humble! He has been visiting Thee." Was the Master referring to Baburam, who later became one of his foremost monastic disciples?

The Master explained the different kinds of samādhi to the devotees. The conversation then turned to the joy and suffering of life. Why did God create so much suffering?

M: "Once Vidyāsāgar said in a mood of pique: 'What is the use of calling on God? Just think of this one incident: On one occasion Genghis Khan plundered a country and imprisoned many people. The number of prisoners rose to about a hundred thousand. The commander of his army said to him: "Your Majesty, who will feed them? It is risky to keep them with us. It will be equally dangerous to release them. What shall I do?" Genghis Khan said: "That's true. What can be done? Well, have them all killed." The order was accordingly given to cut them to pieces. Now, God saw this slaughter, didn't He? But He didn't stop it in any way. Therefore I don't need God, even if He exists. I don't derive any good from Him.' "

MASTER: "Is it possible to understand God's action and His motive? He creates, He preserves, and He destroys. Can we ever understand why He destroys? I say to the Divine Mother: 'O Mother, I do not need to understand. Please give me love for Thy Lotus Feet.' The aim of human life is to attain bhakti. As for other things, the Mother knows best. I have come to the garden to eat mangoes. What is the use of my calculating the number of trees, branches, and leaves? I only

eat the mangoes; I don't need to know the number of
trees and leaves."

Baburam, M, and Ramdayal slept that night on the
floor of the Master's room.

It was an early hour of the morning, about two or
three o'clock. The room was dark. Sri Ramakrishna
was seated on his bed and now and then conversed
with the devotees.

MASTER: "Remember that dayā, compassion, and
māyā, attachment, are two different things. Attachment
means the feeling of 'my-ness' toward one's relatives.
It is the love one feels for one's parents, one's brother,
one's sister, one's wife and children. Compassion is the
love one feels for all beings of the world. It is an attitude of same-sightedness. If you see anywhere an
instance of compassion, as in Vidyāsāgar, know that
it is due to God's grace. Through compassion one serves
all beings. Māyā also comes from God. Through māyā
God makes one serve one's relatives. But one thing
should be remembered: māyā keeps us in ignorance
and entangles us in the world, whereas dayā makes
our hearts pure and gradually unties our bonds.

"God cannot be realized without purity of heart.
One receives God's grace by subduing the passions—
lust, anger, and greed. Then one sees God. I tried
many things in order to conquer lust.

"When I was ten or eleven years old and lived at
Kāmārpukur, I first experienced samādhi. There are
certain characteristics of God-vision. One sees light,
feels joy, and experiences the upsurge of a great current in one's chest, like the bursting of a rocket."

The next day Baburam and Ramdayal returned to
Calcutta. M spent the day and night with the Master.

-»» 5 «-

THE MASTER AND VIJAY GOSWĀMI

Thursday, December 14, 1882

IT WAS AFTERNOON. Sri Ramakrishna was sitting on his bed after a short noonday rest. Vijay, Balaram, M, and a few other devotees were sitting on the floor with their faces toward the Master. They could see the sacred river Ganges through the door. Since it was winter all were wrapped up in warm clothes. Vijay had been suffering from colic and had brought some medicine with him.

Vijay was a paid preacher in the Sādhāran Brāhmo Samāj, but there were many things about which he could not agree with the Samāj authorities. He came from a very noble family of Bengal noted for its piety and other spiritual qualities. Advaita Goswāmi, one of his remote ancestors, had been an intimate companion of Sri Chaitanya. Thus the blood of a great lover of God flowed in Vijay's veins. As an adherent of the Brāhmo Samāj, he no doubt meditated on the formless Brahman; but his innate love of God, inherited from his distinguished ancestors, had merely been waiting for the proper time to manifest itself in all its sweetness. That is why Vijay was irresistibly attracted by the God-intoxicated state of Sri Ramakrishna and often sought his company. He listened to the Master's words with great respect and they danced together in an ecstasy of divine love.

It was a weekday. Generally devotees came to the Master in large numbers on Sundays; hence those who wanted to have intimate talks with him visited him on weekdays.

A boy named Vishnu, living in Āriādaha, had recently committed suicide by cutting his throat with a razor. The talk turned to him.

MASTER: "I felt very badly when I heard of the boy's passing away. He was a pupil in a school and used to come here. He often said to me that he couldn't enjoy worldly life. He had lived with some relatives in the western provinces and at that time used to meditate in solitude, in the meadows, hills, and forests. He told me he had visions of many divine forms.

"Perhaps this was his last birth. He must have finished most of his duties in his previous birth. The little that had been left undone was perhaps finished in this one."

A DEVOTEE: "I am frightened to hear of the suicide."

MASTER: "Suicide is a heinous sin, undoubtedly. A man who kills himself must return again and again to this world and suffer its agony.

"But I don't call it suicide if a person leaves his body after having the vision of God. There is no harm in giving up one's body that way. After attaining Knowledge some people give up their bodies. After the gold image has been cast in the clay mould, you may either preserve the mould or break it.

"Many years ago a young man of about twenty used to come to the temple garden from Barānagore; his name was Gopal Sen. In my presence he used to experience such intense ecstasy that Hriday had to support him for fear he might fall to the ground and break his limbs. That young man touched my feet one day and said: 'Sir, I shall not be able to see you any more. Let me bid you good-bye.' A few days later I learnt that he had given up his body."

Sri Ramakrishna began to describe worldly people.

MASTER: "Bound creatures, entangled in worldliness, will not come to their senses at all. They suffer so much misery and agony, they face so many dangers, and yet they will not wake up.

"The camel loves to eat thorny bushes. The more it eats the thorns, the more the blood gushes from its mouth. Still it must eat thorny plants and will not give them up. The man of worldly nature suffers so much sorrow and affliction, but he forgets it all in a few days and begins his old life over again. Suppose a man has lost his wife or she has turned unfaithful. Lo! He marries again.

"Or take the instance of a mother: her son dies and she feels bitter grief; but after a few days she forgets all about it. The mother, so overwhelmed with sorrow a few days before, now attends to her toilet and puts on her jewelry. A father becomes bankrupt through the marriage of his daughters, yet he goes on having children year after year. People are ruined by litigation, yet they go to court all the same. There are men who cannot feed the children they have, who cannot clothe them or provide decent shelter for them; yet they have more children every year.

"Again, the worldly man is like a snake trying to swallow a mole. The snake can neither swallow the mole nor give it up. The bound soul may have realized that there is no substance to the world—that the world is like a hog plum, only stone and skin—but still he cannot give it up and turn his mind to God.

"I once met a relative of Keshab Sen, fifty years old.

He was playing cards. As if the time had not yet come for him to think of God!

"There is another characteristic of the bound soul. If you remove him from his worldly surroundings to a spiritual environment, he will pine away. The worm that grows in filth feels very happy there. It thrives in filth. It will die if you put it in a pot of rice."

All remained silent.

VIJAY: "What must the bound soul's condition of mind be in order to achieve liberation?"

MASTER: "He can free himself from attachment to 'woman' and 'gold' if, by the grace of God, he cultivates a spirit of strong renunciation. What is this strong renunciation? One who has only a mild spirit of renunciation says, 'Well, all will happen in the course of time; let me now simply repeat God's name.' But a man possessed of a strong spirit of renunciation feels restless for God, as a mother feels for her child. A man of strong renunciation seeks nothing but God. He regards the world as a deep well and feels as if he were going to be drowned in it. He looks on his relatives as venomous snakes; he wants to fly away from them. And he goes away, too. He never says to himself, 'Let me first make some arrangement for my family and then I shall think of God.' He has great inward resolution.

"Let me tell you a story about strong renunciation. At one time there was a drought in a certain part of the country. The farmers began to cut long channels to bring water to their fields. One farmer was a man of stubborn determination. He took a vow that he would not stop digging until the channel connected his field with the river. He set to work. The time came for his bath, and his wife sent their daughter to him with oil. 'Father,' said the girl, 'it is already late. Rub your body with oil and take your bath.' 'Go away!' thundered the farmer. 'I have too much to do now.' It was past midday and the farmer was still at work in his field. He didn't even think of his bath. Then his wife came and said: 'Why haven't you taken your bath? The food is getting cold. You overdo everything. You can finish the rest tomorrow or even today after dinner.' The farmer scolded her furiously and ran at her, spade in hand, crying: 'What? Have you no sense? There's no rain. The crops are dying. What will the children eat? You'll all starve to death. I have taken a vow not to think of bath and food today before I bring water to my field.' The wife saw his state of mind and ran away in fear. Through a whole day's back-breaking labour the farmer managed by evening to connect his field with the river. Then he sat down and watched the water flowing into the field with a mur-muring sound. His mind was filled with peace and joy. He went home, called his wife, and said to her, 'Now give me some oil and prepare me a smoke.' With serene mind he finished his bath and meal, retired to bed, and snored to his heart's content. The determina-tion he showed is an example of strong renunciation.

"Now, there was another farmer who was also dig-ging a channel to bring water to his field. His wife, too, came to the field and said to him: 'It's very late. Come home. It isn't necessary to overdo things.' The farmer didn't protest much, but put aside his spade and said to his wife, 'Well, I'll go home since you ask me to.' (*All laugh.*) That man never succeeded in irrigat-ing his field. This is a case of mild renunciation.

"As without strong determination the farmer cannot

bring water to his field, so also without intense yearning a man cannot realize God. (*To Vijay*) Why don't you come here now as frequently as before?"

VIJAY: "Sir, I wish to very much, but I am not free. I have accepted work in the Brāhmo Samāj."

MASTER: "It is 'woman' and 'gold' that bind man and rob him of his freedom. It is woman that creates the need for gold. For woman one man becomes the slave of another and so loses his freedom. Then he cannot act as he likes.

"The priests in the temple of Govindaji at Jaipur were celibates at first, and at that time they had fiery natures. Once the King of Jaipur sent for them but they didn't obey him. They said to the messenger, 'Ask the king to come here and see us.' After consultation, the king and his ministers arranged marriages for them. From then on the king didn't have to send for them. They would come to him of themselves and say: 'Your Majesty, we have come with our blessings. Here are the sacred flowers from the temple. Please accept them.' They themselves came to the palace, for now they always wanted money for one thing or another: the building of a house, the rice-eating ceremony of their babies, or the rituals connected with the beginning of their children's education.

(*To Vijay*) "You yourself perceive how far you have gone down by being a servant of others. Again, one finds that people with many university degrees, scholars with their vast English education, accept service under their English masters and are daily trampled under their boots. The one cause of all this is woman. They have married and set up a 'gay fair' with their wives and children. Now they cannot go back, much as they would like to. Hence all these insults and humiliations, all this suffering from slavery.

"Once a man realizes God through intense dispassion, he is no longer attached to woman. Even if he must lead the life of a householder, he is free from fear of woman and attachment to her. Suppose there are two magnets, one big and the other small. Which one will attract the iron? The big one, of course. God is the big magnet. Compared to Him, woman is a small one. What can woman do?"

A DEVOTEE: "Sir, shall we hate women then?"

MASTER: "He who has realized God does not look upon a woman with the eye of lust; so he is not afraid of her. He perceives clearly that women are but so many aspects of the Divine Mother. He worships them all as the Mother Herself.

(To Vijay) "Come here now and then. I like to see you very much."

VIJAY: "I have to do my various duties in the Brāhmo Samāj; that is why I can't always come here. But I shall visit you whenever I find it possible."

MASTER (to Vijay): "The task of a religious teacher is indeed difficult. One cannot teach men without a direct command from God. People won't listen to you if you teach without such authority. Such teaching has no force behind it. One must first of all attain God through spiritual discipline or some other means. Thus armed with authority from God, one can deliver lectures."

VIJAY: "Don't the teachings of the Brāhmo Samāj bring men salvation?"

MASTER: "How is it ever possible for one man to liberate another from the bondage of the world? God alone, the Creator of this world-bewitching māyā, can save men from māyā. There is no other refuge but that great Teacher, Satchidānanda. How is it ever possible for men who have not realized God or received His command, and who are not strengthened with divine strength, to save others from the prison-house of the world?

"One day as I was passing the Panchavati on my way to the pine-grove, I heard a bullfrog croaking. I thought it must have been seized by a snake. After some time, as I was coming back, I could still hear its terrified croaking. I looked to see what was the matter, and found that a water snake had seized it. The snake could neither swallow it nor give it up. So there was no end to the frog's suffering. I thought that had it been seized by a cobra it would have been silenced after three croaks at the most. As it was only a water snake, both of them had to go through this agony. A man's ego is destroyed after three croaks, as it were, if he gets into the clutches of a real teacher. But if the teacher is an 'unripe' one, then both the teacher and the disciple undergo endless suffering. The disciple cannot get rid either of his ego or of the shackles of the world. If a disciple falls into the clutches of an incompetent teacher, he doesn't attain liberation."

VIJAY: "Sir, why are we bound like this? Why don't we see God?"

MASTER: "Māyā is nothing but the egotism of the embodied soul. This egotism has covered everything like a veil. 'All troubles come to an end when the ego dies.' If by God's grace a man but once realizes that he is not the doer, then he at once becomes a jivanmukta: though living in the body, he is liberated. He has nothing else to fear.

"This māyā, that is to say, the ego, is like a cloud.

The sun cannot be seen on account of a thin patch of cloud; when that disappears one sees the sun. If by the guru's grace one's ego vanishes, then one sees God.

"The jiva is nothing but the embodiment of Satchidānanda. But since māyā, or ego, has created various upādhis, he has forgotten his real Self.

"Each upādhi changes man's nature. If even a sickly man puts on high boots, he begins to whistle and climbs the stairs like an Englishman, jumping from one step to another. If a man but holds a pen in his hand, he scribbles on any paper he can get hold of—such is the power of the pen!

"Money is also a great upādhi. The possession of money makes such a difference in a man! He is no longer the same person. A brāhmin used to frequent the temple garden. Outwardly he was very modest. One day I went to Konnagar with Hriday. No sooner had we got off the boat than we noticed the brāhmin seated on the bank of the Ganges. We thought he had been enjoying the fresh air. Looking at us, he said: 'Hello there, priest! How do you do?' I marked his tone and said to Hriday: 'The man must have got some money. That's why he talks that way.' Hriday laughed.

"A man can get rid of the ego after the attainment of Knowledge. On attaining Knowledge he goes into samādhi and the ego disappears. But it is very difficult to obtain such Knowledge.

"The 'I' that makes one a worldly person and attaches one to 'woman' and 'gold' is the 'wicked I.' The intervention of this ego creates the difference between jiva and Ātman. Water appears to be divided into two parts if one puts a stick across it. But in reality there is only one expanse of water. It appears as two on account of the stick. This 'I' is the stick. Remove the stick and there remains only one expanse of water as before.

"Now, what is this 'wicked I'? It is the ego that says: 'What? Don't they know me? I have so much money! Who is wealthier than I?' If a thief robs such a man of only ten rupees, first of all he wrings the money out of the thief, then he gives him a good beating. But the matter doesn't end there: the thief is handed over to the police and is eventually sent to jail. The 'wicked I' says: 'What? Doesn't the rogue know whom he has robbed? To steal my ten rupees! How did he dare?'"

VIJAY: "If without destroying the 'I' a man cannot get rid of attachment to the world and consequently cannot experience samādhi, then it would be wise for him to follow the path of Brahmajnāna to attain samādhi. If the 'I' persists in the path of devotion, then one should rather choose the path of knowledge."

MASTER: "It is true that one or two can get rid of the 'I' through samādhi; but these cases are very rare. You may indulge in thousands of reasonings, but still the 'I' comes back. You may cut the peepal-tree to the very root today, but you will notice a sprout springing up tomorrow. Therefore if the 'I' must remain, let the rascal remain as the 'servant I.' As long as you live, you should say, 'O God, Thou art the Master and I am Thy servant.' The 'I' that feels, 'I am the servant of God, I am His devotee' does not injure one."

VIJAY (to the Master): "Sir, you ask us to renounce the 'wicked I.' Is there any harm in the 'servant I'?"

MASTER: "The 'servant I'—that is, the feeling, 'I am the servant of God, I am the devotee of God'—does not injure one. On the contrary, it helps one realize God."

VIJAY: "Well, sir, what becomes of the lust, anger, and other passions of one who keeps the 'servant I'?"

MASTER: "If a man truly feels like that, then he has only the semblance of lust, anger, and the like. If, after attaining God, he looks on himself as the servant or the devotee of God, then he cannot injure anyone. By touching the philosopher's stone a sword is turned into gold. It keeps the appearance of a sword but cannot injure.

"When the dry branch of a coconut palm drops to the ground, it leaves only a mark on the trunk indicating that once there was a branch at that place. In like manner, he who has attained God keeps only an appearance of ego; there remains in him only a semblance of anger and lust. He becomes like a child. A child has no attachment to the three gunas—sattva, rajas, and tamas. He becomes as quickly detached from a thing as he becomes attached to it. You can cajole him out of a cloth worth five rupees with a doll worth an ānnā, though at first he may say with great determination: 'No, I won't give it to you. My daddy bought it for me.' Again, all persons are the same to a child. He has no feeling of high and low in regard to persons. So he doesn't discriminate about caste. The child doesn't know hate or what is holy or unholy.

"Even after attaining samādhi some retain the 'servant ego' or the 'devotee ego.' The bhakta keeps this 'I-consciousness.' He says, 'O God, Thou art the Master and I am Thy servant; Thou art the Lord and I am Thy devotee.' He feels that way even after the realization of God. His 'I' is not completely effaced. Again, by constantly practising this kind of 'I-consciousness,' one ultimately attains God. This is called bhaktiyoga.

"One can attain the Knowledge of Brahman, too, by following the path of bhakti. God is all-powerful. He may give His devotee Brahmajnāna also, if He so wills. But the devotee generally doesn't seek the Knowledge of the Absolute. He would rather have the consciousness that God is the Master and he the servant, or that God is the Divine Mother and he the child."

VIJAY: "But those who discriminate according to the Vedānta philosophy also realize Him in the end, don't they?"

MASTER: "Yes, one may reach Him by following the path of discrimination too: that is called jnānayoga. But it is an extremely difficult path. If a man acquires the firm knowledge that Brahman alone is real and the world illusory, then his mind merges in samādhi. But, as I told you, in the Kaliyuga the life of a man depends entirely on food. How can he have the consciousness that Brahman alone is real and the world illusory? In the Kaliyuga it is difficult to have the feeling, 'I am not the body, I am not the mind, I am not the twenty-four cosmic principles, I am beyond pleasure and pain, I am above disease and grief, old age and death.' However you may reason and argue, the feeling that the body is identical with the soul will somehow crop up from an unexpected quarter. One cannot get rid of this identification with the body; therefore the path of bhakti is best for the people of the Kaliyuga. It is an easy path.

"And there is the saying: 'I don't want to become sugar; I want to eat it.' I never feel like saying, 'I am Brahman.' I say, 'Thou art my Lord and I am Thy servant.' My desire is to sing God's name and glories. It is very good to look on God as the Master and on oneself as His servant. Further, you see, people speak

of the waves as belonging to the Ganges; but no one
says that the Ganges belongs to the waves. The feeling
'I am He' is not wholesome. A man who entertains
such an idea, while looking on his body as the Self,
causes himself great harm. He cannot go forward in
spiritual life; he drags himself down. He deceives himself as well as others. He cannot understand his own
state of mind.

"But it isn't any and every kind of bhakti that enables one to realize God. One cannot realize God without premā-bhakti. Another name for premā-bhakti is
rāga-bhakti.[1] God cannot be realized without love and
longing. Unless one has learnt to love God, one cannot
realize Him.

"There is another kind of bhakti, known as vaidhi-
bhakti, according to which one must repeat God's
name a fixed number of times, fast, make pilgrimages
laid down in the scriptures, worship God with prescribed offerings, make a number of sacrifices, and so
forth and so on. By continuing such practices a long
time one gradually acquires rāga-bhakti. God cannot be
realized until one has rāga-bhakti. One must love God.
In order to realize God one must be completely free
from worldliness and direct all of one's mind to Him.

"But some acquire rāga-bhakti directly. It is innate
in them. They have it from their very childhood. Even
at an early age they weep for God. Vaidhi-bhakti is
like moving a fan to make a breeze. One needs the
fan to make the breeze. Similarly, one practises japa,
austerity, and fasting, in order to acquire love of God.
But the fan is set aside when the southern breeze
blows of itself. Such actions as japa and austerity drop
away when one spontaneously feels love of God. Who,

[1] Supreme love, which makes one attached only to God.

indeed, will perform the ceremonies enjoined in the scriptures, when mad with love of God?

"Devotion to God may be said to be 'green' so long as it doesn't grow into love of God; but it becomes 'ripe' when it has grown into such love.

"A man with 'green' bhakti cannot assimilate spiritual talk and instruction; but one with 'ripe' bhakti can. The image that falls on a photographic plate covered with black film[2] is retained. On the other hand, thousands of images may be reflected on a bare piece of glass, but not one of them is retained. As the object moves away, the glass becomes the same as it was before. One cannot assimilate spiritual instruction unless one has already developed love of God."

VIJAY: "Is bhakti alone sufficient for the attainment of God, for His vision?"

MASTER: "Yes, one can see God through bhakti alone. But it must be 'ripe' bhakti, premā-bhakti and rāga-bhakti. When one has that bhakti, one loves God even as the mother loves the child, the child the mother, or the wife the husband.

"When one has such love for God, one doesn't feel any physical attraction to wife, children, relatives, and friends. One retains only compassion for them. To such a man the world appears as a foreign land, a place where he has merely to perform his duties. It is like a man's having his real home in the country, but coming to Calcutta for work; he has to rent a house in Calcutta for the sake of his duties. When one develops love of God, one completely gets rid of one's attachment to the world and worldly wisdom.

"A man cannot see God if he has even the slightest trace of worldliness. Match-sticks, if damp, won't

[2] Silver nitrate.

strike fire though you rub a thousand of them against the match-box. You only waste a heap of sticks. The mind soaked in worldliness is like a damp match-stick.

"If the devotee but once feels this attachment, this ecstatic love for God, this mature devotion and longing, then he sees God in both His aspects: with form and without form."

VIJAY: "How can one see God?"

MASTER: "One cannot see God without purity of heart. Through attachment to 'woman' and 'gold' the mind has become stained—covered with dirt, as it were. A magnet cannot attract a needle if the needle is covered with mud. Wash away the mud and the magnet will draw it. Likewise, the dirt of the mind can be washed away with the tears of our eyes. This stain is removed if one sheds tears of repentance and says, 'O God, I shall never again do a wicked thing.' Thereupon God, who is like the magnet, draws to Himself the mind, which is like the needle. Then the devotee goes into samādhi and obtains the vision of God.

"You may try thousands of times, but nothing can be achieved without God's grace. One cannot see God without His grace. Is it an easy thing to receive grace? One must altogether renounce egotism; one cannot see God as long as one feels, 'I am the doer.'

"God doesn't easily appear in the heart of a man who feels himself to be his own master. But God can be seen the moment His grace descends. He is the Sun of Knowledge. One single ray of His has illumined the world with the light of knowledge. That is how we are able to see one another and acquire varied knowledge. One can see God only if He turns His light toward His own face.

"The police sergeant goes his rounds in the dark of night with a lantern[3] in his hand. No one sees his face; but with the help of that light the sergeant sees everybody's face, and others, too, can see one another. If you want to see the sergeant, however, you must pray to him: 'Sir, please turn the light on your own face. Let me see you.' In the same way one must pray to God: 'O Lord, be gracious and turn the light of knowledge on Thyself, that I may see Thy face.' A house without light indicates poverty. So one must light the lamp of Knowledge in one's heart."

Vijay had brought medicine with him; the Master asked a devotee to give him some water. He was indeed a fountain of compassion. He had arranged for Vijay's boat fare, since the latter was too poor to pay it. Vijay, Balaram, M, and the other devotees left for Calcutta in a country boat.

Friday, March 9, 1883

About nine o'clock in the morning the Master was seated in his room with Rakhal, M, and a few other devotees. It was the day of the new moon. As usual with him on such a day, Sri Ramakrishna entered again and again into communion with the Divine Mother.

The conversation was about the householder's life in the world.

DEVOTEE: "Sir, why has God put us in the world?"

MASTER: "The world is the field of action. Through action one acquires knowledge. The guru instructs the disciple to perform certain works and refrain from others. Again, he advises the pupil to perform action without desiring the result. The impurity of the mind

---

[3] A reference to the lantern carried by the night-watch, which has dark glass on three sides.

is destroyed through the performance of duty. It is like getting rid of a disease by means of medicine, under the instruction of a competent physician.

"Why doesn't God free us from the world? Ah, He will free us when the disease is cured. He will liberate us from the world when we are through with the enjoyment of 'woman' and 'gold.' "

During these days Sri Ramakrishna's heart overflowed with motherly love. So he kept Rakhal with him. Rakhal felt toward the Master as a child feels toward its mother. He would sit leaning on the Master's lap as a young child leans on its mother while sucking her breast.

Rakhal was thus seated leaning on the Master when a man entered the room and said that a high tide was coming in the Ganges. The Master and the devotees ran to the Panchavati to see it. At the sight of a boat being tossed by the tide, Sri Ramakrishna exclaimed: "Look! Look! I hope nothing happens to it."

They all sat in the Panchavati. The Master asked M to explain the cause of the tide. M drew on the ground the figures of the sun, moon, and earth and tried to explain gravitation, ebb tide, flood tide, new moon, full moon, eclipse, and so forth.

MASTER (to M): "Stop it! I can't follow you. It makes me dizzy. My head is aching. Well, how can they know of things so far off?

"You see, during my childhood I could paint well; but arithmetic would make my head spin. I couldn't learn even simple arithmetic."

The Master enjoyed a nap after his noon meal. Adhar and other devotees gradually gathered. This was Adhar's first visit. He was a deputy magistrate and about thirty years old.

MASTER: "One should not reason too much; it is enough if one loves the Lotus Feet of the Mother. Too much reasoning throws the mind into confusion. You get clear water if you drink from the surface of a pool. Put your hand deeper and stir the water, and it becomes muddy. Therefore pray to God for devotion."

DEVOTEE: "Can one see God?"

MASTER: "Yes, *surely*. One can see both of God's aspects: with form and without form. One can see God with form, the Embodiment of Spirit. Again, God can be directly perceived in a tangible human form. To see an Incarnation of God is the same as to see God Himself. God is born on earth as man in every age."

Sunday, March 11, 1883

It was Sri Ramakrishna's birthday.[4] Many of his disciples and devotees wanted to celebrate the happy occasion at the Dakshineswar temple garden.

From early morning the devotees streamed in, alone or in parties. After the morning worship in the temples sweet music was played in the nahabat. It was springtime. The trees, creepers, and plants were covered with new leaves and blossoms. The very air seemed laden with joy. And the hearts of the devotees were glad on this auspicious day.

M arrived early in the morning and found the Master talking smilingly to Bhavanath, Rakhal, and Kalikrishna. M prostrated himself before him.

MASTER (*to M*): "I am glad you have come.

(*To the devotees*) "One cannot be spiritual as long

[4] In India the birthday is a movable celebration, and is determined each year by the position of the moon at the time the person was born.

as one feels shame, hatred, or fear. Great will be the joy today. But those fools who will not sing or dance, mad with God's name, will never attain God. How can one feel any shame or fear when the names of God are sung? Now sing, all of you."

Bhavanath and his friend Kalikrishna sang. As Sri Ramakrishna listened to the song he remained absorbed in meditation. After a while Kalikrishna whispered something to Bhavanath. Then he bowed before the Master and rose. Sri Ramakrishna was surprised. He asked, "Where are you going?"

BHAVANATH: "He is going away on a little business."

MASTER: "What is it about?"

BHAVANATH: "He is going to the Barānagore Workingmen's Institute."

MASTER: "It's his bad luck. A stream of bliss will flow here today. He could have enjoyed it. But how unlucky!"

Sri Ramakrishna did not feel well; so he decided not to bathe in the Ganges. About nine o'clock a few jars of water were taken from the river, and with the help of the devotees he finished his bath on the verandah east of his room. The Master put on a new wearing-cloth, all the while chanting God's name. Accompanied by one or two disciples he walked across the courtyard to the temple of Kāli, still chanting Her hallowed name. His eyes had an indrawn look, like that of a bird hatching her eggs.

On entering the temple, he prostrated himself before the image and then worshipped the Divine Mother. But he did not observe any of the prescribed rituals of worship. Now he would offer flowers and sandal-paste at the feet of the image, and now he would put them on his own head. After finishing the worship in his own way, he asked Bhavanath to carry the green coconut that had been offered to the Mother. He also visited the images of Rādhā and Krishna in the Vishnu temple.

When the Master returned to his room, he found that other devotees had arrived, among them Ram, Nityagopal, and Kedar. They all saluted the Master, who greeted them cordially.

MASTER (*to the devotees*): "Ordinary people do not recognize the advent of an Incarnation of God. He comes in secret. Only a few of His intimate disciples can recognize Him. That Rāma was both Brahman Absolute and a perfect Incarnation of God in human form was known only to twelve rishis. The other sages said to Him, 'Rāma, we know You only as Daśaratha's son.' "

Presently some devotees from Konnagar arrived, singing kirtan to the accompaniment of drums and cymbals. As they reached the northeast verandah of Sri Ramakrishna's room, the Master joined in the music, dancing with them intoxicated with divine joy. Now and then he went into samādhi, standing still as a statue. While he was in one of these states of divine unconsciousness, the devotees put thick garlands of jasmine around his neck. The enchanting form of the Master reminded them of Chaitanya, another Incarnation of God. The Master passed alternately through three moods of divine consciousness: the inmost, when he lost all knowledge of the outer world; the semi-conscious, when he danced with the devotees in an ecstasy of love; and the conscious, when he joined them in loud singing. It was indeed a sight for the gods to see the Master standing motionless in samādhi, with fragrant garlands hanging from his neck, his countenance beaming with love, and the devotees singing and dancing around him.

When it was time for his noon meal, Sri Ramakrishna put on a new yellow cloth and sat on the small couch. His golden complexion, blending with his yellow cloth, enchanted the eyes of the devotees.

After his meal Sri Ramakrishna rested a little on the small couch. Devotees crowded inside and outside his room—among them Kedar, Suresh, Ram, Manomohan, Girindra, Rakhal, Bhavanath, and M. Rakhal's father also was present.

A Vaishnava goswāmi was seated in the room. The Master said to him: "Well, what do you say? What is the way?"

GOSWĀMI: "Sir, the chanting of God's name is enough. The scriptures emphasize the sanctity of God's name for the Kaliyuga."

MASTER: "Yes, there is no doubt about the sanctity of God's name. But can a mere name achieve anything, without the yearning of the devotee behind it? One should feel great restlessness of soul for the vision of God. Suppose a man repeats God's name mechanically while his mind is absorbed in 'woman' and 'gold.' Can he achieve anything? Suppose a man becomes pure by chanting God's holy name, but immediately afterwards commits many sins. He has no strength of mind. He doesn't take a vow not to repeat his sins. A bath in the Ganges undoubtedly absolves one of all sins; but what does that avail? They say that the sins perch on the trees along the banks of the Ganges. No sooner does the man come back from the holy waters than the old sins jump on his shoulders from the trees. (*All laugh.*) The same old sins take possession of him again. He is hardly out of the water before they fall upon him.

"Therefore I say, chant God's name, and with it pray to Him that you may have love for Him. Pray to God that your attachment to such transitory things as wealth, name, and creature comforts may become less and less every day.

(*To the goswāmi*) "With sincerity and earnestness one can realize God through all religions. The Vaishnavas will realize God, and so will the Śāktas, the Vedāntists, and the Brāhmos. The Mussalmāns and Christians will realize Him too. All will certainly realize God if they are earnest and sincere.

"Some people indulge in quarrels, saying, 'One cannot attain anything unless one worships our Krishna,' or, 'Nothing can be gained without the worship of Kāli, our Divine Mother,' or, 'One cannot be saved without accepting the Christian religion.' This is pure dogmatism. The dogmatist says, 'My religion alone is true, and the religions of others are false.' This is a bad attitude. God can be reached by different paths.

"Further, some say that God has form and is not formless. Thus they start quarrelling. A Vaishnava quarrels with a Vedāntist.

"One can rightly speak of God only after one has seen Him. He who has seen God knows really and truly that God has form and that He is formless as well. He has many other aspects that cannot be described.

"Once some blind men chanced to come near an animal that someone told them was an elephant. They were asked what the elephant was like. The blind men began to feel its body. One of them said the elephant

was like a pillar; he had touched only its leg. Another
said it was like a winnowing-fan; he had touched only
its ear. In this way the others, having touched its
tail or belly, gave their different versions of the elephant. Just so, a man who has seen only one aspect
of God limits God to that alone. It is his conviction
that God cannot be anything else.

(*To the goswāmi*) "How can you say that the only
truth about God is that He has form? It is undoubtedly
true that God comes down to earth in a human form, as
in the case of Krishna. And it is true as well that God
reveals Himself to His devotees in various forms. But
it is also true that God is formless; He is the Indivisible Existence-Knowledge-Bliss Absolute. He has
been described in the Vedas both as formless and as
endowed with form. He is also described there both
as attributeless and as endowed with attributes."

KEDAR: "It is said in the *Bhāgavata* that Vyāsa
asked God's forgiveness for his three transgressions.
He said: 'O Lord, Thou art formless, but I have thought
of Thee in my meditation as endowed with form;
Thou art beyond speech, but I have sung hymns to
Thee; Thou art the All-pervading Spirit, but I have
made pilgrimages to sacred places. Be gracious, O
Lord, and forgive these three transgressions of mine.'"

MASTER: "Yes, God has form and He is formless
too. Further, He is beyond both form and formlessness.
No one can limit Him."

Later in the afternoon the devotees sang in the
Panchavati, where the Master joined them. It was a
very happy day for all.

About six o'clock in the evening the Master was
sitting with the devotees on the southeast verandah
of his room.

MASTER: "A holy man who has renounced the world will of course chant God's name. That is only natural. He has no other duties to perform. If he meditates on God it shouldn't surprise anybody. On the other hand, if he fails to think of God or chant His holy name, then people will think ill of him.

"But it is a great deal to his credit if a householder utters the Lord's name. Think of King Janaka. What courage he had, indeed! He fenced with two swords, the one of knowledge and the other of work. He possessed the perfect Knowledge of Brahman and also was devoted to his royal duties. An unchaste woman attends to the minutest duties of the world, but her mind always dwells on her paramour.

"The constant company of holy men is necessary. They introduce one to God."

The devotees were ready to return home. One by one they saluted the Master. At the sight of Bhavanath Sri Ramakrishna said: "Don't go away today. The very sight of you inspires me." Bhavanath had not yet entered into worldly life. A youth of twenty, he had a fair complexion and handsome features. He shed tears of joy on hearing God's name. The Master looked on him as the embodiment of Nārāyana.

6

IN THE COMPANY OF DEVOTEES

Sunday, April 8, 1883

IT WAS SUNDAY MORNING. The Master, looking like a boy, was seated in his room, and near him was another boy, his beloved disciple Rakhal. M entered and saluted the Master. Ramlal also was in the room, and Kishori, Manilal Mallick, and several other devotees gathered by and by.

Manilal Mallick, a business man, had recently been to Benares, where he owned a bungalow.

MASTER: "So you have been to Benares. Did you see any holy men there?"

MANILAL: "Yes, sir. I paid my respects to Trailanga Swami, Bhaskarananda, and others. Trailanga Swami keeps a strict vow of silence. Unlike him, Bhaskarananda is friendly with all."

MASTER: "Did you have any conversation with Bhaskarananda?"

MANILAL: "Yes, sir. We had a long talk. Among other things we discussed the problem of good and evil. He said to me: 'Don't follow the path of evil. Give up sinful thoughts. That is how God wants us to act. Perform only those duties that are virtuous.'"

MASTER: "Yes, that is also a path, meant for the worldly-minded. But those whose spiritual consciousness has been awakened, who have realized that God alone is real and all else is illusory, cherish a different

243

ideal. They are aware that God alone is the Doer and others are His instruments.

"Those whose spiritual consciousness has been awakened never make a false step. They do not have to reason in order to shun evil. They are so full of love of God that whatever action they undertake is a good action. They are fully conscious that they are not the doers of their actions, but mere servants of God.

"Fully awakened souls are beyond virtue and vice. They realize that it is God who does everything.

"There was a monastery in a certain place. The monks residing there went out daily to beg their food. One day a monk, while out for his alms, saw a landlord beating a man mercilessly. The compassionate monk stepped in and asked the landlord to stop. But the landlord was filled with anger and turned his wrath against the innocent monk. He beat the monk till he fell unconscious on the ground. Someone reported the matter to the monastery. The monks ran to the spot and found their brother lying there. Four or five of them carried him back and laid him on a bed. He was still unconscious. The other monks sat around him sad at heart; some were fanning him. Finally someone suggested that he should be given a little milk to drink. When it was poured into his mouth he regained consciousness. He opened his eyes and looked around. One of the monks said, 'Let us see whether he is fully conscious and can recognize us.' Shouting into his ear, he said, 'Revered sir, who is giving you milk?' 'Brother,' replied the holy man in a low voice, 'He who beat me is now giving me milk.'

"But one does not attain such a state of mind without the realization of God."

MANILAL: "Sir, what you have just said applies to a man of a very lofty spiritual state. I talked on such topics in a general way with Bhaskarananda."

The worship was over in the temples and the bells rang for the food offerings in the shrines. As it was a summer noon the sun was very hot. The flood tide started to rise in the Ganges and a breeze came up from the south. Sri Ramakrishna was resting in his room after his meal.

Presently a few elderly members of the Brāhmo Samāj arrived. The room was full of devotees. Sri Ramakrishna was sitting on his bed, facing the north. He kept smiling and talked to the Brāhmo devotees in a joyous mood.

MASTER: "You talk glibly about prema. But is it such a commonplace thing? There are two characteristics of prema, ecstatic love of God. First, it makes a man forget the world. So intense is his love of God that he becomes unconscious of outer things. Second, he has no feeling of 'my-ness' toward the body, which is so dear to all. He wholly gets rid of the feeling that the body is the soul.

"There are certain signs of God-realization. A man who longs for God is not far from attaining Him. What are the outer indications of such longing? They are discrimination, dispassion, compassion for living beings, serving holy men, loving their company, chanting God's name and glories, telling the truth, and the like. When you see those signs in an aspirant, you can rightly say that for him the vision of God is not far to seek.

"The state of a servant's house will tell you unmistakably if his master has decided to visit it. First, the rubbish and jungle around the house are cleared up. Second, the soot and dirt are removed from the rooms. Third, the courtyard, floors, and other places are swept clean. Finally the master himself sends various things to the house, such as a carpet, a hubble-bubble for smoking, and the like. When you see these things coming, you conclude that the master will very soon arrive."

A DEVOTEE: "Sir, should one first practise discrimination to attain self-control?"

MASTER: "That is also a path. It is called the path of vichára, reasoning. But the inner organs[1] are brought under control through the path of devotion as well. This self-control is rather easily accomplished that way. Sense pleasures appear more and more tasteless as love for God grows."

DEVOTEE: "How can I develop love for God?"

MASTER: "Repeat His name, and sins will disappear. Thus you will destroy lust, anger, the desire for creature comforts, and so on."

DEVOTEE: "How can I take delight in God's name?"

MASTER: "Pray to God with a yearning heart that you may take delight in His name. He will certainly fulfil your heart's desire.

"As is a man's feeling, so is his gain. Once two friends were going along the street, when they saw some people listening to a reading of the *Bhágavata*. 'Come, friend,' said the one to the other. 'Let us hear the sacred book.' So saying he went in and sat down. The second man peeped in and went away. He entered a house of ill fame. But very soon he felt disgusted with the place. 'Shame on me!' he said to himself.

[1] Mind (manas), intelligence (buddhi), mind-stuff (chitta), and ego (ahamkára).

'My friend has been listening to the sacred words about Hari; and see where I am!' But the friend who had been listening to the *Bhāgavata* also became disgusted. 'What a fool I am!' he said. 'I have been listening to this fellow's blah-blah, and my friend is having a grand time.' In course of time they both died. The messenger of Death came for the soul of the one who had listened to the *Bhāgavata* and dragged it off to hell. The messenger of God came for the soul of the other, who had been to the house of prostitution, and led it up to heaven.

"Verily, the Lord looks into a man's heart and does not judge him by what he does or where he lives.

"Everyone can attain Knowledge. There are two entities: jivātmā, the individual soul, and Paramātmā, the Supreme Soul. Through prayer all individual souls can be united to the Supreme Soul. Every house has a connexion for gas, by which gas can be obtained from the main storage tank of the gas company. Apply to the company and it will arrange for your supply of gas. Then your house will be lighted.

"In some people spiritual consciousness has already been awakened; but they have special marks. They do not enjoy hearing or talking about anything but God. They are like the chātak bird, which prays for rainwater though the seven oceans, the Ganges, the Jamunā, and other rivers near by are filled with water. The bird won't drink anything but rainwater, even though its throat is burning with thirst.

"Bound souls, worldly people, are like silkworms. The worms can cut through their cocoons if they want, but having woven the cocoons themselves, they are too much attached to them to leave them. And so they die there.

"Free souls are not under the control of 'woman' and 'gold.' There are some silkworms that cut through the cocoon they have made with such great care. But they are few and far between.

"It is māyā that deludes. Only a few become spiritually awakened and are not deluded by the spell of māyā. They do not come under the control of 'woman' and 'gold.'

"There are two classes of perfect souls: those who attain perfection through spiritual practice, and those who attain it through the grace of God. Some farmers irrigate their fields with great labour. Only then can they grow crops. But there are some who do not have to irrigate at all; their fields are flooded by rain. They don't have to take the trouble to draw water. One must practise spiritual discipline laboriously in order to avoid the clutches of māyā. Those who attain liberation through God's grace do not have to labour. But they are few indeed.

"Then there is the class of the ever-perfect. They are born every time with their spiritual consciousness already awakened. Think of a spring whose outlet is obstructed. While looking after various things in the garden, the plumber accidentally clears away the obstruction and the water gushes out. People are amazed to see the first manifestations of an ever-perfect soul's zeal for God. They say, 'Where was all this devotion and renunciation and love?' "

The conversation turned to the spiritual zeal of devotees, as illustrated in the earnestness of the gopis of Vrindāvan. Ramlal sang:

Thou art my all in all, O Lord—the life of my life, my inmost being;

I have none else but Thee, in the three worlds, to call
    my own.
Thou art my peace, my joy, my hope; Thou my support,
    my wealth, my glory;
Thou my wisdom and my strength.

Thou art my home, my place of rest; my dearest
    friend, my next of kin;
My present and my future, Thou; my heaven and my
    salvation.
Thou art my scriptures, my commandments; Thou art
    my ever gracious guru;
Thou the spring of my boundless bliss.

Thou art the way, and Thou the goal; Thou the
    Adorable One, O Lord;
Thou art the Mother tender-hearted; Thou the chastis-
    ing Father;
Thou the Creator and Protector; Thou the Helmsman
    who dost steer
My craft across the sea of life.

MASTER (*to the devotees*): "Ah! What a beautiful
song!—'Thou art my all in all.'"

Ramlal sang again, this time describing the pangs of
the gopis on being separated from their beloved
Krishna. The Master went into deep samādhi. His
body was motionless, and he sat with folded hands as
in his photograph. Tears of joy flowed from the corners
of his eyes. After a long time his mind came down to
the ordinary plane of consciousness. He mumbled
something, of which only a word now and then could
be heard by the devotees in the room.

Continuing, the Master said: "I see everything like
a man with jaundiced eyes. I see Thee alone everywhere. O Krishna, Friend of the lowly! O eternal
Consort of my soul! O Govinda!"

Uttering the words "O eternal Consort of my soul! O Govinda!", the Master again went into samādhi. There was complete silence in the room. The eager and unsatiated eyes of the devotees were fixed on the Master, a God-man of infinite moods.

Adhar Sen arrived with several of his friends. This was his second visit to the Master. He was accompanied by his friend Saradacharan, who was extremely unhappy because of the death of his eldest son. A retired deputy inspector of schools, Saradacharan devoted himself to meditation and prayer. Adhar had brought his friend to the Master for consolation in his afflicted state of mind.

Coming down from samādhi, the Master found the eyes of the devotees fixed on him. He muttered to himself, still in an abstracted mood. Then, addressing the devotees, he said: "The spiritual wisdom of worldly people is seen only on rare occasions. It is like the flame of a candle. No, it is rather like a single ray of the sun passing through a chink in a wall. Worldly people chant God's name, but there is no zeal behind it. It is like children's swearing by God, having learnt the word from the quarrels of their aunts. Worldly people have no grit. If they succeed in an undertaking, it is all right, but if they don't succeed, it scarcely bothers them at all."

By this time Sri Ramakrishna had become better acquainted with Adhar, who related the cause of his friend's grief. The Master said: "What can you do? Be ready for Death. Death has entered the house. You must fight him with the weapon of God's holy name. God alone is the Doer. I say: 'O Lord, I do as Thou doest through me. I speak as Thou speakest through me.' Give your power of attorney to God. One doesn't come to grief if one lets a good man assume one's responsibilities. Let His will be done.

"House, wife, and children are all transitory; they have only a momentary existence. The palm-tree alone is real. One or two fruits have dropped off. Why lament?

"God is engaged in three kinds of activity: creation, preservation, and destruction. Death is inevitable. All will be destroyed at the time of dissolution. Nothing will remain. At that time the Divine Mother will gather up the seeds for the future creation. She will use them again at the time of the new creation."

Sunday, April 22, 1883

Sri Ramakrishna paid a visit to Benimadhav Pal's garden house at Sinthi, near Calcutta, on the occasion of the semi-annual festival of the Brāhmo Samāj. Many devotees of the Samāj were present and sat around the Master. Now and then some of them asked him questions.

A BRĀHMO DEVOTEE: "Sir, what is the way?"

MASTER: "Attachment to God, or, in other words, love for Him. And secondly, prayer."

BRĀHMO DEVOTEE: "Which one is the way—love or prayer?"

MASTER: "First love and then prayer."

Continuing, the Master said: "And one must always chant God's name and glories and pray to Him. An old metal pot must be scrubbed every day. What is the use of cleaning it only once? Further, one must practise discrimination and renunciation; one must be conscious of the unreality of the world."

BRĀHMO: "Is it good to renounce the world?"

MASTER: "Not for all. Those who have not yet

come to the end of their enjoyments should not renounce the world."

BRĀHMO: "What is the meaning of the 'end of
enjoyments'?"

MASTER: "I mean the enjoyment of 'woman' and
'gold.' Most people don't feel any longing for God
unless they have once passed through the experience
of wealth, name, fame, creature comforts, and the
like, that is to say, unless they have seen through these
enjoyments."

BRĀHMO: "Who is really bad, man or woman?"

MASTER: "As there are women endowed with spiritual knowledge, so also there are women who are
ignorant. A woman endowed with knowledge leads
a man to God, but a woman who is the embodiment
of delusion makes him forget God and drowns him in
the ocean of worldliness.

"This universe is created by the Mahāmāyā[2] of
God. Mahāmāyā contains both vidyāmāyā, the illusion
of knowledge, and avidyāmāyā, the illusion of ignorance. Through the help of vidyāmāyā one cultivates
such virtues as the taste for holy company, knowledge,
devotion, love, and renunciation. Avidyāmāyā consists
of the five elements and the objects of the five senses—
form, flavour, smell, touch, and sound. These make
one forget God."

BRĀHMO: "If the power of avidyā is the cause of
ignorance, then why has God created it?"

MASTER: "That is His play. The glory of light
cannot be appreciated without darkness. Happiness
cannot be understood without misery. Knowledge of
good is possible because of knowledge of evil.

"Further, the mango grows and ripens on account

[2] The inscrutable Power of Illusion.

of the covering skin. You throw away the skin when the mango is fully ripe and ready to be eaten. It is possible for a man to attain gradually to the Knowledge of Brahman because of the covering skin of māyā. Māyā in its aspects of vidyā and avidyā may be likened to the skin of the mango. Both are necessary."

BRĀHMO: "How does one cultivate the spirit of dispassion? Why don't all attain it?"

MASTER: "Dispassion is not possible unless there is satiety through enjoyment. You can easily cajole a small child with candies or toys. But after eating the candies and finishing its play, it cries, 'I want to go to my mother.' Unless you take the child to its mother, it will throw away the toy and scream at the top of its voice."

The members of the Brāhmo Samāj are opposed to the traditional guru system of orthodox Hinduism. Therefore the Brāhmo devotee asked the Master about it.

BRĀHMO: "Is spiritual knowledge impossible without a guru?"

MASTER: "Satchidānanda alone is the Guru. If a man in the form of a guru awakens spiritual consciousness in you, then know for certain that it is God the Absolute who has assumed that human form for your sake. The guru is like a companion who leads you by the hand. After realizing God, one loses the distinction between the guru and the disciple. The relationship between them remains as long as the disciple does not see God."

After dusk the preacher of the Brāhmo Samāj conducted the service from the pulpit. The service was interspersed with recitations from the Upanishads and the singing of Brāhmo songs.

After the service the Master and the preacher conversed.

MASTER: "It seems to me that both the formless Deity and God with form are real. What do you say?"

PREACHER: "Sir, I compare the formless God to the electric current, which is not seen with the eyes but can be felt."

MASTER: "Yes, both are true. God with form is as real as God without form. Do you know what the describing of God as formless only is like? It is like a man's playing only a monotone on his flute, though it has seven holes. But on the same instrument another man plays different melodies. Likewise, in how many ways the believers in a Personal God enjoy Him! They enjoy Him through many different attitudes: the serene attitude, the attitude of a servant, a friend, a mother, a husband, or a lover.

"The nature of Brahman cannot be described. About It one remains silent. Who can explain the Infinite in words? However high a bird may soar, there are regions higher still.

"After having the vision of God man is overpowered with bliss. He becomes silent. Who will speak? Who will explain?"

PREACHER: "Yes, sir, it is so described in Vedānta."

MASTER: "Under the spell of God's māyā man forgets his true nature. He forgets that he is heir to the infinite glories of his Father. This divine māyā is made up of three gunas. And all three are robbers; for they rob man of all his treasures and make him forget his true nature. The three gunas are sattva, rajas, and tamas. Of these, sattva alone points the way to God. But even sattva cannot take a man to God.

"Let me tell you a story. Once a rich man was passing through a forest, when three robbers surrounded him and robbed him of everything he had. Then one of the robbers said: 'What's the good of keeping the man alive? Kill him.' He was about to strike their victim with his sword, when the second robber intervened and said: 'There's no use in killing him. Let us bind him fast and leave him here. Then he won't be able to tell the police.' Accordingly the robbers tied him with a rope and went away.

"After a while the third robber returned to the rich man and said: 'Ah! You're badly hurt, aren't you? Come, I'm going to release you.' The robber set the man free and led him out of the forest. When they came near the highway, the robber said, 'Follow this road and you will reach home easily.' 'But you must come with me too,' said the man. 'You have done so much for me. All my people will be happy to see you.' 'No,' said the robber, 'it is not possible for me to go there. The police will arrest me.' So saying, he left the rich man after pointing out his way.

"Now, the first robber, who said: 'What's the good of keeping the man alive? Kill him,' is tamas. It destroys. The second robber is rajas, which binds a man to the world and entangles him in a variety of activities. Rajas makes him forget God. Sattva alone shows the way to God. It produces virtues like compassion, righteousness, and devotion. Again, sattva is like the last step of the stairs. Next to it is the roof. The Supreme Brahman is man's own abode. One cannot attain the Knowledge of Brahman unless one transcends the three gunas."

PREACHER: "You have given us a fine talk, sir."

MASTER (*with a smile*): "You are a preacher and teach so many people! You are a steamship and I am a mere fishing-boat." (*All laugh.*)

Monday, June 4, 1883

About nine o'clock in the morning the devotees began to arrive at the temple garden. Sri Ramakrishna was sitting on the porch of his room facing the Ganges. M, who had spent the previous night with the Master, sat near him. Balaram and several other devotees were present. Rakhal lay on the floor, resting his head on the Master's lap. The Master asked Balaram to stay for his midday meal. Sri Ramakrishna described to the devotees the days of his God-intoxication.

MASTER: "Oh, what a state of mind I passed through! When I first had that experience, I could not perceive the coming and going of day or night. People said I was insane. What else could they say? They made me marry. I was then in a state of God-intoxication. At first I felt worried about my wife. Then I thought she too would live like me.

"I visited my father-in-law's house. They arranged a kirtan. It turned into a big religious festival and there was much singing of God's holy name. Now and then I would wonder about my future. I would say to the Divine Mother, 'Mother, I shall take my spiritual experiences to be genuine if the landlords of the country show me respect.' They too came of their own accord and talked with me.

"Oh, what an ecstatic state it was! Even the slightest suggestion would awaken my spiritual consciousness. I worshipped the Divine Mother in a girl fourteen years old. I saw that she was the personification of the Mother.

"At that time I used to invite maidens here and worship them. I found them to be the embodiments of the Divine Mother Herself.

"One day I had gone to the Maidān in Calcutta for fresh air. A great crowd had assembled there to watch a balloon ascension. Suddenly I saw an English boy leaning against a tree. As he stood there his body was bent in three places. The vision of Krishna came before me in a flash.[3] I went into samādhi.

"At that time I was almost unconscious of the outer world. Mathur Babu kept me at his Jānbāzār mansion a few days. While living there I regarded myself as the handmaid of the Divine Mother. The ladies of the house didn't feel at all bashful with me. They felt as free before me as women feel before a small boy or girl.

"Even now the slightest thing awakens God-Consciousness in me. Rakhal used to repeat God's name half aloud. At such times I couldn't control myself. It would rouse my spiritual consciousness and overwhelm me."

After his noon meal the Master took a short rest. Manilal Mallick, an old member of the Brāhmo Samāj, entered the room and sat down after saluting the Master, who was still lying on his bed. Manilal asked him questions now and then, and the Master, still half asleep, answered with a word or two. Then Sri Ramakrishna sat up. He spoke reassuringly to the devotees.

MASTER (to M): "Some think: 'Oh, I am a bound soul. I shall never acquire knowledge and devotion.'

[3] In the usual image of Krishna one sees His body bent in three places.

But if one receives the guru's grace, one has nothing to fear. Once a tigress attacked a flock of goats. As she sprang on her prey she gave birth to a cub and died. The cub grew up in the company of the goats. The goats ate grass and the cub followed their example. They bleated; the cub bleated too. Gradually it grew to a big tiger. One day another tiger attacked the same flock. It was amazed to see the grass-eating tiger. Running after it, the wild tiger at last seized it, whereupon the grass-eating tiger began to bleat. The wild tiger dragged it to the water and said: 'Look at your face in the water. It is just like mine. Here is a little meat. Eat it.' Saying this, it thrust some meat into its mouth. But the grass-eating tiger would not swallow it and began to bleat again. Gradually, however, it got the taste for blood and came to relish the meat. Then the wild tiger said: 'Now you see there is no difference between you and me. Come away and follow me into the forest.'

"So there can be no fear if the guru's grace falls on you. He will let you know who you are and what your real nature is.

"If the devotee practises spiritual discipline a little, the guru explains everything to him. Then the disciple understands for himself what is real and what is unreal."

One of the devotees said to himself: "Is the world unreal, then? What, then, will happen to those who are living in the world? Must they too renounce it?" Sri Ramakrishna, who could see into a man's innermost thought, said very tenderly: "Suppose an office clerk has been sent to jail. He undoubtedly leads a prisoner's life there. But when he is released from jail, does he cut capers in the street? Not at all. He gets a job as a clerk again and goes on working as before. Even after attaining Knowledge through the guru's grace, one can very well live in the world as a jivanmukta." Thus did Sri Ramakrishna reassure those who were living as householders.

It was a hot day in June 1883. Sri Ramakrishna was sitting on the steps of the Siva temples in the temple garden. M arrived with ice and other offerings and sat down on the steps after saluting the Master.

MASTER (*to M*): "The husband of Mani Mallick's granddaughter was here. He read in a book[4] that God could not be said to be quite wise and omniscient; otherwise, why should there be so much misery in the world? As regards death, it would be much better to kill a man at once instead of putting him through slow torture. Further, the author writes that if he himself were the Creator, he would have created a better world."

M listened to these words in surprise and made no comment.

MASTER (*to M*): "Can a man ever understand God's ways? I too think of God sometimes as good and sometimes as bad. He has kept us deluded by His great illusion. Sometimes He wakes us up and sometimes He keeps us unconscious. One moment the ignorance disappears, and the next moment it covers our mind. If you throw a brickbat into a pond covered with moss, you get a glimpse of the water. But a few moments later the moss comes dancing back and covers the water.

[4] The autobiography of John Stuart Mill.

"One is aware of pleasure and pain, birth and death, disease and grief, as long as one is identified with the body. All these belong to the body alone, and not to the Soul. After the death of the body, perhaps God carries one to a better place. It is like the birth of the child after the pain of delivery. Attaining Self-Knowledge, one looks on pleasure and pain, birth and death, as a dream. How little we know! Can a one-seer pot hold ten seers of milk?"

At dusk the evening service began in the different temples. The Master was sitting on the small couch in his room, absorbed in contemplation of the Divine Mother. Several devotees also were there. M intended to spend the night with the Master.

A little later Sri Ramakrishna began to talk to a devotee on the verandah north of his room. He said: "It is good to meditate in the small hours of the morning and at dawn. One should also meditate daily after dusk." He instructed the devotee about meditation on the Personal God and on the Impersonal Reality.

After a time he sat on the semicircular porch west of his room. It was about nine o'clock.

MASTER: "Those who come here will certainly have all their doubts removed. What do you say?"

M: "That is true, sir."

A boat was moving in the Ganges, far away from the bank. The boatman began to sing. The sound of his voice floating over the river reached the Master's ears, and he went into a spiritual mood. The hair on his body stood on end. He said to M, "Just feel my body." M was greatly amazed.

After a time Sri Ramakrishna began to converse again.

MASTER: "Those who come here must have been born with good tendencies. Isn't that true?"

M: "It is true, sir."

MASTER: "A guileless man easily realizes God. There are two paths: the path of righteousness and the path of wickedness. One should follow the path of righteousness."

Saturday, July 21, 1883

It was about four o'clock in the afternoon when Sri Ramakrishna, with Ramlal and one or two other devotees, started from Dakshineswar for Calcutta in a carriage. As the carriage passed the gate of the Kāli temple, they met M coming on foot with four mangoes in his hand. The carriage stopped and M saluted the Master.

MASTER (*to M, with a smile*): "Come with us. We are going to Adhar's house."

M got joyfully into the carriage. Having received an English education, he did not believe in the tendencies inherited from previous births. But he had admitted a few days before that it was on account of Adhar's good tendencies from past births that he showed such great devotion to the Master. Later on he had thought about this subject and had discovered that he was not yet completely convinced about inherited tendencies. He had come to Dakshineswar that day to discuss the matter with Sri Ramakrishna.

MASTER: "Well what do you think of Adhar?"

M: "He has great yearning for God."

MASTER: "Adhar, too, speaks very highly of you."

M remained silent awhile and then began to speak of past tendencies.

M: "I haven't much faith in rebirth and inherited

tendencies. Will that in any way injure my devotion to God?"

MASTER: "It is enough to believe that all is possible in God's creation. Never allow the thought to cross your mind that your ideas are the only true ones and that those of others are false. Then God will explain everything.

"How much can a man understand of God's activities? The facets of God's creation are infinite. I do not try to understand God's actions at all. I have heard that everything is possible in God's creation, and I always bear that in mind. Therefore I do not give a thought to the world, but meditate on God alone.

"Can one ever understand God's work? He is so near; still it is not possible for us to know Him."

M: "That is true, sir."

MASTER: "God has covered all with His māyā. He doesn't let us know anything. Māyā is 'woman' and 'gold.' He who puts māyā aside to see God, can see Him. Once, when I was explaining God's actions to someone, God suddenly showed me the lake at Kāmār-pukur. I saw a man pushing aside the green scum and drinking the water. The water was clear as crystal. God revealed to me that Satchidānanda is covered by the scum of māyā. He who pushes the green scum aside can drink the water.

"The universe is conscious on account of the Consciousness of God. Sometimes I find that this Consciousness wriggles about, as it were, even in small fish."

The carriage came to the crossing at Shovābāzār in Calcutta. The Master continued, saying, "Sometimes I find that the universe is saturated with God's Consciousness, as the earth is soaked with water in the rainy season.

"Well, I see so many visions, but I never feel vain about them."

M (*with a smile*): "That you should speak of vanity, sir!"

MASTER: "Upon my word, I don't feel vanity even in the slightest degree."

M: "There once lived a man in Greece, Socrates by name. A voice from heaven said that he was wise among men. Socrates was amazed at this revelation. He meditated on it a long time in solitude and then realized its significance. He said to his friends, 'I alone of all people have understood that I do not know anything.' But every man believes he is wise. In reality all are ignorant."

MASTER: "Now and then I say to myself, 'What is it I know that makes so many people come to me?' Vaishnavcharan was a great pundit. He used to say to me: 'I can find in the scriptures all the things you talk about. But do you know why I come to you? I come to hear them from your mouth.'"

M: "All your words tally with the scriptures."

MASTER: "Have you found anyone else resembling me—any pundit or holy man?"

M: "God has created you with His own hands, whereas He has made others by machine. All others He has created according to law."

MASTER (*laughing, to Ramlal and the other devotees*): "Did you hear what he said?"

Sri Ramakrishna laughed for some time and said at last, "Really and truly I have no pride—no, not even the slightest bit."

M: "Knowledge does us good in one respect at least; it makes us feel that we do not know anything, that we are nothing."

MASTER: "Right you are! I am nothing. I am nobody. "Do you believe in English astronomy?"

M: "It is possible to make new discoveries by applying the laws of Western astronomy. Observing the irregular movement of Uranus, the astronomers looked through their telescopes and discovered Neptune shining in the sky. They can also foretell eclipses."

MASTER: "Yes, that is so."

The carriage drove on. They were approaching Adhar's house. Sri Ramakrishna said to M, "Dwell in the truth and you will certainly realize God."

Sri Ramakrishna arrived at Adhar's house and took a seat in the parlour. Ramlal, Adhar, M, and the other devotees sat near him. Rakhal was staying with his father in Calcutta.

MASTER (to Adhar): "Didn't you tell Rakhal that I was coming?"

ADHAR: "Yes, sir. I have sent him word."

Finding that the Master was eager to see Rakhal, Adhar at once sent his carriage to fetch him. Adhar had felt a yearning to see the Master that day, but he had not definitely known that Sri Ramakrishna was coming.

ADHAR: "You haven't been here in a long time. I prayed to God today that you might come. I even shed tears."

The Master was pleased and said with a smile, "You don't mean that!"

It was dusk and the lamps were lighted. Sri Ramakrishna saluted the Divine Mother with folded hands and sat quietly absorbed in meditation. Then he began to chant the names of God in his sweet voice: "Govinda! Govinda! Satchidānanda! Hari! Hari!" Every word he uttered showered nectar on the ears of the devotees.

Adhar served Sri Ramakrishna with fruits and sweets.

Sunday, July 22, 1883

Taking advantage of the holiday, many householder devotees visited Sri Ramakrishna in his room at the Dakshineswar temple garden. Adhar, Rakhal, and M had come from Calcutta in a hired carriage.

Sri Ramakrishna had enjoyed a little rest after his midday meal. The room had an atmosphere of purity and holiness. On the walls hung pictures of gods and goddesses, among them one of Christ rescuing the drowning Peter. Outside the room were plants laden with fragrant flowers, and the Ganges could be seen flowing toward the south. The Master was seated on the small couch, facing the north, and the devotees sat on mats and carpets spread on the floor. All eyes were directed toward him.

A DEVOTEE: "Sir, you met Pundit Vidyāsāgar. What did you think of him?"

MASTER: "Vidyāsāgar has both scholarship and compassion, but he lacks inner vision. Gold lies hidden within him. Had he but found it out, his activities would have been reduced; finally they would have stopped altogether. Had he but known that God resides in his heart, his mind would have been directed to God in thought and meditation. Some persons must perform selfless work a long time before they can practise dispassion and direct their minds to the spiritual ideal. In the end they too are absorbed in God.

"The activities that Vidyāsāgar is engaged in are good. Compassion is a noble quality. There is a great deal of difference between dayā, compassion, and māyā, attachment. Dayā is good, but māyā is not. Māyā is love for one's relatives—one's wife, children, brother, sister, nephew, father, and mother. But dayā is the same love for all created beings without any distinction."

M: "Is dayā also a bondage?"

MASTER: "Yes, it is. But that concept is something far beyond the ordinary man. Dayā springs from sattva. Sattva preserves, rajas creates, and tamas destroys. But Brahman is beyond the three gunas. It is beyond Prakriti. What Brahman is cannot be described. Even he who knows It cannot talk about It.

"Once four friends, in the course of a walk, saw a place enclosed by a wall. The wall was very high. They all became eager to know what was inside. One of them climbed to the top of the wall. What he saw on looking inside made him speechless with wonder. He only cried, 'Ah! Ah!' and jumped in. He could not give any information about what he saw. The others, too, climbed the wall, uttered the same cry, 'Ah! Ah!,' and jumped in. Now who could tell what was inside?"

DEVOTEE: "Can one keep up an organization after attaining the Knowledge of Brahman?"

MASTER: "Once I talked to Keshab Sen about the Knowledge of Brahman. He asked me to explain it further. I said, 'If I proceed further, then you won't be able to preserve your organization and following.' 'Then please stop here!' replied Keshab. (All laugh.) But still I said to Keshab: ' "I" and "mine" indicate ignorance. Without ignorance one cannot have such a feeling as "I am the doer; these are my wife, children, and possessions." ' Thereupon Keshab said, 'Sir, if one gave up the "I," nothing whatsoever would remain.' I reassured him and said: 'I am not asking you to give up all of the "I." You should give up only the "unripe I." The "unripe I" makes one feel: "I am the doer. These are my wife and children. I am a teacher." Renounce this "unripe I" and keep the "ripe I," which will make you feel that you are God's servant, His devotee, and that God is the Doer and you are His instrument.'

"I asked Keshab to give up this 'unripe I.' The ego that feels, 'I am the servant of God and lover of God' does not injure one. I said to him: 'You have been constantly talking of your organization and your following. But people also go away from your organization.' Keshab answered: 'It is true, sir. After staying in it several years, people go to another organization. What is worse, on deserting me they abuse me right and left.' 'Why don't you study their nature beforehand?' I said. 'Is there any good in making anybody and everybody a disciple?'

"It is extremely difficult to go beyond the three gunas. One cannot reach that state without having realized God. Man dwells in the realm of māyā. Māyā does not permit him to see God. It has made him a victim of ignorance.

"Once Hriday brought a bull calf here. I saw, one day, that he had tied it with a rope in the garden so that it might graze there. I asked him, 'Hriday, why do you tie the calf there every day?' 'Uncle,' he said, 'I am going to send this calf to our village. When it grows strong I shall yoke it to the plough.' As soon as I heard these words I was stunned to think: 'How inscrutable is the play of the divine māyā! Kāmārpukur and Sihore[5] are so far away from Calcutta! This poor calf must go all that way. Then it will grow, and at length it will be yoked to the plough. This is indeed the world! This is indeed māyā!' I fell down unconscious. Only after a long time did I regain consciousness."

Wednesday, September 26, 1883

M arrived in the afternoon and found the Master seated on the small couch.

MASTER (*to M*): "How is it that you are here today? Have you no school?"

M: "Our school closed today at half-past one."

MASTER: "Why so early?"

M: "Vidyāsāgar visited the school. He owns the school. So the boys get a half holiday whenever he comes."

MASTER: "Why doesn't Vidyāsāgar keep his word? The other day he said he would come here and visit me. But he hasn't kept his word.

"There is a big difference between a scholar and a holy man. The mind of a mere scholar is fixed on 'woman' and 'gold,' but the sādhu's mind is on the Lotus Feet of Hari. A scholar says one thing and does another. But it is quite a different matter with a sādhu. The words and actions of a man who has given his mind to God are altogether different.

"Once a Vedāntic monk came here. He used to dance at the sight of a cloud. He would go into an ecstasy of joy over a rainstorm. He would get very angry if anyone went near him when he meditated.

[5] Hriday's birthplace.

One day I came to him while he was meditating, and that made him very cross. He discriminated constantly: 'Brahman alone is real and the world is illusory.' Since the appearance of diversity is due to māyā, he walked about with a prism from a chandelier in his hand. One sees different colours through the prism; in reality there is no such thing as colour. Likewise, nothing exists, in reality, except Brahman. But there is an appearance of the manifold because of māyā, egotism. He would not look at an object more than once, lest he should be deluded by māyā and attachment. He stayed here for three days. One day he heard the sound of a flute near the embankment and said that a man who had realized Brahman would go into samādhi at such a sound."

While talking about the monk, the Master showed his devotees the manners and movements of a paramahamsa: the gait of a child, his face beaming with laughter, eyes swimming in joy, and body completely naked. Then he again took his seat on the small couch and poured out his soul-enthralling words.

MASTER (to M): "I learnt Vedānta from Nangtā: 'Brahman alone is real; the world is illusory.' The magician performs his magic. He produces a mango-tree which even bears mangoes. But this is all sleight of hand. The magician alone is real."

M: "It seems that the whole of life is a long sleep. This much I understand, that we are not seeing things rightly. We perceive the world with a mind by which we cannot comprehend even the nature of the sky. So how can our perceptions be correct?"

MASTER: "How can a man see correctly? His mind is delirious, like the mind of a typhoid patient."

The Master sang in his sweet voice:

What a delirious fever is this that I suffer from!
Mother, Thy grace is my only cure. . . .

Continuing, the Master said: "Truly it is a state
of delirium. Just see how worldly men quarrel among
themselves. No one knows what they quarrel about.
Oh, how they quarrel! How much shouting! How
much abuse!"

The Master and M went toward the Kāli temple.

MASTER: "This world may be a 'framework of
illusion,' but it is also described as a 'mansion of mirth.'
One can turn this world into a mansion of mirth."

M: "But where is unbroken bliss in this world?"

MASTER: "Indeed, it's true, isn't it?"

Sri Ramakrishna stood in front of the shrine of
Kāli and prostrated himself before the Divine Mother.
M followed him. Then the Master sat on the lower
floor in front of the shrine room, facing the blissful
image. He wore a red-bordered cloth, part of which
was on his shoulder and back. M sat by his side.

M: "Since there is no unbroken happiness in the
world, why should one assume a body at all? I know
that the body is meant only to reap the results of
past action. But who knows what sort of action it is
performing now? The unfortunate part is that we
are being crushed. There are the eight bonds."

MASTER: "They are not eight bonds, but eight
strong fetters. But what if they are? These fetters fall
off in a moment, by God's grace. Do you know what
it is like? Suppose a room has been kept dark a
thousand years. The moment a man brings a light into
it, the darkness vanishes. Not little by little. Haven't
you seen the magician's feat? He takes a string with
many knots, and ties one end to something, keeping
the other in his hand. Then he shakes the string once

or twice, and immediately all the knots come undone. But another man cannot untie the knots however he may try. All the knots of ignorance come undone in the twinkling of an eye, through the guru's grace.

"Do not reason. Who can ever know God? I have heard it from Nangtā, once for all, that this whole universe is only a fragment of Brahman.

"Hazra is given to too much calculation. He says, 'This much of God has become the universe and this much is the balance.' My head aches at his calculations. I know that I know nothing. Sometimes I think of God as good, and sometimes as bad. What can I know of Him?"

M: "It is true, sir. Can anyone ever know God? Each thinks, with his little bit of intelligence, that he has understood all of God."

MASTER: "Who can ever know God? I don't even try. I only call on Him as Mother. Let Mother do whatever She likes. I shall know Her if it is Her will; but I shall be happy to remain ignorant if She wills otherwise. The young child wants only his mother. He doesn't know how wealthy his mother is, and he doesn't even want to know. All that he knows is, 'I have a mother; why should I worry?' Even the child of the maidservant knows that he has a mother. If he quarrels with the master's son, he says: 'I shall tell my mother. I have a mother.' My attitude, too, is that of a child."

Suddenly Sri Ramakrishna caught M's attention and said, touching his own chest: "Well, there must be something here. Isn't that so?"

M looked wonderingly at the Master. He said to himself: "Does the Mother Herself dwell in the Master's heart? Is it the Divine Mother who has assumed this human body for the welfare of humanity?"

Sri Ramakrishna was praying to the Divine Mother: "O Mother! O Embodiment of Om! Mother, how many things people say about Thee! But I don't understand any of them. I don't know anything, Mother. I have taken refuge at Thy feet. I have sought protection in Thee. O Mother, I pray only that I may have pure love for Thy Lotus Feet, love that seeks no return. And Mother, do not delude me with Thy world-bewitching māyā. I seek Thy protection. I have taken refuge in Thee."

The evening worship in the temples was over. Sri Ramakrishna was again seated in his room with M.

MASTER: "You have accepted an ideal, that of God without form—isn't that so?"

M: "Yes, sir. But I also believe what you say—that all is possible with God. It is quite possible for God to have forms."

MASTER: "Good. Remember further that, as Consciousness, He pervades the entire universe of the living and non-living. Let me ask you one thing: do you feel attracted to money?"

M: "No, sir. But I think of earning money in order to be free from anxiety, to be able to think of God without worry."

MASTER: "Oh, that's perfectly natural."

M: "Is it greed? I don't think so."

MASTER: "You are right. Otherwise, who will look after your children? What will become of them if you feel that you are not the doer?"

M: "I have heard that one cannot attain Knowledge as long as one has the consciousness of duty. Duty is like the scorching sun."

MASTER: "Keep your present attitude. It will be

different when the consciousness of duty drops away
of itself."

Wednesday, November 28, 1883

At two o'clock in the afternoon M was pacing the
footpath of the Circular Road in front of the Lily
Cottage, where Keshab Chandra Sen lived. He was
eagerly awaiting Sri Ramakrishna's arrival. Keshab's
illness had taken a serious turn, and there was very
little chance of his recovery. Since the Master loved
Keshab dearly, he was coming from Dakshineswar to
see him.

About five o'clock a carriage stopped in front of the
Lily Cottage and Sri Ramakrishna got out with Latu
and several other devotees, including Rakhal. He was
received by Keshab's relatives, who led him and the
devotees upstairs to the verandah south of the drawing-room. The Master seated himself on a couch.

After a long wait he became impatient to see Keshab.
Keshab's disciples said that he was resting and would
be there presently. Sri Ramakrishna became more and
more impatient and said to Keshab's disciples: "Look
here, what need is there of his coming to me? Why
can't I go in and see him?"

PRASANNA (*humbly*): "Sir, he will come in a few
minutes."

MASTER: "Go away! It is you who are making all
this fuss. Let me go in."

Prasanna began to talk about Keshab in order to
divert the Master's attention. He said: "Keshab is now
an altogether different person. Like you, sir, he talks
to the Divine Mother. He hears what the Mother says,
and laughs and cries."

When he was told that Keshab talked to the Divine Mother and laughed and cried, the Master became ecstatic. Presently he went into samādhi.

It was winter and the Master was wearing a green flannel coat with a shawl thrown over it. He sat straight, with his eyes fixed, deep in ecstasy. A long time passed this way. There was no indication of his returning to the normal plane of consciousness.

Gradually it became dark. Lamps were lighted in the drawing-room, where the Master was now to go. While he was slowly coming down to the plane of ordinary consciousness, he was taken there, though with great difficulty. The room was well furnished. At the sight of the furniture, the Master muttered to himself, "These things were necessary before, but of what use are they now?"

The Master was in a state of intense divine intoxication. In the well-lighted room the Brāhmo devotees sat around the Master; Latu, Rakhal, and M remained near him. He was saying to himself, still filled with divine fervour: "The body and the soul! The body was born and it will die. But for the soul there is no death. It is like the betel-nut. When the nut is ripe it does not stick to the shell. But when it is green it is difficult to separate it from the shell. After realizing God one does not identify oneself any more with the body. Then one knows that body and soul are two different things."

At this moment Keshab entered the room. He came through the east door. Those who remembered the man who had preached in the Town Hall or the Brāhmo Samāj temple were shocked to see this skeleton covered with skin. He could hardly stand. He walked holding to the wall for support. With great difficulty he sat down in front of the couch. In the mean time Sri Ramakrishna had got down from the couch and was sitting on the floor. Keshab bowed low before the Master and remained in that position a long time, touching the Master's feet with his forehead. Then he sat up. Sri Ramakrishna was still in a state of ecstasy. He muttered to himself. He talked to the Divine Mother.

Raising his voice, Keshab said: "I am here, sir. I am here." He took Sri Ramakrishna's left hand and stroked it gently. But the Master was in deep samādhi, completely intoxicated with divine love. A stream of words came from his lips as he talked to himself, and the devotees listened to him spellbound.

MASTER: "As long as a man associates himself with upādhis, so long he sees the many, such as Keshab, Prasanna, Amrita, and so on; but on attaining Perfect Knowledge he sees only one Consciousness everywhere. The same Perfect Knowledge, again, makes him realize that the one Consciousness has become the universe and its living beings and the twenty-four cosmic principles. But the manifestations of Divine Power are different in different beings. It is He, undoubtedly, who has become everything; but in some cases there is a greater manifestation than in others.

"The soul through which God sports is endowed with His special power. The landlord may reside in any part of his mansion, but he is generally to be found in a particular drawing-room. The devotee is God's drawing-room. God loves to sport in the heart of His devotee. It is there that His special power is manifest. What is the sign of such a devotee? When you see a man doing great works, you may know that God's special power is manifested through him.

"After realizing God, one sees Him in all beings. But His greater manifestation is in man. Again, among men, God manifests Himself more clearly in those devotees who are sāttvic, in those who have no desire whatever to enjoy 'woman' and 'gold.' Where else can a man of samādhi rest his mind after coming down from the plane of samādhi? That is why he feels the need of seeking the company of pure-hearted devotees endowed with sattva and free from attachment to 'woman' and 'gold.' How else can such a person occupy himself in the relative plane of consciousness?

"My Mother! Who is my Mother? Ah, She is the Mother of the Universe. It is She who creates and preserves the world, who always protects Her children, and who grants whatever they desire: dharma, artha, kāma, moksha. A true son cannot live away from his mother. The mother knows everything. The child only eats, drinks, and makes merry; he doesn't worry himself about the things of the world."

KESHAB: "Yes, sir. It is quite true."

While talking, Sri Ramakrishna regained the normal consciousness of the world. With a smile on his face he conversed with Keshab. The roomful of men watched them eagerly and listened to their words. Everybody was amazed to find that neither Keshab nor the Master inquired about each other's health. They talked only of God.

MASTER (to Keshab): "Why do the members of the Brāhmo Samāj dwell so much on God's glories? Is there any great need of repeating such things as 'O God, Thou hast created the moon, the sun, and the stars?' Most people are filled with admiration for the garden only. How few care to see its owner! Who is greater, the garden or its owner?

"Shall I tell you the truth? Man loves his own riches, and so he thinks that God loves His, too. He thinks that God will be pleased if we glorify His riches.

"Can one ever bring God under control through wealth? He can be tamed only through love. What does He want? Certainly not wealth! He wants from His devotees love, devotion, feeling, discrimination, and renunciation.

(*To Keshab, with a smile*) "Why is it that you are ill? There is a reason for it. Many spiritual emotions have passed through your body; therefore it has fallen ill. At the time an emotion is aroused, one understands very little about it. The blow that it delivers to the body is felt only after a long while. I have seen big steamers going by on the Ganges, at the time hardly noticing their passing. But oh, my! What a terrific noise is heard after a while, when the waves splash against the banks! Perhaps a piece of the bank breaks loose and falls into the water.

"An elephant entering a hut creates havoc within and ultimately shakes it down. The elephant of divine emotion enters the hut of this body and shatters it to pieces.

"Do you know what actually happens? When a house is on fire, at first a few things inside burn. Then comes the great commotion. Just so, the fire of Knowledge at first destroys such enemies of spiritual life as passion, anger, and so forth. Then comes the turn of ego. And lastly a violent commotion is seen in the physical frame.

"You may think that everything is going to be over. But God will not release you as long as the slightest trace of your illness is left. You simply cannot leave the hospital if your name is registered there. As long as the illness is not perfectly cured, the doctor won't give you the permit to go. Why did you register your name in the hospital at all?" (*All laugh.*)

Keshab laughed again and again at the Master's allusion to the hospital. Then Sri Ramakrishna spoke of his own illness.

MASTER (*to Keshab*): "Hriday used to say, 'Never before have I seen such ecstasy for God, and never before have I seen such illness.' I was then seriously ill with stubborn diarrhoea. It was as if millions of ants were gnawing at my brain. But all the same, spiritual talk went on day and night. Dr. Rama of Nātāgore was called in to see me. He found me engaged in spiritual discussion. 'What a madman!' he said. 'Nothing is left of him but a few bones, and still he goes on reasoning like that!'

"In order to take full advantage of the dew, the gardener removes the soil from the Basrā rose down to the very root. The plant thrives better on account of the moisture. Perhaps that is why you too are being shaken to the very root. (*Keshab and the Master laugh.*) It may be that you will do tremendous things when you come back.

"Whenever I heard that you were ill I became extremely restless. After hearing of your last illness I used to weep to the Divine Mother in the small hours of the morning. I offered fruits and sweets to the Divine Mother with a prayer for your well-being."

The devotees were deeply touched to hear of Sri Ramakrishna's love for Keshab and his solicitude for the Brāhmo leader.

MASTER: "But this time, to tell the truth, I didn't

feel anxious to that extent. Only for two or three days did I feel a little worried."

Keshab's venerable mother came to the east door of the room, the same door through which Keshab had entered. Umanath said aloud to the Master, "Sir, here is mother saluting you."

Sri Ramakrishna smiled. Umanath said again, "Mother asks you to bless Keshab that he may be cured of his illness."

MASTER (to Keshab's mother): "Please pray to the Divine Mother, who is the Bestower of all bliss. She will take away your troubles.

(To Keshab) "Don't spend long hours in the inner apartments. You will sink down and down in the company of women. You will feel better if you hear only talk of God."

The Master uttered these words in a serious voice and then began to laugh like a boy. He said to Keshab, "Let me see your hand." He weighed it playfully, like a child. At last he said: "No, your hand is light. Hypocrites have heavy hands." (All laugh.)

Umanath again said to the Master from the door, "Mother asks you to bless Keshab."

MASTER (gravely): "What can I do? God alone blesses all. 'Thou doest Thine own work; men only call it theirs.'

"God laughs on two occasions. He laughs when two brothers divide land between them. They put a string across the land and say to each other, 'This side is mine, and that side is yours.' God laughs and says to Himself, 'Why, this whole universe is Mine; and about a little clod they say, "This side is mine, and that side is yours!"'

"God laughs again when the physician says to the mother weeping bitterly because of her child's desperate illness: 'Don't be afraid, mother. I shall cure your child.' The physician does not know that no one can save the child if God wills that he should die." (*All are silent.*)

Just then Keshab was seized with a fit of coughing, which lasted for a long time. The sight of his suffering made everyone sad. He became exhausted and could stay no longer. He bowed low before the Master and left the room, holding to the wall as before.

Some refreshments had been arranged for the Master. Keshab's eldest son was seated near him. Amrita introduced the boy and requested Sri Ramakrishna to bless him. The Master said, "It is not given to me to bless anyone." With a sweet smile he gently stroked the boy's body.

AMRITA (*with a smile*): "All right, then do as you please."

MASTER (*to the devotees*): "I cannot say such a thing as 'May you be healed.' I never ask the Divine Mother to give me the power of healing. I pray to Her only for pure love."

After partaking of the refreshments the Master was ready to leave. The Brāhmo devotees accompanied him to the cab, which was standing in the street. While coming down the stairs the Master noticed that there was no light on the ground floor. He said to Amrita and Keshab's other disciples: "These places should be well lighted. A house without light becomes stricken with poverty. Please see that it doesn't happen again."

Then Sri Ramakrishna left for Dakshineswar with one or two devotees.

7

PUNDIT SHASHADHAR

Saturday, February 2, 1884

IT WAS THREE O'CLOCK in the afternoon. Sri Ramakrishna had been conversing with Rakhal, Mahimacharan, Hazra, and other devotees, when M entered
the room and saluted him. He brought with him
splint, pad, and lint to bandage the Master's injured
arm.

Some days before, while going toward the pine-
grove, Sri Ramakrishna had fallen near the railing
and dislocated a bone in his left arm. He had been in
an ecstatic mood at the time and no one had been with
him.

MASTER (*to Mahima*): "Well, if I am the machine
and God is its Operator, then why should this have
happened to me?"

Weeping like a child, he said to the Divine Mother:
"O Brahmamayi! O Mother! Why hast Thou done this
to me? My arm is badly hurt. (*To the devotees*) Will
I be all right again?" They consoled him, as one would
a child, and said: "Surely. You will be quite well
again."

MASTER (*to Rakhal*): "You aren't to blame for it,
though you are living here to look after me; for even
if you had accompanied me, you certainly wouldn't
have gone up to the railing."

The Master again went into a spiritual mood and

said: "Om! Om! Om! Mother, what is this that I am saying? Don't make me unconscious, Mother, with the Knowledge of Brahman. Don't give me Brahmajnāna. I am but Thy child. I am easily worried and frightened. I want a Mother. A million salutations to the Knowledge of Brahman! Give it to those who seek it. O Ānandamayi! O Blissful Mother!"

Uttering loudly the word "Ānandamayi," he burst into tears and said:

Mother, this is the grief that sorely grieves my heart,
That even with Thee for Mother, and though I am
   wide awake,
There should be a robbery in my house.

Again he said to the Divine Mother: "What wrong have I done, Mother? Do I ever do anything? It is Thou, Mother, who doest everything. I am the machine and Thou art its Operator."

The Master was again talking and laughing, like a child who, though ailing, sometimes forgets his illness and laughs and plays about.

MASTER (to the devotees): "It will avail you nothing unless you realize Satchidānanda. There is nothing like discrimination and renunciation. The worldly man's devotion to God is momentary—like a drop of water on a red-hot frying pan. Perchance he looks at a flower and exclaims, 'Ah, what a wonderful creation of God!'

"One must be restless for God. God will certainly listen to your prayers if you feel restless for Him. Since He has begotten us, surely we can claim our inheritance from Him. He is our own Father, our own Mother. We can force our demand on Him. We can say to Him, 'Reveal Thyself to me or I shall cut my throat with a knife!'"

Sri Ramakrishna was teaching the devotees how to call on the Divine Mother.

MASTER: "I used to pray to Her in this way: 'O Mother! O Blissful One! Reveal Thyself to me. Thou must!' Again, I would say to Her: 'O Lord of the lowly! O Lord of the universe! Surely I am not outside Thy universe. I am bereft of knowledge. I am without discipline. I have no devotion. I know nothing. Thou must be gracious and reveal Thyself to me.' "

Thus the Master taught the devotees how to pray. They were deeply touched. Tears filled Mahimacharan's eyes.

Several devotees arrived from Shibpur. Since they had come from a great distance the Master could not disappoint them. He told them some of the essentials of spiritual life.

At five o'clock in the afternoon Dr. Madhusudan arrived. He was ready to bandage the Master's arm. A bed was spread on the floor and the Master, laughing, lay down upon it. After his arm was bandaged he said: "I haven't very much faith in your Calcutta physicians. When Sambhu became delirious, Dr. Sarvadhikari said: 'Oh, it is nothing. It is just grogginess from the medicine.' And a little while after, Sambhu breathed his last."

It was evening and the worship in the temples was over. A few minutes later Adhar arrived from Calcutta to see the Master. Mahimacharan, Rakhal, and M were in the room.

ADHAR: "How are you?"

MASTER (affectionately): "Look here. How my arm hurts! (Smiling) You don't have to ask how I am!"

Adhar sat on the floor with the devotees. The Master

said to him, "Please stroke here gently." Adhar sat on the end of the couch and gently stroked Sri Ramakrishna's feet.

The Master conversed with Mahimacharan.

MASTER: "It will be very good if you can practise unselfish love for God. A man who has such love says: 'O Lord, I do not seek salvation, fame, wealth, or cure of disease. None of these do I seek. I want only Thee.' Many are the people who come to a rich man with various desires. But if someone comes to him simply out of love, not wanting any favour, then the rich man feels attracted to him."

Mahimacharan sat silent. The Master turned to him.

MASTER: "Now let me tell you something that will agree with your mood. According to Vedānta one has to know the real nature of one's own Self. But such knowledge is impossible without the renunciation of ego. The ego is like a stick that seems to divide the water in two. It makes you feel that you are one and I am another. When the ego disappears in samādhi one realizes Brahman as one's own inner consciousness.

"One cannot obtain the Knowledge of Brahman unless one is extremely cautious about women. Therefore it is very difficult for those who live in the world to get such Knowledge. However clever you may be, you will stain your body if you live in a sooty room. The company of a young woman evokes lust even in a lustless man.

"A sannyāsi must renounce both 'woman' and 'gold.' As he must not look even at the portrait of a woman, so also he must not touch gold, that is to say, money. It is bad for him even to keep money near him, for it brings in its train calculation, worry, insolence, anger, and such evils. There is the instance of the sun: it shines brightly; suddenly a cloud appears and hides it.

"Why all these strict rules for a sannyāsi? It is for the welfare of mankind as well as for his own good. A sannyāsi may himself lead an unattached life and may have controlled his passion, but he must altogether renounce 'woman' and 'gold' to set an example to the world.

"A man will have the courage to practise renunciation if he sees one hundred per cent renunciation in a sannyāsi. Then only will he try to give up 'woman' and 'gold.' If a sannyāsi does not set this example, then who will?"

It was about eight o'clock in the evening. Sri Ramakrishna asked Mahimacharan to recite a few hymns from the scriptures. Mahima read the first verse of the *Uttara Gītā*, describing the nature of the Supreme Brahman:

He, Brahman, is one, partless, stainless, and beyond the ākāśa;
Without beginning or end, unknowable by mind or intelligence.

Finally he came to the seventh verse of the third chapter, which reads:

The twice-born[1] worship the Deity in fire,
The munis contemplate Him in the heart,
Men of limited wisdom see Him in the image,
And the yogis who have attained samesightedness
Behold Him everywhere.

No sooner had the Master heard the words "the yogis who have attained samesightedness" than he

[1] A man belonging to the brāhmin, kshatriya, or vaiśya caste, who has his second or spiritual birth at the time of his spiritual initiation.

stood up and went into samādhi, his arm supported by the splint and bandage. Speechless, the devotees looked at this yogi who had himself attained the state of same-sightedness.

After a long time the Master regained consciousness of the outer world and took his seat. Mahima read from the *Yatipanchaka*:

I am She, the Divine Mother, in whom the illusion of the universe of animate and inanimate things is seen, as in magic, and in whom the universe shines, being the play of Her mind. I am She, the Embodiment of Consciousness, who is the Self of the universe, the only Existence, Knowledge, and Bliss.

When the Master heard the line "I am She, the Embodiment of Consciousness," he said with a smile, "Whatever is in the microcosm is also in the macrocosm."

Mahima recited the description of Om:

It is like the unceasing flow of oil, like the long peal of a bell.

About the characteristics of samādhi he read: "The man established in samādhi sees the upper region filled with Ātman, the nether region filled with Ātman, the middle region filled with Ātman. He sees all filled with Ātman."

Adhar and Mahima saluted the Master and departed.

Sunday, February 24, 1884

Sri Ramakrishna was resting in his room after his midday meal, and Mani Mallick was sitting on the floor beside him, when M arrived. M saluted the

Master and sat down beside Mani. The Master's injured arm was bandaged.

MASTER (to M): "How did you come?"

M: "I came as far as Ālambāzār in a carriage and from there I walked."

MANILAL: "Oh, he is so hot!"

MASTER (with a smile): "This makes me think that my visions are not mere fancies of my brain. Otherwise why should these 'Englishmen'[2] take so much trouble to come here?"

Sri Ramakrishna began to talk to them about his health and his injured arm.

MASTER: "Now and then I become impatient about my arm. I show it to this or that man and ask him whether I shall get well again. That makes Rakhal angry. He doesn't understand my mood. Now and then I say to myself, 'Let him go away.' Again I say to the Mother: 'Mother, where will he go? Why should he burn himself in the frying pan of the world?'

"This childlike impatience of mine is nothing new. I used to ask Mathur Babu to feel my pulse and tell me whether I was ill.

(To M) "Can you tell me why I am so impatient?"

M: "Your mind, sir, is always absorbed in samādhi. You have kept a fraction of it on your body for the welfare of the devotees. Therefore you feel impatient now and then for your body's safety."

MASTER: "That is true. A little of the mind is attached to the body. It wants to enjoy the love of God and the company of the devotees."

Mani Mallick told the Master about an exhibition that was being held in Calcutta.

[2] Sri Ramakrishna used this word to denote Europeans in general, and also those Indians whose ways and thoughts were largely influenced by Western ideas.

MANILAL: "If you were not unwell, you could visit the exhibition in the Maidān."

MASTER (*to M and the others*): "I shan't be able to see everything even if I go. Perhaps my eyes will fall on some certain thing and I shall become unconscious. Then I shall not be able to see the rest. I was taken to the Zoological Garden. I went into samādhi at the sight of the lion, for the carrier[3] of the Mother awakened in my mind the consciousness of the Mother Herself. In that state who could see the other animals? I had to return home after seeing only the lion. Hence Jadu Mallick's mother first suggested that I should go to the exhibition, and then said I should not."

Mani Mallick, about sixty-five years old, had been a member of the Brāhmo Samāj for many years, and Sri Ramakrishna gave him instruction that would agree with his mood.

MASTER: "Pundit Jaynarayan had very liberal views. I visited him once and liked his attitude. He told me he intended to go to Benares and live there, and at last he carried out his intention; for later on he did live in Benares and die there. When one grows old one should retire, like Jaynarayan, and devote oneself to the thought of God. What do you say?"

MANILAL: "True, sir. I don't relish the worries and troubles of the world."

MASTER (*to Manilal*): "Please tell them that little story of yours."

MANILAL (*smiling*): "Once several men were crossing the Ganges in a boat. One of them, a pundit, was making a great display of his erudition, saying that he had studied various books—the Vedas, the Vedānta,

[3] In Hindu mythology the lion is the carrier of Durgā, the Divine Mother.

and the six systems of philosophy. He asked a fellow passenger, 'Do you know the Vedānta?' 'No, revered sir.' 'The Sāmkhya and the Pātanjala?' 'No, revered sir.' 'Have you read no philosophy whatsoever?' 'No, revered sir.' The pundit was talking in this vain way and the passenger sitting in silence, when a great storm arose and the boat was about to sink. The passenger said to the pundit, "Sir, can you swim?' 'No,' replied the pundit. The passenger said, 'I don't know the Sāmkhya or the Pātanjala, but I can swim.' "

MASTER (*smiling*): "What will a man gain by knowing many scriptures? The one thing needful is to know how to cross the river of the world. God alone is real and all else is illusory.

"While Arjuna was aiming his arrow at the eye of the bird, Drona asked him: 'What do you see? Do you see these kings?' 'No, sir,' replied Arjuna. 'Do you see me?' 'No.' 'The tree?' 'No.' 'The bird on the tree?' 'No.' 'What do you see, then?' 'Only the bird's eye.'

"He who sees only the eye of the bird can hit the mark. He alone is clever who sees that God is real and all else is illusory. What need have I of other information?

(*To M*) "Since my arm was injured a deep change has come over me. I now delight only in the Naralilā, the human manifestation of God. There are two aspects of Reality: Nitya and Lilā. The Nitya, or the Absolute, is the Indivisible Satchidānanda, and the Lilā, or Sport, takes various forms, such as the Lilā as God, the Lilā as the deities, the Lilā as man, and the Lilā as the universe.

"Vaishnavcharan used to say that one has attained Perfect Knowledge if one believes in God sporting as man. I wouldn't admit it then. But now I realize that

he was right. Vaishnavacharan liked pictures of man
expressing tenderness and love.

(*To Manilal*) "It is God Himself who is sporting in
the form of man. It is He alone who has become Mani
Mallick. The Śikhs teach: 'Thou art Satchidānanda.'

"Now and then a man catches a glimpse of his real
Self and becomes speechless with wonder. At such
times he swims in an ocean of joy. It is like suddenly
meeting a dear relative.

"Why do people worship virgins? All women are so
many forms of the Divine Mother. But Her manifestation is greatest in pure-souled virgins.

(*To M*) "Why do I become impatient when I am
ill? Because the Mother has placed me in the state of
a child. The child depends entirely on its mother.

"I was taken to Rādhābāzār to be photographed. It
had been arranged that I should go to Rajendra Mitra's
house that day. I heard that Keshab would be there.
I planned to tell them certain things, but I forgot it all
when I went to Rādhābāzār. I said: 'O Mother, Thou
wilt speak. What shall I say?'

"I have not the nature of a jnāni. He considers himself great. He says, 'What? How can I be ill?'

"Koar Singh once said to me, 'You still worry about
your body.' But it is my nature to believe that my
Mother knows everything. It was She who would speak
at Rajendra Mitra's house. Hers are the only effective
words. One ray of light from the Goddess of Wisdom
stuns a thousand scholars.

"The Mother has kept me in the state of a bhakta,
a vijnāni. That is why I joke with Rakhal and the
others. Had I been in the condition of a jnāni I couldn't
do that.

"In this state I realize that it is the Mother alone

who has become everything. I see Her everywhere. In the Kāli temple I found that the Mother Herself had become everything—even the wicked.

"Once I was about to scold Ramlal's mother, but I had to restrain myself. I saw her to be a form of the Divine Mother. I worship virgins because I see in them the Divine Mother."

Sunday, March 2, 1884

Sri Ramakrishna was sitting on the small couch in his room, listening to devotional music by Trailokya Sannyal of the Brāhmo Samāj. He had not yet recovered from the effects of the injury to his arm, which was still supported by a splint. Many devotees, including Narendra, Surendra, and M, were sitting on the floor.

Narendra's father, a lawyer of the High Court of Calcutta, had passed away suddenly. He had not been able to make provision for the family, which consequently faced grave financial difficulties. The members of the family sometimes had to go without food. Narendra was therefore passing his days in great anxiety.

Trailokya sang:

> Seeking a shelter at Thy feet,
> I have for ever set aside
> My pride of race and caste, O Lord,
> And turned my back on fear and shame.
> A lonely pilgrim on life's path,
> Where shall I go for succour now?
> For Thy sake, Lord, I bear men's blame:
> They rail at me with bitter words
> And hate me for my love of Thee.
> Both friends and strangers use me ill.

Thou art the guardian of my name;
Thou mayest save or slay me, Lord.
Upon the honour of Thy servant
Rests Thy own good name as well.
Thou art the ruler of my soul,
The glow of love within my heart;
Do with me as it pleases Thee.

Addressing Trailokya, the Master said: "Ah! How touching your songs are! They are genuine. Only he who has gone to the ocean can fetch its water."

Trailokya sang again:

Thou it is that dancest, Lord,
And Thou that singest the song;
Thou it is that clappest Thy hands
In time with the music's beat;
But man, who is an onlooker merely,
Foolishly thinks it is he.

Though but a puppet, man becomes
A god if he moves with Thee;
Thou art the mover of the machine,
The driver of the car;
But man is weighted down with woe,
Dreaming that he is free.

Thou art the root of everything,
Thou the Soul of our souls;
Thou art the master of our hearts;
Through Thine unbounded grace
Thou turnest even the meanest sinner
Into the mightiest saint.

The singing came to an end. The Master engaged in conversation with the devotees.

MASTER: "There are three classes of devotees. The lowest one says, 'God is up there,' and he points to heaven. The mediocre devotee says that God dwells

in the heart as the 'Inner Controller.' But the highest
devotee says: 'God alone has become everything. All
things that we perceive are so many forms of God.'
Narendra used to make fun of me and say: 'Yes, God
has become all! Then a pot is God, a cup is God!'
(*Laughter.*)

"All doubts disappear when one sees God. It is one
thing to hear of God, but quite a different thing to see
Him. A man cannot have one hundred per cent conviction through mere hearing. But if he beholds God
face to face, then he is wholly convinced.

"Formal worship drops away after the vision of God.
It was thus that my worship in the temple came to an
end. I used to worship the Deity in the Kāli temple.
It was suddenly revealed to me that everything is
Pure Spirit. The utensils of worship, the altar, the door-
frame—all Pure Spirit. Men, animals, and other living
beings—all Pure Spirit. Then like a madman I began
to shower flowers in all directions. Whatever I saw I
worshipped.

"One day, while worshipping Śiva, I was about to
offer a bel-leaf on the head of the image, when it was
revealed to me that this Virāt, this Universe, itself is
Śiva. After that my worship of Śiva through the image
came to an end. Another day I had been plucking
flowers, when it was revealed to me that the flowering
plants were so many bouquets."

TRAILOKYA: "Ah! How beautiful is God's creation!"

MASTER: "Oh no, it is not that. It was revealed to
me in a flash. I didn't calculate about it. It was shown
to me that each plant was a bouquet adorning the
Universal Form of God. That was the end of my plucking flowers. I look on man in just the same way. When
I see a man, I see that it is God Himself who walks

on earth, as it were, rocking to and fro like a pillow floating on the waves. The pillow moves with the waves. It bobs up and down.

"The body has, indeed, only a momentary existence. God alone is real. Now the body exists, and now it does not. Years ago, when I had been suffering terribly from indigestion, Hriday said to me, 'Do ask the Mother to cure you.' I felt ashamed to speak to Her about my illness. I said to Her: 'Mother, I saw a skeleton in the Asiatic Society Museum. It was pieced together with wires into a human form. O Mother, please keep my body together a little, like that, so that I may sing Thy name and glories.

"Without desires the body cannot live. (*Smiling*) I had one or two desires. I prayed to the Mother, 'O Mother, give me the company of those who have renounced "woman" and "gold." ' I said further: 'I should like to enjoy the society of Thy jnānis and bhaktas. So give me a little strength that I may walk hither and thither and visit those people.' But She did not give me the strength to walk."

TRAILOKYA (*smiling*): "Have all the desires been fulfilled?"

MASTER (*smiling*): "No, there are still a few left. (*All laugh.*)

"The body is really impermanent. When my arm was broken I said to the Mother, 'Mother, it hurts me very much.' At once She revealed to me a carriage and its driver. Here and there a few screws were loose. The carriage moved as the driver directed it. It had no power of its own.

"Why, then, do I take care of the body? It is to enjoy God, to sing His name and glories, and to go about visiting His jnānis and bhaktas."

Narendra was sitting on the floor in front of the Master.

MASTER (*to Trailokya and the other devotees*): "The joys and sorrows of the body are inevitable. Look at Narendra. His father is dead, and his people have been put to extreme suffering. He can't find any way out of it. God places one sometimes in happiness and sometimes in misery."

TRAILOKYA: "Revered sir, God will be gracious to Narendra."

MASTER (*with a smile*): "But when? Once Hriday asked Sambhu Mallick for some money. Sambhu held the views of 'Englishmen' on such matters. He said to Hriday: 'Why should I give you money? You can earn your livelihood by working. Even now you are earning something. The case of a very poor person is different. The purpose of charity is fulfilled if one gives money to the blind or the lame.' Thereupon Hriday said: 'Sir, please don't say that. I don't need your money. May God help me not to become blind or deaf or extremely poor! I don't want you to give, and I don't want to receive.'"

The Master spoke as if piqued because God had not yet shown His kindness to Narendra. Now and then he cast an affectionate glance at his beloved disciple.

NARENDRA: "I am now studying the views of the atheists."

MASTER: "There are two doctrines: one about the existence of God, and the other about His non-existence. Why don't you accept the first?"

SURENDRA: "God is just. He must look after His devotees."

MASTER: "It is said in the scriptures that only those who have been charitable in their former births get money in this life. But to tell you the truth, this world is God's māyā. And there are many confusing things in this realm of māyā. One cannot comprehend them.

"God has revealed to me that only the Paramātman, whom the Vedas describe as the Pure Soul, is immutable, like Mount Sumeru, unattached, and beyond pain and pleasure. There is much confusion in this world of His māyā. One can by no means say that 'this' will come after 'that' or 'this' will produce 'that.'"

Saturday, April 5, 1884

It was about eight o'clock in the morning when M arrived at the temple garden and found Sri Ramakrishna seated on the small couch in his room. A few devotees were sitting on the floor. The Master was talking to them. Prankrishna Mukherji was there.

Prankrishna belonged to an aristocratic family and lived in the northern part of Calcutta. He held a high post in an English business firm. He was very much devoted to Sri Ramakrishna and, though a householder, derived great pleasure from the study of Vedānta philosophy. He was a frequent visitor at the temple garden. Once he invited the Master to his house in Calcutta and held a religious festival. Every day, early in the morning, he bathed in the holy water of the Ganges. Whenever convenient, he came to Dakshineswar in a hired country boat.

PRANKRISHNA: "Sir, what is the nature of the life after death?"

MASTER: "Keshab Sen, too, asked that question. As long as a man remains ignorant, that is to say, as long as he has not realized God, so long will he be born. But after attaining Knowledge he will not have to come back to this earth or go to any other plane of existence.

"The potter puts his pots in the sun to dry. Haven't you noticed that among them there are both baked and unbaked ones? When a cow happens to walk over them, some are broken to pieces. The broken pots that are already baked, the potter throws away, since they are of no more use to him. But the soft ones, though broken, he gathers up. He makes them into a lump and out of this forms new pots. In the same way, so long as a man has not realized God, he will have to come back to the Potter's hand, that is, he will have to be born again and again.

"What is the use of sowing a boiled paddy grain? It will never bring forth a shoot. Likewise, if a man is boiled by the fire of Knowledge, he will not be used for new creation. He is liberated.

"According to the Purānas, the bhakta and the Bhagavān, the devotee and God, are two separate entities. 'I' am one and 'You' are another. The body is a plate, as it were, containing the water of mind, intelligence, and ego. Brahman is like the sun. It is reflected in the water. Therefore the devotee sees the divine form.

"According to Vedānta, Brahman alone is real and all else is māyā, dreamlike and unsubstantial. The ego, like a stick, lies across the Ocean of Satchidānanda. (To M) Listen to what I am saying. When this ego is taken away, there remains only one undivided Ocean of Satchidānanda. But as long as the stick of ego remains, there is an appearance of two: here is one part of the water and there another part. Attaining the Knowledge of Brahman one is established in samādhi. Then the ego is effaced.

"But Śankarāchārya retained the 'ego of Knowledge'[4] in order to teach men. (*To Prankrishna*) But there are signs that distinguish the man of Knowledge. Some people think they have Knowledge. What are the characteristics of Knowledge? A jnāni cannot injure anybody. He becomes like a child.

"From a distance a burnt string lying on the ground may look like a real one; but if you come near and blow at it, it disappears altogether. The anger and egotism of a jnāni are mere appearances; they are not real.

"A child has no attachment. He makes a play house, and if anyone touches it he will jump about and cry. The next moment he himself will break it. This moment he may be very much attached to his cloth and say: 'My daddy gave it to me. I won't part with it.' But the next moment you can cajole him out of it with a toy. He will go away with you, leaving the cloth behind.

"These are the characteristics of a jnāni. Perhaps he has many luxuries at home—couch, chairs, paintings, and equipage. But any day he may leave all these and go off to Benares."

Prankrishna took leave of the Master. M bathed in the river. Then he went to the temples of Rādhākānta

[4] The ego illumined and purified by the Knowledge of God. Following the method of discrimination, the jnāni, in samādhi, merges his ego in Brahman. Thereafter he may come down to the relative plane with an appearance of individuality, but even then he is always conscious of his identity with Brahman. This apparent ego is called the "ego of Knowledge." A bhakta, following the path of love, realizes his eternal relationship with God. He too keeps an appearance of individuality on the relative plane. This ego has none of the characteristics of the worldly ego and is called the "ego of Devotion." The two egos here described refer to practically the same state of realization.

and Kāli and prostrated himself before the images. He
said to himself: "I have heard that God has no form.
Then why do I bow before these images? Is it because
Sri Ramakrishna believes in gods and goddesses with
form? I don't know anything about God, nor do I
understand Him. The Master believes in images; then
why shouldn't I accept them? I am such an insignificant
creature."

The midday worship and the offering of food in
the temples were over. The bells, gongs, and cymbals
of the ārati were being played, and the temple garden
was filled with joyful activity. Beggars, sādhus, and
guests hurried to the guest-house for the noonday meal,
carrying leaf or metal plates in their hands. M also
took some of the prasād from the Kāli temple.

Sri Ramakrishna had been resting awhile after his
meal when several devotees, including Ram and Girindra, arrived. They sat down after saluting the Master.

GIRINDRA: "The Brāhmos say that you have no
faculty for organization [said in English]."

MASTER: "What does that mean?"

M: "That you don't know how to lead a sect; that
your intellect is rather dull. They say things like that."
(*All laugh.*)

MASTER (*to Ram*): "Now tell me why my arm
was hurt. Stand up and deliver a lecture on that.
(*Laughter.*)

"The Brāhmos insist that God is formless. What if
they do? It is enough to call on Him with sincerity of
heart. If the devotee is sincere, then God, who is the
Inner Guide of all, will certainly reveal to the devotee
His true nature.

"But it is not good to say that what we ourselves
think of God is the only truth and what others think

is false; that because we think of God as formless, therefore He is formless and cannot have any form; that because we think of God as having form, therefore He has form and cannot be formless. Can a man really fathom God's nature?

"I see people who talk about religion constantly quarrelling with one another. Hindus, Mussalmāns, Brāhmos, Śāktas, Vaishnavas, Śaivas, all quarrel with one another. They haven't the intelligence to understand that He who is called Krishna is also Śiva and the Primal Śakti, and that it is He, again, who is called Jesus and Āllāh. 'There is only one Rāma and He has a thousand names.' Truth is one; It is only called by different names. All people are seeking the same Truth; the disagreement is due to differences in climate, temperament, and names. Everyone is going toward God. They will all realize Him if they have sincerity and longing of heart."

Saturday, May 24, 1884

It was about five o'clock in the afternoon. Sri Ramakrishna was sitting on the steps of the Śiva temples. Adhar, Dr. Nitai, M, and several other devotees were with him.

MASTER (*to the devotees*): "I want to tell you something. A change has been coming over my nature."

The Master came down a step and sat by the devotees. It seemed that he intended to communicate some of his deeper experiences to them.

MASTER: "You are devotees. I have no hesitation in telling you this. Nowadays I don't see the Spirit-form of God. He is revealed to me in human form. My nature is such that I enjoy seeing the form of God, touching and embracing Him. God is saying to me,

'You have assumed a body; therefore enjoy God through His human forms.'

"God no doubt dwells in all, but He manifests Himself more through man than through other beings. Is man an insignificant thing? He can think of God, he can think of the Infinite, while other living beings cannot. God exists in other living beings —animals, plants, nay, in all beings—but He manifests Himself more through man than through these others. Fire exists in all beings, in all things; but its presence is felt more in wood.

"But in the Incarnation there is a greater manifestation of God than in other men. Rāma said to Lakshmana, 'Brother, if you see in a man ecstatic love of God, if he laughs, weeps, and dances in divine ecstasy, then know for certain that I dwell in him.'"

The Master remained silent. After a few minutes he resumed the conversation.

MASTER: "Keshab Sen used to come here frequently. As a result he changed a great deal. Of late he became quite a remarkable man. Many a time he came here with his party; but he also wanted to come alone. In the earlier years of his life Keshab didn't have much of an opportunity to live in the company of holy men.

"I once visited him at his house in Coolootolā Street. Hriday was with me. We were shown into the room where Keshab was working. He was writing something. After a long while he put aside his pen, got off his chair, and sat on the floor with us. He didn't salute us, however, or show us respect in any other way. But when he and his friends came here, I saluted them before they bowed to me. Thus they gradually learnt to salute a holy man, touching the ground with their foreheads.

"One day Keshab came here with his followers. They

stayed till ten at night. We were all seated in the Panchavati. Pratap and several others said they would like to spend the night here. Keshab said: 'No, I must go. I have some work to do.' I laughed and said: 'Can't you sleep without the smell of your "fish-basket"? Once a fishwife was a guest in the house of a gardener who raised flowers. She came there with her empty basket, after selling fish in the market, and was asked to sleep in a room where flowers were kept. But because of the fragrance of the flowers she couldn't get to sleep for a long time. Her hostess saw her condition and said, "Hello! Why are you tossing from side to side so restlessly?" The fishwife said: "I don't know, friend. Perhaps the smell of the flowers has been disturbing my sleep. Can you give me my fish-basket? Perhaps that will put me to sleep." The basket was brought to her. She sprinkled water on it and set it near her nose. Then she fell sound asleep and snored all night.'

"At this story Keshab's followers burst into loud laughter.

"Keshab conducted the prayer that evening at the bathing-ghāt on the river. After the worship I said to him: 'It is God who manifests Himself, in one aspect, as the scriptures; therefore one should worship the sacred books, such as the Vedas, the Purānas, and the Tantras. In another aspect He has become the devotee. The heart of the devotee is God's drawing-room. One can easily find one's master in the drawing-room. Therefore by worshipping His devotee one worships God Himself.'

(To the devotees) "You see, Keshab was a great scholar. He lectured in English. Many people honoured him. Queen Victoria herself talked to him. But when Keshab came here he would be bare-bodied and

bring some fruit, as one should when visiting a holy
man. He was totally free from egotism."

Wednesday, June 25, 1884

It was the day of the Rathayātrā, the Car Festival
of the Hindus. At Ishan's invitation Sri Ramakrishna
went to his house in Calcutta. For some time the
Master had had a desire to meet Pundit Shashadhar
Tarkachudāmani, who had been staying with one of
Ishan's neighbours.

About four o'clock in the afternoon the Master left
in a carriage for the house where Pundit Shashadhar
was staying. As soon as Sri Ramakrishna got into the
carriage he went into samādhi. His physical frame was
very tender as a result of the austerities he had under-
gone during the long years of his spiritual discipline
and his constant absorption in God-Consciousness.
The Master would suffer from the slightest physical
discomfort and even from the vibration of worldly
thoughts around him. Once Keshab Chandra Sen
said that Sri Ramakrishna, Christ, and Sri Chaitanya
belonged to a delicate species of humanity that should
be kept in a glass case and protected from the vulgar
contact of the world.

It was the rainy season, and a fine drizzle of rain
had made the road wet. The sky was overcast. The
devotees followed the carriage on foot. As the carriage
stopped in front of the house, the host and his relatives
welcomed the Master and took him upstairs to the
drawing-room. There the Master met the pundit.

Pundit Shashadhar, a man of fair complexion and
no longer young, had a string of rudrāksha beads
around his neck. He was one of the renowned Sanskrit
scholars of his time—a pillar of orthodox Hinduism,

which had reasserted itself after the first wave of
Christianity and Western culture had passed over
Hindu society. His clear exposition of the Hindu
scriptures, his ringing sincerity, and his stirring elo-
quence had brought back a large number of the
educated young Hindus of Bengal to the religion of
their forefathers.

The pundit saluted the Master with reverence.
Narendra, Rakhal, Ram, Hazra, and M, who had
come with the Master, seated themselves in the room
as near the Master as they could, anxious not to miss
one of his words.

At the sight of the pundit the Master again went
into samādhi. After a while, still in that state, he looked
at the pundit and said with a smile, "Very well, very
well." Then, addressing the pundit, the Master said,
"Tell me how you give lectures."

PUNDIT: "Sir, I try to explain the injunctions of the
Hindu scriptures."

MASTER: "For the Kaliyuga the path of devotion
described by Nārada is best. Where can people find
time now to perform rituals according to the scriptural
injunctions? Nowadays the decoctions of roots and
herbs of the orthodox Hindu physicians cannot be
given to a fever patient. By the time that kind of
medicine begins its slow process of curing, the patient
is done for. Therefore only a drastic medicine like the
allopathic 'fever mixture' is effective now. You may
ask people to practise scriptural rites and rituals; but
when prescribing the rituals, please ask them to
remove the 'head and tail.'[5]

"You may deliver thousands of lectures, but they

[5] The non-essential parts. The allusion is to the head and
tail of a fish, which are non-essential.

won't make the slightest impression on worldly people.
Can one drive a nail into a stone wall? The point of
the nail will sooner break than make a dent in the
stone. What will you gain by striking the tough skin
of the crocodile with a sword? Your lectures are not
helping worldly people very much; and you will realize
this by and by.

"You cannot distinguish a lover of God from a
worldly person. It isn't your fault, of course. When
the first onrush of the gale shakes the trees, it is impossible to distinguish one tree from another—the
mango from the tamarind, for instance."

Presently the Master went into samādhi. His face
radiated a heavenly light. Bereft of outer consciousness, he could not utter another word. His gaze was
indrawn and transfixed in communion with the Self.
After a long time the Master began to recognize the
world around him and said, like a child, "I will have
a drink of water." Whenever after samādhi the Master
asked for a drink of water, his devotees knew that he
was gradually becoming conscious of the outer world.

Still lingering in the state of ecstasy, he said to the
Divine Mother: "O Mother, the other day You showed
me Pundit Iswar Chandra Vidyāsāgar. Then I told
You that I should like to see another pundit, and so
You have brought me here."

Looking at the pundit, he said: "My child, add a
little more to your strength. Practise spiritual discipline
a few days more. You have hardly set your foot on
the tree, yet you expect to lay hold of a big cluster of
fruit. But, of course, you are doing all this for the
welfare of others." With these words he bowed his
head before the pundit.

The Master continued: "When I first heard about

you, I inquired whether you were merely erudite or whether you had discrimination and renunciation. A pundit who doesn't know how to discriminate between the Real and the unreal is no pundit at all.

"There is no harm in teaching others if the preacher has a commission from the Lord. Nobody can confound a preacher who teaches people after having received the command of God. Getting a ray of light from the goddess of learning, a man becomes so powerful that before him even big scholars seem mere earthworms.

"When the lamp is lighted the moths come in swarms. They don't have to be invited. In the same way, the preacher who has a commission from God need not invite people to hear him. He doesn't have to announce the time of his lectures. He possesses such irresistible attraction that people come to him of their own accord. People of all classes, even kings and aristocrats, gather around him.

"Does the magnet say to the iron, 'Come near me'? That is not necessary. Because of the attraction of the magnet, the iron rushes to it.

"Such a preacher may not be a scholarly person, but don't conclude from that that he has any lack of wisdom. Does book learning ever make one wise? He who has a commission from God never runs short of wisdom. That wisdom comes from God; it is inexhaustible. It never comes to an end.

"Can a preacher ever lack knowledge if but once he is favoured with a benign glance from the Divine Mother? Therefore I ask you whether you have received any commission from God."

HAZRA: "Oh yes, he must have it. (*To the pundit*) Isn't it true, sir?"

PUNDIT: "Commission? No, sir, I am afraid I haven't received any such thing."

HOST: "He may not have received the commission, but he preaches from a sense of duty."

MASTER: "What will a man accomplish by mere lectures without the commission from God? Once a Brāhmo preacher said in the course of his sermon, 'Friends, how much I used to drink!' and so on. Hearing this the people began to whisper among themselves: 'What is this fool saying? He used to drink!' Now these words produced a very unfavourable effect. This shows that preaching cannot bring a good result unless it comes from a good man.

"So I say, a worthless man may talk his head off preaching, and yet he will produce no effect. But people will listen to him if he is armed with a badge of authority from God. A teacher of men must have great power. Therefore I say to you, dive into the Ocean of Satchidānanda. Nothing will ever worry you if you but realize God. Then you will get His commission to teach people."

PUNDIT: "How far did you go in visiting the sacred places?"

MASTER: "Oh, I visited a few places. (*With a smile*) But Hazra went farther and also climbed higher. He visited Hrishikesh,[6] but I didn't go so far or so high.

"You must have noticed kites and vultures soaring very high in the sky; but their eyes are always fixed on the charnel-pits. Do you know the meaning of 'charnel-pits'? It is 'woman' and 'gold.'

"What is the use of making pilgrimages if you can attain love of God remaining where you are? I have

[6]A holy place on the Ganges at the foot of the Himālayas.

been to Benares and noticed the same trees there as here. The same green tamarind-leaves!

"Pilgrimage becomes futile if it does not enable you to attain love of God. Love of God is the one essential and necessary thing. Do you know the meaning of 'kites' and 'vultures'? There are many people who talk big and who say that they have performed most of the duties enjoined in the scriptures. But with all that their minds are engrossed in worldliness and deeply preoccupied with money, riches, name, fame, creature comforts, and such things."

The Master was about to take his leave. The pundit and his friends bowed low before him.

It was not yet dusk, and Sri Ramakrishna returned to Ishan's house with the devotees. The Master took his seat in the drawing-room with Ishan and his sons, a pundit, and a few devotees.

MASTER (smiling, to Ishan): "I said to Pundit Shashadhar: 'You have hardly set your foot on the tree, and yet you aspire to lay hold of a big bunch of fruit. First of all practise some spiritual discipline; then you may teach others.'"

ISHAN: "Every preacher thinks that he enlightens others. The glow-worm also may think that it illuminates the world. Imagining this to be the glow-worm's feeling, someone said to it: 'O glow-worm, how can you bring light to the world? You only reveal the intensity of the darkness.'"

MASTER (with a smile): "But Shashadhar is not just a scholar. He also has a little discrimination and dispassion."

The Master was about to leave for Dakshineswar. Ishan and the other devotees stood around him while he gave Ishan various words of advice.

MASTER: "A devotee who can call on God while living a householder's life is a hero indeed. God thinks: 'He who has renounced the world for My sake will surely pray to Me; he must serve Me. Is there anything very remarkable about it? People will cry shame on him if he fails to do so. But he is blessed indeed who prays to Me in the midst of his worldly duties. He is trying to find Me, overcoming a great obstacle—pushing away, as it were, a huge block of stone weighing a ton. Such a man is a real hero.'

"Live in the world like an ant. The world contains a mixture of truth and untruth, sugar and sand. Be an ant and take the sugar.

"Again, the world is a mixture of milk and water, the bliss of God-Consciousness and the pleasure of sense enjoyment. Be a swan and drink the milk, leaving the water aside.

"Live in the world like a waterfowl. The water clings to the bird, but the bird shakes it off. Live in the world like a mudfish. The fish lives in the mud, but its skin is always bright and shiny.

"The world is indeed a mixture of truth and make-believe. Discard the make-believe and take the truth."

Sri Ramakrishna got into the carriage and left for Dakshineswar.

Monday, June 30, 1884

Sri Ramakrishna was in his room, sitting on a mat spread on the floor. Pundit Shashadhar and a few devotees were with him on the mat, and the rest sat on the bare floor. Surendra, Baburam, M, Harish, Latu, Hazra, and others were present. It was about four o'clock in the afternoon.

Sri Ramakrishna had met Pundit Shashadhar six

days before in Calcutta, and now the pundit had come to Dakshineswar to visit the Master. The pundit had studied the Vedas and the other scriptures. He loved to discuss philosophy. The Master, seated on the couch, cast his benign look on the pundit and gave him counsel through parables.

MASTER (*to the pundit*): "There are many scriptures like the Vedas. But one cannot realize God without austerity and spiritual discipline. 'God cannot be found in the six systems, the Vedas, or the Tantra.'

"But one should learn the contents of the scriptures and then act according to their injunctions. Once a man lost a letter. He couldn't remember where he had left it. He began to search for it with a lamp. After two or three people had searched, the letter was at last found. The message in the letter was: 'Please send us five seers of sandesh and a piece of wearing-cloth.' The man read it and then threw the letter away. There was no further need of it; now all he had to do was to buy the five seers of sandesh and the piece of cloth.

"Better than reading is hearing, and better than hearing is seeing. One understands the scriptures better by hearing them from the lips of the guru or of a holy man. Then one doesn't have to think about their non-essential part.

"But seeing is far better than hearing. Then all doubts disappear. It is true that many things are recorded in the scriptures; but all these are useless without the direct realization of God, without devotion to His Lotus Feet, without purity of heart. The almanac forecasts the rainfall of the year. But not a drop of water will you get by squeezing the almanac. No, not even one drop."

A DEVOTEE: "Does the body remain even after the realization of God?"

MASTER: "The present body remains alive as long as its momentum[7] is not exhausted; but future births are no longer possible. The wheel moves as long as the impulse that has set it in motion lasts. Then it comes to a stop. In the case of such a person, passions like lust and anger are burnt up. Only the body remains alive to perform a few actions."

The Master remained silent a few moments and then asked Pundit Shashadhar to have a smoke. The pundit went to the southeast verandah to smoke. Soon he came back to the room and sat on the floor with the devotees. Seated on the small couch, the Master continued the conversation.

MASTER (to the pundit): "Let me tell you something. There are three kinds of ānanda, joy: the joy of worldly enjoyment, the joy of worship, and the Joy of Brahman. The joy of worldly enjoyment is the joy of 'woman' and 'gold,' which people always love. The joy of worship one feels while chanting God's name and glories. And the Joy of Brahman is the joy of God-vision. After experiencing the joy of God-vision the rishis of olden times went beyond all rules and conventions.

"What is samādhi? It is the complete merging of the mind in God-Consciousness. The jnāni experiences jada samādhi, in which no trace of 'I' is left. The samādhi attained through the path of bhakti is called 'chetana samādhi.' In this samādhi there remains the consciousness of 'I'—the 'I' of the servant-and-Master relationship, of the lover-and-Beloved relationship, of

[7] The momentum of the actions of his previous birth, which has given rise to a man's present body.

the enjoyer-and-Food relationship. God is the Master; the devotee is the servant. God is the Beloved; the devotee is the lover. God is the Food; and the devotee is the enjoyer. 'I don't want to *be* sugar. I want to eat it.'

"God keeps a little of 'I' in his devotee even after giving him the Knowledge of Brahman. That 'I' is the 'I of the devotee,' the 'I of the jnāni.' Through that 'I' the devotee enjoys the infinite play of God.

"It is a joy to merge the mind in the Indivisible Brahman through contemplation. And it is also a joy to keep the mind on the Lilā, the Relative, without dissolving it in the Absolute.

"A mere jnāni is a monotonous person. He always analyses, saying: 'It is not this, not this. The world is like a dream.' "

A DEVOTEE: "Does this 'I' of the devotee never disappear altogether?"

MASTER: "Yes, it disappears at times. Then one attains the Knowledge of Brahman and goes into samādhi. I too lose it, but not for all the time. I pray to the Divine Mother, 'O Mother, do not give me Brahmajnāna.' Formerly believers in God with form used to visit me a great deal. Then the modern Brahmajnānis[8] began to arrive. During that period I used to remain unconscious in samādhi most of the time. Whenever I regained consciousness, I would say to the Divine Mother, 'O Mother, please don't give me Brahmajnāna.' "

PUNDIT: "Does God listen to our prayers?"

MASTER: "God is the Kalpataru, the Wish-fulfilling Tree. You will certainly get whatever you ask of Him. But you must pray standing near the Kalpataru.

[8] The members of the Brāhmo Samāj, who believe in the formless Brahman.

Only then will your prayer be fulfilled. But you must remember another thing. God knows our inner feeling. A man gets the fulfilment of the desire he cherishes while practising sādhanā. As one thinks, so one receives.

"I used to weep, praying to the Divine Mother, 'O Mother, destroy with Thy thunderbolt my inclination to reason.'"

PUNDIT: "Then you too had an inclination to reason?"

MASTER: "Yes, once."

PUNDIT: "Then please assure us that we shall get rid of that inclination too. How did you get rid of yours?"

MASTER: "Oh, somehow or other."

Sri Ramakrishna was silent awhile. Then he went on with his conversation.

MASTER: "God is the Kalpataru. One should pray standing near it. Then one will get whatever one desires.

"How many things God has created! Infinite is His universe. But what need have I to know about His infinite splendours? If I must know these, let me first realize Him. Then God Himself will tell me all about them. What need have I to know how many houses and how many government securities Jadu Mallick possesses? All that I need is somehow to converse with Jadu Mallick. I may succeed in seeing him by jumping over a ditch, or through a petition, or after being pushed about by his gatekeeper. Once I get a chance to talk to him, he himself will tell me all about his possessions if I ask him. If one becomes acquainted with the master, then one is respected by his officers too." (*All laugh.*)

The Master was pleased with the pundit's humility. He praised him to the devotees.

MASTER: "He has such a nice nature. You find no difficulty in driving a nail into a mud wall. But its point breaks if you try to drive it against a stone; and still it will not pierce it. There are people whose spiritual consciousness is not at all awakened even though they hear about God a thousand times. They are like a crocodile, on whose hide you cannot make any impression with a sword."

PUNDIT: "But one can hurt a crocodile by throwing a spear into its belly." (*All laugh.*)

MASTER (*smiling*): "What good is there in reading a whole lot of scriptures? What good is there in the study of philosophy? What is the use of talking big? In order to learn archery one should first aim at a banana tree, then at a reed, then at a wick, and last at a flying bird. At the beginning one should concentrate on God with form.

"The way to realize God is through discrimination, renunciation, and yearning for Him. What kind of yearning? One should yearn for God as the cow, with yearning heart, runs after its calf."

PUNDIT: "The same thing is said in the Vedas: 'O God, we call on Thee as the cow lows for the calf.'"

MASTER: "Add your tears to your yearning. And if you can renounce everything through discrimination and dispassion, then you will be able to see God. That yearning brings about God-intoxication, whether you follow the path of knowledge or the path of devotion.

"There is a great deal of difference between the knowledge of a householder and that of an all-renouncing sannyāsi. The householder's knowledge is

like the light of a lamp, which illumines only the
inside of a room. He cannot see anything, with the
help of such knowledge, except his own body and his
immediate family. But the knowledge of the all-renouncing monk is like the light of the sun. Through
that light he can see both inside and outside the
room. Chaitanyadeva's knowledge had the brilliance
of the sun—the Sun of Knowledge. Further, he
radiated the soothing light of the Moon of Devotion.
He was endowed with both—the Knowledge of
Brahman and ecstatic love of God."

The pundit and Mani Mallick became engaged in
conversation. Mani was a member of the Brāhmo
Samāj. The pundit argued vehemently about the good
and bad sides of the Samāj.

With a smile Sri Ramakrishna said to the pundit:
"Mani Mallick has been following the tenets of the
Brāhmo Samāj a long time. You can't convert him to
your views. Is it an easy thing to destroy old tendencies? Once there lived a very pious Hindu who
always worshipped the Divine Mother and chanted
Her name. When the Mussalmāns conquered the
country, they forced him to embrace Islām. They said
to him: 'You are now a Mussalmān. Say "Āllāh." From
now on you must repeat only Āllāh's name.' With
great difficulty he repeated the word 'Āllāh,' but every
now and then blurted out 'Jagadambā.'[9] At that the
Mussalmāns were about to beat him. Thereupon he
said to them: 'I beseech you! Please do not kill me.
I have been trying my utmost to repeat the name of
Āllāh, but our Jagadambā has filled me up to the
throat. She pushes out your Āllāh.' (All laugh.)

[9] "The Mother of the Universe," a name of the Divine
Mother.

(*To the pundit*) "Please don't say anything to Mani Mallick. You must know that there are different tastes. There are also different powers of digestion. God has made different religions and creeds to suit different aspirants. By no means all are fit for the Knowledge of Brahman. Therefore the worship of God with form has been provided."

All sat in silence. Sri Ramakrishna said to the pundit, "Go and visit the temples and take a stroll in the garden." It was about half-past five in the afternoon. The pundit left the room with his friends and several of the devotees.

After a while the Master went with M toward the bathing-ghāt on the Ganges. On the bank of the river he met the pundit and said to him, "Aren't you going to the Kāli temple?" The pundit said: "Yes, sir. Let us go together." They came to the temple. Sri Ramakrishna saluted the Divine Mother, touching the ground with his forehead.

Red hibiscus flowers and vilwa-leaves adorned the Mother's feet. Her three eyes radiated love for Her devotees. Two of Her hands were raised as if to give them boons and reassurance; the other two hands held symbols of death. She was clothed in a sāri of Benares silk and was decked with ornaments. Referring to the image, one of the party remarked, "I heard it was made by the sculptor Nabin." The Master answered: "Yes, I know. But to me She is the Embodiment of Spirit."

It was dusk. The Master was sitting on the semi-circular porch west of his room. Baburam and M sat near him. He was in a mood of partial ecstasy.

Rakhal was not then living with Sri Ramakrishna

and therefore the Master was having difficulties about his personal needs. Several devotees lived with him, but he could not bear the touch of everyone during his spiritual moods. He hinted to Baburam: 'Do stay with me. It will be very nice. In this mood I cannot allow others to touch me.'

(*To M, tenderly*): "Why don't you come here so frequently now?"

M: "Not for any special reason. I have been rather busy at home."

MASTER: "Yesterday I came to know Baburam's inner nature. That is why I have been trying so hard to persuade him to live with me. The mother bird hatches the egg in proper time. Boys like Baburam are pure in heart. They have not yet fallen into the clutches of 'woman' and 'gold.' Isn't that so?"

M: "It is true, sir. They are still stainless."

MASTER: "They are like a new pot. Milk kept in it will not sour."

M: "Yes, sir."

MASTER: "I need Baburam here. I pass through certain spiritual states when I need someone like him. He says he must not, all at once, live with me permanently, for it will create difficulties. His relatives will make trouble. I am asking him to come here Saturdays and Sundays."

The pundit entered the room with his friends.

MASTER (*to the pundit*): "You have read the Gītā, no doubt. It says that there is a special power of God in the man who is honoured and respected by all."

The pundit quoted the verse from the Gītā.

MASTER: "You surely possess divine power."

PUNDIT: "Shall I work with perseverance to finish the task that I have accepted?"

Sri Ramakrishna forced himself, as it were, to say, "Yes." He soon changed the conversation.

The pundit and his friends saluted the Master and were about to take their leave. Sri Ramakrishna said to the pundit: "Come again. One hemp-smoker rejoices in the company of another hemp-smoker. They even embrace each other. But they hide from people not of their own kind. A cow licks the body of her calf, but she threatens a strange cow with her horns." (All laugh.)

The pundit left the room. With a smile the Master said: "He has become 'diluted' even in one day. Did you notice how modest he was? And he accepted everything I said."

Moonlight flooded the semicircular porch. Sri Ramakrishna was still seated there. M was about to leave.

MASTER (tenderly): "Must you go now?"

M: "Yes, sir. Let me say good-bye."

MASTER: "I have been thinking of visiting the houses of the devotees. I want to visit yours also. What do you say?"

M: "That will be very fine."

Thursday, July 3, 1884

Sri Ramakrishna was sitting in Balaram Bose's house in Calcutta. Near him were Ram, Balaram, Balaram's father, M, Manomohan, and several young devotees.

Sri Ramakrishna went to the porch for a few minutes and then returned. As he was going out, Vishvamvhar's daughter, six or seven years old, saluted him. On returning to the room, the Master began talking to the little girl and her companions, who were of the same age.

THE CHILD (*to the Master*): "I saluted you and you didn't even notice it."

MASTER (*smiling*): "Did you? I really didn't notice."

CHILD: "Then wait. I want to salute you again—the other foot too."

Sri Ramakrishna laughed and sat down. He returned the salute and bowed to the child, touching the ground with his forehead. He asked her to sing. The child said, "I swear I don't sing." When the Master pressed her again, she said, "Should you press me when I said 'I swear'?" The Master was very happy with the children and sang light songs to entertain them.

He sang:

> Come, let me braid your hair,
> Lest your husband should scold you
> When he beholds you!

The children and the devotees laughed.

MASTER (*to the devotees*): "The paramahamsa is like a five-year-old child. He sees everything filled with Consciousness. At one time I was staying at Kāmār-pukur when Shivaram[10] was four or five years old. One day he was trying to catch grasshoppers near the pond. The leaves were moving. To stop their rustling he said to the leaves: 'Hush! Hush! I want to catch a grasshopper.' Another day it was stormy. It rained hard. Shivaram was with me inside the house. There were flashes of lightning. He wanted to open the door and go out. I scolded him and stopped him, but still he peeped out now and then. When he saw the lightning he exclaimed, 'There, uncle! They are striking matches again!'

[10] A nephew of the Master.

"The paramahamsa is like a child. He cannot distinguish between a stranger and a relative. He isn't particular about worldly relationships. One day Shivaram said to me, 'Uncle, are you my father's brother or his brother-in-law?'

"The paramahamsa is like a child. He doesn't keep any track of his whereabouts. He sees everything as Brahman. He is indifferent to his own movements. Shivaram went to Hriday's house to see the Durgā Pujā. He slipped out of the house and wandered away. A passer-by saw the child, who was then only four years old, and asked, 'Where do you come from?' He couldn't say much. He only said the word 'hut.' He was speaking of the big hut in which the image of the Divine Mother was being worshipped. The stranger asked him further, 'Whom are you living with?' He only said the word 'brother.'

"Sometimes the paramahamsa behaves like a mad-man. A few days after the dedication of the temple at Dakshineswar, a madman came there who was really a sage endowed with the Knowledge of Brahman. He had a bamboo twig in one hand and a potted mango-plant in the other, and was wearing torn shoes. He didn't follow any social conventions. After bathing in the Ganges he didn't perform any religious rites. He ate something that he carried in a corner of his wearing-cloth. Then he entered the Kāli temple and chanted hymns to the Deity. The temple seemed to tremble. Haladhari was then in the shrine. The mad-man wasn't allowed to eat at the guest-house, but he paid no attention to this slight. He searched for food in the rubbish heap where the dogs were eating crumbs from the discarded leaf-plates. Now and then he pushed the dogs aside to get his crumbs. The dogs

didn't mind either. Haladhari followed him and asked:
'Who are you? Are you a perfect knower of Brahman?'
The madman whispered, 'Sh! Yes, I am a perfect
knower of Brahman.' My heart began to palpitate
as Haladhari told me about it. I clung to Hriday. I
said to the Divine Mother, 'Mother, shall I too have
to pass through such a state?' We all went to see the
man. He spoke words of great wisdom to us but behaved like a madman before others. Haladhari followed
him a great way when he left the garden. After passing
the gate he said to Haladhari: 'What else shall I say
to you? When you no longer make any distinction
between the water of this pool and the water of the
Ganges, then you may know that you have Perfect
Knowledge.' Saying this he walked rapidly away."

Sri Ramakrishna began to talk with M. Other devotees, too, were present.

MASTER (to M): "How do you feel about Shashadhar?"

M: "He is very nice."

MASTER: "He is very intelligent, isn't he?"

M: "Yes, sir. He is very erudite."

MASTER: "According to the Gitā there is a power
of God in one who is respected and honoured by
many. But Shashadhar has still a few things to
accomplish. What will he gain with mere scholarship?
He needs to practise some austerity. It is necessary to
practise some spiritual discipline."

Sri Ramakrishna went to the inner apartments to
see the Deity. He offered some flowers. The ladies
of Balaram's family were pleased to see him.

The Master came back to the drawing-room and said:
"The worldly-minded practise devotions, japa, and
austerity only by fits and starts. But those who know

nothing else but God repeat His name with every breath. Some always repeat mentally, 'Om Rāma.' Even the followers of the path of knowledge repeat, 'Soham,' 'I am He.' There are others whose tongues are always moving, repeating God's name. One should remember and think of God constantly."

Pundit Shashadhar entered the room with one or two friends and saluted the Master.

MASTER (smiling): "We are like the bridesmaids waiting near the bed for the arrival of the groom."

The pundit laughed. The room was filled with devotees, among them Dr. Pratap and Balaram's father. The Master continued his talk.

MASTER (to Shashadhar): "The first sign of knowledge is a peaceful nature, and the second is absence of egotism. You have both. There are other indications of a jnāni. He shows intense dispassion in the presence of a sādhu, is a lion when at work, for instance, when he lectures, and is full of wit before his wife. (All laugh.)

"But the nature of the vijnāni is quite different, as was the case with Chaitanyadeva. He acts like a child or a madman or an inert creature or a ghoul. While in the mood of a child, he sometimes shows childlike guilelessness, sometimes the frivolity of adolescence, and sometimes, while instructing others, the strength of a young man."

All sat in silence. Again the Master spoke, addressing the pundit.

MASTER: "Formerly many great men used to come here."

SHASHADHAR: "You mean rich people?"

MASTER: "No. Great scholars."

SHASHADHAR (*humbly*): "Sir, please tell us what kind of yearning gives one the vision of God."

MASTER: "Once a guru said to his disciple: 'Come with me. I shall show you what kind of longing will enable you to see God.' Saying this, he took the disciple to a pond and pressed his head under the water. After a few moments he released the disciple and asked, 'How did you feel?' The disciple answered: 'Oh, I felt as if I were dying! I was longing for a breath of air.' "

SHASHADHAR: "Yes! Yes! That's it. I understand it now."

MASTER: "To love God is the whole thing. Bhakti alone is the essence. Nārada said to Rāma, 'May I always have pure love for Your Lotus Feet, and may I not be deluded by Your world-bewitching māyā!' Rāma said to him, 'Ask for some other boon.' 'No,' said Nārada, 'I don't want anything else. May I have love for Your Lotus Feet. This is my only prayer. "

Pundit Shashadhar was ready to leave. Sri Ramakrishna asked a devotee to bring a carriage for the pundit.

It was dusk. Sri Ramakrishna began to chant the names of the Divine Mother, Krishna, Rāma, and Hari. The devotees sat in silence. The Master chanted the names in such sweet tones that the hearts of the devotees were deeply touched.

8

GOD-INTOXICATED STATE

I T WAS MAHĀLAYĀ, a sacred day of the Hindus, and the day of the new moon. At two o'clock in the afternoon Sri Ramakrishna was sitting in his room with Mahendra Mukherji, Priya Mukherji, M, Baburam, Harish, Kishori, and ᴌatu. Some were sitting on the floor, some standing, and others moving about. Hazra was sitting on the porch. Rakhal was at Vrindāvan with Balaram.

MASTER (*to Mahendra Mukherji and the others*): "I shall feel ᴠery happy to know that you are being benefited by your visits here. (*To M*) Why do people come here? I don't know much of reading and writing."

M: "God's power is in you. That is why there is such attraction. It is the Divine Spirit that attracts."

MASTER: "By no means all people are attracted to God. There are special souls who feel so. To love God one must be born with good tendencies. Otherwise, why should you alone of all the people of Bāghbāzār come here? You can't expect anything good in a dung-hill.

(*To the Mukherji brothers*) "You are well off. If a man slips from the path of yoga, then he is reborn in a prosperous family and starts again his spiritual practice for the realization of God."

324

MAHENDRA: "Why does one slip from the path of yoga?"

MASTER: "While thinking of God the aspirant may feel a craving for material enjoyment. It is this craving that makes him slip from the path. In his next life he will be born with the spiritual tendencies that he failed to translate into action in his present life."

MAHENDRA: "Then what is the way?"

MASTER: "No salvation is possible for a man as long as he has desire, as long as he hankers for worldly things.

"It is not good to cherish desires and hankerings. For that reason I used to fulfil whatever desires came to my mind. Once I saw some coloured sweetmeats at Burrabāzār and wanted to eat them. They brought me the sweets and I ate a great many. The result was that I fell ill.

"In my boyhood days, while bathing in the Ganges, I saw a boy with a gold ornament around his waist. During my state of divine intoxication I felt a desire to have a similar ornament myself. I was given one, but I couldn't keep it on very long. When I put it on, I felt within my body the painful uprush of a current of air. It was because I had touched gold to my skin. I wore the ornament a few moments and then had to put it aside. Otherwise I should have had to tear it off.

"At that time many holy men used to visit the temple garden. A desire arose in my mind that there should be a separate storeroom to supply them with their provisions. Mathur Babu arranged for one. The sādhus were given food-stuffs, fuel, and the like from that storeroom.

"Once the idea came to me to put on a very expensive robe embroidered with gold and to smoke a

silver hubble-bubble. Mathur Babu sent me the new
robe and the hubble-bubble. I put on the robe. I also
smoked the hubble-bubble in various fashions. Sometimes I smoked reclining this way, and sometimes that
way, sometimes with head up, and sometimes with
head down. Then I said to myself, 'O mind, this is
what they call smoking a silver hubble-bubble.' Immediately I renounced it. I kept the robe on my body
a few minutes longer and then took it off. I began to
trample it underfoot and spit on it, saying: 'So this is
an expensive robe! But it only increases a man's rajas.' "

Rakhal had been staying at Vrindāvan with Balaram.
At first he had written excited letters praising the holy
place. He had written to M: "It is the best of all
places. Please come here. The peacocks dance around,
and one always hears and sees religious music and
dancing. There is an unending flow of divine bliss."
But then Rakhal had been laid up with an attack of
fever. Sri Ramakrishna was very much worried about
him and vowed to worship the Divine Mother for his
recovery. He began to talk about Rakhal.

MASTER: "Rakhal had his first religious ecstasy
while sitting here massaging my feet. A *Bhāgavata*
scholar had been expounding the sacred book in the
room. As Rakhal listened to his words, he shuddered
every now and then. Then he became altogether still.

"His second ecstasy was at Balaram Bose's house.
In that state he could not keep himself sitting upright;
he lay flat on the floor. Rakhal belongs to the realm
of the Personal God. He leaves the place if one talks
about the Impersonal.

"I have taken a vow to worship the Divine Mother
when he recovers. You see, he has renounced his home
and relatives and completely surrendered himself to

me. It was I who sent him to his wife now and then. He still had a little desire for enjoyment.

(*Pointing to M*) "Rakhal has written him from Vrindāvan that it is a grand place—the peacocks dance around. Now let the peacocks take care of him. He has really put me in a fix.

"Why am I so fond of the youngsters? They are still untouched by 'woman' and 'gold.' I find that they belong to the class of the ever-perfect.

"When Narendra first came here he was dressed in dirty clothes; but his eyes and face betokened some inner stuff. At that time he did not know many songs. He sang one or two: 'Let us go back once more, O mind, to our own abode,' and 'O Lord, must all my days be spent utterly in vain?'

"Whenever he came here, I would talk only with him, though the room was filled with people. He would say to me, 'Please talk to them,' and then I would talk with the others.

"I became mad for the sight of him and wept for him in Jadu Mallick's garden house. I wept here, too, holding Bholanath's hand. Bholanath said, 'Sir, you shouldn't behave that way for a mere kāyastha boy.' One day the 'fat brāhmin'[1] said to me about Narendra, with folded hands, 'Sir, he has very little education; why should you be so restless for him?'

"Can you tell me why all these youngsters, and you people, too, visit me? There must be something in me; or why should you all feel such a pull, such attraction?

"Once I visited Hriday's house at Sihore. From there I was taken to Śyāmbāzār. For seven days and nights I was surrounded by a huge crowd of people. Such attraction! Nothing but kirtan and dancing day and

[1] A nickname for Prankrishna, a devotee of the Master.

night. People stood in rows on the walls and even were in the trees. The rumour spread everywhere that a man had arrived who died[2] seven times and came back to life again. Hriday would drag me away from the crowd to a paddy-field for fear I might have an attack of heat apoplexy. The crowd would follow us there like a line of ants. Hriday scolded them and said: 'Why do you bother us like this? Have we never heard kirtan?'

"People came thronging from distant villages. They even spent the night there. At Śyāmbāzār I learnt the meaning of divine attraction. When God incarnates Himself on earth He attracts people through the help of Yogamāyā, His Divine Power. People become spellbound."

Sri Ramakrishna talked to the Mukherji brothers. Mahendra, the elder, had his own business. Priyanath, the younger, had been an engineer. After making some provision for himself he had given up his job. Mahendra was thirty-five or thirty-six years old. The brothers had homes both in the country and in Calcutta.

MASTER (smiling): "Don't sit idle simply because your spiritual consciousness has been awakened a little. Go forward. Beyond the forest of sandalwood there are other and more valuable things—silver-mines, gold-mines, and so on."

PRIYA (smiling): "Sir, our legs are in chains. We cannot go forward."

MASTER: "What if the legs are chained? The important thing is the mind. Bondage is of the mind, and freedom also is of the mind."

PRIYA: "But the mind is not under my control."

MASTER: "How is that? There is such a thing as

[2] Referring to the Master's samādhi.

abhyāsayoga, yoga through practice. Keep up the practice and you will find that your mind will follow in
whatever direction you lead it."

It was dusk. They heard the sound of gongs, cymbals,
and other instruments used in the evening service in
the temples. The Master said to Baburam, "Come with
me to the Kāli temple." He and Baburam went toward
the temple, accompanied by M. At the sight of Harish
sitting on the porch the Master said: "What is this?
Is he in ecstasy?"

Going through the courtyard, the Master and the
devotees stopped a minute in front of the Rādhākānta
temple to watch the worship. Then they proceeded to
the shrine of Kāli. With folded hands the Master
prayed to the Divine Mother: "O Mother! O Divine
Mother! O Brahmamayi!"

Reaching the cement platform in front of the shrine,
he bowed low before the image. The ārati was going
on. He entered the shrine and fanned the image.

The evening worship was over. The devotees bowed
before the Deity. It was the night of the new moon.
The Master was in a spiritual mood. Gradually his
mood deepened into intense ecstasy. He returned to
his room, reeling like a drunkard and holding to Baburam's hand.

A lamp was lighted on the west porch. The Master
sat there a few minutes, chanting: "Hari Om! Hari
Om! Hari Om!" and other mystic syllables of the Tantra. Presently he returned to his room and sat on the
small couch, facing the east. He was still completely
absorbed in divine fervour. He said to the Divine
Mother: "Mother, that I should first speak and You
then act—oh, that's nonsense! What is the meaning of

talk? It is nothing but a sign. One man says, 'I shall eat.' Again, another says, 'No! I won't hear of it.' Well, Mother, suppose I had said I would not eat; wouldn't I still feel hungry? Is it ever possible that You should listen only when one prays aloud and not when one feels an inner longing? You are what You are. Then why do I speak? Why do I pray? I do as You make me do. Oh, what confusion! Why do You make me reason?"

As Sri Ramakrishna was thus talking to God, the devotees listened wonderstruck to his words. The Master's eyes fell upon them.

MASTER (*to the devotees*): "One must inherit good tendencies to realize God. One must have done something, some form of tapasyā, either in this life or in another."

Hazra entered the room. He had been living with Sri Ramakrishna in the temple garden for the past two years and had first met the Master in 1880 at Sihore in the house of Hriday, the Master's nephew. Hazra's native village was near Sihore, and he owned some property there. He had a wife and children and also some debts. From youth he had felt a spirit of renunciation and sought the company of holy men and devotees. The Master had asked him to live with him at Dakshineswar and looked after his necessities. Hazra's mind was a jumble of undigested religious moods. He professed the path of knowledge and disapproved of Sri Ramakrishna's attitude of bhakti and his longing for the young devotees. Now and then he thought of the Master as a great soul, but again he slighted him as an ordinary human being. He spent much of his time in telling his beads, and he criticized Rakhal and the other young men for their indifference to the practice. He was a strong advocate of religious conventions and rules of conduct, and made a fad of them. He was about thirty-eight years old.

As Hazra came in, the Master became a little abstracted and in that mood began to talk.

MASTER (*to Hazra*): "What you are doing is right in principle, but the application is not quite correct. Don't find fault with anyone, not even with an insect. As you pray to God for devotion, so also pray that you may not find fault with anyone."

HAZRA: "Does God listen to our prayer for bhakti?"

MASTER: "Surely. I can assure you of that a hundred times. But the prayer must be genuine and earnest. Do worldly-minded people weep for God as they do for wife and children? The wife of a certain man fell ill. He thought she would not recover; he began to tremble and was about to faint. Who feels that way for God?"

Hazra was about to take the dust of the Master's feet.

MASTER (*shrinking*): "What is this?"

HAZRA: "Why should I not take the dust of his feet who has so kindly kept me with him?"

MASTER: "Satisfy God and everyone will be satisfied. 'If He is pleased the world is pleased.'

(*To Hazra*) "A perfect soul, even after attaining Knowledge, practises devotions or observes religious ceremonies to set an example to others. I go to the Kāli temple and I bow before the holy pictures in my room; therefore others do the same. Further, if a man has become habituated to such ceremonies, he feels restless if he does not observe them.

"If there is knowledge of one, there is also knowledge of many. What will you achieve by mere study of the scriptures? The scriptures contain a mixture of sand and sugar, as it were. It is extremely difficult to separate the sugar from the sand. Therefore one should learn the essence of the scriptures from the teacher or from a sādhu. Afterwards what does one care for books?

(To the devotees) "Gather all the information and then plunge in. Suppose a pot has dropped in a certain part of a lake. Locate the spot and dive there.

"One should learn the essence of the scriptures from the guru and then practise sādhanā. If one rightly follows spiritual discipline, then one directly sees God. The discipline is said to be rightly followed only when one plunges in. What will a man gain by merely reasoning about the words of the scriptures? Ah, the fools! They reason themselves to death over information about the path. They never take the plunge. What a pity!

"God made me pass through the disciplines of various paths. First according to the Purāna, then according to the Tantra. I also followed the disciplines of the Vedas. At first I practised sādhanā in the Panchavati. I made a grove of tulsi-plants and used to sit inside it and meditate. Sometimes I cried with a longing heart, 'Mother! Mother!' Or again, 'Rāma! Rāma!'

"I practised the discipline of the Tantra under the bel-tree. At that time I could see no distinction between the sacred tulsi and any other plant. Sometimes I rode on a dog and fed him with luchi, also eating part of the bread myself. I realized that the whole world was filled with God alone.

"While practising the disciplines of the Vedas I became a sannyāsi. I used to lie down in the chāndni and say to Hriday: 'I am a sannyāsi. I shall take my meals here.'[3]

"I vowed to the Divine Mother that I would kill myself if I did not see God. I said to Her: 'O Mother, I am a fool. Please teach me what is contained in the Vedas, the Purānas, the Tantras, and the other scriptures.' The Mother said to me, 'The essence of the Vedānta is that Brahman alone is real and the world illusory.' The essence of the Gītā is what you get by repeating the word ten times. It is reversed into 'tāgi,' which refers to renunciation.

"After the realization of God, how far below lie the Vedas, Vedānta, the Purānas, and Tantra! (To Hazra) I cannot utter the word 'Om' in samādhi. Why is that? I cannot say 'Om' unless I come down very far from the state of samādhi.

"I had all the experiences that one should have, according to the scriptures, after one's direct perception of God. I behaved like a child, like a madman, like a ghoul, and like an inert thing.

"I saw the visions described in the scriptures. Sometimes I saw the universe filled with sparks of fire. Sometimes I saw all the quarters glittering with light, as if the world were a lake of mercury. Sometimes I saw the world as if made of liquid silver. Sometimes, again, I saw all the quarters illumined as if with the light of Roman candles. So you see my experiences tally with those described in the scriptures.

"It was revealed to me further that God Himself has become the universe and all its living beings and the

[3] The chāndni is an open portico in the temple garden with steps descending to the Ganges. According to the orthodox Hindu tradition, a monk is forbidden to live in a house.

twenty-four cosmic principles. It is like the process of evolution and involution.[4]

"Oh, what a state God kept me in at that time! One experience would hardly be over before another overcame me.

"I would see God in meditation, in the state of samādhi, and I would see the same God when my mind came back to the outer world. When looking at this side of the mirror I would see Him alone, and when looking on the reverse side I saw the same God."

The devotees listened to these words with rapt attention.

The Mukherji brothers saluted the Master. Their carriage was ready near the verandah north of the room. The Master stood facing the north. On his left was the Ganges; in front of him were the nahabat, the garden, and the kuthi; and to his right was the road leading to the gate. The night was dark, and a devotee had brought a lantern to show the visitors their way. One by one the devotees bowed and took the dust of the Master's feet. The carriage seemed too heavily loaded for the horses. The Master said, "Aren't there too many people in the carriage?"

Sri Ramakrishna remained standing. As the carriage rolled away, the devotees looked back at the Master's face beaming with compassion and love.

Friday, September 26, 1884

Sri Ramakrishna had come to Calcutta. It was the first day of the Durgā Pujā, the great religious festival, and the Hindus of the metropolis were celebrating it.

---

[4] That is to say, God Himself evolves as the universe at the time of creation, and names and forms are involved back into God at the time of dissolution.

The Master intended to visit the image of the Divine Mother at Adhar's house. He also wanted to see Shivanath, a Brāhmo devotee.

It was about midday. Umbrella in hand, M was pacing the footpath in front of the Brāhmo Samāj temple. Two hours had passed but the Master had not yet appeared. Now and then M sat down on the steps of Dr. Mahalnavish's dispensary and watched the joy and mirth of the people, young and old, who were celebrating the Pujā.

A little after three the Master's carriage drove up. As soon as Sri Ramakrishna stepped out he saluted the temple of the Brāhmo Samāj with folded hands. Hazra and a few other devotees were with him. M bowed before the Master and took the dust of his feet. The Master told him that he was going to Shivanath's house. A few minutes later several members of the Brāhmo Samāj arrived and took him to Shivanath's. But Shivanath was not at home. Shortly afterwards Vijay Goswāmi, Mahalnavish, and several other Brāhmo leaders greeted the Master and took him inside the Brāhmo temple.

Sri Ramakrishna was in a happy mood. He was given a seat below the altar. There the Brāhmo devotees sang their devotional music. Vijay and the Brāhmo devotees sat in front of the Master.

MASTER (to Vijay, with a smile): "I was told that you had put up a 'signboard' here saying that people belonging to other faiths were not allowed to come in. Narendra, too, said to me: 'You shouldn't go to the Brāhmo Samāj. You had better visit Shivanath's house.

"But I say that we are all calling on the same God. Jealousy and malice need not be. Some say that God is formless, and some that God has form. I say, let one man meditate on God with form if he believes in form, and let another meditate on the formless Deity if he does not believe in form. What I mean is that dogmatism is not good. It is not good to feel that my religion alone is true and other religions are false. The correct attitude is this: My religion is right, but I do not know whether other religions are right or wrong, true or false. I say this because one cannot know the true nature of God unless one realizes Him. Kabir used to say: 'God with form is my Mother, the Formless is my Father. Which shall I blame? Which shall I praise? The two pans of the scales are equally heavy.'

"Do you know what the truth is? God has made different religions to suit different aspirants, times, and countries. All doctrines are only so many paths; but a path is by no means God Himself. Indeed, one can reach God if one follows any of the paths with whole-hearted devotion. Suppose there are errors in the religion that one has accepted; if one is sincere and earnest, then God Himself will correct those errors. Suppose a man has set out with a sincere desire to visit Jagannāth at Puri and by mistake has gone north instead of south; then certainly someone meeting him on the way will tell him: 'My good fellow, don't go that way. Go to the south.' And the man will reach Jagannāth sooner or later.

"If there are errors in other religions, that is none of our business. God, to whom the world belongs, takes care of that. Our duty is somehow to visit Jagannāth. (To the Brāhmos) The view you hold is good indeed. You describe God as formless. That is fine. One may eat a cake with icing, either straight or sidewise. It will taste sweet either way.

"God has been described in the Vedas as both with

attributes and without. You describe Him as without
form only. That is one-sided. But never mind. If you
know one of His aspects truly, you will be able to
know His other aspects too. God Himself will tell you
all about them."

Vijay still belonged to the Sādhāran Brāhmo Samāj.
He was a salaried preacher of that organization but
could not obey all its rules and regulations. He mixed
with those who believed in God with form. This was
creating a misunderstanding between him and the
Brāhmo authorities. Many Brāhmos disapproved of his
conduct. The Master suddenly looked at Vijay and began to talk to him.

MASTER (to Vijay, smiling): "I understand that
they have been finding fault with you for mixing with
those who believe in God with form. Is that true? He
who is a devotee of God must have an understanding
that cannot be shaken under any conditions. He must
be like the anvil in a blacksmith's shop. It is constantly
being struck by the hammer; still it rémains unshaken.
Bad people may abuse you very much and speak ill of
you; but you must bear with them all if you sincerely
seek God. Isn't it possible to think of God in the midst
of the wicked? Just think of the rishis of ancient times.
They used to meditate on God in the forest, surrounded
on all sides by tigers, bears, and other ferocious beasts.
Wicked men have the nature of tigers and bears. They
will pursue you to do you an injury.

"One must be careful about these few things. First,
an influential man who has much money and many men
under his control. He can injure you if he wants; you
must be careful while talking to him; perhaps you may
have to approve what he says. Second, a dog. When it
chases you or barks at you, you must stand still, talk

to it gently, and pacify it. Third, a bull. If it runs after you with lowered horns, you must calm it with a gentle voice. Fourth, a drunkard. If you arouse his anger, he will abuse you, naming fourteen generations of your family. You should say to him: 'Hello uncle! How are you?' Then he will be mightily pleased and sit by you and smoke.

"In the presence of a wicked person I become alert. Some people have the nature of a snake: they will bite you without warning. You have to discriminate a great deal in order to avoid the bite; otherwise your passion will be stirred up to such an extent that you will feel like doing injury in return. The companionship of a holy man is greatly needed now and then. It enables one to discriminate between the Real and the unreal."

VIJAY: "I have no time, sir. I am entangled in my duties here."

MASTER: "You are a religious teacher. Others have holidays, but not so a religious teacher. When the manager of an estate brings order to one part of it, the landlord sends him to another part. So you have no leisure." (All laugh.)

VIJAY (with folded hands): "Sir, please give me your blessing."

MASTER: "Now you are talking like an ignorant person. It is God alone who blesses."

VIJAY: "Revered sir, please give us some instruction."

MASTER: "One can realize God in the world, too, if only one is sincere. 'I' and 'mine'—that is ignorance. But, 'O God! Thou and Thine'—that is knowledge.

"I ask people to renounce mentally. I do not ask them to give up the world. If one lives in the world unattached and seeks God with sincerity, then one is able to attain Him.

(*To Vijay*) "There was a time when I too would meditate on God with my eyes closed.[5] Then I said to myself: 'Does God exist only when I think of Him with my eyes closed? Doesn't He exist when I look around with my eyes open?' Now, when I look around with my eyes open, I see that God dwells in all beings. He is the Indwelling Spirit of all—men, animals and other living beings, trees and plants, sun and moon, land and water."

Sri Ramakrishna was about to depart. The Brāhmo devotees bowed low before him and he returned their salute. Then, getting into the carriage, he set out for Adhar's house to see the image of the Divine Mother.

Saturday, October 11, 1884

Sri Ramakrishna lay on the small couch in his room at the Dakshineswar temple garden. It was about two in the afternoon. M and Priya Mukherji were sitting on the floor. M had left his school at one o'clock and had just arrived at Dakshineswar.

The Master warned the devotees about the danger of lust and greed.

MASTER: "Those who develop dispassion from early youth, those who roam about yearning for God from boyhood, those who renounce all worldly life, belong to a different class. They belong to an unsullied aristocracy. People who practise renunciation from early youth belong to a very high level. Their ideal is very pure. They are stainless."

A brāhmin from Sinthi entered the room and saluted

[5] An allusion to the Brāhmo way of meditating on God.

Sri Ramakrishna. He had studied Vedānta in Benares. He was stout and had a smiling face.

MASTER: "Hello! How are you? You haven't been here in a long time. Why so?"

PUNDIT (*smiling*): "Worldly duties, sir. You know I have very little leisure."

The pundit sat down, and the Master began to talk with him.

MASTER: "You spent a long time in Benares. Tell us what you saw there. Tell us something about Dayananda."

PUNDIT: "Yes, I met him. You also met him. I saw Colonel Olcott too. The Theosophists believe in the existence of mahātmās. They also speak of the 'lunar,' 'solar,' 'stellar,' and other planes. A Theosophist can go in his 'astral body' to all these planes. Oh, Olcott said many such things. Well, sir, what do you think of Theosophy?"

MASTER: "The one essential thing is bhakti, loving devotion to God. Do the Theosophists seek bhakti? They are good if they do. If Theosophy makes the realization of God the goal of life, then it is good. One cannot seek God if one constantly busies oneself with the mahātmās and the lunar, solar, and stellar planes. A man should practise spiritual discipline and pray to God with a longing heart for love at His Lotus Feet. He should direct his mind to God alone, withdrawing it from the various objects of the world.

"You may speak of the scriptures, of philosophy, of Vedānta; but you will not find God in any of these. You will never succeed in realizing God unless your soul becomes restless for Him. One must practise intense spiritual discipline. Can one obtain the vision of God all of a sudden, without any preparation?

"A man asked me, 'Why don't I see God?' I said to him, as the idea came to my mind: 'You want to catch a big fish. First make arrangements for it. Throw spiced bait into the water. Get a line and a rod. At the smell of the bait the fish will come from the deep water. By the movement of the water you will know that a big fish has come.'

"You want to eat butter. But what will you achieve by simply repeating that there is butter in milk? You have to work hard for it. Only thus can you separate butter from milk. Can one see God by merely repeating, 'God exists'? One needs to practise spiritual discipline.

(*To the pundit*) "It is good to live in the company of holy men now and then. The disease of worldliness has become chronic in man. It is mitigated, to a great extent, in holy company.

" 'I' and 'mine'—that is ignorance. True knowledge makes one feel: 'O God, You alone do everything. You alone are my own. And to You alone belong houses, buildings, family, relatives, friends, the whole world. All is Yours.' But ignorance makes one feel: 'I am doing everything. I am the doer. House, buildings, family, children, friends, and property are all mine.'

"Once a teacher was explaining all this to a disciple. He said, 'God alone, and no one else, is your own.' The disciple said: 'But, revered sir, my mother, my wife, and my other relatives take very good care of me. They see nothing but darkness when I am not present. How much they love me!' The teacher said: 'There you are mistaken. I shall show you presently that nobody is your own. Take these few pills with you. When you go home, swallow them and lie down in bed. People will think you are dead, but you will remain conscious of the outside world and will see and hear everything. Then I shall visit your home.'

"The disciple followed the instructions. He swallowed the pills and lay as if unconscious in his bed. His mother, wife, and other relatives began to cry. Just then the teacher arrived, in the guise of a physician, and asked the cause of their grief. When they had told him everything, he said to them: 'Here is a medicine for him. It will bring him back to life. But I must tell you something. This medicine must first be taken by one of his relatives and then given to him. But the relative who takes it first will die. I see his mother, his wife, and others here. Certainly one of you will volunteer to take the medicine. Then the young man will come back to life.'

"The disciple heard all this. First the physician called his mother, who was weeping and rolling on the ground in grief. He said to her: 'Mother, you don't need to weep any more. Take this medicine and your son will come to life. But you will die.' The mother took the medicine in her hand and began to think. After much reflection she said to the physician, with tears in her eyes: 'My son, I have a few more children. I have to think about them too. I am wondering what will happen to them if I die. Who will feed them and look after them?' The physician next called the wife and handed the medicine to her. She had been weeping bitterly too. With the medicine in her hand she also began to reflect. She had heard that she would die from the effect of the medicine. At last, with tears in her eyes, she said: 'He has met his fate. If I die, what will happen to my young children? Who will keep them alive? How can I take the medicine?' In the mean time the disciple had got over the effect of the pills. He was now convinced that nobody was really his own. He jumped out of bed and left the place with his teacher. The guru said to him, 'There is only one whom you may call your own, and that is God.'

"Therefore a man should act in such a way that he may have bhakti at God's Lotus Feet and love God as his very own. You see this world around you. It exists for you only for a couple of days. There is nothing to it."

PUNDIT (*smiling*): "Revered sir, I feel a spirit of total renunciation when I am here. I feel like going away, giving up the world."

MASTER: "No, no! Why should you give up? Give up mentally. Live unattached in the world.

"Surendra wanted to spend the night here occasionally. He brought a bed and even spent a day or two here. Then his wife said to him, 'You may go anywhere you like during the daytime, but at night you must not leave home.' What could poor Surendra do? Now he has no way of spending the night away from home."

The pundit from Sinthi left. It was dusk. Twilight hung over the Panchavati, the temples, and the river. Evening worship began in the different temples. Sri Ramakrishna bowed before the pictures of the deities in his room. He was sitting on the small couch in an abstracted mood. A few devotees were on the floor. There was silence in the room.

An hour passed. Ishan and Kishori entered and sat down on the floor after saluting Sri Ramakrishna. Ishan was a great ritualist, devoted to the performance of the various rites and ceremonies prescribed by the scriptures. The Master opened the conversation.

MASTER: "Can one attain knowledge of God by merely repeating the word 'God'? There are two indications of such knowledge. First, longing, that is to say, love for God. You may indulge in reasoning or discussion, but if you feel no longing or love, it is all futile. Second, the awakening of the Kundalini. As long as the Kundalini remains asleep, you have not attained knowledge of God. You may be spending hours poring over books or discussing philosophy, but if you have no inner restlessness for God, you have no knowledge of Him.

"When the Kundalini is awakened, one develops feeling, devotion, and love for God. This is the path of devotion.

"The path of karma[6] is very difficult. Through it one obtains some powers—I mean occult powers."

ISHAN: "Let me go and see Hazra."

Sri Ramakrishna sat in silence. After a while Ishan returned to the room accompanied by Hazra. The Master was still silent. A few moments later Hazra whispered to Ishan: "Let's leave him alone. Perhaps he will meditate now." Both left the room.

Sri Ramakrishna was still silent. In a few moments the devotees noticed that he was really meditating. Then he performed japa. He placed his right hand on his head, then on his forehead, then on his throat, then on his heart, and last of all on his navel. Was it meditation on the Kundalini in the six centres of the body?

Ishan and Hazra had gone to the Kāli temple. Sri Ramakrishna was absorbed in meditation. Meanwhile Adhar had arrived. It was about half-past seven.

A little later the Master went to the Kāli temple. He looked at the image, took some sacred flowers from the Feet of the Mother, and placed them on his head.

[6] Here signifying religious rites and rituals.

He prostrated himself before the Mother and went round the image. He waved the chāmara. He appeared ecstatic with divine fervour. Coming out, he found Ishan performing ritualistic worship.

MASTER (to Ishan): "What? You are still here? Are you still engaged in rituals? Listen to a song:

Why should I go to Gayā or Gangā, to Kāśi, Kānchi, or Prabhās,
So long as I can breathe my last with Kāli's name upon my lips?
What need of worship has a man, what need of rituals any more,
If he repeats his Mother's name during the three holy hours?
Rituals may pursue him close, but they can never overtake him.
Charity, vows, and giving of gifts have no appeal for Madan's mind;
The blissful Mother's Lotus Feet are his prayer and sacrifice. . . .

"How long must a man continue formal worship? As long as he has not developed love for God's Lotus Feet, as long as he does not shed tears and his hair does not stand on end when he repeats God's name.

"When the fruit grows, the flower drops off. When one has developed love of God and has beheld Him, then one gives up rites.

"You cannot achieve anything by moving at such a slow pace. You need stern renunciation. Can you achieve anything by counting fifteen months as a year? You seem to have no strength, no grit. You are as mushy as flattened rice soaked in milk. Be up and doing! Gird your loins!

"I don't like that song:

Brother, joyfully cling to God;
So striving, some day you may attain Him.

I don't care for the line, 'So striving, some day you may attain Him.' You need stern renunciation. I say the same thing to Hazra.

"You ask me why you don't feel stern renunciation. There is a reason for it. You have desires and hidden tendencies within you. The same is true of Hazra. In our part of the country I have seen peasants bringing water into their paddy-fields. The fields have low ridges on all sides to prevent the water from leaking out; but these are made of mud and often have holes here and there. The peasants work themselves to death to bring the water, which, however, leaks out through the holes. Desires are the holes. You practise japa and austerities, no doubt, but they all leak out through the holes of your desires. If there are no desires, the mind naturally looks up toward God. Do you know what it is like? It is like the needles of a balance. On account of the weight of 'woman' and 'gold' the two needles are not in line. It is 'woman' and 'gold' that make a man stray from the path of yoga. Haven't you noticed the flame of a candle? The slightest wind makes it waver. The state of yoga is like the steady flame in a windless place.

"The mind is dispersed. Part of it has gone to Dāccā, part to Delhi, and another part to Coochbehār. That mind is to be gathered in; it must be concentrated on one object. If you want sixteen ānnās' worth of cloth, then you have to pay the merchant the full sixteen ānnās. Yoga is not possible if there is the slightest obstacle. If there is a tiny break in the telegraph wire, then the news cannot be transmitted.

"You are no doubt in the world. What of that? You must surrender the fruit of your action to God. You must not seek any result for yourself. But remember one thing: the desire for bhakti cannot be called a desire. You may desire bhakti and pray for it. Practise the tamas of bhakti and force your demand upon the Divine Mother.

"God is your own Mother. Is She a stepmother? Is it an artificial relationship? If you cannot force your demand on Her, then on whom can you force it? Say to Her:

Mother, am I Thine eight-months child?[7] Thy red eyes cannot frighten me!

"God is your own Mother. Enforce your demand. If you are a part of a thing, you feel its attraction. Because of the element of the Divine Mother in me I feel attracted to Her.

"Nowadays you don't have to attend to worldly duties. Spend a few days thinking of God. You have seen that there is nothing to the world."

The Master sang:

Remember this, O mind—nobody is your own;
Vain is your wandering in this world.
Trapped in the subtle snare of māyā, as you are,
Do not forget your Mother's name.

Only a day or two men honour you on earth
As lord and master; all too soon
This form, so honoured now, must needs be cast away,
When Master Death takes hold of you.

[7] A premature child is generally weak and fearful.

Even your beloved wife, for whom, while yet you live,
  You fret yourself continually,
Cannot go with you then; she too will say farewell
  And shun your corpse as an evil thing.

Continuing, the Master said: "What are these things you busy yourself with—this arbitration and leadership? I hear that you settle people's quarrels and that they make you the arbiter. You have been doing this kind of work a long time. Let those who care for such things do them. Now devote your mind more and more to God's Lotus Feet.

"Sambhu, too, said, 'I shall build hospitals and dispensaries.' He was a devotee of God; so I said to him, 'Will you ask God for hospitals and dispensaries when you see Him?'

"Keshab Sen asked me, 'Why do I not see God?' I said, 'You do not see God because you busy yourself with such things as name and fame and scholarship.' The mother does not come to the child as long as it sucks its toy—a red toy. But when, after a few minutes, it throws the toy away and cries, then the mother takes down the rice-pot from the hearth and comes running to the child.

"You are engaged in arbitration. The Divine Mother says to Herself: 'My child is now busy arbitrating and is very happy. Let him be.'"

In the mean time Ishan had been holding Sri Ramakrishna's feet. He said humbly, "It is not my will that I should do those things."

MASTER: "I know it. This is the Divine Mother's play—Her lilā. It is the will of the Great Enchantress that many should remain entangled in the world. Do you know what it is like?

> How many are the boats, O mind,
> That float on the ocean of this world!
> How many are those that sink!

Again,

> Out of a hundred thousand kites,
> At best but one or two break free;
> And Thou dost laugh and clap Thy hands,
> O Mother, watching them.

Only one or two in a hundred thousand get liberation. The rest are entangled through the will of the Divine Mother.

"Haven't you seen the game of hide-and-seek? It is the 'granny's' will that the game should continue. If all touch her and are released, then the playing comes to a stop. Therefore it is not her will that all should touch her.

"I prayed to the Divine Mother: 'O Mother, I don't want name and fame. I don't want the eight occult powers. I don't want a hundred occult powers. O Mother, I have no desire for creature comforts. Please, Mother, grant me the boon that I may have pure love for Thy Lotus Feet.'"

The devotees listened spellbound to Sri Ramakrishna. His burning words entered their souls, spurring them along the path of renunciation.

Now he spoke to Ishan in a serious voice.

MASTER: "Don't forget yourself because of what you hear from your flatterers. Flatterers gather around a worldly man. Vultures gather around the carcass of a cow.

"Worldly people have no stuff in them. Flatterers come to them and say: 'You are so charitable and wise!

You are so pious!' These are not mere words but pointed bamboos thrust at them. How foolish it is! To be surrounded day and night by a bunch of worldly brāhmin pundits and hear their flattery!

"Worldly men are slaves of three things: they are slaves of their wives, slaves of their money, slaves of their masters. Can they have any inner stuff?

"Arbitration and leadership? How trifling these are! Charity and doing good to others? You have had enough of these. Those who are to devote themselves to such things belong to a different class. Now the time is ripe for you to devote your mind to God's Lotus Feet. If you realize God you will get everything else. First God, then charity, doing good to others, doing good to the world, and redeeming people. Why need you worry about these things?

"That's the trouble with you. It will be very good if a world-renouncing sannyāsi gives you some spiritual instruction. The advice of the worldly man will not be right, be he a brāhmin pundit or anyone else.

"Be mad! Be mad with love of God! Let people know that Ishan has gone mad and cannot perform worldly duties any more. Then people will no longer come to you for leadership and arbitration. Throw aside these articles of worship and justify your name of Ishan."[8]

Ishan quoted:

Mother, make me mad with Thy Love.
What need have I of knowledge or reason?

MASTER: "Mad! That's the thing! Shivanath once said that one 'loses one's head' by thinking too much of God. 'What?' said I. 'Can anyone ever become un-

[8] An epithet of the all-renouncing Śiva.

conscious by thinking of Consciousness? God is of the nature of Eternity, Purity, and Consciousness. Through His Consciousness one becomes conscious of everything; through His Intelligence the whole world appears intelligent.'"

Ishan was seated touching Sri Ramakrishna's feet and listening to his words. Now and then he cast a glance at the basalt image of Kāli in the shrine. In the light of the lamp She appeared to be smiling. It was as if the living Deity, manifesting Herself through the image, was delighted to hear the Master's words, holy as the words of the Vedas.

ISHAN (*pointing to the image*): "Those words from your sacred lips have really come from there."

MASTER: "I am the machine and She is the Operator. I move as She moves me; I speak as She speaks through me. In the Kaliyuga one does not hear God's voice, it is said, except through the mouth of a child or a madman or some such person."

The Master rose. He mounted the platform in front of the shrine and saluted the Mother, touching the ground with his forehead. The devotees quickly gathered around him and fell at his feet. They all begged his grace.

Sunday, October 26, 1884

It was afternoon, and many devotees were present in the Master's room. Among them were Manomohan, Mahimacharan, and M. They were joined later by Ishan and Hazra.

A DEVOTEE: "Sir, we hear that you see God. If you do, please show Him to us."

MASTER: "Everything depends on God's will. What can a man do? While chanting God's name, sometimes tears flow and at other times the eyes remain dry. While meditating on God, some days I feel a great deal of inner awakening and some days I feel nothing.

"A man must work. Only then can he see God. One day, in an exalted mood, I had a vision of the Hāldār-pukur. I saw a low-caste villager drawing water after pushing aside the green scum. Now and then he took up the water in the palm of his hand and examined it. In that vision it was revealed to me that the water cannot be seen without pushing aside the green scum that covers it; that is to say, one cannot develop love of God or obtain the vision of Him without work. Work means meditation, worship and the like. The chanting of God's name and glories is work too. You may also include charity, sacrifice, and so on."

MAHIMACHARAN: "That is true, sir. Work is certainly necessary. One must labour hard. Only then does one succeed. There is so much to read! The scriptures are endless."

MASTER (to Mahimacharan): "How much of the scriptures can you read? What will you gain by mere reasoning? Try to realize God before anything else. Have faith in the guru's words, and work. If you have no guru, then pray to God with a longing heart. He will let you know what He is like.

"What will you learn of God from books? As long as you are at a distance from the market-place you hear only an indistinct roar. But it is quite different when you are actually there. Then you hear and see everything distinctly. You hear people saying: 'Here are your potatoes. Take them and give me the money.'

"From a distance you hear only the rumbling noise of the ocean. Go near it and you will see many boats sailing about, birds flying, and waves rolling.

"One cannot get true feeling about God from the study of books. This feeling is something very different from book-learning. Books, the scriptures, and science appear as mere dirt and straw after the realization of God."

MAHIMACHARAN: "By what kind of work can one realize God?"

MASTER: "It is not that God can be realized by this work and not by that. The vision of God depends on His grace. Still a man must work a little with longing for God in his heart. If he has longing he will receive God's grace.

"To attain God a man must have certain favourable conditions: the company of holy men, discrimination, and the blessings of a real teacher. Perhaps his elder brother takes the responsibility for the family; perhaps his wife has spiritual qualities and is very virtuous; perhaps he is not married at all or entangled in worldly life. He succeeds when conditions like these are fulfilled.

"You should renounce mentally. Live the life of a householder in a spirit of detachment. Where will you go away from the world? Live in the world like a cast-off leaf in a gale. Such a leaf is sometimes blown inside a house and sometimes to a rubbish heap. The leaf goes wherever the wind blows it—sometimes to a good place and sometimes to a bad. Now God has put you in the world. That is good. Stay here. Again, when He lifts you from here and puts you in a better place, there will be time enough to think about what to do then.

"God has put you in the world. What can you do about it? Resign everything to Him. Surrender yourself at His feet. Then there will be no more confusion.

Then you will realize that it is God who does everything. All depends on 'the will of Rāma.' "

A DEVOTEE: "What is the story about 'the will of
Rāma'?"

MASTER: "In a certain village there lived a weaver.
He was a very pious soul. Everyone trusted him and
loved him. He used to sell his goods in the market-place.
When a customer asked him the price of a piece of
cloth, the weaver would say: 'By the will of Rāma
the price of the yarn is one rupee and the labour four
ānnās; by the will of Rāma the profit is two ānnās. The
price of the cloth, by the will of Rāma, is one rupee
and six ānnās.' Such was the people's faith in the
weaver that the customer would at once pay the price
and take the cloth. The weaver was a real devotee of
God. After finishing his supper in the evening, he
would spend long hours in the worship hall meditating
on God and chanting His name and glories. Now, late
one night the weaver couldn't get to sleep. He was
sitting in the worship hall, smoking now and then,
when a band of robbers happened to pass that way.
They wanted a man to carry their goods and said to
the weaver, 'Come with us.' So saying, they led him
off by the hand. After committing a robbery in a house,
they put a load of things on the weaver's head, com-
manding him to carry them. Suddenly the police arrived and the robbers ran away. But the weaver, with
his load, was arrested. He was kept in the lock-up for
the night. Next day he was brought before the magistrate for trial. The villagers learnt what had happened
and came to court. They said to the magistrate, 'Your
Honour, this man could never commit a robbery.'
Thereupon the magistrate asked the weaver to make
his statement.

"The weaver said: 'Your Honour, by the will of Rāma I finished my meal at night. Then by the will of Rāma I was sitting in the worship hall. It was quite late at night by the will of Rāma. By the will of Rāma I had been thinking of God and chanting His name and glories, when by the will of Rāma a band of robbers passed that way. By the will of Rāma they dragged me with them; by the will of Rāma they committed a robbery in a house; and by the will of Rāma they put a load on my head. Just then by the will of Rāma the police arrived and by the will of Rāma I was arrested. Then by the will of Rāma the police kept me in the lock-up for the night, and this morning by the will of Rāma I have been brought before Your Honour.' The magistrate realized that the weaver was a pious man and ordered his release. On his way home the weaver said to his friends, 'By the will of Rāma I have been released.'

"Whether a man should be a householder or a monk depends on the will of Rāma. Surrender everything to God and do your duties in the world. What else can you do?

"If the householder becomes a jivanmukta, then he can easily live in the world if he likes. A man who has attained Knowledge does not differentiate between 'this place' and 'that place.' All places are the same to him. He who thinks of 'that place' also thinks of 'this place.'

"When I first met Keshab at Jaygopal's garden house, I remarked, 'He is the only one who has dropped his tail.' At this people laughed. Keshab said to them: 'Don't laugh. There must be some meaning in his words. Let us ask him.' Thereupon I said to Keshab: 'The tadpole, so long as it has not dropped its tail, lives only in the water. It cannot move about on dry land. But as soon as it drops its tail it hops out on the bank; then it can live both on land and in water. Likewise, as long as a man has not dropped his tail of ignorance, he can live only in the water of the world. But when he drops his tail, that is to say, when he attains the Knowledge of God, then he can roam about as a free soul or live as a householder if he likes.' "

Mahimacharan and the other devotees remained absorbed, listening to the Master's words.

MASTER: "Once I visited Devendranath Tagore[9] with Mathur Babu. I had said to Mathur: 'I have heard that Devendra Tagore thinks of God. I should like to see him.' 'All right,' said Mathur, 'I will take you to him. We were fellow students in the Hindu College and I am very friendly with him.' We went to Devendra's house. Mathur and Devendra had not seen each other for a long time. Devendra said to Mathur: 'You have changed a little. You have grown fat around the stomach.' Mathur said, referring to me: 'He has come to see you. He is always mad about God.' I wanted to see Devendra's physical marks and said to him, 'Let me see your body.' He pulled up his shirt and I found that he had very fair skin tinted red. His hair had not yet turned grey.

"At the outset I noticed a little vanity in Devendra. And isn't that natural? He had such wealth, such scholarship, such name and fame! Noticing that streak of vanity, I asked Mathur: 'Well, is vanity the outcome of knowledge or ignorance? Can a knower of Brahman have such a feeling as, "I am a scholar; I am a jnāni; I am rich"?'

"While I was talking to Devendra, I suddenly got into that state of mind in which I can see through a

[9] The father of Rabindranath Tagore.

man. I was convulsed with laughter inside. In that state I regard scholars and the book-learned as mere straw. If I see that a scholar has no discrimination and renunciation, I regard him as worthless straw. I see that he is like a vulture, which soars high but fixes its look on a charnel-pit down below.

"I found that Devendra had combined both yoga and bhoga in his life. He had a number of children, all young. The family physician was there. Thus, you see, though he was a jnāni, yet he was preoccupied with worldly life. I said to him: 'I have heard that you live in the world and think of God; so I have come to see you. Please tell me something about God.'

"He recited some texts from the Vedas. He said, 'This universe is like a chandelier and each living being is a light in it.' Once, while I was meditating in the Panchavati, I too had had a vision like that. I found his words agreed with my vision, and I thought he must be a very great man. I asked him to explain his words. He said: 'God has created men to manifest His own glory; otherwise, who could know this universe? Everything becomes dark without the lights in the chandelier. One cannot even see the chandelier itself.'

"We talked a long time. Devendra was pleased and said to me, 'You must come to our Brāhmo Samāj festival.' 'That,' I said, 'depends on God's will. You can see my state of mind. There's no knowing when God will put me into a particular state.' Devendra insisted: 'No, you must come. But put on your cloth and wear a shawl over your body. Someone might say something unkind about your untidiness, and that would hurt me.' 'No,' I replied, 'I cannot promise that. I cannot be a babu.' Devendra and Mathur laughed.

"The very next day Mathur received a letter from

Devendra forbidding me to go to the festival. He wrote that it would be ungentlemanly of me not to cover my body with a shawl. (*All laugh.*)

"There is another big man: Captain.[10] Though a man of the world, he is a great lover of God. (*To Mahima*) Talk to him some time. He knows the Vedas, Vedānta, the Gītā, and other scriptures by heart. You will find that out when you talk to him.

"Captain's wife said to me: 'He doesn't enjoy worldly life. That is why he once said he would renounce the world.' True, every now and then he expresses that desire.

"Captain was born in a family of devotees. His father was a soldier. I have heard that on the battle-field he would worship Śiva with one hand and hold a naked sword in the other.

"Captain is a strong upholder of orthodox conventions. Because of my visiting Keshab Chandra Sen he stopped coming here for a month. He said to me that Keshab had violated the social conventions: he dined with the English, had married his daughter into another caste, and had lost his own caste. I said to Captain: 'What do I care for such things? Keshab chants the name of God; so I go to him to hear about God. I eat only the plum; what do I care about the thorns?' But Captain remained stubborn. He said to me, 'Why do you see Keshab?' I answered him rather sharply: 'But I don't go to him for money; I go there to hear the name of God. And how is it that you visit the Viceroy's house? He is a mlechchha. How can you be in his company?' That silenced him a little.

"But he is a great devotee. At the time of worship he

[10] See Introduction, p. 57.

performs ārati with camphor. When he recites hymns he becomes a totally different person. He remains absorbed.

(*To Mahima*) "You explain 'Aum' with reference to 'a,' 'u,' and 'm' only."

MAHIMA: " 'A,' 'u,' and 'm' mean creation, preservation, and destruction."

MASTER: "But I give the illustration of the sound of a gong: 'tom,'[11] t—o—m. It is the merging of the Līlā in the Nitya: the gross, the subtle, and the causal merge in the Great Cause; waking, dream, and deep sleep merge in Turiya. The striking of the gong is like the falling of a heavy weight into a big ocean. Waves begin to rise: the Relative rises from the Absolute; the causal, subtle, and gross bodies appear out of the Great Cause; from Turiya emerge the states of deep sleep, dream, and waking. These waves arising from the Great Ocean merge again in the Great Ocean. From the Absolute to the Relative, and from the Relative to the Absolute. Therefore I give the illustration of the gong's sound: 'tom.' I have clearly perceived all these things. It has been revealed to me that there exists an Ocean of Consciousness without limit. From It come all things of the relative plane, and in It they merge again."

MAHIMA: "Those to whom such things were revealed did not write the scriptures. They were rapt in their own experiences; when would they write? One needs a somewhat calculating mind to write. Others learnt these things from the seers and wrote the books."

[11] The "o" is to be pronounced as "aw" in dawn.

Saturday, December 6, 1884

Adhar lived in Sobhābāzār, in the northern section of Calcutta. Almost every day, after finishing his hard work at the office and returning home in the late afternoon, he paid Sri Ramakrishna a visit. From his home in Calcutta he would go to Dakshineswar in a hired carriage. His one delight was to see the Master. But he would hear very little of what Sri Ramakrishna said; for, after saluting the Master and visiting the temples, he would lie down, at the Master's request, on a mat spread on the floor and would soon fall asleep. At nine or ten o'clock he would be awakened to return home. He considered himself blessed, however, to be able to see the God-man of Dakshineswar. At Adhar's request Sri Ramakrishna often visited his home. His visits were occasions for religious festivals. Devotees in large numbers would assemble, and Adhar would feed them sumptuously.

Sri Ramakrishna arrived at Adhar's house with his attendants. Everyone was in a joyous mood. Adhar had arranged a rich feast. Many strangers were present. At Adhar's invitation several other deputy magistrates had come; they wanted to watch the Master and judge his holiness. Among them was Bankim Chandra Chatterji, perhaps the greatest literary figure of Bengal during the later part of the nineteenth century. He was one of the creators of modern Bengali literature and wrote on social and religious subjects. Bankim was a product of the contact of India with England. He gave modern interpretations of the Hindu scriptures and advocated drastic social reforms.

Sri Ramakrishna had been talking happily with the

devotees when Adhar introduced several of his
personal friends to him.

ADHAR (introducing Bankim): "Sir, he is a great
scholar and has written many books. He has come
here to see you. His name is Bankim Babu."

MASTER (smiling): "Bankim![12] Well, what has
made you bent?"

BANKIM (smiling): "Why, sir, boots are responsible
for it. The kicks of our white masters have bent my
body."

MASTER: "No, my dear sir! Sri Krishna was bent
on account of His ecstatic love. His body was bent
in three places owing to His love for Rādhā. That is
how some people explain Sri Krishna's form. Do you
know why He has a deep-blue complexion? And why
He is of such small stature—only three and a half
cubits measured by His own hand? God looks so as
long as He is seen from a distance. So the water of
the ocean looks blue from afar. But if you go near the
ocean and take the water in your hand, you will no
longer find it blue; it will be very clear, transparent.
So the sun appears small because it is very far away; if
you go near it you will no longer find it small. When
one knows the true nature of God, He appears neither
blue nor small. But that is a far-off vision: one does
not see it except in samādhi. As long as 'I' and 'you'
exist, name and form will also exist. Everything is
God's lilā, His sportive pleasure. As long as a man
is conscious of 'I' and 'you,' he will experience the
manifestations of God through diverse forms."

BANKIM: "Sir, why don't you preach?"

MASTER (smiling): "Preaching? It is only a man's
vanity that makes him think of preaching. A man is

[12] Literally the word means "bent" or "curved."

but an insignificant creature. It is God alone who will preach—God, who has created the sun and moon and so illumined the universe. Is preaching such a trifling affair? You cannot preach unless God reveals Himself to you and gives you the command to preach. Of course, no one can stop you from lecturing. You haven't received the command, but still you cry yourself hoarse. People will listen to you a couple of days and then forget all about it. It is like any other sensation: as long as you speak, people will say, 'Ah! He speaks well'; and the moment you stop, everything will disappear. If God reveals Himself to you and gives you the command, then you can preach and teach people. Otherwise, who will listen to you?"

The visitors were listening seriously.

MASTER (to Bankim): "I understand you are a great pundit and have written many books. Please tell me what you think about man's duties? What will accompany him after death? You believe in the hereafter, don't you?"

BANKIM: "The hereafter? What is that?"

MASTER: "True. When a man dies after attaining Knowledge, he doesn't have to go to another plane of existence; he isn't born again. But as long as he has not attained Knowledge, as long as he has not realized God, he must come back to the life of this earth; he can never escape it. For such a person there is a hereafter. A man is liberated after attaining Knowledge, after realizing God. For him there is no further coming back to earth. If a boiled paddy-grain is sown it doesn't sprout. Just so, if a man is boiled by the fire of Knowledge, he cannot take part any more in the play of creation. What will you gain by sowing boiled paddy?

(*To Bankim, smiling*) "Well, what do you say about man's duties?"

BANKIM (*smiling*): "If you ask me about them, I should say they are eating, sleeping, and sex-life."

MASTER (*sharply*): "Eh? You are very saucy! What you do day and night comes out through your mouth. A man belches what he eats. If he eats radish he belches radish; if he eats green coconut he belches green coconut. Day and night you live in the midst of 'woman' and 'gold'; so your mouth utters words about them alone. By constantly thinking of worldly things a man becomes calculating and deceitful. On the other hand, he becomes guileless by thinking of God. A man who has seen God will never say what you have just said. What will a pundit's scholarship profit him if he does not think of God and has no discrimination and renunciation?

"The pundit has no doubt studied many books and scriptures; he may rattle off their texts or he may have written books. But if he is attached to women, if he thinks of money and honour as the essential things, will you call him a pundit? How can a man be a pundit if his mind does not dwell on God?

"Some may say about the devotees: 'Day and night these people speak about God. They are crazy; they have lost their heads. But how clever we are! How we enjoy pleasure—money, honour, the senses!' The crow, too, thinks he is a clever bird; but the first thing he does when he wakes up in the early morning is to fill his stomach with nothing but others' filth. Haven't you noticed how he struts about? Very clever indeed!"

There was dead silence.

Sri Ramakrishna continued: "But like the swan are those who think of God, who pray day and night to get rid of their attachment to worldly things, who do not enjoy anything except the nectar of the Lotus Feet of the Lord, and to whom worldly pleasures taste bitter. If you put a mixture of milk and water before the swan, it will leave the water and drink only the milk. And haven't you noticed the gait of a swan? It goes straight ahead in one direction. So it is with genuine devotees: they go toward God alone. They seek nothing else; they enjoy nothing else.

(*Tenderly to Bankim*) "Please don't take offence at my words."

BANKIM: "Sir, I haven't come here to hear sweet things."

MASTER (*to Bankim*): " 'Woman' and 'gold' alone are the world; they alone constitute māyā. Because of them you cannot see or think of God. After the birth of one or two children, husband and wife should live as brother and sister and talk only of God. Then the minds of both will be drawn to God, and the wife will be a help to the husband on the path of spirituality. None can taste divine bliss without giving up his animal feeling. A devotee should pray to God to help him get rid of this feeling. It must be a sincere prayer. God is our Inner Controller; He will certainly listen to our prayer if it is sincere.

"And 'gold.' Sitting on the bank of the Ganges below the Panchavati, I used to say, 'Rupee is clay and clay is rupee.' Then I threw both into the Ganges."

BANKIM: "Indeed! Money is clay! Sir, if you have a few pennies you can help the poor. If money is clay, then a man cannot give in charity or do good to others."

MASTER (*to Bankim*): "Charity! Doing good! How dare you say you can do good to others? Man boasts so much; but if one pours foul water into his mouth

when he is asleep, he doesn't even know it; his mouth
overflows with it. Where are his boasting, his vanity,
his pride, then?

"If a householder is a genuine devotee, he performs
his duties without attachment; he surrenders the
fruit of his work to God—his gain or loss, his pleasure
or pain—and day and night he prays for devotion and
for nothing else. This is called motiveless work, the
performance of duty without attachment. A sannyāsi,
too, must do all his work in that spirit of detachment;
but he has no worldly duties to attend to, like a householder.

"If a householder gives in charity in a spirit of detachment, he is really doing good to himself and not
to others. It is God alone that he serves—God, who
dwells in all beings; and when he serves God, he is
really doing good to himself and not to others. If a man
thus serves God through all beings, not through men
alone but through animals and other living beings as
well; if he doesn't seek name and fame, or heaven
after death; if he doesn't seek any return from those
he serves; if he can carry on his work of service in
this spirit—then he performs truly selfless work, work
without attachment. Through such selfless work he
does good to himself. This is called karmayoga. This
too is a way to realize God. But it is very difficult, and
not suited to the Kaliyuga.

"Therefore I say, he who works in such a detached
spirit—who is kind and charitable—benefits only himself. Helping others, doing good to others—this is the
work of God alone, who has created for men the sun
and moon, father and mother, fruits, flowers, and
corn. The love that you see in parents is God's love:
He has given it to them to preserve His creation. The

compassion that you see in the kindhearted is God's compassion: He has given it to them to protect the helpless. Whether you are charitable or not, He will have His work done somehow or other. Nothing can stop His work.

"What, then, is man's duty? What else can it be? It is just to take refuge in God and pray to Him with a yearning heart for the vision of Him.

(*To Bankim*) "Some people think that God cannot be realized without studying books and the scriptures. They think that first of all one should learn of this world and its creatures; that first of all one should study 'science.' They think that one cannot realize God without first understanding His creation. Which comes first, 'science' or God? What do you say?"

BANKIM: "I too think that we should first of all know about the different things of the world. How can we know of God without knowing something of this world? We should first learn from books."

MASTER: "That's the one cry from all of you. But God comes first and then the creation. When you know God you know all else; but then you don't care to know small things. The same thing is stated in the Vedas. You talk about the virtues of a person as long as you haven't seen him, but as soon as he appears before you all such talk stops. You are beside yourself with joy simply to be with him. You feel overwhelmed by simply conversing with him. You don't talk about his virtues any more.

"First realize God, then think of the creation and other things. If you know one you know all. If you put fifty zeros after a one, you have a large sum; but erase the one and nothing remains. It is the one that makes the many. First one, then many. First God, then His creatures and the world.

"Pray to God with a longing heart. He will surely listen to your prayer if it is sincere. Perhaps He will direct you to holy men with whom you can keep company; and that will help you on your spiritual path. Perhaps someone will tell you, 'Do this and you will attain God.'

"One must have faith in the guru's words. The guru is none other than Satchidānanda. God Himself is the guru. If you only believe his words like a child, you will realize God. God cannot be realized by a mind that is hypocritical, calculating, or argumentative. One must have faith and sincerity. Hypocrisy will not do. To the sincere, God is very near; but He is far, far away from the hypocrite.

"One must have for God the yearning of a child. The child sees nothing but confusion when his mother is away. You may try to cajole him by putting a sweetmeat in his hand; but he will not be fooled. He only says, 'No, I want to go to my mother.' One must feel such yearning for God. Ah, what yearning! How restless a child feels for his mother! Nothing can make him forget his mother. He to whom the enjoyment of worldly happiness appears tasteless, he who takes no delight in anything of the world—money, name, creature comforts, sense pleasure—becomes sincerely grief-stricken for the vision of the Mother. And to him alone the Mother comes running, leaving all Her other duties.

"Ah, that restlessness is the whole thing. Whatever path you follow—whether you are a Hindu, a Mussalmān, a Christian, a Śākta, a Vaishnava, or a

Brāhmo—the vital point is restlessness. God is our Inner Guide. It doesn't matter if you take a wrong path—only you must be restless for Him. He Himself will put you on the right path."

Trailokya of the Brāhmo Samāj began to sing. Presently Sri Ramakrishna stood up and lost consciousness of the outer world. He became completely indrawn, absorbed in samādhi. The devotees stood around him in a circle. Pushing aside the crowd, Bankim came near the Master and began to watch him attentively. He had never seen anyone in samādhi.

After a few minutes Sri Ramakrishna regained partial consciousness and began to dance in an ecstatic mood. It was a never-to-be-forgotten scene. Bankim and his Anglicized friends looked at him in amazement. They said to themselves, "Is this the God-intoxicated state?" The devotees also watched him with wondering eyes.

The singing and dancing over, the Master took his seat and all sat around him.

BANKIM (to the Master): "Sir, how can one develop divine love?"

MASTER: "Through restlessness—the restlessness a child feels for his mother. The child feels bewildered when he is separated from his mother, and weeps longingly for her. If a man can weep like that for God he can even see Him.

"At the approach of dawn the eastern horizon becomes red. Then one knows it will soon be sunrise. Likewise, if you see a person restless for God, you can be pretty certain that he hasn't long to wait for His vision.

(To Bankim) "Let me tell you something. What will you gain by floating on the surface? Dive a little under the water. The gems lie deep under the water; so what is the good of throwing your arms and legs about on the surface? A real gem is heavy. It doesn't float; it sinks to the bottom. To get the real gem you must dive deep."

BANKIM: "Sir, what can we do? We are tied to a cork. It prevents us from diving." (All laugh.)

MASTER: "All sins vanish if one only remembers God. His name breaks the fetters of death. You must dive; otherwise you can't get the gem."

Bankim bowed low before the Master. He was about to take his leave.

BANKIM: "Sir, I am not such an idiot as you may think. I have a prayer to make. Please be kind enough to grace my house with the dust of your holy feet."

MASTER: "That's nice. I shall go if God wills."

Bankim took his leave; but he was absent-minded. When he reached the door he discovered that he had dropped his shawl in the room; he was in his shirtsleeves. A gentleman handed him his shawl.

Adhar entertained the Master and the devotees with a feast. It was quite late in the evening when the devotees returned home, cherishing in their hearts the image of the Master in his spiritual ecstasy and remembering his words of great wisdom.

Since Bankim had invited Sri Ramakrishna to visit his home, the Master a few days later sent Girish and M to his Calcutta residence. At that time Bankim had a long discussion with these two devotees about the Master. He told them that he wanted to visit Sri Ramakrishna again. But his desire was not fulfilled.

9

SOME INTIMATE DISCIPLES

Wednesday, March 11, 1885

AFTER SCHOOL HOURS M went to Balaram's house and found the Master sitting in the drawing-room, surrounded by his devotees and disciples. The Master's face was beaming with a sweet smile, which was reflected in the happy faces of those in the room. M was asked to take a seat by the Master's side.

MASTER (*to Girish*): "You had better argue this point with Narendra and see what he has to say."

GIRISH: "Narendra says that God is infinite; we cannot even so much as say that the things or persons we perceive are parts of God. How can Infinity have parts? It cannot."

MASTER: "However great and infinite God may be, His Essence can and does manifest itself through man by His mere will. God's Incarnation as a man cannot be explained by analogy. One must feel it for oneself and realize it by direct perception. An analogy can give us only a little glimpse. By touching the horns, legs, or tail of a cow, we in fact touch the cow herself; but for us the essential thing about a cow is her milk, which comes through the udder. The Divine Incarnation is like the udder. God incarnates Himself as man from time to time in order to teach people devotion and divine love."

GIRISH: "Narendra says: 'Is it ever possible to know all of God? He is infinite.'"

MASTER (to Girish): "Who can comprehend everything about God? It is not given to man to know any aspect of God, great or small. And what need is there to know everything about God? It is enough if we only see Him. And we see God Himself if we but see His Incarnation. Suppose a person goes to the Ganges and touches its water. He will then say, 'Yes, I have seen and touched the Ganges.' To say this it is not necessary for him to touch the whole length of the river from Hārdwār to Gangāsāgar. (Laughter.)

"If I touch your feet, surely that is the same as touching you. (Laughter.) If a person goes to the ocean and touches but a little of its water, he has surely touched the ocean itself. Fire, as an element, exists in all things, but in wood it is present to a greater degree."

GIRISH (smiling): "I am looking for fire. Naturally I want to go to a place where I can get it."

MASTER (smiling): "Yes, fire, as an element, is present more in wood than in any other object. If you seek God, then seek Him in man; He manifests Himself more in man than in any other thing. If you see a man endowed with ecstatic love, overflowing with prema, mad after God, intoxicated with His love, then know for certain that God has incarnated Himself through that man.

(To M) "There is no doubt that God exists in all things; but the manifestations of His Power are different in different beings. The greatest manifestation of His Power is through an Incarnation. Again, in some Incarnations there is a complete manifestation of God's Power."

GIRISH: "Narendra says that God is beyond our words and thought."

MASTER: "That is not altogether true. He is, no doubt, unknowable by this ordinary mind, but He can indeed be known by the pure mind. The mind and intellect become pure the moment they are free from attachment to 'woman' and 'gold.' The pure mind and pure intellect are one and the same. God is known by the pure mind. Didn't the sages and seers of olden times see God? They realized the All-pervading Consciousness by means of their inner consciousness."

GIRISH (with a smile): "I defeated Narendra in the argument."

MASTER: "Oh, no! He said to me: 'When Girish Ghosh has so much faith in God's Incarnation as man, what can I say to him? It is not proper to meddle with such faith.'

"Narendra is a boy of a very high order. He excels in everything: vocal and instrumental music and studies. Again, he has control over his sense-organs. He is truthful and has discrimination and dispassion. So many virtues in one person! (To M) What do you say? Isn't he unusually good?"

M: "Yes, sir, he is."

MASTER (aside to M): "He [meaning Girish] has great earnestness and faith."

M looked at Girish and marvelled at his tremendous faith. Girish had been coming to Sri Ramakrishna only a short time and had already recognized his spiritual power. To M he seemed a familiar friend and kinsman, related to him by the strong bond of spirituality. Girish was one of the gems in the necklace of the Master's devotees.

Gradually it became dusk. The shadow of evening

fell on Calcutta. For the moment the noise of the busy metropolis was subdued. Gongs and conch-shells proclaimed the evening worship in many Hindu homes. Devotees of God set aside their worldly duties and turned their minds to prayer and meditation. This joining of day and night, this mystic twilight, always created an ecstatic mood in the Master.

The devotees seated in the room looked at Sri Ramakrishna as he began to chant the sweet name of the Divine Mother. After the chanting he began to pray. What was the need of prayer to a soul in constant communion with God? Did he not rather want to teach erring mortals how to pray? Addressing the Divine Mother, he said: "O Mother, I throw myself on Thy mercy; I take shelter at Thy Hallowed Feet. I do not want bodily comforts: I do not crave name and fame; I do not seek the eight occult powers. Be gracious and grant that I may have pure love for Thee, a love unsmitten by desire, untainted by any selfish ends—a love craved by the devotee for the sake of love alone. And grant me the favour, O Mother, that I may not be deluded by Thy world-bewitching māyā, that I may never be attached to the world, to 'woman' and 'gold,' conjured up by Thy inscrutable māyā! O Mother, there is no one but Thee whom I may call my own. Mother, I do not know how to worship; I am without austerity; I have neither devotion nor knowledge. Be gracious, Mother, and out of Thy infinite mercy grant me love for Thy Lotus Feet."

Every word of this prayer, uttered from the depths of his soul, stirred the minds of the devotees. The melody of his voice and the childlike simplicity of his face touched their hearts.

Girish invited the Master to his house, saying that he must go there that very night.

MASTER: "Don't you think it will be late?"

GIRISH: "No, sir. You may return any time you like. I shall have to go to the theatre tonight to settle a quarrel there."

It was nine o'clock in the evening when the Master was ready to start for Girish's house. Since Balaram had prepared supper for him, Sri Ramakrishna said to Balaram: "Please send the food you have prepared for me to Girish's. I shall enjoy it there." He did not want to hurt Balaram's feelings.

As the Master was coming down from the second floor of Balaram's house, he became filled with divine ecstasy. He looked as if he were drunk. Narayan and M were by his side; a little behind came Ram, Chuni, and the other devotees. No sooner had he reached the ground floor than he became totally overwhelmed. Narayan came forward to hold him by the hand lest he should miss his footing and fall. The Master expressed annoyance at this. A few minutes later he said to Narayan affectionately: "If you hold me by the hand people may think I am drunk. I shall walk by myself."

Girish's house was not far away. The Master passed the crossing at Bosepārā Lane. Suddenly he began to walk faster. The devotees were left behind. Presently Narendra was seen coming from a distance. At other times the Master's joy would have been unbounded at the thought of Narendra or at the mere mention of his name; but now he did not even exchange a word with his beloved disciple. As the Master and the devotees entered the lane where Girish lived, he was able to utter words. He said to Narendra: "Are you quite

well, my child? I could not talk to you then." Every
word the Master spoke was full of infinite tenderness.

Girish stood at the door to welcome the Master. As
Sri Ramakrishna entered the house, Girish fell at his
feet and lay there on the floor like a rod. At the
Master's bidding he stood up, touching the Master's
feet with his forehead. Sri Ramakrishna was taken to
the drawing-room on the second floor. The devotees
followed him and sat down, eager to get a view of the
Master and catch every word that fell from his lips.

As Sri Ramakrishna was about to take the seat reserved for him, he saw a newspaper lying near it. He
signed to someone to remove the paper. Since a newspaper contains worldly matters—gossip and scandal
—he regarded it as unholy. After the paper was removed he took his seat.

Many of his devotees were in the room: Narendra,
Girish, Ram, Haripada, Chuni, Balaram, and M.
Narendra did not believe that God could incarnate
Himself in a human body. But Girish differed with
him; he had the burning faith that from time to time
the Almighty Lord, through His inscrutable Power,
assumes a human body and descends to earth to serve
a divine purpose.

The Master said to Girish, "I should like to hear you
and Narendra argue in English."

The discussion began; but they talked in Bengali.
Narendra said: "God is Infinity. How is it possible
for us to comprehend Him? He dwells in every human
being. It is not that He manifests Himself through one
person only."

SRI RAMAKRISHNA (tenderly): "I quite agree with
Narendra. God is everywhere. But then you must remember that there are different manifestations of His

power in different beings. At some places there is a manifestation of His power of ignorance, at others a manifestation of His power of knowledge. Through different instruments God's power is manifest in different degrees, greater and smaller. Therefore all men are not equal."

RAM: "What is the use of these futile arguments?"

MASTER (sharply): "No! No! There is a meaning in all this."

GIRISH (to Narendra): "How do you know that God does not assume a human body?"

NARENDRA: "God is 'beyond words and thought.'"

MASTER: "No, that is not true. He can be known by the pure buddhi, which is the same as the Pure Self. The seers of old directly perceived the Pure Self through their pure buddhi."

GIRISH (to Narendra): "Unless God Himself teaches men through His human Incarnation, who else will teach them spiritual mysteries? God takes a human body to impart to men divine knowledge and divine love. Otherwise, who will teach?"

NARENDRA: "Why, God dwells in our own heart; He will certainly teach us from within the heart."

MASTER (tenderly): "Yes, yes. He will teach us as our Inner Guide."

Gradually Narendra and Girish became involved in a heated discussion. If God is Infinity, how can He have parts? What did Hamilton say? What were the views of Herbert Spencer, of Tyndall, of Huxley? And so forth and so on.

MASTER (to M): "I don't enjoy these discussions. Why should I argue at all? I clearly see that God is everything; He Himself has become all. I see that whatever is, is God. He is everything; again, He is beyond everything. I come to a state in which my mind and intellect merge in the Indivisible.

"But without awakening one's own inner consciousness one cannot realize the All-pervading Consciousness. How long does a man reason? So long as he has not realized God. But mere words will not do. As for myself, I clearly see that He Himself has become everything. The inner consciousness must be awakened through God's grace. Through this awakening a man goes into samādhi. He often forgets that he has a body. He does not enjoy any talk unless it is about God. Worldly talk gives him pain. Through the awakening of the inner consciousness one realizes the All-pervading Consciousness."

The discussion came to a close. Sri Ramakrishna said to M: "I have observed that a man acquires one kind of knowledge about God through reasoning and another kind through meditation; but he acquires a third kind of knowledge about God when God reveals Himself to him, His devotee. If God Himself reveals to His devotee the nature of Divine Incarnation—how He plays in human form—then the devotee doesn't have to reason about the problem or need an explanation. Do you know what it is like? Suppose a man is in a dark room. He goes on rubbing a match against a matchbox and all of a sudden light comes. Likewise, if God gives us this flash of divine light, all our doubts are destroyed. Can one ever know God by mere reasoning?"

Sri Ramakrishna asked Narendra to sit by his side. He tenderly inquired about his health and showed him much affection.

NARENDRA (to the Master): "Why, I have meditated on Kāli for three or four days, but nothing has come of it."

MASTER: "All in good time, my child. Kāli is none other than Brahman. That which is called Brahman is really Kāli. She is the Primal Energy. When that Energy remains inactive, I call It Brahman, and when It creates, preserves, or destroys, I call It Śakti or Kāli. What you call Brahman I call Kāli."

It was late at night. Girish asked Haripada to call a cab, for he had to go to the theatre.

GIRISH: "That I should have to go to the theatre and leave you here!"

MASTER: "No, no. You must hold to both."

GIRISH: "I have been thinking of leaving the theatre to the youngsters."

MASTER: "No, no. It is all right. You are doing good to many."

Narendra said in a whisper, "Just a moment ago he [meaning Girish] was calling him [meaning Sri Ramakrishna] God, an Incarnation, and now he is attracted to the theatre!"

Narendra was sitting beside the Master. The latter looked at him intently and suddenly moved closer to his beloved disciple. Narendra did not believe in God's assuming a human body; but what did that matter? Sri Ramakrishna's heart overflowed with love for his disciple. He said to Narendra: "As long as a man argues about God, he has not realized Him. You two were arguing. I didn't like it.

"The nearer you approach God, the less you reason and argue. When you attain Him, then all sounds— all reasoning and disputing—come to an end. Then you go into samādhi, into communion with God in silence."

The Master gently stroked Narendra's body and affectionately touched his chin, uttering sweetly the holy words "Hari Om! Hari Om! Hari Om!" He was fast becoming unconscious of the outer world. His hand was on Narendra's foot. Still in that mood he gently stroked Narendra's body. Slowly a change came over his mind. With folded hands he said to Narendra: "Sing a song, please; then I shall be all right. How else shall I be able to stand on my own feet?"

Then the Master completely forgot the outer world. He did not notice anyone in the room, not even his beloved Narendra seated by his side. He did not know where he himself was seated. He was totally merged in God. Suddenly he stood up, shouting, "Deep drunk with the Wine of Divine Love!" As he took his seat again, he muttered, "I see a light coming, but I know not whence it comes."

Now Narendra sang:

> Lord, Thou hast lifted all my sorrow
> With the vision of Thy face,
> And the magic of Thy beauty
> Has bewitched my mind;
> Beholding Thee, the seven worlds
> Forget their never-ending woe;
> What shall I say, then, of myself,
> A poor and lowly soul?

Listening to the song, Sri Ramakrishna again went into deep samādhi. His eyes were closed and his body was transfixed.

Coming down from the ecstatic mood he looked around and said, "Who will take me to the temple garden?" He appeared like a child who felt confused in the absence of his companion.

It was late in the evening. The night was dark. The devotees stood by the carriage that had been brought to take the Master to Dakshineswar. They helped him in gently, for he was still in deep ecstasy. The carriage moved down the street and they looked after it with wistful eyes.

Soon the devotees turned homeward, a gentle south wind blowing in their faces. Some were humming the lines of the song:

> Lord, Thou hast lifted all my sorrow
> With the vision of Thy face,
> And the magic of Thy beauty
> Has bewitched my mind.

Saturday, May 9, 1885

It was about three o'clock in the afternoon. Sri Ramakrishna sat in Balaram's drawing-room in a happy mood. Many devotees were present. Balaram was not there. He had gone to Monghyr for a change of air. His eldest daughter had invited Sri Ramakrishna and the devotees and celebrated the occasion with a feast. The Master was resting after the meal.

Again and again the Master asked M: "Am I liberal-minded? Tell me."

BHAVANATH (*smiling*): "Why do you ask him? He will only keep quiet."

A DEVOTEE: "Sir, how does one receive God's grace?"

MASTER: "God has the nature of a child. A child is sitting with gems in the skirt of his cloth. Many a person passes by him along the road. Many of them pray to him for gems. But he hides the gems with his hands and says, turning away his face, 'No, I will not give any away.' But another man comes along. He doesn't ask for the gems and yet the child runs after him and offers him the gems, begging him to accept them.

"One cannot realize God without renunciation. Who will accept my words? I have been seeking a companion, a sympathetic soul who will understand my feelings. When I see a great devotee, I say to myself, 'Perhaps he will accept my ideal.' But later on I find that he behaves in a different way.

"Once Mathur Babu was in an ecstatic mood. He behaved like a drunkard and could not look after his work. At this all said: 'Who will look after his estate if he behaves like that? Certainly the young priest[1] has cast a spell upon him.'

"During one of Narendra's early visits I touched his chest and he became unconscious. Regaining consciousness, he wept and said: 'Oh, why did you do that to me? I have a father! I have a mother!' This 'I' and 'mine' spring from ignorance."

NARENDRA: "How can I believe, without proof, that God incarnates Himself as a man?"

GIRISH: "Faith alone is sufficient. What is the proof that these objects exist here? Faith alone is the proof."

A DEVOTEE: "Have philosophers been able to prove that the external world exists outside us? But they say we have an irresistible belief in it."

GIRISH (to Narendra): "You wouldn't believe, even if God appeared before you. God Himself might say that He was God born as a man, but perhaps you would say that He was a liar and a cheat."

[1] Referring to Sri Ramakrishna, who was at that time a priest in the Kāli temple.

JOGIN (*smiling*): "He [meaning the Master] doesn't accept Narendra's words any more."

MASTER (*smiling*): "At Jadu Mallick's garden house Narendra said to me, 'The forms of God that you see are the fiction of your mind.' I was amazed and said to him, 'But they speak too!' Narendra answered, 'Yes, you may think so.' I went to the temple and wept before the Mother. 'O Mother,' I said, 'what is this? Then is this all false? How could Narendra say that?' Instantly I had a revelation. I saw Consciousness—Indivisible Consciousness—and a divine being formed of that Consciousness. The divine form said to me, 'If your words are untrue, how is it that they tally with the facts?' Thereupon I said to Narendra: 'You rogue! You created unbelief in my mind. Don't come here any more.' "

The discussion continued. Narendra was arguing. He was then slightly over twenty-two years of age.

NARENDRA (*to Girish, M, and the others*): "How am I to believe in the words of scripture? The *Mahānirvāna Tantra* says, in one place, that unless a man attains the Knowledge of Brahman he goes to hell; and the same book says, in another place, that there is no salvation without the worship of Pārvati, the Divine Mother. Manu writes about himself in the *Manusamhitā*; Moses describes his own death in the Pentateuch.

"The Sāmkhya philosophy says that God does not exist, because there is no proof of His existence. Again, the same philosophy says that one must accept the Vedas and that they are eternal.

"But I don't say that these are not true. I simply don't understand them. Please explain them to me. People have explained the scriptures according to their fancy. Which explanation shall we accept? White light coming through a red medium appears red, through a green medium, green."

A DEVOTEE: "The Gitā contains the words of God."

MASTER: "Yes, the Gitā is the essence of the scriptures. A sannyāsi may or may not keep with him another book, but he always carries a pocket Gitā."

A DEVOTEE: "The Gitā contains the words of Krishna."

NARENDRA: "Yes, Krishna or any fellow for that matter!"

Sri Ramakrishna was amazed at these words of Narendra.

MASTER: "This is a fine discussion. There are two interpretations of the scriptures: the literal and the real. One should accept the real meaning alone— what agrees with the words of God. There is a vast difference between the words written in a letter and the direct words of its writer. The scriptures are like the words of the letter; the words of God are direct words. I do not accept anything unless it agrees with the direct words of the Divine Mother."

The conversation again turned to Divine Incarnation.

NARENDRA: "It is enough to have faith in God. I don't care about what He is doing or what He hangs from. Infinite is the universe; infinite are the Incarnations."

As Sri Ramakrishna heard the words "Infinite is the universe; infinite are the Incarnations," he said with folded hands, "Ah!"

M whispered something to Bhavanath.

BHAVANATH: "M says: 'As long as I have not seen the elephant, how can I know whether it can pass through the eye of a needle? I do not know God; how can I understand through reason whether or not He can incarnate Himself as man?' "

MASTER: "Everything is possible for God. It is He who casts the spell. The magician swallows the knife and takes it out again; he swallows stones and bricks."

A DEVOTEE: "The Brāhmos say that a man should perform his worldly duties. He must not renounce them."

GIRISH: "Yes, I saw something like that in one of their newspapers. But a man cannot even finish all the works that are necessary for him in order to know God, and still he speaks of worldly duties."

Sri Ramakrishna smiled a little, looked at M, and made a sign with his eye, as if to say, "What he says is right."

M understood that this question of performing duties was an extremely difficult one.

Purna arrived.

MASTER: "Who told you about our being here?"

PURNA: "Sarada."

MASTER (to the women devotees): "Give him some refreshments."

Narendra was preparing to sing. The Master and the devotees were eager to hear his music. Narendra sang:

> Śiva, Thy ready thunderbolt
> Rules over meadows, hills, and sky!
> O God of gods! O Slayer of Time!
> Thou the Great Void, the King of Dharma!
> Śiva, Thou Blessed One, redeem me;
> Take away my grievous sin.

At Narayan's request Narendra sang:

Come. Come, Mother. Doll of my soul! My heart's
    delight!
In my heart's lotus come and sit, that I may see Thy
    face.
Alas! sweet Mother, even from birth I have suffered
    much;
But I have borne it all, Thou knowest, gazing at Thee.
Open the lotus of my heart, dear Mother. Reveal Thy-
    self there.

Sri Ramakrishna was in samādhi. He was sitting on
a pillow, dangling his feet, facing the north and
leaning against the wall. The devotees were seated
around him. The Master gradually regained consciousness of the outer world.

It was late in the evening. Lamps were burning
in the drawing-room.

MASTER (*in an ecstatic mood*): "There is no one
else here; so I am telling you this. He who from the
depth of his soul seeks to know God will certainly
realize Him. He must. He alone who is restless for
God and seeks nothing but Him will certainly realize
Him."

Saturday, June 13, 1885

About three o'clock in the afternoon Sri Ramakrishna was resting in his room after the midday meal.
A pundit was sitting on a mat on the floor. Near the
north door of the room stood a brāhmin woman who
had recently lost her only daughter and was stricken
with grief. Kishori, too, was in the room. M arrived
and saluted the Master. He was accompanied by
Dwija and a few other devotees.

Sri Ramakrishna was not well. He had been suffering from an inflamed throat. These were the hot days of summer. M was not keeping well either, and of late he had not been able to visit Sri Ramakrishna frequently.

MASTER (*to M*): "How are you? It is nice to see you. The bel-fruit you sent me the other day was a very good one."

M: "I am slightly better now, sir."

MASTER: "It is very hot. Take a little ice now and then. I have been feeling the heat very much myself; so I ate a great deal of ice cream. That is why I have this sore throat. The saliva smells very bad.

"I have said to the Divine Mother: 'Mother, make me well. I shall not eat ice cream any more.' Next I said to Her that I wouldn't eat ice either. Since I have given my word to the Mother, I shall certainly not eat these things. But sometimes I become forgetful. Once I said that I wouldn't eat fish on Sundays; but one Sunday I forgot and ate fish. But I cannot consciously go back on my word."

A devotee had brought some ice. Again and again the Master asked M, "Shall I eat it?"

M said humbly, "Please don't eat it without consulting the Mother." Sri Ramakrishna did not take the ice. The Master began to talk about Divine Incarnation.

MASTER (*to M*): "Do you know why God incarnates Himself as a man? It is because through a human body one can hear His words. He sports through it. He tastes Divine Bliss through a human body. But through His other devotees God manifests only a small part of Himself. A devotee is like something you get a little juice from after much sucking

—like a flower you get a drop of honey from after much sucking. (*To M*) Do you understand this?"

M: "Yes, sir. Very well."

MASTER: "There is such a thing as inborn tendencies. After performing many good deeds in his previous lives, when a man is born for the last time, he becomes guileless; he acts somewhat like a madcap.

"To tell you the truth, everything happens by God's will. When He says 'Yea,' everything comes to pass, and when He says 'Nay,' everything comes to a standstill."

The brāhmin lady still stood near the north door. She was a widow. Her only daughter had been married to a very aristocratic man, a landlord in Calcutta with the title of Rājā. Whenever the daughter visited her she was escorted by liveried footmen. Then the mother's heart swelled with pride. Just a few days ago the daughter had died, and now she was beside herself with sorrow. For the last few days she had been running to the Master from her home at Bāghbāzār like an insane person. She was eager to know whether Sri Ramakrishna could suggest any remedy for her unquenchable grief. Sri Ramakrishna resumed the conversation.

MASTER (*to M*): "The truth is that God alone is real and all else unreal. Men, universe, house, children—all these are like the magic of the magician. The magician strikes his wand and says: 'Come delusion! Come confusion!' Then he says to the audience, 'Open the lid of the pot; see how the birds fly into the sky.' But the magician alone is real and his magic unreal. The unreal exists for a second and then vanishes.

"God is like an ocean, and living beings are its

bubbles. They are born there and they die there. Children are like the few small bubbles around a big one.

"God alone is real. Make an effort to cultivate love for Him and find out the means to realize Him. What will you gain by grieving?"

All sat in silence. The brāhmin lady said, "May I go home now?" The Master said to her tenderly: "Do you want to go now? It is very hot. Why now? You can go later in a carriage with the devotees."

Captain arrived with his children.

Sri Ramakrishna said to Kishori, "Please show the temples to the children." He began to talk to Captain. Sri Ramakrishna was sitting on the small couch, facing the north, and he asked Captain to sit in front of him on the same couch.

A DEVOTEE: "Bankim has written a life of Krishna."

MASTER: "I hear that Bankim says that one needs passions such as lust."

A DEVOTEE: "He has written in his magazine that the purpose of religion is to give expression to our various faculties: physical, mental, and spiritual."

CAPTAIN: "I see. He believes that lust and so forth are necessary. But he doesn't believe that Sri Krishna could enjoy His sportive pleasure in the world, that God could incarnate Himself in a human form and sport in Vrindāvan with Rādhā and the gopis."

MASTER (smiling): "But these things are not written in the newspaper. How could he believe them?

"A man said to his friend, 'Yesterday, as I was passing through a certain part of the city, I saw a house fall with a crash.' 'Wait,' said the friend. 'Let me look it up in the newspaper.' But this incident wasn't mentioned in the paper. Thereupon the man said, 'But the paper doesn't mention it.' His friend replied, 'I saw it with my own eyes.' 'Be that as it may,' said the man, 'I can't believe it as long as it isn't in the paper.'

"How can Bankim believe that God sports about as a man? He doesn't get it from his English education. It is very hard to explain how God fully incarnates Himself as man. Isn't that so? The manifestation of Infinity in this human body only three and a half cubits tall!"

CAPTAIN: "Krishna is God Himself. In describing Him we have to use such terms as 'whole' and 'part.' "

MASTER: "Whole and part are like fire and its sparks. An Incarnation of God is for the sake of the bhaktas and not of the jnanis."

Sri Ramakrishna was talking thus to Captain and the devotees when Jaygopal Sen and Trailokya of the Brāhmo Samāj arrived. They saluted the Master and sat down. Sri Ramakrishna looked at Trailokya with a smile and continued the conversation.

MASTER: "It is on account of the ego that one is not able to see God. In front of the door of God's mansion lies the stump of ego. One cannot enter the mansion without jumping over the stump.

"There was once a man who had acquired the power to tame ghosts. One day, at his summons, a ghost appeared. The ghost said: 'Now tell me what you want me to do. The moment you cannot give me any work I shall break your neck.' The man had many things to accomplish, and he had the ghost do them all, one by one. At last he could find nothing more for the ghost to do. 'Now,' said the ghost, 'I am going to break your neck.' 'Wait a minute,' said the man. 'I shall return presently.' He ran to his teacher and said: 'Revered sir, I am in great danger. This is my trouble.' And he told his teacher his trouble and asked, 'What shall I do now?' The teacher said: 'Do this. Tell the ghost to straighten this kinky hair.' The ghost devoted itself day and night to straightening the hair. But how could it make a kinky hair straight? The hair remained kinky.

"Likewise, the ego seems to vanish this moment, but it reappears the next. Unless one renounces the ego, one does not receive God's grace.

"A guardian is appointed only for a minor. A boy cannot safeguard his property; therefore the king assumes responsibility for him. God does not take over our responsibilities unless we renounce our ego.

"Once Lakshmi and Nārāyana were seated in Vaikuntha, when Nārāyana suddenly stood up. Lakshmi had been stroking His feet. She said, 'Lord, where are You going?' Nārāyana answered: 'One of My devotees is in great danger. I must save him.' With these words He went out. But He came back immediately. Lakshmi said, 'Lord, why have You returned so soon?' Nārāyana smiled and said: 'The devotee was going along the road overwhelmed with love for Me. Some washermen were drying clothes on the grass, and the devotee unknowingly walked over the clothes. At this the washermen chased him and were going to beat him with their sticks. So I ran out to protect him.' 'But why have You come back?' asked Lakshmi. Nārāyana laughed and said: 'I saw the devotee himself picking up a brick to throw at them. (*All laugh.*) So I came back.'"

TRAILOKYA: "It is very difficult to get rid of the ego. People only think they are free from it."

MASTER: "Gauri would not refer to himself as 'I'

lest he should feel egotistic. He would say 'this' instead. I followed his example and would refer to myself as 'this' instead of 'I.' Instead of saying, 'I have eaten,' I would say, 'This has eaten.' Mathur noticed it and said one day: 'What is this, revered father? Why should you talk that way? Let them talk that way. They have their egotism. You are free from it; you don't have to talk like them.'

"During the stage of sādhanā one should describe God by all His attributes. One day Hazra said to Narendra: 'God is Infinity. Infinite is His splendour. Do you think He will accept your offerings of sweets and bananas or listen to your music? This is a mistaken notion of yours.' Narendra at once sank ten fathoms. So I said to Hazra, 'You villain! Where will these youngsters be if you talk to them like that?' How can a man live if he gives up devotion? No doubt God has infinite splendour; yet He is under the control of His devotees. A rich man's gatekeeper came to the parlour where his master was seated with his friends. He stood on one side of the room. In his hand he had something covered with a cloth. He was very hesitant. The master asked him, 'Well, gatekeeper, what have you in your hand?' Very hesitantly the servant took out a custard-apple from under the cover, placed it in front of his master, and said, 'Sir, it is my desire that you eat this.' The master was impressed with his servant's devotion. With great love he took the fruit in his hand and said: 'Ah! This is a very nice custard-apple. Where did you pick it? You must have taken a great deal of trouble to get it.'

"A man cannot renounce action as long as he desires worldly enjoyment. As long as one cherishes a desire for enjoyment, one performs action.

"A bird sat absent-mindedly on the mast of a ship anchored in the Ganges. Slowly the ship sailed out into the ocean. When the bird came to its senses, it could find no shore in any direction. It flew toward the north hoping to reach land; it went very far and grew very tired but could find no shore. What could it do? It returned to the ship and sat on the mast. After a long while the bird flew away again, this time toward the east. It couldn't find land in that direction either; everywhere it saw nothing but limitless ocean. Very tired, it again returned to the ship and sat on the mast. After resting a long while the bird went toward the south, and then toward the west. When it found no sign of land in any direction, it came back and settled down on the mast. It did not leave the mast again, but sat there without making any further effort. It no longer felt restless or worried. Because it was free from worry it made no further effort."

CAPTAIN: "Ah, what an illustration!"

MASTER: "Worldly people wander about to the four quarters of the earth for the sake of happiness. They don't find it anywhere; they only become tired and weary. When through their attachment to 'woman' and 'gold' they only suffer misery, they feel an urge toward dispassion and renunciation. Most people cannot renounce 'woman' and 'gold' without first enjoying them.

"But what is there to enjoy in the world? The pleasure is only transitory. One moment it exists and the next moment it disappears.

"The world is like an overcast sky that steadily pours down rain: the face of the sun is seldom seen. There is mostly suffering in the world. On account of the cloud of 'woman' and 'gold' one cannot see the sun. Some people ask me: 'Sir, why has God created

such a world? Is there no way out for us?' I say to
them: 'Why shouldn't there be a way out? Take
shelter with God and pray to Him with a yearning
heart for a favourable wind, that you may have things
in your favour. If you call on Him with yearning,
He will surely listen to you.'"

It was evening. A lamp was lighted in Sri Ramakrishna's room and incense was burnt. Lamps also
were lighted in the different temples and buildings.
The orchestra was playing in the nahabat. Soon the
evening service would begin in the temples.

Sri Ramakrishna sat on the small couch. After chanting the names of the different deities, he meditated
on the Divine Mother. The evening service was over.
Sri Ramakrishna paced the room, now and then talking
to the devotees.

Presently Narendra arrived. He was accompanied
by Sarat and one or two other young devotees. They
all saluted the Master.

At the sight of Narendra Sri Ramakrishna's love
overflowed. He tenderly touched Narendra's chin as
one touches a baby's to show one's love. He said in
a loving voice, "Ah, you have come!"

Tuesday, July 28, 1885

Sri Ramakrishna paid a visit to Nanda Bose's
mansion to see his collection of pictures of the Hindu
deities. From there he went to the house of the brāhmani[2] who was grief-stricken on account of her daughter's death. It was an old brick house. Entering it, the
Master passed the cowshed on his left. He and the
devotees went to the roof, where they took seats.

----

[2] Brāhmin lady.

People were standing there in rows. Others were seated. They were all eager to get a glimpse of Sri Ramakrishna.

The brāhmani had a sister; both of them were widows. Their brothers also lived in the house with their families. The brāhmani had been busy all day making arrangements to entertain Sri Ramakrishna. While the Master was at Nanda Bose's house she had been extremely restless, going out of her house every few minutes to see if he was coming. He had promised to come to her place from Nanda's. Because of his delay she had thought perhaps he would not come at all.

Sri Ramakrishna was seated on a carpet. M, Narayan, Jogin, Devendra, and others were seated on a mat. A few minutes later the younger Naren and some other devotees arrived. The brāhmani's sister came to the Master and saluted him. She said: "Sister has just gone to Nanda Bose's house to inquire the reason for your delay in coming. She will return presently."

A sound was heard downstairs and she exclaimed, "There she comes!" She went down. But it was not the brāhmani.

Sri Ramakrishna sat there smiling, surrounded by devotees.

M (to Devendra): "What a grand sight! All these people—young and old, men and women—standing in lines, eager to have a glimpse of him and hear his words."

DEVENDRA (to the Master): "M says that this place is better than Nanda's. The devotion of these people is amazing."

Sri Ramakrishna laughed.

The brāhmani's sister exclaimed, "Here comes sister!" The brāhmani came and saluted the Master. She was beside herself with joy. She did not know what to say. In a half-choked voice she said: "This joy is too much for me. Perhaps I shall die of it. Tell me, friends, how I shall be able to live. I did not feel such a thrill even when Chandi, my daughter, used to visit the house accompanied by liveried footmen, with armed guards lining both sides of the street. Oh! Now I have no trace of my grief at her death. I was afraid he[3] would not come. Then I thought, if that happened, I should throw into the Ganges all the things I had arranged for his reception and entertainment. I should not speak to him any more. If he visited a place, I should go there, look at him from a distance, and then come away.

"Let me go and tell everybody how happy I am. Let me go and tell Yogin of my good luck."

Still overwhelmed with joy she said: "A labourer won a hundred thousand rupees in a lottery. The moment he heard the news he died of sheer joy. Yes, he really and truly died. I am afraid the same thing is going to happen to me. Please bless me, friends, or else I shall certainly die."

The brāhmani was extremely happy at the sight of the devotees. She said: "I am so happy to see you all here. I have brought the younger Naren; without him, who would there be to make us laugh?"

She was talking like this when her sister came up and said: "Come down, sister! How can I manage things if you stay here? Can I do it all by myself?"

But the brāhmani was overwhelmed with joy. She could not take her eyes from the Master and the devotees.

After a while she very respectfully took Sri Rama-

[3] Meaning Sri Ramakrishna.

krishna to another room and offered him sweets and other refreshments. The devotees were entertained on the roof.

It was about eight o'clock in the evening. Sri Ramakrishna was ready to leave. When he came to the door, the brāhmani asked her sister-in-law to salute the Master. Next, one of her brothers took the dust of the Master's feet. Referring to him, she said: "He is one of my brothers. He is a little foolish." "No, no!" said the Master. "They are all good."

A man showed the way with a light. At places it was dark. Sri Ramakrishna stood in front of the cowshed. The devotees gathered around him. M saluted the Master, who was about to go to the house of Ganu's mother.

Sri Ramakrishna was seated in the drawing-room of Ganu's mother's house. It was on the street floor. The room was used by a concert party. Several young men played on their instruments now and then for the pleasure of the Master. It was eight-thirty in the evening. Moonlight flooded the streets, the houses, and the sky. It was the first day after the full moon.

The brāhmani, who had also come, was visiting the drawing-room and the inner apartments alternately. Every few minutes she would come to the door of the drawing-room and look at the Master. Some youngsters from the neighbourhood also looked at him through the windows. The people of the locality, young and old, came thronging to see the saint.

The younger Naren saw the boys in the street climbing the windows. He said to them: "Why are you here? Get away! Go home!" The Master said tenderly,

"Let them stay." Every now and then he chanted: "Hari Om! Hari Om!" A few minutes later the brāhmani said to Sri Ramakrishna, "Please come inside."

MASTER: "Why?"

BRĀHMANI: "The refreshments are served there. Please come."

MASTER: "Why not bring them here?"

BRĀHMANI: "Ganu's mother requests you to bless the room with the dust of your feet. Then the room will be turned into Benares and anyone dying in it will have no trouble hereafter."

Sri Ramakrishna went inside accompanied by the brāhmani and the young men of the family. The devotees were strolling outside in the moonlight. M and Binode were pacing the street south of the house and recalling the various incidents in the life of their beloved Master.

Sri Ramakrishna had returned to Balaram's house. He was resting in the small room to the west of the drawing-room. It was quite late, almost a quarter to eleven.

Sri Ramakrishna said to Jogin, "Please rub my feet gently." M was sitting near by. While Jogin was rubbing his feet the Master said suddenly: "I feel hungry. I should like some farina pudding."

The brāhmani had accompanied the Master and the devotees to Balaram's house. Her brother knew how to play the drums. Sri Ramakrishna said, "It will be helpful to get her brother when Narendra or some other singer wants to sing."

Sri Ramakrishna ate a little pudding. Jogin and the

other devotees left the room. M was stroking the Master's feet. They talked together.

MASTER (*referring to the brāhmani and her relatives*): "Ah! How happy they were!"

M: "How amazing! A similar thing happened with two women at the time of Jesus. They too were sisters and devoted to Christ. Martha and Mary."

MASTER (*eagerly*): "Tell me the story."

M: "Jesus Christ, like you; went to their house with His devotees. At the sight of Him one of the sisters was filled with ecstatic happiness. The other sister, all by herself, was arranging the food to entertain Jesus. She complained to the Master, saying: 'Lord, please judge for yourself—how wrong my sister is! She is sitting in your room and I am doing all these things by myself.' Jesus said: 'Your sister indeed is blessed. She has developed the only thing needful in human life: love of God.'"

MASTER: "Well, after seeing all this, what do you feel?"

M: "I feel that Christ, Chaitanyadeva, and yourself —all three are one and the same. It is the same Person that has become all these three."

MASTER: "Yes, yes! One! One! It is indeed one. Don't you see that it is He alone who dwells here in this way?"

As he said this, Sri Ramakrishna pointed with his finger to his own body.

M: "You explained clearly, the other day, how God incarnates Himself on earth."

MASTER: "Tell me what I said."

M: "You told us to imagine a field extending to the horizon and beyond. It extends without any obstruction;

but we cannot see it on account of a wall in front of us. In that wall there is a round hole. Through the hole we see a part of that infinite field."

MASTER: "Tell me what that hole is."

M: "You are that hole. Through you can be seen everything—that infinite field without any end."

Sri Ramakrishna was very much pleased. Patting M's back, he said: "I see you have understood. That's fine!"

M: "It is indeed difficult to understand that. One cannot quite grasp how God, Perfect Brahman that He is, can dwell in that small body.

"You also told us about Jesus."

MASTER: "What did I say?"

M: "You went into samādhi at the sight of Jesus Christ's picture in Jadu Mallick's garden house. You saw Jesus come down from the picture and merge in your body."

Sri Ramakrishna was silent a few moments. Then he said to M: "Perhaps there is a meaning in what has happened to my throat [referring to the sore in his throat]. This has happened lest I should make myself light before all; lest I should go to all sorts of places and sing and dance."

Sri Ramakrishna lay down inside the mosquito curtain. M fanned him. The Master turned on his side. He told M how God incarnates Himself in a human body. He told him, further, about his (M's) spiritual ideal.

MASTER: "At the beginning I too passed through such states that I did not see divine forms. Even now I don't see them often."

M: "Among all the forms God chooses for his lilā, I like best His play as a human being."

MASTER: "That is enough. And you are seeing me."

Sunday, August 9, 1885

Sri Ramakrishna was sitting in his room at Dakshineswar. It was eight o'clock in the evening. The Master was talking to Mahimacharan. Rakhal, M, and one or two companions of Mahimacharan were in the room. Mahimacharan was going to spend the night at the temple garden.

MASTER: "It will be sufficient for the youngsters who come here if they know only two things. If they know these, they will not have to practise much discipline and austerity. First, who I am, and second, who they are. Many of the youngsters belong to the inner circle.

"Those belonging to the inner circle will not attain liberation. I shall have to assume a human body again, in a northwesterly direction."

Mahimacharan recited some texts from the scriptures. He also described various mystic rites of the Tantra.

MASTER: "Well, some say that my soul, going into samādhi, flies about like a bird in the Mahākāśa, the Infinite Space.

"Once a sādhu of Hrishikesh came here. He said to me: 'There are five kinds of samādhi. I find you have experienced them all. In these samādhis one feels the movement of the spiritual current to be like that of an ant, a fish, a monkey, a bird, or a serpent.'

"Sometimes the spiritual current rises through the spine, crawling like an ant.

"Sometimes, in samādhi, the soul swims joyfully in the ocean of divine ecstasy, like a fish.

"Sometimes, when I lie down on my side, I feel the spiritual current pushing me like a monkey and playing with me joyfully. I remain still. That current,

like a monkey, suddenly with one jump reaches the
Sahasrāra. That is why you see me jump up with a
start.

"Sometimes, again, the spiritual current rises like a
bird hopping from one branch to another. The place
where it rests feels like fire. It hops from one centre
to another, and thus gradually to the head.

"Sometimes the spiritual current moves like a snake.
Going up in a zigzag way, it at last reaches the head
and I go into samādhi.

"A man's spiritual consciousness is not awakened
unless his Kundalini is aroused.

"The Kundalini dwells in the Mulādhāra. When it
is aroused, it passes along the Sushumnā nerve, goes
through the centres of Svādhisthāna, Manipura, and
so on, and at last reaches the head. This is called the
movement of the mahāvāyu, the great spiritual current.
It culminates in samādhi.

"One's spiritual consciousness is not awakened by the
mere reading of books. One should also pray to God.
The Kundalini is aroused if the aspirant feels restless
for God. To talk of Knowledge from mere study and
hearsay! What will that accomplish?

"Just before my attaining this state of mind it was
revealed to me how the Kundalini is aroused, how the
lotuses of the different centres blossom forth, and how
all this culminates in samādhi. This is a very secret
experience. I saw a boy twenty-two or twenty-three
years old, exactly resembling me, enter the Sushumnā
nerve and commune with the lotuses, touching them
with his tongue. He began with the centre at the
anus and passed through the centres at the sexual
organ, navel, and so on. The different lotuses of those
centres—four-petalled, six-petalled, ten-petalled, and so

forth—had been drooping. At his touch they stood erect.

"When he reached the heart—I distinctly remember it—and communed with the lotus there, touching it with his tongue, the twelve-petalled lotus, which was hanging head down, stood erect and opened its petals. Then he came to the sixteen-petalled lotus in the throat and the two-petalled lotus in the forehead. And last of all, the thousand-petalled lotus in the head blossomed. Since then I have been in this state."

Sri Ramakrishna came down to the floor and sat near Mahimacharan. M and a few other devotees were near him. Rakhal also was in the room.

MASTER (to Mahima): "For a long time I have wanted to tell you my spiritual experiences, but I could not. I feel like telling you today.

"You say that by mere sādhanā one can attain a state of mind like mine. But it is not so. There is something special here [referring to himself]."

Rakhal, M, and the others became eager to hear what the Master was going to say.

MASTER: "God talked to me. It was not merely His vision. Yes, He talked to me. Under the banyan-tree I saw Him coming from the Ganges. Then we laughed so much! By way of playing with me He cracked my fingers. Then He talked. Yes, He talked to me.

"For three days I wept continuously. And He revealed to me what is in the Vedas, the Purānas, the Tantras, and the other scriptures.

"One day He showed me the māyā of Mahāmāya. A small light inside a room began to grow, and at last it enveloped the whole universe.

"Further, He revealed to me a huge reservoir of water covered with green scum. The wind moved a little of the scum and immediately the water became visible; but in the twinkling of an eye, scum from all sides came dancing in and again covered the water. He revealed to me that the water was like Satchidānanda, and the scum, like māyā. On account of the māyā, Satchidānanda is not seen. Though now and then one may get a glimpse of It, again māyā covers It.

"God reveals the nature of the devotees to me before they arrive. I saw Chaitanya's party singing and dancing near the Panchavati, between the banyan-tree and the bakul-tree. I noticed Balaram there. If it weren't for him, who would there be to supply me with sugar candy and such things? (*Pointing to M*) And I saw him too.

"I had seen Keshab before I actually met him—I had seen him and his party in my samādhi. In front of me sat a roomful of men. Keshab looked like a peacock sitting with its tail spread out. The tail meant his followers. I saw a red gem on Keshab's head. That indicated his rajas. He said to his disciples, 'Please listen to what he [meaning the Master] is saying.' I said to the Divine Mother: 'Mother, these people hold the views of "Englishmen." Why should I talk to them?' Then the Mother explained to me that it would be like this in the Kaliyuga. Keshab and his followers got from here [meaning himself] the names of Hari and the Divine Mother.

(*Pointing to himself*) "There must be something special here. Long ago a young man named Gopal Sen used to visit me. He who dwells in me placed His foot on Gopal's chest. Gopal said in an ecstatic mood: 'You will have to wait here a long time. I cannot live any more with worldly people.' He took leave of me.

Afterwards I heard that he was dead. Perhaps he was born as Nityagopal.

"I have had many amazing visions. I had a vision of the Indivisible Satchidānanda. Inside It I saw two groups with a fence between them. On one side were Kedar, Chuni, and other devotees who believe in the Personal God. On the other side was a luminous space like a heap of red brick-dust. Inside it was seated Narendra immersed in samādhi. Seeing him absorbed in meditation, I called aloud, 'Oh, Narendra!' He opened his eyes a little. I came to realize that he had been born, in another form, in Simlā[4] in a kāyastha family. At once I said to the Divine Mother, 'Mother, entangle him in māyā; otherwise he will give up his body in samādhi.' Kedar, a believer in the Personal God, peeped in and ran away with a shudder.

"Therefore I feel that it is the Divine Mother Herself who dwells in this body and plays with the devotees. When I first had my exalted state of mind, my body would radiate light. My chest was always flushed. Then I said to the Divine Mother: 'Mother, do not reveal Thyself outwardly. Please go inside.' That is why my complexion is so dull now. If my body were still luminous, people would have tormented me; a crowd would always have thronged here. Now there is no outer manifestation. That keeps weeds away. Only genuine devotees will remain with me now. Do you know why I have this illness? It has the same significance. Those whose devotion to me has a selfish motive behind it will run away at the sight of my illness.

"I cherished a desire. I said to the Mother, 'O Mother, I shall be the king of the devotees.'

[4] The section of Calcutta in which Narendra was born.

"Again, this thought arose in my mind: 'He who sincerely prays to God will certainly come here. He must.' You see, that is what is happening now. Only people of that kind come.

"My parents knew who dwells inside this body. Father had a dream at Gayā. In that dream Raghuvir said to him, 'I shall be born as your son.'

"God alone dwells inside this body. Such renunciation of 'woman' and 'gold'! Could I have accomplished that myself? I have never enjoyed a woman even in a dream.

"Nangtā instructed me in Vedānta. In three days I went into samādhi. At the sight of my samādhi under the mādhavi vine, he was quite taken aback and exclaimed, 'Ah! What is this?' Then he came to know who resides in this body. He said to me, 'Please let me go.' At these words of Totāpuri I went into an ecstatic mood and said, 'You cannot go till I realize the truth of Vedānta.'

"Day and night I lived with him. We talked only Vedānta. The Brāhmani[5] often said to me: 'Don't listen to Vedānta. It will spoil your devotion to God.'

"I said to the Divine Mother: 'Mother, please get me a rich man. If you don't, how shall I be able to protect this body? How shall I be able to keep the sādhus and devotees near me?' That is why Mathur Babu provided for my needs for fourteen years.

"He who dwells in me tells me beforehand what particular class of devotees will come to me. When I have a vision of Gaurānga, I know that devotees of Gaurānga are coming. When I have a vision of Kālī, the Śāktas come.

[5] Refers to the Bhairavi Brāhmani, a brāhmin nun who was one of Sri Ramakrishna's spiritual guides.

"At the time of the evening service I used to cry out from the roof of the kuthi, weeping: 'Oh, where are you all? Come to me!' You see, they are all gathering here, one by one.

"I have practised all kinds of sādhanā: jnānayoga, karmayoga, and bhaktiyoga. I have even gone through the exercises of hathayoga to increase longevity. There is another Person dwelling in this body. Otherwise, after attaining samādhi, how could I live with the devotees and enjoy the love of God? Koar Singh used to say to me: 'I have never before seen a person who has returned from the plane of samādhi. You are none other than Nānak.'

"I live in the midst of worldly people; on all sides I see 'woman' and 'gold.' Nevertheless, this is the state of my mind: unceasing samādhi and bhāva. That is the reason Pratap[6] said, at the sight of my ecstatic mood: 'Good heavens! It is as if he were possessed by a ghost!' "

Rakhal, M, and the others were speechless as they drank in this account of Sri Ramakrishna's unique experiences.

But did Mahimacharan understand the import of these words? Even after hearing them, he said to the Master, "These things have happened to you on account of your meritorious actions in your past births." Mahima still thought that Sri Ramakrishna was a sādhu or a devotee of God. The Master nodded assent to Mahima's words and said: "Yes, the result of past actions. God is like an aristocrat who has many mansions. Here [referring to himself] is one of His drawing-rooms. The bhakta is God's drawing-room."

[6] Pratap Chandra Mazumdar, a distinguished member of the Brāhmo Samāj.

It was one o'clock in the morning, the fourteenth day of the dark fortnight of the moon. There was intense darkness everywhere. One or two devotees were pacing the concrete embankment of the Ganges. Sri Ramakrishna was up. He came out and said to the devotees, "Nangtā told me that at this time, about midnight, one hears the Anāhata sound."

In the early hours of the morning Mahimacharan and M lay down on the floor of the Master's room. Rakhal slept on a camp cot. Now and then Sri Ramakrishna paced up and down the room with his clothes off, like a five-year-old child.

Friday, August 28, 1885

It was dawn. Sri Ramakrishna was awake and meditating on the Divine Mother. On account of his illness the devotees could not enjoy his sweet chanting of the Mother's name.

Sri Ramakrishna was seated on the small couch. He asked M, "Well, why have I this illness?"

M: "People will not have the courage to approach you unless you resemble them in all respects. But they are amazed to find that in spite of such illness you don't know anything but God."

MASTER (*smiling*): "Balaram also said, 'If even you can be ill, then why should we wonder about our illness?' Even Brahman weeps, entangled in the snare of the five elements."

M: "Jesus Christ, too, wept like an ordinary man at the suffering of His devotees."

MASTER: "How was that?"

M: "There were two sisters, Mary and Martha. Lazarus was their brother. All three were devoted to

Jesus. Lazarus died. Jesus was on His way to their house. One of the sisters, Mary, ran out to meet Him. She fell at His feet and said, weeping, 'Lord, if You had been here my brother would not have died!' Jesus wept to see her cry.

"Then Jesus went to the tomb of Lazarus and called him by name. Immediately Lazarus came back to life and walked out of the tomb."

MASTER: "But I cannot do those things."

M: "That is because you don't want to. These are miracles; therefore you aren't interested in them. These things draw people's attention to their bodies and they don't feel genuine devotion for God. That is why you don't perform miracles. But there are many similarities between you and Jesus Christ."

MASTER (smiling): "What else?"

M: "You don't ask your devotees to fast or practise other austerities. You don't prescribe hard and fast rules about food. Christ's disciples did not observe the sabbath; so the Pharisees took them to task. Thereupon Jesus said: 'They have done well to eat. As long as they are with the bridegroom they must make merry.'"

MASTER: "What does that mean?"

M: "Christ meant that as long as the disciples live with the Incarnation of God they should only make merry. Why should they be sorrowful? But when He returns to His own abode in heaven, then will come the days of their sorrow and suffering."

MASTER (smiling): "Do you find anything else in me that is similar to Christ?"

M: "Yes, sir. You say: 'The youngsters are not yet touched by "woman" and "gold"; they will be able to assimilate instruction. It is like keeping milk in a new pot: the milk may turn sour if it is kept in a pot in which curd has been made.' Christ also spoke that way."

MASTER: "What did He say?"

M: " 'If new wine is kept in an old bottle, the bottle may crack. If an old cloth is patched with new cloth, the old cloth tears away.'

"Further, you tell us that you and the Mother are one. Likewise, Christ said, 'I and My Father are one.' "

MASTER (smiling): "Anything else?"

M: "You say to us, 'God will surely listen to you if you call on Him earnestly.' So also Christ said, 'Knock and it shall be opened unto you.' "

MASTER: "Well, if God has incarnated Himself again, is it a fractional or a partial or a complete manifestation of God? Some say it is a complete manifestation."

M: "Sir, I don't quite understand the meaning of complete or partial or fractional Incarnation. But I have understood, as you explained it, the idea of a round hole in a wall."

MASTER: "Tell me about it."

M: "There is a round hole in the wall. Through it one is able to see part of the field on the other side of the wall. Likewise, through you one sees part of the Infinite God."

MASTER: "True. You can see five or six miles of the meadow at a stretch."

M saluted the Master and took his leave. Sri Ramakrishna said to him tenderly: "Come early in the morning tomorrow. The hot sun of the rainy season is bad for the health."

Tuesday, September 1, 1885

Sri Ramakrishna was about to take his bath. A devotee was rubbing his body with oil on the verandah south of his room. M came there after finishing his bath in the Ganges and saluted the Master.

After bathing, Sri Ramakrishna wrapped himself in a towel and with folded hands saluted the deities in the temples from afar. He could not go to the temples because of his illness.

It was the sacred Janmāsthami day, the birthday of Krishna. Ram and other devotees had brought new clothes for Sri Ramakrishna. He put them on and looked charming. Again he saluted the deities.

It was eleven o'clock in the morning. The devotees were gradually arriving from Calcutta. Balaram, Narendra, the younger Naren, Navagopal, and a Vaishnava from Kātoā arrived. Rakhal and Latu were staying with Sri Ramakrishna. A Punjabi sādhu had been staying in the Panchavati for some days. He was going along the footpath in the garden. The Master said: "I don't attract him. He has the attitude of a jnāni. I find him dry as wood."

Sri Ramakrishna and the devotees returned to the Master's room.

The Vaishnava from Kātoā began to ask Sri Ramakrishna questions. He was squint-eyed.

VAISHNAVA: "Sir, is a man born again?"

MASTER: "It is said in the Gitā that a man is reborn with those tendencies which are in his mind at the time of his death. King Bharata thought of his deer at the time of death and was reborn as a deer."

VAISHNAVA: "I could believe in rebirth only if an eye-witness told me about it."

MASTER: "I don't know about that, my dear sir. I cannot cure my own illness, and you ask me to tell you what happens after death!

"What you are talking about only shows your petty mind. Try to cultivate love of God. You are born as a human being only to attain divine love. You have come to the orchard to eat mangoes; what need is there of knowing how many thousands of branches and millions of leaves there are in the orchard? To bother about what happens after death! How silly!"

Girish Ghosh arrived in a carriage with one or two friends. He was drunk. He was weeping as he entered the room. He wept as he placed his head on Sri Ramakrishna's feet.

Sri Ramakrishna affectionately patted him on the back. He said to a devotee, "Prepare a smoke for him."

Girish raised his head and said with folded hands: "You alone are the Perfect Brahman! If that is not so then everything is false.

"It is such a pity that I could not be of any service to you." He uttered these words with a tenderness that made several devotees weep.

Girish continued: "O Lord, please grant me the boon that I may serve you for a year. Who cares for salvation? One finds it everywhere. I spit on it. Please tell me that you will accept my service for one year."

MASTER: "People around here are not good. Some may criticize you for what you have been saying."

GIRISH: "I don't care. Please tell—"

MASTER: "All right. You may serve me when I go to your house—"

GIRISH: "No, it is not that. I want to serve you here."

Girish was insistent. The Master said, "Well, that depends on God's will."

Referring to the Master's throat trouble, Girish said: "Please say, 'Let it be cured.' All right, I shall thrash it out. Kāli! Kāli!"

MASTER: "You will hurt me."

GIRISH: "O throat, be cured! (*He blows at the throat like an exorciser.*) Are you not all right? If you aren't cured by this time, you certainly will be if I have any devotion to your feet. Say that you are cured."

MASTER (*sharply*): "Leave me alone. I can't say those things. I can't ask the Divine Mother to cure my illness.

"All right. I shall be cured if it is God's will."

GIRISH: "You are trying to fool me. All depends on your will."

MASTER: "Shame! Never say that again. I look on myself as a devotee of Krishna, not as Krishna Himself. You may think as you like. You may look on your guru as God. Nevertheless, it is wrong to talk as you are talking. You must not talk that way again."

GIRISH: "Please say that you will be cured."

MASTER: "Very well, if that pleases you."

Girish was still under the influence of drink. Now and then he said to Sri Ramakrishna, "Well, sir, how is it that you were not born this time with your celestial beauty?"

A few moments later he said, "I see, this time it will be the salvation of Bengal."

A devotee said to himself: "Why Bengal alone? It will be the salvation of the whole world."

Girish said, addressing the devotees: "Does any of you understand why he is here? It is for the liberation of men. Their suffering has moved him to assume a human body."

The coachman was calling Girish. He got up and

was going toward the man. The Master said to M: "Watch him. Where is he going? I hope he won't beat the coachman!" M accompanied Girish.

Presently Girish returned. He prayed to Sri Rama-krishna and said, "O Lord, give me purity that I may not have even a trace of sinful thought."

MASTER: "You are already pure. You have such faith and devotion! You are in a state of joy, aren't you?"

GIRISH: "No, sir. I feel bad. I have worries. That is why I have taken so much liquor."

A few minutes afterwards Girish said: "Lord, I am amazed to find that I, even I, have been given the privilege of serving the Perfect Brahman. What aus-terities have I practised to deserve this privilege?"

Sri Ramakrishna took his midday meal. On account of his illness he ate very little.

The Master's natural tendency of mind was to soar into the plane of God-Consciousness. He would force his mind to be conscious of the body. But, like a child, he was incapable of looking after his body. Like a child he said to the devotees: "I have eaten a little. I shall rest now. You may go out for a little while." Sri Ramakrishna rested a few minutes. The devotees re-turned to the room.

The Vaishnava from Kātoā was arguing.

MASTER (to the Vaishnava): "Stop that sizzling noise! When butter containing water is heated over a fire, it makes that sound. If a man but once tastes the joy of God, his desire to argue takes wing. What will you achieve by quoting from books? The pundits recite verses and do nothing else."

Dr. Rakhal arrived to examine Sri Ramakrishna. The Master said to him eagerly, "Come in and sit down."

The conversation with the Vaishnava continued.

MASTER: "Man should possess dignity and alertness. Only he whose spiritual consciousness is awakened possesses this dignity and alertness and can be called a man. Futile is human birth without the awakening of spiritual consciousness."

Like a child Sri Ramakrishna said to the physician, "Sir, please cure my throat."

DOCTOR: "Do you ask me to cure you?"

MASTER: "The physician is Nārāyana Himself. I honour everybody."

The doctor was going to examine Sri Ramakrishna's throat. The Master said, "Dr. Mahendra Sarkar pressed my tongue the way they press a cow's."

Like a child Sri Ramakrishna said to the physician, pulling at his shirt-sleeves again and again, "Sir! My dear sir! Please cure my throat." Looking at the laryngoscope he said with a smile: "I know it. You will see the reflection in it."

Narendra sang. But on account of the Master's illness there was not much music.

→ 10 ←

SRI RAMAKRISHNA AT ŚYĀMPUKUR

Sunday, October 18, 1885

THE DOCTORS had definitely diagnosed Sri Ramakrishna's illness as cancer. No proper arrangement
for his treatment and nursing could be made at Dakshineswar. He needed the constant attention of a
physician, which could not be given at the temple
garden. Furthermore, the devotees who lived in Calcutta found it very inconvenient to attend on him daily
at Dakshineswar. Therefore the older devotees rented
a small two-storey house in Bāghbāzār, Calcutta, and
brought the Master there. Sri Ramakrishna, however,
did not like the place and went to Balaram's house.
In a few days a new house was engaged in Śyāmpukur,
in the northern section of Calcutta. The Master was
taken there and was placed under the treatment of
Dr. Mahendra Lal Sarkar. The new building had two
large rooms and two smaller ones on the second floor.
One of the larger rooms was used as the parlour, and
in the other the Master lived. Of the two smaller
rooms, one was used as a sleeping-room by the devotees,
and the other by the Holy Mother. Near the exit to
the roof was a small, covered, square space, where the
Holy Mother stayed during the day and prepared the
Master's food.

It was afternoon. Dr. Sarkar arrived accompanied by

415

his son Amrita and Hem. Narendra and other devotees were present.

Sri Ramakrishna was talking aside to Amrita. He asked him, "Do you meditate?" He further said to him: "Do you know what one feels in meditation? The mind becomes like a continuous flow of oil—it thinks of one object only, and that is God. It is not aware of anything else."

Sri Ramakrishna was talking to the devotees.

MASTER (to the doctor): "Your son does not believe in the Incarnation of God. That's all right. It doesn't matter if he does not believe in it.

"Your son is a nice boy. Why shouldn't he be? Does a mango-tree of the fine 'Bombay' variety ever bear sour mangoes? How firm his faith in God is! That man is a true man whose mind dwells in God. He alone is a man whose spiritual consciousness has been awakened and who is firmly convinced that God alone is real and all else is illusory. Your son does not believe in Divine Incarnation; but what does that matter? It is enough if he believes that God exists and that all this universe and its living beings are the manifestations of His Power—like a rich man and his garden.

"Some say that there are ten Divine Incarnations, some twenty-four, while others say that there are innumerable Incarnations. If you see anywhere a special manifestation of God's Power, you may know that God has incarnated Himself there. That is my opinion.

"There is another view, according to which God has become all that you see. That which is the Absolute has also its relative aspect, and that which is the Relative has also its absolute aspect. You cannot set aside the Absolute and understand just the Relative. And it is only because there is the Relative that you can transcend it step by step and reach the Absolute. So long as 'I-consciousness' exists, a man cannot go beyond the Relative."

DOCTOR: "Quite true."

In Dr. Sarkar's opinion, God created men and ordained that every soul should make infinite progress. He would not believe that one man was greater than another. That was why he did not believe in the doctrine of Divine Incarnation.

DOCTOR: "I believe in infinite progress. If that is not so, then what is the use of leading a mere five or six years' existence in the world? I would rather hang myself with a rope round my neck.

"Incarnation! What is that? To cower before a man who excretes filth! It is absurd. But if you speak of a man as the reflection of God's Light—yes, that I admit."

GIRISH (smiling): "But you have not seen God's Light."

Dr. Sarkar was hesitating before giving a reply. A friend who sat near him whispered something into his ear.

DOCTOR (to Girish): "You too have not seen anything but a reflection."

GIRISH: "I see it! I see the Light! I shall prove that Sri Krishna is an Incarnation of God or I shall cut out my tongue!"

MASTER: "All this is useless talk. It is like the ravings of a delirious patient. A delirious patient says, 'I will drink a whole tank of water; I will eat a whole pot of rice.' The physician says: 'Yes, yes. You will have all these. We shall give you whatever you want when you are convalescent.' There are signs of Perfect Knowledge. One is that reasoning comes to an end."

DOCTOR: "But can one retain Perfect Knowledge permanently? You say that all is God. Then why have you taken up this profession of a paramahamsa? And why do these people attend on you? Why don't you keep silent?"

MASTER (smiling): "Water is water whether it is still or moves or breaks into waves.

"It is God who dwells within as the Pure Mind and Pure Intelligence. I am the machine and He is its Operator. I am the house and He is the Indweller."

DOCTOR: "Let me ask you something. Why do you ask me to cure your illness?"

MASTER: "I talk that way as long as I am conscious of the 'jar' of the 'ego.' Think of a vast ocean filled with water on all sides. A jar is immersed in it. There is water both inside and outside the jar; but the water does not become one unless the jar is broken. It is God who has kept this 'jar' of 'ego' in me."

DOCTOR: "What is the meaning of 'ego' and all that you are talking about? You must explain it to me. Do you mean to say that God is playing tricks on us?"

GIRISH: "Sir, how do you know that He is not playing tricks?"

MASTER (smiling): "It is God who has kept this 'ego' in us. All this is His play, His lilā. A king has four sons. They are all princes; but when they play, one becomes a minister, another a police officer, and so on. Though a prince, he plays as a police officer.

(To the doctor) "Listen. If you realize Ātman you will see the truth of all I have said. All doubts disappear after the vision of God."

DOCTOR: "But is it ever possible to get rid of all doubts?"

MASTER: "Learn from me as much as I have told

you. But if you want to know more, you must pray to
God in solitude. Ask Him why He has so ordained."

The doctor remained silent.

MASTER: "Well, you love reasoning. Listen a little
to the Vedāntic reasoning. A magician came to a king
to show his magic. When the magician moved away a
little the king saw a rider on horseback approaching
him. He was brilliantly arrayed and had various weapons in his hands. The king and the audience began to
reason out what was real in the phenomenon before
them. Evidently the horse was not real, nor the robes,
nor the armour. At last they found out beyond the
shadow of a doubt that the rider alone was there. The
significance of this is that Brahman alone is real and
the world unreal. Nothing whatsoever remains if you
analyse."

DOCTOR: "I don't object to this."

MASTER: "But it is not easy to get rid of illusion.
It lingers even after the attainment of Knowledge. A
man dreamt of a tiger. Then he woke up and his
dream vanished. But his heart continued to palpitate.

"Some thieves came to a field. A straw figure resembling a man had been put there to frighten in-
truders. The thieves were scared by the figure and
could not persuade themselves to enter the field. One
of them, however, went near and found that it was
only a figure made of straw. He came back to his companions and said, 'There is nothing to be afraid of.'
But still they refused to go; they said that their hearts
were beating fast. Then the daring thief laid the figure
on the ground and said, 'It is nothing, it is nothing.'
This is the process of 'Neti, neti.' "

DOCTOR: "These are fine words."

MASTER (smiling): "What kind of words?"

DOCTOR: "Fine."

MASTER: "Then give me a 'thank you.'" [The Master said the words "thank you" in English.]

DOCTOR: "Don't you know what is in my mind? I go to so much trouble to come and visit you!"

Sri Ramakrishna asked Dr. Sarkar to have some refreshments. The devotees served him with sweets.

DOCTOR (*while eating*): "Now I say 'thank you' for the sweets; but it is not for your teachings. Why should I give that 'thank you' in words?"

October 22, 1885

It was Thursday evening, a few days after the Durgā Pujā. Sri Ramakrishna sat on his bed in his room on the second floor, with Dr. Sarkar, Ishan, and several of the devotees. Although Dr. Sarkar was a very busy physician, he would spend a long time—sometimes six or seven hours—in Sri Ramakrishna's company. He had great love for the Master and looked on the devotees as his own kith and kin. A lamp was burning in the room. Moonlight illumined the outside world.

Addressing Ishan, a householder devotee, the Master said: "Blessed indeed is the householder who, while he performs his duties in the world, cherishes love for the Lotus Feet of God. He is indeed a hero. He is like a man who carries a heavy load of two maunds on his head and at the same time watches a bridal procession. One cannot lead such a life without great spiritual power. Again, such a man is like the mudfish, which lives in the mud but is not stained by it. Or again, such a householder may be compared to a waterfowl, which is constantly diving under water, and yet, by fluttering its wings only once, shakes off all trace of wet.

"You may ask, 'Is there any difference between the

realizations of two jnānis, one a householder and the other a monk?' The reply is that the two belong to one class. Both of them are jnānis; they have the same experience. But a householder jnāni has reason to fear. He cannot altogether get rid of his fear as long as he is to live in the midst of 'woman' and 'gold.' If you constantly live in a room full of soot, you are sure to soil your body, be it ever so little, no matter how clever you may be.

"When they parch rice, a few grains jump out of the frying pan to the ground. These are white, like mallikā flowers, without the slightest stain on them. But the grains that remain in the pan are also good, though not as immaculate as the fresh mallikā flower. They are a little stained. In the same way, if a monk who has renounced the world attains divine wisdom, he appears as spotless as the white flower; but one who stays in the frying pan of the world after attaining Knowledge may get a little blemish. (*All laugh.*)

"Although a jnāni living in the world may have a little blemish, yet this does not injure him. The moon undoubtedly has dark spots, but these do not obstruct its light."

DOCTOR: "It is very hard to control the sense-organs. They are like restive horses, whose eyes must be covered with blinkers. In the case of some horses it is necessary to prevent them from seeing at all."

MASTER: "A man need not fear anything if but once he receives God's grace, if but once he obtains the vision of God, if but once he attains Self-Knowledge. Then the six passions cannot do him any harm.

"Eternally perfect souls like Nārada and Prahlāda did not have to take the trouble to put blinkers on their eyes. The child who holds his father's hand, while walking along a narrow ridge in the paddy-field, may loosen his hold in a moment of carelessness and slip into the ditch. But it is quite different if the father holds the child's hand. Then the child never falls into the ditch."

DOCTOR: "But it is not proper for a father to hold his child by the hand."

MASTER: "It is not quite like that. Great sages have childlike natures. Before God they are always like children. They have no pride. Their strength is the strength of God, the strength of their Father. They have nothing to call their own. They are firmly convinced of that."

DOCTOR: "Can you make a horse move forward without first covering his eyes with blinkers? Can one realize God without first controlling the passions?"

MASTER: "What you say is according to the path of discrimination. Through that path, too, one attains God. The jnānis say that an aspirant must, first of all, purify his heart. First he needs spiritual exercises; then he will attain Knowledge.

"But God can also be realized through the path of devotion. Once the devotee develops love for the Lotus Feet of God and enjoys the singing of His name and attributes, he does not have to make a special effort to restrain his senses. For such a devotee the sense-organs come under control of themselves.

"Suppose a man has just lost his son and is mourning his death. Can he be in a mood to quarrel with others that very day, or enjoy a feast in a friend's house? Can he, that very day, show his pride before others or enjoy sense pleasures?

"If a moth discovers light, can it remain in darkness any longer?"

DOCTOR (*with a smile*): "Of course it cannot. It would rather fly into the flame and perish."

MASTER: "Oh no, that's not so. A lover of God does not burn himself to death, like the moth. The light to which he rushes is like the light of a gem. That light is brilliant, no doubt, but it is also cooling and soothing. That light does not scorch his body; it gives him joy and peace.

"One realizes God by following the path of discrimination and knowledge. But this is an extremely difficult path. It is easy enough to say such things as: 'I am not the body, mind, or intellect; I am beyond grief, disease, and sorrow; I am the embodiment of Existence-Knowledge-Bliss Absolute; I am beyond pain and pleasure; I am not under the control of the sense-organs'; but it is very hard to assimilate these ideas and practise them. Suppose I *see* my hand cut by a thorn and blood gushing out; then it is not right for me to say: 'Why, my hand is not cut by the thorn! I am all right.' In order to be able to say that, I must first of all burn the thorn itself in the fire of Knowledge."

DOCTOR (*to the devotees*): "If he [meaning Sri Ramakrishna] had studied books he could not have acquired so much knowledge. Faraday communed with nature; that is why he was able to discover many scientific truths. He could not have known so much from the mere study of books. Mathematical formulas only throw the brain into confusion and bar the path to original inquiry."

MASTER: "There was a time when I lay on the ground in the Panchavati and prayed to the Divine Mother: 'O Mother, reveal to me what the karmis[1] have realized through their ritualistic worship, what

[1] The ritualists.

the yogis have realized through yoga, and what the jnānis have realized through discrimination.' How intensely I communed with the Divine Mother! How can I describe it all? Ah, what a state I passed through! Sleep left me completely."

He continued: "I have not read books. But people show me respect because I chant the Divine Mother's name. Sambhu Mallick said about me, 'Here is a great hero without a sword or shield!' (Laughter.)

(To the doctor) "It is very difficult to understand that God can be a finite human being and at the same time the all-pervading Soul of the universe. The Absolute and the Relative are His two aspects. How can we say emphatically with our small intelligence that God cannot assume a human form? Can we ever understand all these ideas with our little intellect?

"Therefore one should trust in the words of holy men and great souls, those who have realized God. They constantly think of God, as a lawyer of his lawsuits.

"Unless a man is guileless, he cannot easily have faith in God. God is far, far away from the mind steeped in worldliness. Worldly intelligence creates many doubts and many forms of pride—pride of learning, wealth, and the rest. (Pointing to the doctor) But he is guileless.

"For seekers of God the constant company of holy men is necessary. The disease of worldly people has become chronic, as it were. They should carry out the instruction of holy men. What will they gain by merely hearing their advice? They must not only take the prescribed medicine but also follow a strict diet. Diet is important."

DOCTOR: "Yes, it is the diet, more than anything else, that causes the cure."

GIRISH (*to the doctor, with a smile*): "You have already spent three or four hours here. What about your patients?"

DOCTOR: "Well, hang my practice and patients! I see I shall lose everything on account of your paramahamsa! (*All laugh.*)

(*To Girish, M, and the other devotees*) "My friends, consider me as one of you. I am not saying this as a physician. But if you think of me as your own, then I am yours.

(*To the Master*) "The illness you are suffering from does not permit the patient to talk with people. But my case is an exception. You may talk with me when I am here." (*All laugh.*)

MASTER: "Please cure my illness. I cannot chant God's name and glories."

DOCTOR: "Meditation is enough."

MASTER: "What do you mean? Why should I lead a monotonous life? I enjoy my fish in a variety of dishes: curried fish, fried fish, pickled fish, and so forth! Sometimes I worship God with rituals, sometimes I repeat His name, sometimes I meditate on Him, sometimes I sing His name and glories, sometimes I dance in His name."

DOCTOR: "Neither am I monotonous."

MASTER: "Your son Amrita does not believe in God's Incarnation. What is the harm in that? One realizes God if one believes Him to be formless. One also realizes God if one believes that He has form. Two things are necessary for the realization of God: faith and self-surrender. Man is ignorant by nature. Errors are natural to him. Whatever path you may follow, you must pray to God with a restless heart. He is the Ruler of the soul within. He will surely listen to your prayer if it is sincere. Whether you follow the ideal of the Personal God or that of the Impersonal Truth, you will realize God alone, provided you are restless for Him.

"Your son Amrita is a nice boy."

DOCTOR: "He is your disciple."

MASTER (*with a smile*): "There is not a fellow under the sun who is my disciple. On the contrary, I am everybody's disciple. All are the children of God. All are His servants. I too am God's child. I too am His servant. 'Uncle Moon' is every child's uncle!"

Saturday, October, 24, 1885

It was about one o'clock in the afternoon. Sri Ramakrishna was seated on the second floor of the house at Śyāmpukur. Dr. Sarkar, Narendra, Mahimacharan, M, and other devotees were in the room. Referring to the homoeopathic system of medicine, the Master said to Dr. Sarkar, "This treatment of yours is very good."

DOCTOR: "According to homoeopathy the physician has to check up the symptoms of the disease with the medical book. It is like Western music. The singer follows the score.

"Where is Girish Ghosh? Never mind. Don't trouble him. He didn't sleep last night."

MASTER: "Well, when I am in samādhi I feel intoxicated as if I were drunk with siddhi. What have you to say about that?"

DOCTOR (*to M*): "In that state the nerve centres cease to function. Hence the limbs become numb. Again, the legs totter because all the energy rushes toward the brain. Life consists of the nervous system. There is a nerve centre in the nape of the neck called the medulla oblongata. If that is injured one may die."

Mahima Chakravarty began to describe the Kundalini. He said: "The Sushumnā nerve runs through the spinal cord in a subtle form. None can see it. That is what Śiva says."

DOCTOR: "Śiva examined man only in his maturity. But the Europeans have examined man in all stages of his life from the embryo to maturity. It is good to know comparative history. From the history of the Sonthāls one learns that Kāli was a Sonthāl woman. She was a valiant fighter. (*All laugh.*)

"Don't laugh, please. Let me tell you how greatly the study of comparative anatomy has benefited men. The difference between the actions of the pancreatic juice and bile was at first unknown. But later Claude Bernard examined the stomach, liver, and other parts of the rabbit and demonstrated that the action of bile is different from the action of the pancreatic juice. Therefore it stands to reason that we should watch the lower animals as well. The study of man alone is not enough.

"Similarly, the study of comparative religion is highly beneficial.

"Why do his [meaning the Master's] words go straight to our hearts? He has experienced the truths of different religions. He himself has practised the disciplines of the Hindu, Christian, Mussalmān, Śākta, and Vaishnava religions. The bees can make good honey only if they gather nectar from different flowers."

Sri Ramakrishna asked Narendra to sing. Narendra sang:

> O King of kings, reveal Thyself to me.
> I crave Thy mercy. Cast on me Thy glance.
> At Thy feet I dedicate my life,
> Seared in the fiery furnace of the world.
>
> My heart, alas, is deeply stained with sin;
> Ensnared in māyā, I am all but dead.
> Compassionate Lord, revive my fainting soul
> With the life-giving nectar of Thy grace.

MASTER: "And sing that one—'All that exists art Thou.'"

DOCTOR: "Ah!"

Narendra sang the song.

The singing was over. Dr. Sarkar sat there almost spellbound. After a time, with folded hands, he said very humbly to Sri Ramakrishna: "Allow me to take my leave now. I shall come again tomorrow."

Dr. Sarkar took his leave. It was evening, the first night after the full moon. Sri Ramakrishna stood up, lost in samādhi. Nityagopal stood beside him in a reverent attitude.

Sri Ramakrishna took his seat. Nityagopal was stroking his feet. Devendra, Kalipada, and many other devotees were seated by his side.

It was arranged that a few of the younger men should stay to nurse the Master by turns. M also was going to spend the night there.

Sunday, October 25, 1885

It was about half-past six in the morning when M arrived at Śyāmpukur and asked Sri Ramakrishna about his health. He was on his way to Dr. Sarkar to report the Master's condition. The Master said to M: "Tell the doctor that during the early hours of the morning my mouth becomes filled with water and I cough. Also ask him if I may take a bath."

After seven o'clock M came to Dr. Sarkar's house and told him about the Master's condition. The physician's old teacher and one or two friends were in the room. Dr. Sarkar said to his teacher: "Sir, I have been thinking of the Paramahamsa[2] since three in the morning. I couldn't sleep at all. Even now he is in my mind."

One of the doctor's friends said to him: "Sir, I hear that some speak of the Paramahamsa as an Incarnation of God. You see him every day. How do you feel about it?"

DOCTOR: "I have the greatest regard for him as a man."

M (to the doctor's friend): "It is very kind of Dr. Sarkar to treat him."

DOCTOR: "Kindness? What do you mean?"

M: "Not toward him, but toward us."

DOCTOR: "You see, you don't know my actual loss on account of the Paramahamsa. Every day I fail to see two or three patients. When the next day I go to their houses, of my own accord, I cannot accept any fee since I am seeing them without being called. How can I charge them for my visit?"

M requested the doctor to visit Sri Ramakrishna and returned home.

In the afternoon, about three o'clock, M came to the Master and repeated the conversation he had had with Dr. Sarkar.

[2] Refers to Sri Ramakrishna.

M: "He told me that he had waked at three in the morning and had been thinking of you ever since. When I saw him it was eight o'clock. He said to me, 'Even now the Paramahamsa is in my mind.'"

MASTER (*laughing*): "You see, he has studied English. I cannot ask him to meditate on me; but he is doing it all the same, of his own accord."

M: "He also said about you, 'I have the greatest regard for him as a man.'"

MASTER: "Did you talk of anything else?"

M: "I asked him, 'What is your suggestion today about the patient?' He said: 'Suggestion? Hang it! I shall have to go to him again myself. What else shall I suggest?' (*Sri Ramakrishna laughs.*) Further he said: 'You don't know how much money I am losing every day. Every day I miss two or three calls.'"

There were many devotees, including Narendranath, in the room. Vijaykrishna Goswāmi arrived and respectfully took the dust of the Master's feet. Several Brāhmo devotees came with him. Vijay had cut off his connexion with the Brāhmo Samāj and was practising spiritual discipline independently. Sri Ramakrishna was very fond of him on account of his piety and devotion. Though not a disciple of the Master, Vijay held him in very high respect. He had lived in Dāccā a long time. Recently he had visited many sacred places in upper India.

MAHIMA CHAKRAVARTY (*to Vijay*): "Sir, you have visited many holy places and new countries. Please tell us some of your experiences."

VIJAY: "What shall I say? I realize that everything is here where we are sitting now. This roaming about is useless. At other places I have seen two, five, ten, or twenty-five per cent of him [meaning the Master], at the most. Here alone I find the full one hundred per cent manifestation of God."

MAHIMA: "You are right, sir. Again, it is he [the Master] who makes us roam about or remain in one place."

MASTER (to Narendra): "See what a change has come over Vijay's mind. He is an altogether different person. He is like thick milk from which all the water has been boiled off. You see, I can recognize a paramahamsa by his neck and forehead. Yes, I can recognize a paramahamsa."

MAHIMA (to Vijay): "Sir, you seem to eat less now. Isn't that so?"

VIJAY: "Perhaps you are right. (To the Master) I heard about your illness and have come to see you. Again, in Dāccā—"

MASTER: "What about Dāccā?"

Vijay did not reply and was silent a few moments.

VIJAY: "It is difficult to understand him [meaning the Master] unless he reveals himself. Here alone is the one hundred per cent manifestation of God."

MASTER: "Kedar said the other day, 'At other places we hardly get anything to eat, but here we get a stomachful!'"

MAHIMA: "Why a stomachful? It overflows the stomach."

VIJAY (to the Master, with folded hands): "I have now realized who you are. You don't have to tell me."

MASTER (in a state of ecstasy): "If so, then so be it!"

Saying, "Yes, I have understood," Vijay fell prostrate before the Master. He held the Master's feet on his chest and clung to them. The Master was in deep samādhi, motionless as a picture. The devotees were overwhelmed by this sight. Some burst into tears and some chanted sacred hymns. All eyes were riveted on Sri Ramakrishna. They viewed him in different ways, according to their spiritual unfoldment: some as a great devotee, some as a holy man, some as God Incarnate.

Mahimacharan sang, with tears in his eyes: "Behold, behold the embodiment of Love Divine!"

Now and then he chanted, as if enjoying a glimpse of Brahman:

The Transcendental, beyond the One and the many,
    Existence-Knowledge-Bliss Absolute.

Navagopal was weeping. Bhupati sang:

Hallowed be Brahman, the Absolute, the Infinite, the
    Fathomless,
Higher than the highest, deeper than the deepest
    depths!
Thou art the Light of Truth, the Fount of Love, the
    Home of Bliss:
This universe with all its manifold and blessed modes
Is the enchanting poem of Thine inexhaustible
    thought;
Its beauty overflows on every side.

O Thou Poet, great and primal, in the rhythm of Thy
    thought
Sun and moon arise and move toward their setting;
The stars, gleaming like bits of gems, are the clear
    characters
In which Thy song is written across the blue expanse
    of sky;
The year, with its six seasons, in tune with the
    happy earth,
Proclaims Thy glory to the end of time.

The colours of the flowers reveal Thy flawless beauty,
The waters in their stillness, Thy deep serenity;
The thunder-clap unveils to us the terror of Thy law.
Deep is Thy essence, truly; how can a foolish mind
    perceive it?
Wondering, it meditates on Thee from yuga to yuga's
    end;
Millions upon millions of suns and moons and stars
Bow down to Thee, O Lord, in rapturous awe.

Beholding Thy creation, men and women weep for joy;
The gods and angels worship Thee, O All-pervading
    Presence.
O Thou, the Source of Goodness, bestow on us Thy
    Knowledge,
Bestow on us devotion, bestow pure love and perfect
    peace,
And grant us shelter at Thy hallowed feet.

After a long time Sri Ramakrishna regained consciousness of the world.

MASTER (*to M*): "Something happens to me in that state of intoxication. Now I feel ashamed of myself. In that state I feel as if I were possessed by a spirit. I cease to be my own self. While coming down from that state I cannot count correctly. Trying to count, I say, 'One, seven, eight,' or some such thing."

NARENDRA: "It is because everything is one."

MASTER: "No, it is beyond one and two."

MAHIMA: "Yes, you are right. 'It is neither one nor two.'"

MASTER: "There reason withers away. God cannot be realized through scholarship. He is beyond the scriptures—the Vedas, Purānas, and Tantras."

The conversation was thus going on, when Dr.

Sarkar came into the room and took a seat. He said to the Master: "I woke up at three this morning, greatly worried that you might catch cold. Oh, I thought many other things about you."

MASTER: "I have been coughing and my throat is sore. In the small hours of the morning my mouth was filled with water. My whole body is aching."

DOCTOR: "Yes, I heard all about it this morning."

Mahimacharan told of his trip to various parts of India and said that in Ceylon no man laughed. Dr. Sarkar said, "It may be so; but I shall have to investigate it." (All laugh.)

The conversation turned to the duties of life.

MASTER (to the doctor): "Many think that the duty of a physician is a very noble one. The physician is undoubtedly a noble man if he treats his patients free, out of compassion and moved by their suffering. Then his work may be called very uplifting. But a physician becomes cruel and callous if he carries on his profession for money."

DOCTOR: "You are right. It is undoubtedly wrong for a physician to perform his duties in that spirit. But I don't like to brag before you—"

MASTER: "But the medical profession is certainly very noble if the physician devotes himself to the welfare of others in an unselfish spirit.

"Whatever may be a householder's profession, it is necessary for him to live in the company of holy men now and then. If a man loves God, he will himself seek the company of holy men."

Dr. Sarkar inquired if anybody would sing that day.

MASTER (to Narendra): "Why don't you sing a little?"

Narendra sang:

> Mother, make me mad with Thy love.
> What need have I of knowledge or reason?
> Make me drunk with Thy love's wine;
> O Thou who stealest Thy bhaktas' hearts,
> Drown me deep in the sea of Thy love!
> Here in this world, this madhouse of Thine,
> Some laugh, some weep, some dance for joy:
> Jesus, Buddha, Moses, Gaurānga,
> All are drunk with the wine of Thy love.
> Mother, when shall I be blessed
> By joining their blissful company?

A strange transformation came over the devotees. They all became mad, as it were, with divine ecstasy. The pundit stood up, forgetting the pride of his scholarship, and cried:

> Mother, make me mad with Thy love.
> What need have I of knowledge or reason?

Vijay was the first on his feet, carried away by divine intoxication. Then Sri Ramakrishna stood up, forgetting all about his painful and fatal illness. The doctor, who had been sitting in front of him, also stood up. Both patient and physician forgot themselves in the spell created by Narendra's music. The younger Naren and Latu went into deep samādhi. The atmosphere of the room became electric. Everyone felt the presence of God. Dr. Sarkar, eminent scientist that he was, stood breathless, watching this strange scene. He noticed that the devotees who had gone into samādhi were utterly unconscious of the outer world. All were motionless and transfixed. After a while, as they came down a little to the plane of the relative world, some laughed and some wept. An outsider, entering the room, would have thought that a number of drunkards were assembled there.

A little later Sri Ramakrishna resumed his conversation, the devotees taking their seats. It was about eight o'clock in the evening.

MASTER: "You have just noticed the effect of divine ecstasy. What does your 'science' say about that? Do you think it is a mere hoax?"

DOCTOR (*to the Master*): "I must say that this is all natural, when so many people have experienced it. It cannot be a hoax. (*To Narendra*) When you sang the lines:

> Mother, make me mad with Thy love.
> What need have I of knowledge or reason?

I could hardly control myself. I was about to jump to my feet. With great difficulty I suppressed myself. I said to myself, 'No, I must not display my feelings.'"

MASTER (*with a smile, to the doctor*): "You are unshakable and motionless, like Mount Sumeru. You are a very deep soul. If an elephant enters a small pool, there is a splashing of water on all sides. But this does not happen when it plunges into a big lake; hardly anyone notices it."

DOCTOR: "Nobody can beat you in talk!" (*Laughter.*)

The conversation turned to other things. Sri Ramakrishna described to the doctor his ecstasies at Dakshineswar. He also told him how to control anger, lust, and the other passions.

DOCTOR: "I have heard the story that you were once lying on the ground unconscious in samādhi when a wicked man kicked you with his boots."

MASTER: "You must have heard it from M. The man was Chandra Haldar, a priest of the Kāli temple at Kālighāt; he often came to Mathur Babu's house. One day I was lying on the ground in an ecstatic mood. The room was dark. Chandra Haldar thought I was feigning that state in order to win Mathur's favour. He entered the room and kicked me several times with his boots. It left black marks on my body. Everybody wanted to tell Mathur Babu about it, but I forbade them."

DOCTOR: "This is also due to God's will. Thus you have taught people how to control anger and practise forgiveness."

In the mean time Vijay had become engaged in conversation with the other devotees.

VIJAY: "I feel as if someone were always moving with me. He shows me what is happening even at a distance."

NARENDRA: "Like a guardian angel."

VIJAY: "I have seen him [meaning the Master] in Dāccā. I even touched his body."

MASTER (with a smile): "It must have been someone else."

NARENDRA: "I too have seen him many a time. (To Vijay) How can I say I do not believe your words?"

Tuesday, October 27, 1885

It was half-past five in the afternoon when Dr. Sarkar came to the Master's room at Śyāmpukur, felt his pulse, and prescribed the necessary medicine. Many devotees were present, including Narendra, Girish, Dr. Dukari, the younger Naren, Rakhal, M, Sarat, and Shyam Basu.

Dr. Sarkar talked a little about the Master's illness and watched him take the first dose of medicine.

Then Sri Ramakrishna began to talk to Shyam Basu. Dr. Sarkar started to leave, saying, "Now that you are talking to Shyam Basu, I shall say good-bye to you."

The Master and a devotee asked the doctor if he would like to hear some songs.

DR. SARKAR (to the Master): "I should like it very much. But music makes you frisk about like a kid and cut all sorts of capers. You must suppress your emotion."

Dr. Sarkar took his seat once more, and Narendra began to sing in his sweet voice, to the accompaniment of the tānpurā and mridanga:

In dense darkness, O Mother, Thy formless beauty
    sparkles;
And therefore the yogis meditate in a dark mountain
    cave.
In the lap of boundless dark, upborne on Mahānirvāna's
    waves,
Peace flows serene and inexhaustible.

Taking the form of the Void, enwrapped in the robe
    of darkness,
Who art Thou, Mother, seated alone in the shrine
    of samādhi?
From the Lotus of Thy fear-scattering feet flash Thy
    love's lightnings;
Thy Spirit-face shines forth with laughter terrible and
    loud!

Dr. Sarkar said to M, "This song is dangerous for him." Sri Ramakrishna asked M what the doctor had said. M replied, "The doctor is afraid that this song may throw your mind into samādhi."

In the mean time the Master had partially lost consciousness of the outer world. Looking at the phy-

sician, he said with folded hands: "No, no. Why
should I go into samādhi?" Hardly had he spoken
these words when he went into a deep ecstasy. His
body became motionless, his eyes fixed, his tongue
silent. He sat there like a statue cut in stone, completely unconscious of the outer world. Turned inward were his mind, ego, and all the organs of
perception. He seemed an altogether different person.

Narendra continued his singing, pouring his entire
heart and soul into it:

What matchless beauty! What a bewitching face I
    behold!
The Sovereign of my soul has entered my lowly hut;
The springs of my love are welling forth on every side.
Tell me, my Beloved! O Thou, the Lord of my heart!
What treasure shall I lay before Thy Lotus Feet?
Take Thou my life, my soul; what more can I offer
    Thee?
Take everything that is mine. Deign to accept my all.

In the midst of the singing Sri Ramakrishna had regained consciousness of the outer world. When
Narendra finished the song, the Master continued his
conversation, keeping them all under a spell. The devotees looked at his face in wonder. It did not show
the slightest trace of the agonizing pain of his illness.
It shone with heavenly joy.

Addressing the doctor, the Master said: "Give up
this false modesty. Why should you feel shy about
singing God's name? The proverb says very truly:
'One cannot realize God if one is a victim of shame,
hatred, or fear.' Give up such foolish notions as:
'I am such a great man! Shall I dance chanting the
name of God? What will other great men think of me
on hearing of this? They may say that the doctor, poor

fellow, has been dancing, chanting Hari's name, and thus pity me.' Give up all these foolish notions."

DOCTOR: "I never bother about what people say. I don't care a straw about their opinions."

MASTER: "Yes, I know of your strong feeling about that. (*All laugh.*)

"Go beyond knowledge and ignorance; only then can you realize God. To know many things is ignorance. Pride of scholarship is also ignorance. The unwavering conviction that God alone dwells in all beings is jnāna, knowledge. To know Him intimately is vijnāna, a richer Knowledge. God is beyond both knowledge and ignorance."

SHYAM BASU: "Sir, what remains after one goes beyond both ignorance and knowledge?"

MASTER: "*Nityaśuddhabodharupam*—the Eternal and Ever-pure Consciousness. How can I make it clear to you? A young girl once asked her friend: 'Well, friend, your husband is here. What sort of pleasure do you enjoy with him?' The friend answered: 'My dear, you will know it for yourself when you get a husband. How can I explain it to you?'

"What Brahman is cannot be described in words. One cannot describe in words the joy of play and communion with Satchidānanda. He alone knows, who has realized it."

Addressing Dr. Sarkar, Sri Ramakrishna continued: "Look here. One cannot attain Knowledge unless one is free from egotism. There is a saying:

> When shall I be free?
> When 'I' shall cease to be.

'I' and 'mine'—that is ignorance. 'Thou' and 'Thine' —that is Knowledge. A true devotee says: 'O God,

Thou alone art the Doer; Thou alone doest all. I am a mere instrument; I do as Thou makest me do. All these—wealth, possessions, nay, the universe itself—belong to Thee. This house and these relatives are Thine alone, not mine. I am Thy servant; mine is only the right to serve Thee according to Thy bidding.'

"Those who have read a few books cannot get rid of conceit. Once I had a talk with Kalikrishna Tagore about God. At once he said, 'I know all about that.' I said to him: 'Does a man who has visited Delhi brag about it? Does a gentleman go about telling everyone that he is a gentleman?' "

SHYAM: "But Kalikrishna Tagore has great respect for you."

MASTER: "Oh, how vanity turns a person's head! There was a scavenger woman in the temple garden at Dakshineswar. And her pride! And all because of a few ornaments. One day some men were passing her on the path and she shouted at them, 'Hey! Get out of the way, you people!' If a scavenger woman could talk that way, what can one say about the vanity of others?"

SHYAM: "Sir, if God alone does everything, how is it that man is punished for his sins?"

MASTER: "How like a goldsmith you talk!"

NARENDRA: "In other words, Shyam Babu has a calculating mind, like a goldsmith, who weighs things with his delicate balance."

MASTER: "I say: 'O my foolish boy, eat the mangoes and be happy. What is the use of your calculating how many hundreds of trees, how many thousands of branches, and how many millions of leaves there are in the orchard? You have come to the orchard to eat mangoes. Eat them and be contented.'

(To Shyam) "You have been born in this world

as a human being to worship God; therefore try to acquire love for His Lotus Feet. Why do you trouble yourself to know a hundred other things? What will you gain by discussing 'philosophy'? Look here. One ounce of liquor is enough to intoxicate you. What is the use of your trying to find out how many gallons of liquor there are in the tavern?"

DOCTOR: "Quite so. And what is more, the Wine in God's Tavern is beyond all measure. There is no limit to it."

MASTER (to Shyam): "Why don't you give your power of attorney to God? Rest all your responsibilities on Him. If you entrust an honest man with your responsibilities, will he misuse his power over you? God alone knows whether or not He will punish you for your sins."

DOCTOR: "God alone knows what is in His mind. How can a man guess it? God is beyond all our calculations."

MASTER (to Shyam): "That's the one theme of you Calcutta people. You all say, 'God is stained by the evil of inequality,' because He has made one person happy and another miserable. What these rascals see in themselves they see in God, too."

SHYAM: "We hear a great deal about the subtle body. Can anyone show it to us? Can anyone demonstrate that when a man dies the subtle body leaves the gross body and goes away?"

MASTER: "True devotees don't care a rap about showing you these things. What do they care whether some fool of a big man respects them or not? The desire to have a big man under their control never enters their minds."

SHYAM: "What is the distinction between the gross body and the subtle body?"

MASTER: "The body consisting of the five gross elements is called the gross body. The subtle body is made up of the mind, the ego, the discriminating faculty, and the mind-stuff. There is also a causal body, by means of which one enjoys the Bliss of God and holds communion with Him. Beyond all these is the Mahākāraṇa, the Great Cause. That cannot be expressed by words.

"What is the use of merely listening to words? Do something! How can a man recognize yarns of different counts, such as number forty and number forty-one, unless he is in the trade? Those who deal in yarn do not find it at all difficult to describe a thread of a particular count. Therefore I say, practise a little spiritual discipline; then you will know all these—the gross, the subtle, the causal, and the Great Cause. While praying to God, ask only for love for His Lotus Feet.

"I prayed to the Divine Mother only for love. I offered flowers at Her Lotus Feet and said with folded hands: 'O Mother, here is Thy ignorance and here is Thy knowledge; take them both and give me only pure love for Thee. Here is Thy holiness and here is Thy unholiness; take them both and give me only pure love for Thee. Here is Thy virtue and here is Thy sin; here is Thy good and here is Thy evil; take them all and give me only pure love for Thee. Here is Thy dharma and here is Thy adharma; take them both and give me only pure love for Thee.'

"Dharma means good actions, like giving in charity. If you accept dharma, righteousness, you have to accept adharma, unrighteousness, too. If you accept virtue you have to accept sin. If you accept knowledge you have to accept ignorance. If you accept holiness you have to accept unholiness. It is like a man's being aware of light, in which case he is aware of darkness too. If a man is aware of one he is aware of many too. If he is aware of good he is aware of evil too.

"Blessed is the man who retains his love for the Lotus Feet of God even though he eats pork. But if a man is attached to the world, even though he lives only on boiled vegetables and rice, then—"

DOCTOR: "He is a wretch. But let me interrupt you here and say something. Buddha once ate pork and as a result had colic. To get rid of the pain he would take opium and thus become unconscious. Do you know the meaning of Nirvāna and such stuff? Buddha would become stupefied after eating opium. He would have no consciousness of the outer world. This is what they call Nirvāna!"

All laughed to hear this novel interpretation of Nirvāna. The conversation went on.

SHYAM: "Sir, what do you think of Theosophy?"

MASTER: "The long and short of the matter is that those who go about making disciples belong to a very inferior level. So also do those who want occult powers to walk over the Ganges and to report what a person says in a far-off country and so on. It is very hard for such people to have pure love for God."

SHYAM: "But the Theosophists have been trying to re-establish the Hindu religion."

MASTER: "I don't know much about them."

SHYAM: "You can learn from Theosophy where the soul goes after death—whether to the lunar sphere or the stellar sphere or some other region."

MASTER: "That may be. But let me tell you my

own attitude. Once a man asked Hanumān, 'What day of the lunar fortnight is it?' Hanumān replied: 'I know nothing about the day of the week, the day of the lunar fortnight, the position of the stars in the sky, or any such things. On Rāma alone I meditate.' That is my attitude too."

SHYAM: "The Theosophists believe in the existence of mahātmās. Do you believe in them, sir?"

MASTER: "If you believe in my words, I say yes. But now please leave these matters alone. Come here again when I am a little better. Some way will be found for you to attain peace of mind, if you have faith in me. You must have noticed that I don't accept any gift of money or clothes. We do not take any collection here. That is why so many people come. (*Laughter.*)

(*To the doctor*) "If you won't take offence, I shall tell you something. It is this: You have had enough of such things as money, honour, lecturing, and so on. Now for a few days direct your mind to God. And come here now and then. Your spiritual feeling will be kindled by hearing words about God."

After a little while, as the doctor stood up to take his leave, Girish Chandra Ghosh entered the room and bowed low before the Master. Dr. Sarkar was pleased to see him and took his seat again.

DOCTOR (*pointing to Girish*): "Of course he would not come as long as I was here. No sooner am I about to leave than he enters the room."

Girish and Dr. Sarkar began to talk about the Science Association established by the latter.

MASTER: "Will you take me there one day?"

DOCTOR: "If you go there you will lose all consciousness at the sight of the wondrous works of God."

MASTER: "Oh, indeed!"

DOCTOR (to Girish): "Whatever you may do, please do not worship him as God. You are turning the head of this good man."

GIRISH: "What else can I do? Oh, how else shall I regard a person who has taken me across this ocean of the world, and what is still more, the ocean of doubt? There is nothing in him that I do not hold sacred."

DOCTOR: "Do you think I can't take the dust of his feet? Look here."

The doctor saluted Sri Ramakrishna and touched the Master's feet with his forehead.

GIRISH: "Oh, the angels are saying, 'Blessed, blessed be this auspicious moment!'"

DOCTOR: "What is there to marvel at in taking the dust of a man's feet? I can take the dust of everybody's feet. Give me, all of you, the dust of your feet."

The doctor touched the feet of all the devotees.

NARENDRA (to the doctor): "We think of him [meaning the Master] as a person who is like God. Do you know, sir, what it is like? There is a point between the vegetable creation and the animal creation where it is very difficult to determine whether a particular thing is a vegetable or an animal. Likewise, there is a stage between the man-world and the God-world where it is extremely hard to say whether a creature is a man or God."

DOCTOR: "Well, my dear young friend, one cannot apply analogies to things divine."

NARENDRA: "I do not say that he is God. What I am saying is that he is a godlike man."

DOCTOR: "One should suppress one's feelings in such a matter. It is bad to give vent to them. Alas! No

one understands my own feelings. Even my best friend
thinks of me as a stern and cruel person. Even people
like you will perhaps one day throw me out after
beating me with your shoes."

MASTER: "Don't say such a thing! They love you
so much! They await your coming as eagerly as the
bridesmaids in the bridal chamber await the coming
of the groom."

GIRISH: "Everyone has, the greatest respect for
you."

DOCTOR: "My son and even my wife think of me
as a hard-hearted person. My only crime is that I do
not display my feelings."

GIRISH: "In that case, sir, it would be wise for you
to open the door of your heart, at least out of pity
for your friends; for you see that your friends cannot
otherwise understand you."

DOCTOR: "Will you believe me when I say that my
feelings get worked up even more than yours? (*To
Narendra*) I shed tears in solitude.

(*To Sri Ramakrishna*) "Well, may I say something?
When you are in ecstasy you place your foot on others'
bodies. That is not good."

MASTER: "Do you think I know at that time that I
am touching another with my foot?"

DOCTOR: "You feel that it is not the right thing to
do, don't you?"

MASTER: "How can I explain to you what I experience in samādhi? After coming down from that
state I think, sometimes, that my illness may be due to
samādhi. The thing is, the thought of God makes me
mad. All this is the result of my divine madness. How
can I help it?"

DOCTOR: "Now he accepts my view. He expresses regret for what he does. He is conscious that the act is sinful."

MASTER (to Narendra): "You are very clever. Why don't you answer? Explain it all to the doctor."

GIRISH (to the doctor): "Sir, you are mistaken. He is not expressing regret for touching the bodies of his devotees during samādhi. His own body is pure, untouched by any sin. That he touches others in this way is for their good. Sometimes he thinks he may have got this illness by taking their sins upon himself.

"Think of your own case. Once you suffered from colic. Didn't you have regrets at that time for sitting up and reading till very late at night? Does that prove that reading till the late hours of the night is, in itself, a bad thing? He [meaning Sri Ramakrishna] too may be sorry that he is ill. But that does not make him feel that it is wrong on his part to touch others for their welfare."

Dr. Sarkar felt rather embarrassed and said to Girish: "I confess my defeat at your hands. Give me the dust of your feet." He saluted Girish.

DOCTOR (to Narendra): "Whatever else one may say about him [meaning Girish], one must admit his intellectual powers."

NARENDRA (to the doctor): "You may look at the thing from another standpoint. You can devote your life to scientific research without giving a thought to your health or comfort. But the science of God is the grandest of all sciences. Isn't it natural for him to risk his health to realize God?"

DOCTOR: "All religious reformers, including Jesus, Chaitanya, Buddha, and Mohammed, were in the end filled with egotism. They all said, 'Whatever I say is alone true.' How shocking!"

GIRISH (to the doctor): "Now, sir, you are committing the same mistake. You are accusing them all of egotism. You are finding fault with them. For that very reason you too can be accused of egotism."

Dr. Sarkar remained silent.

NARENDRA (to the doctor): "We offer worship to him bordering on divine worship."

At these words the Master laughed like a child.

Thursday, October 29, 1885

It was about ten o'clock in the morning when M arrived at Dr. Sarkar's house in Sānkhāritolā, Calcutta, to report Sri Ramakrishna's condition. Soon afterwards they got into the doctor's carriage. The doctor visited many patients. He entered a house of the Tagore family at Pāthuriāghātā and was detained there by the head of the family. Returning to the carriage, he began to talk to M about Sri Ramakrishna's illness and how he should be taken care of.

DOCTOR: "Do you intend to send him back to Dakshineswar?"

M: "No, sir. That would greatly inconvenience the devotees. They can always visit him if he is in Calcutta."

DOCTOR: "But it is very expensive here."

M: "The devotees don't mind that. All they want is to be able to serve him. As regards the expense, it must be borne whether he lives in Calcutta or at Dakshineswar. But if he goes back to Dakshineswar the devotees won't always be able to visit him, and that will cause them great worry."

Dr. Sarkar and M arrived at Śyāmpukur and found

the Master sitting with the devotees in his room. Dr. Bhaduri also was there.

Dr. Sarkar examined the Master's pulse and inquired about his condition. The conversation turned to God.

DR. BHADURI: "Shall I tell you the truth? All this is unreal, like a dream."

DR. SARKAR: "Is everything delusion? Then whose is this delusion? And why this delusion? If all know it to be delusion, then why do they talk? I cannot believe that God is real and His creation unreal."

MASTER: "That is a good attitude. It is good to look on God as the Master and oneself as His servant. As long as a man feels the body to be real, as long as he is conscious of 'I' and 'you,' it is good to keep the relationship of master and servant; it is not good to cherish the idea of 'I am He.'

"Let me tell you something else. You see the same room whether you look at it from one side or from the middle of the room."

DR. BHADURI (to Dr. Sarkar): "What I have just said you will find in Vedānta. You must study the scriptures. Then you will understand."

DR. SARKAR: "Why so? Has he [meaning the Master] acquired all this wisdom by studying the scriptures? He too supports my view. Can't one be wise without reading the scriptures?"

MASTER: "But how many scriptures I have heard!"

DR. SARKAR: "A man may mistake the meaning if he only hears. In your case it is not mere hearing."

MASTER (to Dr. Sarkar): "I understand that you spoke of me as insane. That is why they (pointing to M and the others) don't want to go to you."

DR. SARKAR (looking at M): "Why should I call

you [meaning the Master] insane? But I mentioned
your egotism. Why do you allow people to take the
dust of your feet?"

M: "Otherwise they weep."

DR. SARKAR: "That is their mistake. They should
be told about it."

M: "Why should you object to their taking the dust
of his feet? Doesn't God dwell in all beings?"

DR. SARKAR: "I don't object to that. Then you must
take the dust of everyone's feet."

M: "But there is a greater manifestation of God
in some men than in others. There is water everywhere;
but you see more of it in a lake, a river, or an ocean.
Will you show the same respect to a new Bachelor of
Science as you do to Faraday?"

DR. SARKAR: "I agree with that. But why do you
call him God?"

M: "Why do we salute each other? It is because
God dwells in everybody's heart. You haven't given
much thought to this subject."

MASTER (to Dr. Sarkar): "I have already told you
that some people reveal more of God than others. Earth
reflects the sun's rays in one way, a tree in another
way, and a mirror in still another way. You see a better
reflection in a mirror than in other objects."

Dr. Sarkar did not reply. All were silent.

MASTER (to Dr. Sarkar): "You see, you have love
for this [meaning himself]. You told me that you
loved me."

DR. SARKAR: "You are a child of nature. That is
why I tell you all this. It hurts me to see people salute
you by touching your feet. I say to myself, 'They
are spoiling such a good man.' Keshab Sen, too, was
spoiled that way by his devotees. Listen to me—"

MASTER: "Listen to you? You are greedy, lustful, and egotistic."

DR. BHADURI (to Dr. Sarkar): "That is to say, you have the traits of a jiva, an embodied being. These are his traits: lust, egotism, greed for wealth, and a hankering after name and fame. All embodied beings have these traits."

DR. SARKAR (to the Master): "If you talk that way, I shall only examine your throat and go away. Perhaps that is what you want. In that case we should not talk about anything else. But if you want discussion, then I shall say what I think to be right."

All remained silent.

MASTER (to Dr. Sarkar): "Read the Gītā, the Bhāgavata, and the Vedānta, and you will understand all this. Is not God in His creation?"

DR. SARKAR: "Not in any particular object. He is everywhere. And because He is everywhere, He cannot be sought after."

The conversation turned to other things. Sri Ramakrishna constantly experienced ecstatic moods, which the doctor said might aggravate his illness. Dr. Sarkar said to him: "You must suppress your emotion. My feelings, too, are greatly stirred up. I can dance much more than you."

THE YOUNGER NAREN (smiling): "What would you do if your emotion increased a little more?"

DR. SARKAR: "My power of control would also increase."

MASTER AND M: "You may say that now!"

M: "Can you tell us what you would do if you went into an ecstatic mood?"

The conversation turned to money.

MASTER (to Dr. Sarkar): "I don't think about it

at all. You know that very well, don't you? This is not
a pretence."

DR. SARKAR: "Even I have no desire for money—
not to speak of yourself! My cashbox lies open."

MASTER: "Jadu Mallick, too, is absent-minded.
When he takes his meals he sometimes becomes so
absent-minded that he doesn't know whether the
food is good or bad. When someone says to him,
'Don't eat that; it doesn't taste good,' Jadu says: 'Eh?
Is this food bad? Why, that's so!'"

Was the Master hinting that there was an ocean
of difference between absent-mindedness due to the
contemplation of God and absent-mindedness due to
preoccupation with worldly thoughts?

Pointing to Dr. Sarkar, Sri Ramakrishna said to
the devotees, with a smile: "When a thing is boiled
it becomes soft. At first he was very hard. Now he is
softening from inside."

DR. SARKAR: "When a thing is boiled it begins to
soften from the outside. I am afraid that won't happen
to me in this birth." (*All laugh.*)

Dr. Sarkar was about to take his leave. He was
talking to Sri Ramakrishna.

DOCTOR: "Can't you forbid people to salute you by
touching your feet?"

MASTER: "Can all comprehend the Indivisible
Satchidānanda?"

DR. SARKAR: "But shouldn't you tell people what
is right?"

MASTER: "People have different tastes. Besides, all
have not the same fitness for spiritual life."

DR. SARKAR: "How is that?"

MASTER: "Don't you know what difference in taste
is? Some enjoy fish curry; some, fried fish; some,

pickled fish; and again, some, the rich dish of fish
pilau. Then, too, there is difference in fitness. I ask
people to learn to shoot at a banana tree first, then at
the wick of a lamp, and then at a flying bird."

It was dusk. Sri Ramakrishna became absorbed in
contemplation of God. For the time being he forgot
all about his painful disease. Several intimate disciples
sat near him and looked at him intently. After a long
time he became aware of the outer world and said to
M in a whisper: "You see, my mind was completely
merged in the Indivisible Brahman. After that I saw
many things. I found that the doctor will have spiritual
awakening. But it will take some time. I won't have
to tell him much. I saw another person while in that
mood. My mind said to me, 'Attract him too.' I shall
tell you about him later."

Friday, October 30, 1885

About half-past ten M arrived at Dr. Sarkar's house.
He went up to the second floor and sat in a chair
on the porch adjacent to the drawing-room. In front of
Dr. Sarkar was a glass bowl in which goldfish were
kept. Now and then Dr. Sarkar threw some cardamon
shells into the bowl. Again, he threw pellets of flour to
the sparrows. M watched him.

DOCTOR (*smiling, to M*): "You see, these goldfish
are staring at me like devotees staring at God. They
haven't noticed the food I have thrown into the water.
Therefore I say, what will you gain by mere bhakti?
You need knowledge too."

Dr. Sarkar and M entered the drawing-room. There
were shelves all around filled with books. The doctor
rested a little. M looked at the books. He picked up
Canon Farrar's *Life of Jesus* and read a few pages. Dr.

Sarkar told M how the first homoeopathic hospital was started in the teeth of great opposition. He asked M to read the letters relating to it, which had been published in the *Calcutta Journal of Medicine* in 1876. Dr. Sarkar was much devoted to homoeopathy.

M picked up another book, Munger's *New Theology*. Dr. Sarkar noticed it.

DOCTOR: "Munger has based his conclusions on nice argument and reasoning. It is not like your believing a thing simply because a Chaitanya or a Buddha or a Jesus Christ has said so."

M (*smiling*): "Yes, we should not believe Chaitanya or Buddha; but we must believe Munger!"

DOCTOR: "Whatever you say."

M: "We must quote someone as our authority; so it is Munger." (*The doctor smiles.*)

Dr. Sarkar got into his carriage accompanied by M. The carriage proceeded toward Śyāmpukur. It was midday. They gossiped together. The conversation turned to Dr. Bhaduri, who had also been visiting the Master now and then.

M (*smiling*): "Bhaduri said about you that you must begin all over again from the stone and brickbat."

DR. SARKAR: "How is that?"

M: "Because you don't believe in the mahātmās, astral bodies, and so forth. Perhaps Bhaduri is a Theosophist. Further, you don't believe in the Incarnation of God. That is why he said sarcastically that when you died this time you would certainly not be reborn as a human being. That would be far off. You wouldn't be born even as an animal or a bird, or even as a tree or a plant. You would have to begin all over again from stone and brickbat. Then, after many, many births, you might assume a human body."

DR. SARKAR: "Goodness gracious!"

M: "Bhaduri further said that the knowledge of your physical science was a false knowledge and had only temporary value. He gave an analogy. Suppose there are two wells. The one gets its water from an underground spring. The other has no such spring and is filled with rainwater. But the water of the second well does not last a long time. The knowledge of your science is like the rainwater. It dries up."

DR. SARKAR (with a smile): "I see!"

The carriage arrived at Cornwallis Street. Dr. Sarkar picked up Dr. Pratap Mazumdar. Pratap had visited Sri Ramakrishna the previous day. They soon arrived at Śyāmpukur.

Sri Ramakrishna was sitting in his room on the second floor, with several devotees.

Pratap was Dr. Bhaduri's son-in-law. Sri Ramakrishna was speaking to him in praise of his father-in-law.

MASTER (to Pratap): "Ah, what a grand person he has become! He contemplates God and observes purity in his conduct. Further, he accepts both aspects of God: personal and impersonal.

(To Dr. Sarkar) "Do you know what Dr. Bhaduri said about you? He said that, because you didn't believe these things, in the next cycle you would have to begin your earthly life from a stone or brickbat." (All laugh.)

DR. SARKAR (smiling): "Suppose I begin from a stone or brickbat and after many births obtain a human body; but as soon as I come back to this place I shall have to begin over again from a stone or brickbat." (The doctor and all laugh.)

The conversation turned to the Master's ecstasy in spite of his illness.

PRATAP: "Yesterday I saw your ecstatic mood."

MASTER: "It happened of itself; but it was not intense."

DR. SARKAR: "Ecstasy and talking are not good for you now."

MASTER (to Dr. Sarkar): "I saw you yesterday in my samādhi. I found that you are a mine of knowledge; but it is all dry knowledge. You have not tasted divine bliss. (To Pratap, referring to Dr. Sarkar) If he ever tastes divine bliss he will see everything, above and below, filled with it. Then he will not say that whatever he says is right and what others say is wrong. Then he will not utter sharp, strong, pointed words."

The devotees remained silent.

Suddenly Sri Ramakrishna went into a spiritual mood and said to Dr. Sarkar: "Mahindra Babu, what is this madness of yours about money? Why such attachment to wife? Why such longing for name and fame? Give up all these, now, and direct your mind to God with whole-souled devotion. Enjoy the Bliss of God."

Dr. Sarkar sat still without uttering a word. The devotees also remained silent.

MASTER: "Nangtā used to tell me how a jnāni meditates: Everywhere is water; all the regions above and below are filled with water; man, like a fish, is swimming joyously in that water. In real meditation you will actually see all this.

"Do you know another way a jnāni meditates? Think of infinite ākāśa and a bird flying there, joyfully spreading its wings. There is the Chidākāśa, and

Ātman is the bird. The bird is not imprisoned in a cage; it flies in the Chidākāśa. Its joy is limitless."

The devotees listened with great attention to these words about meditation. After a time Pratap resumed the conversation.

PRATAP (to Dr. Sarkar): "When one thinks seriously, one undoubtedly sees everything as a mere shadow."

DR. SARKAR: "If you speak of a shadow, then you need three things: the sun, the object, and the shadow. How can there be any shadow without an object? And you say that God is real and the creation unreal. I say that the creation is real too."

PRATAP: "Very well. As you see a reflection in a mirror, so you see this universe in the mirror of your mind."

DR. SARKAR: "But how can there be a reflection without an object?"

NARENDRA: "Why, God is the object."

Dr. Sarkar remained silent.

MASTER (to Dr. Sarkar): "You said a very fine thing. No one else has said before that samādhi is the result of the union of the mind with God. You alone have said that.

"Shivanath said that one lost one's head by too much thinking of God. In other words, one becomes unconscious by meditating on the Universal Consciousness. Think of it! Becoming unconscious by contemplating Him who is of the very nature of Consciousness and whose Consciousness endows the world with consciousness!

"And what does your 'science' say? This combined with this produces that; that combined with that produces this. One is more likely to lose consciousness by contemplating those things—by handling material things too much."

DR. SARKAR: "One can see God in those things."

M: "If so, one sees God more clearly in man, and still better in a great soul. In a great soul there is a greater manifestation of God."

DR. SARKAR: "Yes, in man, no doubt."

MASTER: "Just fancy, to lose consciousness by contemplating God—through whose Consciousness even inert matter appears to be conscious, and hands, feet, and body move! People say that the body moves of itself; but they do not know that it is God who moves it. They say that water scalds the hand. But water can by no means scald the hand; it is the heat in the water, the fire in the water, that scalds. Man says that the sense-organs do their work of themselves; but he does not know that inside dwells He whose very nature is Consciousness."

Dr. Sarkar stood up. He was about to take his leave. Sri Ramakrishna also stood up.

DR. SARKAR: "People call on God when they are faced with a crisis. Is it for the mere fun of it that they say, 'O Lord! Thou, Thou'? You speak of God because of that trouble in your throat."

MASTER: "There is nothing for me to say."

DR. SARKAR: "Why not? We lie in the lap of God. We feel free with Him. To whom should we speak about our illness if not to Him?"

MASTER: "Right you are. Once in a while I try to speak to Him about it, but I do not succeed."

Dr. Sarkar left. M sat near Sri Ramakrishna and repeated the conversation he had had at Dr. Sarkar's house.

M: "He said: 'Must I believe a thing simply because

a Chaitanya or a Buddha or a Christ has said it? That would not be proper.' "

MASTER: "He has been thinking of this [meaning himself]. His faith is growing. Is it possible to get rid of egotism altogether? Such scholarship! Such fame! And he has so much money! But he doesn't show disrespect for what I say."

Saturday, October 31, 1885

It was about eleven o'clock in the morning. Sri Ramakrishna was sitting in his room with the devotees. He was talking to a Christian devotee named Misra. Misra was born in a Christian family in northwestern India and belonged to the Quaker sect. He was thirty-five years old. Though clad in European fashion he wore the ochre cloth of a sannyāsi under his foreign dress. Two of his brothers had died on the day fixed for the marriage of one of them, and on that very day Misra had renounced the world.

MISRA: " 'It is Rāma alone who dwells in all beings.' "

Sri Ramakrishna said to the younger Naren, within Misra's hearing: "Rāma is one but He has a thousand names. He who is called 'God' by the Christians is addressed by the Hindus as Rāma, Krishna, Iśvara, and other names."

MISRA: "Jesus is not the son of Mary. He is God Himself. (*To the devotees*) Now he (*pointing to Sri Ramakrishna*) appears as you see him—again, he is God Himself. You are not able to recognize him. I have seen him before, in visions, though I see him now directly with my eyes."

MASTER: "Do you see visions?"

MISRA: "Sir, even when I lived at home I used to

see light. Then I had a vision of Jesus. How can I
describe that beauty? How insignificant is the beauty
of a woman compared with that beauty!"

After a while Misra took off his trousers and showed
the devotees the gerruā loincloth that he wore
underneath.

Presently Sri Ramakrishna went out on the porch.
Returning to the room, he said to the devotees, "I saw
him [meaning Misra] standing in a heroic posture." As
he uttered these words he went into samādhi. He stood
facing the west.

Regaining partial consciousness, he fixed his gaze on
Misra and began to laugh. Still in an ecstatic mood,
he shook hands with him and laughed again. Taking
him by the hands, he said, "You will get what you
are seeking."

MISRA (*with folded hands*): "Since that day I have
surrendered to you my mind, soul, and body."

Sri Ramakrishna was laughing, still in an ecstatic
mood.

Dr. Sarkar arrived. At the sight of him Sri Ramakrishna went into samādhi. When his ecstasy abated
a little, he said, "First the bliss of divine inebriation
and then the bliss of Satchidānanda, the Cause of the
cause."

DOCTOR: "Yes."

MASTER: "I am not unconscious."

The doctor realized that the Master was inebriated
with divine bliss. Therefore he said, "No, no! You are
quite conscious."

Sri Ramakrishna smiled and said:

> I drink no ordinary wine,
> But wine of Everlasting Bliss,

As I repeat my Mother Kāli's name;
It so intoxicates my mind
That others take me to be drunk!

As the doctor listened to the words, he too became almost ecstatic. Sri Ramakrishna again went into a deep spiritual mood and placed his foot on the doctor's lap. A few minutes later he became conscious of the outer world and withdrew his foot. He said to the doctor: "Ah, what a splendid thing you said the other day! 'We lie in the lap of God. To whom shall we speak about our illness if not to Him?' If I must pray, I shall certainly pray to Him." As Sri Ramakrishna said these words, his eyes filled with tears. Again he went into ecstasy and said to the doctor, "You are very pure; otherwise I could not have put my foot on your lap." Continuing, he said: " 'He alone has peace who has tasted the Bliss of Rāma.' What is this world? What is there in it? What is there in money, wealth, honour, or creature comforts? 'O mind, know Rāma! Whom else should you know?' "

Friday, November 6, 1885

It was the day of the Kāli Pujā, the worship of the Divine Mother, Sri Ramakrishna's Chosen Ideal. About nine o'clock in the morning the Master, clad in a new cloth, stood in the south room on the second floor of his temporary residence at Śyāmpukur. He had asked M to offer worship to the Divine Mother at Thanthaniā, in the central part of Calcutta, with flowers, green coconut, sugar, and other sweets. After bathing in the Ganges, M had offered the worship and come barefoot to Śyāmpukur. He had brought the prasād with him. Sri Ramakrishna took off his shoes and with great reverence ate a little of the prasād and placed a little on his head.

Sri Ramakrishna was pacing the room with M. He had put on his slippers. In spite of his painful illness his face beamed with joy.

MASTER: "And this song is also very good: 'This world is a framework of illusion.'"

M: "Yes, sir."

Suddenly Sri Ramakrishna gave a start. He put aside his slippers and stood still. He was in deep samādhi. It was the day of the Divine Mother's worship. Was that why he frequently went into samādhi? After a long while he sighed and restrained his emotion as if with great difficulty.

It was about ten o'clock. Sri Ramakrishna was seated on his bed, leaning against the pillow. The devotees sat around him. Ram, Rakhal, Niranjan, Kalipada, M, and many others were present.

Sri Ramakrishna said to M: "It is the day of the Kāli Pujā. It is good to make some arrangements for the worship. Please speak to the devotees about it."

M went to the drawing-room and told the devotees what the Master had said. Kalipada and others busied themselves with the arrangements.

It was the dark night of the new moon. At seven o'clock the devotees made arrangements for the worship of Kāli in Sri Ramakrishna's room on the second floor. Flowers, sandal-paste, vilwa-leaves, red hibiscus, rice pudding, and various sweets and other articles of worship were placed in front of the Master. The devotees were sitting around him. There were present, among others, Sarat, Sashi, Ram, Girish, Chunilal, M, Rakhal, Niranjan, and the younger Naren.

Sri Ramakrishna asked a devotee to bring some incense. A few minutes later he offered all the articles to the Divine Mother. M was seated close to him. Looking at M, he said to the devotees, "Meditate a little." The devotees closed their eyes.

Presently Girish offered a garland of flowers at Sri Ramakrishna's feet. M offered flowers and sandal-paste. Rakhal, Ram, and the other devotees followed him.

Niranjan offered a flower at Sri Ramakrishna's feet, crying, "Brahmamayi! Brahmamayi!" and prostrated himself before him, touching the Master's feet with his head. The devotees cried out, "Jai Mā!," "Hail to the Mother!"

In the twinkling of an eye Sri Ramakrishna went into deep samādhi. An amazing transformation took place in the Master before the very eyes of the devotees. His face shone with a heavenly light. His two hands were raised in the posture of granting boons and giving assurance to the devotees; it was the posture one sees in images of the Divine Mother. His body was motionless; he had no consciousness of the outer world. He sat facing the north. Was the Divine Mother of the Universe manifesting Herself through his person? Speechless with wonder, the devotees looked intently at Sri Ramakrishna, who appeared to them to be the embodiment of the Divine Mother Herself.

The devotees began to sing hymns, one of them leading and the rest following in chorus.

Gradually Sri Ramakrishna came back to the consciousness of the outer world. He asked the devotees to

sing "O Mother Śyāmā, full of the waves of drunkenness divine." They sang the song.

When this song was over, Sri Ramakrishna asked the
devotees to sing "Behold my Mother playing with
Śiva." The devotees sang that one too.

Sri Ramakrishna tasted a little pudding to make the
devotees happy, but immediately went into deep
ecstasy.

A few minutes later the devotees prostrated themselves before the Master and went into the drawing-
room. There they enjoyed the prasād.

It was nine o'clock in the evening. Sri Ramakrishna sent word to the devotees, asking them to go
to Surendra's house to participate in the worship
of Kāli.

They arrived at Surendra's house on Simlā Street
and were received very cordially. Surendra conducted
them to the drawing-room on the second floor. The
house was filled with a festive atmosphere and a veritable mart of joy was created with the songs and
music of the devotees. It was very late at night when
they returned home after enjoying the sumptuous feast
given by Surendra, the Master's beloved disciple.

11

THE MASTER AT COSSIPORE

Wednesday, December 23, 1885

ON FRIDAY, DECEMBER 11, Sri Ramakrishna was moved to a beautiful house at Cossipore, a suburb of Calcutta. The house was situated in a garden covering about five acres of land and abounding in fruit trees and flowering plants. Here the final curtain fell on the Master's life.

At Cossipore he set himself with redoubled energy to the completion of the task of spiritual ministration he had begun long before at Dakshineswar. Realizing that the end of his physical life was approaching, he gave away his spiritual treasures without stint to one and all. He was like one of those fruit-sellers who bring their fruit to the market-place, bargain at first about the prices, but then toward sunset, when the market is about to close, give away the fruit indiscriminately. Here his disciples saw the greatest manifestation of his spiritual powers. Here they saw, also, the fulfilment of his prophecies about his own end: "I shall make the whole thing public before I go." "When people in large numbers come to know and whisper about the greatness of this body, then the Mother will take it back." "The devotees will be sifted into inner and outer circles toward the end." And so on. Here he predicted that a band of young disciples, with Narendranath as their leader, would in due course renounce the world and devote themselves to the realization of God and the service of humanity.

The young devotees had taken up their quarters at the garden house to tend Sri Ramakrishna, although many of them visited their own homes every now and then. The householders came to see the Master almost every day, and some of them occasionally spent the night.

On the morning of December 23 Sri Ramakrishna gave unrestrained expression to his love for the devotees. Touching Kalipada's chest, he said, "May your inner spirit be awakened!" He stroked Kalipada's chin affectionately and said, "Whoever has sincerely called on God or performed his daily religious devotions will certainly come here." In the morning two ladies received his special blessing. In a state of samādhi he touched their hearts with his feet. They shed tears of joy. One of them said to him, weeping, "You are so kind!" His love this day really broke all bounds. He wanted to bless Gopal of Sinthi and said to a devotee, "Bring Gopal here."

It was evening. Sri Ramakrishna was absorbed in meditation on the Mother of the Universe. After a while he began to talk very softly with some of the devotees. Kali, Chunilal, M, Navagopal, Sashi, Niranjan, and a few others were present.

MASTER: "Can you tell me how long it will take to recover from this illness?"

M: "It has been aggravated a little and will take some days."

MASTER: "How long?"

M: "Perhaps five to six months."

Hearing this, Sri Ramakrishna became impatient,

like a child, and said: "So long? What do you mean?"

M: "I mean, sir, for complete recovery."

MASTER: "Oh, that! I am relieved. Can you explain one thing? How is it that in spite of all these visions, all this ecstasy and samādhi, I am so ill?"

M: "Your suffering is no doubt great; but it has a deep meaning."

MASTER: "What is it?"

M: "A change is coming over your mind. It is turning toward the formless aspect of God. Even your 'ego of Knowledge' is vanishing."

MASTER: "That is true. My teaching is coming to an end. I cannot give any more instruction. I see that everything is God Himself. And sometimes I say to myself, 'Whom shall I teach?' You see, because I am living in a rented house all kinds of devotees are coming here. I hope I shall not have to put up a 'signboard,' like Shashadhar or Krishnaprasanna Sen,[1] announcing my lectures." (The Master and M laugh.)

M: "There is yet another purpose in this illness. It is the final sifting of disciples. The devotees have achieved in these few days what they could not have realized by five years' tapasyā. Their love and devotion are growing by leaps and bounds."

MASTER: "That may be true; but Niranjan went back home. (To Niranjan) Please tell me how you feel."

NIRANJAN: "Formerly I loved you, no doubt, but now it is impossible for me to live without you."

M: "One day I found out how great these young men were."

MASTER: "Where?"

[1] Shashadhar and Krishnaprasanna were two well-known Hindu preachers, contemporaries of Sri Ramakrishna.

M: "Sir, one day I stood in a corner of the house at Śyāmpukur and watched the devotees. I clearly saw that every one of them had made his way here through almost insurmountable obstacles and given himself over to your service."

As Sri Ramakrishna listened to these words he became abstracted. He was silent a few moments. Presently he went into samādhi.

Regaining consciousness of the outer world, he said to M: "I saw everything passing from form to formlessness. I want to tell you all the things I saw, but I cannot. Well, this tendency of mine toward the formless is only a sign of my nearing dissolution. Isn't that so?"

M (wonderingly): "It may be."

MASTER: "Even now I see the Formless Indivisible Satchidānanda—just like that. . . . But I am suppressing my feelings with great difficulty.

"What you said about the sifting of disciples was right: this illness is showing who belong to the inner circle and who to the outer. Those who are living here, renouncing the world, belong to the inner circle; and those who pay occasional visits and ask, 'How are you, sir?' belong to the outer circle.

(To M) "When God assumes a human body for the sake of His devotees, many of His devotees accompany Him to this earth. Some of them belong to the inner circle, some to the outer circle, and some become the suppliers of His physical needs.

"I experienced one of my first ecstasies when I was ten or eleven years old, as I was going through a meadow to a shrine of the Divine Mother. What a vision! I became completely unconscious of the outer world.

"I was twenty-two or twenty-three when the Divine Mother one day asked me in the Kāli temple, 'Do you want to be *Akshara*?' I didn't know what the word meant. I asked Haladhari about it. He said, '*Kshara* means jiva, living being; *Akshara* means Paramātman, the Supreme Soul.'

"At the hour of the evening worship in the Kāli temple I would climb to the roof of the kuthi and cry out: 'O devotees, where are you all? Come to me soon! I shall die in the company of worldly people!' I told all this to the 'Englishmen.'[2] They said it was all an illusion of my mind. 'Perhaps it is,' I said to myself, and became calm. But now it is all coming true; the devotees are coming.

"The Divine Mother also showed me in a vision the five suppliers of my needs; first, Mathur Babu, and second, Sambhu Mallick, whom I had not then met. I had a vision of a fair-skinned man with a cap on his head. Many days later, when I first met Sambhu, I recalled that vision; I realized that it was he whom I had seen in that ecstatic state. I haven't yet found out the three other suppliers of my wants. But they were all of a fair complexion. Surendra looks like one of them.

"In a vision I saw that Sashi and Sarat had been among the followers of Christ.

"Under the banyan-tree in the Panchavati I had a vision of a child. Hriday said to me, 'Then a son will soon be born to you.' I said to him: 'But I regard all women as mother. How can I have a son?' That child is Rakhal.

"Vijay had a vision of this form [meaning himself].

[2] The Master perhaps referred to the English-educated Brāhmos.

How do you account for that? Vijay said to me, 'I touched it exactly as I am touching you now.'

"It was revealed to me in a vision that during my last days I should have to live on pudding. During my present illness my wife was one day feeding me with pudding. I burst into tears and said, 'Is this my living on pudding near the end, and so painfully?'"

Monday, January 4, 1886

It was the fourteenth day of the dark fortnight of the moon. At four o'clock in the afternoon Sri Ramakrishna was sitting in his room. He told M that Ram Chatterji had come from the Kāli temple at Dakshineswar to inquire about his health. He asked M whether it was now very cold at the temple garden.

Narendra arrived. Now and then the Master looked at him and smiled. It appeared to M that that day the Master's love for his beloved disciple was boundless. He indicated to M by a sign that Narendra had wept. Then he remained quiet. Again he indicated that Narendra had cried all the way from home.

No one spoke. Narendra broke the silence.

NARENDRA: "I have been thinking of going there today."

MASTER: "Where?"

NARENDRA: "To Dakshineswar. I intend to light a fire under the bel-tree and meditate."

MASTER: "No. The authorities of the powder-magazine will not allow it. The Panchavati is a nice place. Many sādhus have practised japa and meditation there. But it is very cold there. The place is dark, too."

Again for a few moments all sat in silence.

MASTER (*to Narendra, smiling*): "Won't you continue your studies?"

NARENDRA (*looking at the Master and M*): "I shall feel greatly relieved if I find a medicine that will make me forget all I have studied."

The elder Gopal, who was also in the room, said, "I shall accompany Narendra."

Kalipada Ghosh had brought a box of grapes for Sri Ramakrishna; it lay beside the Master. The Master gave Narendra a few and poured the rest on the floor for the devotees to pick up.

It was evening. Narendra was sitting in a room downstairs. He was smoking and describing to M the yearning of his soul. No one else was with them.

NARENDRA: "I was meditating here last Saturday when suddenly I felt a peculiar sensation in my heart."

M: "It was the awakening of the Kundalini."

NARENDRA: "Probably it was. I clearly perceived the Idā and the Pingalā nerves. I asked Hazra to feel my chest. Yesterday I saw him [meaning the Master] upstairs and told him about it. I said to him: 'All the others have had experiences; please give me some. All have succeeded; shall I alone remain unsatisfied?'"

M: "What did he say to you?"

NARENDRA: "He said: 'Why don't you settle your family affairs first and then come to me? You will get everything. What do you want?' I replied, 'It is my desire to remain absorbed in samādhi continually for three or four days, only once in a while coming down to the sense plane to eat a little food.' Thereupon he said to me: 'You are a very small-minded person. There is a state higher even than that. "All that exists art Thou"—it is you who sing that song.'"

M: "Yes, he always says that after coming down

from samādhi one sees that it is God Himself who has become the universe, the living beings, and all that exists. The Iśvarakotis alone can attain that state. An ordinary man can at the most attain samādhi; but he cannot come down from that state."

NARENDRA: "He [the Master] said: 'Settle your family affairs and then come to me. You will attain a state higher than samādhi.' I went home this morning. My people scolded me, saying: 'Why do you wander about like a vagabond? Your law examination is near at hand and you are not paying any attention to your studies. You wander about aimlessly.'"

M: "Did your mother say anything?"

NARENDRA: "No. She was very eager to feed me. She gave me venison. I ate a little, though I didn't feel like eating meat."

M: "And then?"

NARENDRA: "I went to my study at my grandmother's. As I tried to read I was seized with a great fear, as if studying were a terrible thing. My heart struggled within me. I burst into tears: I never wept so bitterly in my life. I left my books and ran away. I ran along the streets. My shoes slipped from my feet—I didn't know where. I ran past a haystack and got hay all over me. I kept on running along the road to Cossipore."

Narendra remained silent a few minutes and then resumed.

NARENDRA: "Since reading the Vivekachudāmani I have felt very much depressed. In it Śankarāchārya says that only through great tapasyā and good fortune does one acquire these three things: a human birth, the desire for liberation, and refuge with a great soul. I said to myself: 'I have surely gained all these three.

As a result of great tapasyā I have been born a human being; through great tapasyā, again, I have the desire for liberation; and through great tapasyā I have secured the companionship of such a great soul.' "

M: "Ah!"

NARENDRA: "I have no more taste for the world. I do not relish the company of those who live in the world—of course, with the exception of one or two devotees."

Narendra became silent again. A fire of intense renunciation was burning within him. His soul was restless for the vision of God. He resumed the conversation.

NARENDRA (to M): "You have found peace, but my soul is restless. You are blessed indeed."

M did not reply, but sat in silence. He said to himself, "Sri Ramakrishna said that one must pant and pine for God; only then may one have the vision of Him."

Immediately after dusk M went upstairs. He found Sri Ramakrishna asleep.

It was about nine o'clock in the evening. Niranjan and Sashi were sitting near the Master. He was awake. Every now and then he talked of Narendra.

MASTER: "How wonderful Narendra's state of mind is! You see, this very Narendra did not believe in God's forms. And now you see how his soul is panting for God!

"When the soul yearns for God like that, then you will know that you do not have long to wait for His vision. The rosy colour on the eastern horizon shows that the sun will soon rise."

This day Sri Ramakrishna's illness was worse. In

spite of much suffering he said many things about Narendra—though mostly by means of signs.

At night Narendra left for Dakshineswar. It was very dark, being the night of the new moon. He was accompanied by one or two devotees. M spent the night at the Cossipore garden. He dreamt that he was seated in an assembly of sannyāsis.

Sunday, March 14, 1886

Sri Ramakrishna sat facing the north in the large room upstairs. It was evening. He was very ill. Narendra and Rakhal were gently massaging his feet. M sat near by. The Master, by a sign, asked him, too, to stroke his feet. M obeyed.

The previous Sunday the devotees had observed Sri Ramakrishna's birthday with worship and prayer. His birthday the year before had been celebrated at Dakshineswar with great pomp; but this year, on account of his illness, the devotees were very sad and there was no festivity at all.

The Holy Mother busied herself day and night in the Master's service. Among the young disciples, Narendra, Rakhal, Niranjan, Sarat, Sashi, Baburam, Jogin, Latu, and Kali had been staying with him at the garden house. The older devotees visited him daily, and some of them occasionally spent the night there.

That day Sri Ramakrishna was feeling very ill. At midnight the moon was flooding the garden with light, but it could wake no response in the devotees' hearts. They were drowned in a sea of grief. They felt that they were living in a beautiful city besieged by a hostile army. Perfect silence reigned everywhere. Nature was still, except for the gentle rustling of the leaves at the touch of the south wind. Sri Ramakrishna lay awake. One or two devotees sat near him in silence. At times he seemed to doze.

M was seated by his side. Sri Ramakrishna asked him, by a sign, to come nearer. The sight of his suffering was unbearable. In a very soft voice and with great difficulty he said to M:

"I have borne so much suffering for fear of making you all weep. But if you all say: 'Oh, there is so much suffering! Let the body go,' then I can give up the body."

These words pierced the devotees' hearts. And he who was their father, mother, and protector had uttered these words. What could they say? All sat in silence. Some thought, "Is this another crucifixion— the sacrifice of the body for the sake of the devotees?"

It was the dead of night. Sri Ramakrishna's illness was taking a turn for the worse. The devotees wondered what was to be done. One of them left for Calcutta. That very night Girish came to the garden house with two physicians, Upendra and Navagopal.

The devotees sat near the Master. He felt a little better and said to them: "The illness is of the body. That is as it should be; I see that the body is made of the five elements."

Turning to Girish, he said: "I am seeing many forms of God. Among them I find this one also [meaning his own form]."

Monday, March 15, 1886

About seven o'clock in the morning Sri Ramakrishna felt a little better. He talked to the devotees, sometimes in a whisper, sometimes by signs. Narendra, Rakhal, Latu, M, Gopal of Sinthi, and others were in

the room. They sat speechless and looked grave, thinking of the Master's suffering of the previous night.

MASTER (*to the devotees*): "Do you know what I
see right now? I see that it is God Himself who has
become all this. It seems to me that men and other
living beings are made of leather and that it is God
Himself who, dwelling inside these leather cases,
moves the hands, the feet, the heads. I had a similar
vision once before, when I saw houses, gardens, roads,
men, cattle—all made of one substance; it was as if
they were all made of wax.

"I see that it is God Himself who has become the
block, the executioner, and the victim for the sacrifice."

As he described this staggering experience, in which
he realized in full the identity of all within the One
Being, he was overwhelmed with emotion and exclaimed, "Ah! What a vision!"

Immediately Sri Ramakrishna went into samādhi.
He completely forgot his body and the outer world.
The devotees were bewildered. Not knowing what to
do, they sat still.

Presently the Master regained partial consciousness
of the world and said: "Now I have no pain at all. I
am my old self again."

The devotees were amazed to watch this state of
the Master, beyond pleasure and pain, weal and woe.

He cast his glance on Latu and said: "There is Loto.
He bends his head, resting it on the palm of his
hand. I see that it is God Himself who rests His head
on His hand."

Sri Ramakrishna looked at the devotees and his love
for them welled up in a thousand streams. Like a
mother showing her tenderness to her children, he
touched the face and chin of Rakhal and of Narendra.

A few minutes later he said to M, "If the body were to be preserved a few days more, many people would have their spirituality awakened."

He paused a few minutes.

"But this is not to be. This time the body will not be preserved."

The devotees eagerly awaited the Master's next words.

"Such is not the will of God. This time the body will not be preserved, lest, finding me guileless and foolish, people should take advantage of me, and lest I, guileless and foolish as I am, should give away everything to everybody. In this Kaliyuga, you see, people are averse to meditation and japa."

RAKHAL (*tenderly*): "Please speak to God that He may preserve your body some time more."

MASTER: "That depends on God's will."

NARENDRA: "Your will and God's will have become one."

Sri Ramakrishna remained silent. He appeared to be thinking about something.

MASTER (*to Narendra, Rakhal, and the others*): "And nothing will happen if I speak to God. Now I see that I and the Mother have become one."

The devotees sat silently in the room. Sri Rama-krishna looked at them tenderly. Then he placed his hand on his heart. He was about to speak.

MASTER (*to Narendra and the others*): "There are two persons in this. One, the Divine Mother—"

He paused. The devotees eagerly looked at him to hear what he would say next.

MASTER: "Yes, one is She. And the other is Her devotee. It is the devotee who broke his arm, and it is the devotee who is now ill. Do you understand?"

The devotees sat without uttering a word.

MASTER: "Alas! To whom shall I say all this? Who will understand me?"

Pausing a few moments, he said:

"God becomes man, an Avatār, and comes to earth with His devotees. And the devotees leave the world with Him."

RAKHAL: "Therefore we pray that you may not go away and leave us behind."

Sri Ramakrishna smiled and said:

"A band of God's troubadours suddenly appears, dances and sings, and departs in the same sudden manner. They come and they return, but none recognizes them."

The Master and the devotees smiled.

After a few minutes he said:

"Suffering is inevitable when one assumes a human body.

"Every now and then I say to myself, 'May I not have to come back to earth again!' But there is something else. After enjoying sumptuous feasts outside, one does not relish cheap home cooking.

"Besides, this assuming of a human body is for the devotees' sake."

Sri Ramakrishna looked at Narendra very tenderly.

MASTER (to Narendra): "An outcaste was carrying a load of meat. Śankarāchārya, after bathing in the Ganges, was passing by. Suddenly the outcaste touched him. Śankara said sharply: 'What! You touched me!' 'Revered sir,' he replied, 'I have not touched you nor have you touched me. Reason with me: Are you the body, the mind, or the buddhi? Analyse what you are. You are the Pure Ātman, unattached and free, unaffected by the three gunas—sattva, rajas, and tamas.'

"Do you know what Brahman is like? It is like air. Good and bad smells are carried by the air, but the air itself is unaffected."

NARENDRA: "Yes, sir."

MASTER: "He is beyond the gunas and māyā—beyond both the 'māyā of knowledge' and the 'māyā of ignorance.' 'Woman' and 'gold' are the 'māyā of ignorance.' Knowledge, renunciation, devotion, and other spiritual qualities are the splendours of the 'māyā of knowledge.' Śankarāchārya kept this 'māyā of knowledge'; and that you and these others feel concerned about me is also due to this 'māyā of knowledge.' "

NARENDRA: "Some people get angry with me when I speak of renunciation."

MASTER (in a whisper): "Renunciation is necessary. (Pointing to his limbs) "If one limb is placed upon another, you must remove the first to get the second. Can you get the second limb without removing the first?"

NARENDRA: "True, sir."

MASTER (in a whisper, to Narendra): "When one sees everything filled with God alone, does one see anything else?"

NARENDRA: "Must one renounce the world?"

MASTER: "Didn't I say just now: 'When one sees everything filled with God alone, does one see anything else?' Does one then see any such thing as the world?

"I mean mental renunciation. Not one of those who have come here is a worldly person. Some of them had a slight desire—for instance, a fancy for woman. (Rakhal and M smile.) And that desire has been fulfilled."

The Master looked at Narendra tenderly and became filled with love. Looking at the devotees, he said, "Grand!"

With a smile Narendra asked the Master, "What is grand?"

MASTER (smiling): "I see that preparations are going on for a grand renunciation."

Narendra and the devotees looked silently at the Master. Rakhal resumed the conversation.

RAKHAL (smiling, to the Master): "Narendra is now beginning to understand you rather well."

Sri Ramakrishna laughed and said: "Yes, that is so. I see that many others, too, are beginning to understand. (To M) Isn't that so?"

M: "Yes, sir."

Sri Ramakrishna turned his eyes to Narendra and M and by a sign of his finger drew the devotees' attention to them. He first pointed out Narendra and then M. Rakhal understood the Master's hint and said to him with a smile, 'Don't you mean that Narendra has the attitude of a hero, and he [meaning M] that of a handmaid of God?"

Sri Ramakrishna laughed.

NARENDRA (smiling, to Rakhal): "He [meaning M] doesn't talk much and is bashful. Is that why you say he is a handmaid of God?"

MASTER (smiling, to Narendra): "Well, what do you think of me?"

NARENDRA: "You are a hero, a handmaid of God, and everything else."

These words filled Sri Ramakrishna with divine emotion. He placed his hand on his heart and was about to say something.

He said to Narendra and the other devotees:

"I see that all things—everything that exists—have come from this."

He asked Narendra by a sign, "What did you understand?"

NARENDRA: "All created objects have come from you."

The Master's face beamed with joy. He said to Rakhal, "Did you hear what he said?"

Sri Ramakrishna asked Narendra to sing. Narendra intoned a hymn. His mind was full of renunciation. He sang:

> Unsteady is water on the lotus petal;
> Quite as unsteady is the life of man.
> One moment with a sādhu is the boat
> With which to cross the ocean of this world. . . .

Narendra had hardly finished one or two lines, when Sri Ramakrishna said to him by a sign: "What are you singing? That is a very insignificant attitude, a very commonplace thing."

Now Narendra sang about the love of the gopis for Krishna, impersonating one of them:

> How strange, O friend, are the rules of life and death!
> The Youth of Braja has fled away,
> And this poor maid of Braja soon will die.
> Mādhava is in love with other maids
> More beautiful than I.
> Alas! He has forgotten the milkman's artless daughter.
>
> Who would ever have guessed, dear friend, that He,
> A Lover so tender, so sublime,
> Could go a-begging simply for outward charm?
> I was a fool not to have seen it before;
> But carried away by His beauty,
> I yearned alone to hold His two feet to my breast.

Now I shall drown myself in the Jamunā's stream
Or take a draught of poison, friend!
Or I shall bind a creeper round my neck
And hang myself from a young tamāla tree;
Or, failing all of these,
Destroy my wretched self by chanting Krishna's name.

Sri Ramakrishna and the devotees were greatly
moved by the song. The Master and Rakhal shed tears
of love. Narendra was intoxicated with the love of
the gopis of Braja for their Sweetheart, Sri Krishna,
and sang:

O Krishna, Beloved, You are mine.
What shall I say to You, O Lord?
What shall I ever say to You?
Only a woman am I,
And never fortune's favourite;
I do not know what to say.

You are the mirror for the hand
And You are the flower for the hair.
O Friend, I shall make a flower of You
And wear You in my hair;
Under my braids I shall hide You, Friend!
No one will see You there.

You are the betel-leaf for the lips,
The dark collyrium for the eyes;
O Friend, with You I shall stain my lips,
With You I shall paint my eyes.

You are the sandal-paste for the body;
You are the necklace for the neck.
I shall anoint myself with You,
My fragrant Sandal-paste,
And soothe my body and my soul.

I shall wear You, my lovely Necklace,
Here about my neck,
And You will lie upon my bosom,
Close to my throbbing heart.

You are the Treasure in my body;
You are the Dweller in my house.
You are to me, O Lord,
What wings are to a bird,
What water is to a fish.

Friday, April 9, 1886

It was five o'clock in the afternoon. Narendra, Kali,
Niranjan, and M were talking downstairs in the Cossipore garden house. Narendra had just returned from a
visit to Bodh-Gayā, where he had gone with Kali and
Tarak. In that sacred place he had been absorbed in
deep meditation before the image of Buddha. He had
paid his respects to the Bodhi-tree, which is an offshoot
of the original tree under which Buddha attained
Nirvāna.

It was evening. Sri Ramakrishna sat on his bed in the
big hall upstairs. M was alone in the room, fanning
the Master. Latu came in a little later. Narendra
entered the room and took a seat. Sashi, Rakhal, and
one or two other devotees came in. The Master asked
Narendra to stroke his feet. He also asked him whether
he had taken his meal.

MASTER (*smiling, to M*): "He went there [referring
to Bodh-Gayā]."

M (*to Narendra*): "What are the doctrines of
Buddha?"

NARENDRA: "He could not express in words what he
had realized by his tapasyā. So people say he was an
atheist."

MASTER (*by signs*): "Why atheist? He was not an atheist. He simply could not express his inner experiences in words. Do you know what 'Buddha' means? It is to become one with Bodha, Pure Intelligence, by meditating on That which is of the nature of Pure Intelligence; it is to become Pure Intelligence Itself."

NARENDRA: "Yes, sir. There are three classes of Buddhas: Buddha, Arhat, and Bodhisattva."

MASTER: "This too is sport of God, a new lila of God.

"Why should Buddha be called an atheist? When one realizes Svarupa, the true nature of one's Self, one attains a state that is something between asti, *is*, and nāsti, *is-not*."

NARENDRA (*to M*): "It is a state in which contradictions meet. A combination of hydrogen and oxygen produces cool water; and the same hydrogen and oxygen are used in the oxy-hydrogen blowpipe.

"In that state both activity and non-activity are possible; that is to say, one then performs unselfish action.

"Worldly people, who are engrossed in sense objects, say that everything exists—*asti*. But the māyāvādis, the illusionists, say that nothing exists—*nāsti*. The experience of a Buddha is beyond both 'existence' and 'non-existence.' "

MASTER: "This 'existence' and 'non-existence' are attributes of Prakriti. The Reality is beyond both."

The devotees remained silent a few moments.

MASTER (*to Narendra*): "What did Buddha preach?"

NARENDRA: "He did not discuss the existence or non-existence of God. But he showed compassion for others all his life.

"A hawk pounced upon a bird and was about to devour it. In order to save the bird, Buddha offered the hawk his own flesh."

Sri Ramakrishna remained silent. Narendra became more and more enthusiastic about Buddha.

NARENDRA: "How great his renunciation was! Born a prince, he renounced everything! If a man has nothing, no wealth at all, what does his renunciation amount to? After attaining Buddhahood and experiencing Nirvāna, Buddha once visited his home and exhorted his wife, his son, and many others of the royal household to embrace the life of renunciation. How intense his renunciation was! But look at Vyāsa's conduct! He forbade his son Śukadeva to give up the world, saying, 'My son, practise religion as a householder.' "

Sri Ramakrishna was silent. As yet he had not uttered a word.

NARENDRA: "Buddha did not care for Śakti or any such thing. He sought only Nirvāna. Ah, how intense his dispassion was! When he sat down under the Bodhi-tree to meditate, he took this vow: 'Let my body wither away here if I do not attain Nirvāna.' Such a firm resolve!

"This body, indeed, is the great enemy. Can anything be achieved without chastising it?"

SASHI: "But it is you who say that one develops sattva by eating meat. You insist that one should eat meat."

NARENDRA: "I eat meat, no doubt, but I can also live on rice, mere rice, even without salt."

After a few minutes Sri Ramakrishna broke his silence. He asked Narendra, by a sign, if he had seen a tuft of hair on Buddha's head.

NARENDRA: "No, sir. He seems to have a sort of crown; his head seems to be covered by strings of rudrāksha beads placed on top of one another."

MASTER: "And his eyes?"

NARENDRA: "They show that he is in samādhi."

Sri Ramakrishna again became silent. Narendra and the other devotees looked at him intently. Suddenly a smile lighted his face and he began to talk with Narendra. M was fanning him.

MASTER (to Narendra): "Well, here you find everything—even ordinary red lentils and tamarind. Isn't that so?"

NARENDRA: "After experiencing all those states, you are now dwelling on a lower plane."

M (to himself): "Yes, after realizing all those ideals, he is now living as a bhakta, a devotee of God."

MASTER: "Someone seems to be holding me to a lower plane."

Saying this, Sri Ramakrishna took the fan from M's hand and said: "As I see this fan, *directly* before me, in exactly the same manner have I seen God. And I have seen—"

With these words he placed his hand on his heart and asked Narendra, by a sign, "Can you tell me what I said?"

NARENDRA: "I have understood."

MASTER: "Tell me."

NARENDRA: "I didn't hear you well."

Sri Ramakrishna said again, by a sign, "I have seen that He and the one who dwells in my heart are one and the same Person."

NARENDRA: "Yes, yes! *Soham*—I am He."

MASTER: "But only a line divides the two—that I may enjoy divine bliss."

NARENDRA (to M): "Great souls, even after their own liberation, retain the ego and experience the pleasure and pain of the body that they may help others to attain liberation.

"It is like coolie work. We perform coolie work under compulsion, but great souls do so of their own sweet pleasure."

Again all fell into silence. After a time Sri Ramakrishna resumed the conversation.

MASTER (to Narendra and the others): "The roof is clearly visible, but extremely hard to reach."

NARENDRA: "Yes, sir."

MASTER: "But if someone who has already reached it drops down a rope, he can pull another person up."

RAKHAL (to the other devotees): "Let us stop here. He has already talked a great deal. It will aggravate his illness."

Tuesday, April 13, 1886

Sri Ramakrishna was seated with the devotees. A crazy woman had been troubling everybody in order to see the Master. She had assumed toward him the attitude of a lover and often ran into the garden house and burst into the Master's room. She had even been beaten by the devotees; but that did not stop her.

SASHI: "If she comes again I shall shove her out of the place!"

MASTER (tenderly): "No, no! Let her come and go away."

RAKHAL: "At the beginning I too used to feel jealous of others when they visited the Master. But he graciously revealed to me that my guru is also the guru of the universe. Has he taken this birth only for a few of us?"

SASHI: "I don't mean that. But why should she trouble him when he is ill? And she is such a nuisance!"

RAKHAL: "We all give him trouble. Did we all come to him after attaining perfection? Haven't we caused him suffering? How Narendra and some of the others behaved in the beginning! How they argued with him!"

SASHI: "Whatever Narendra expressed in words he carried out in his actions."

RAKHAL: "How rude Dr. Sarkar has been to him! No one is guiltless, if it comes to that."

MASTER (to Rakhal, tenderly): "Will you eat something?"

RAKHAL: "Not now. Later on."

Sri Ramakrishna asked M, by a sign, whether he was going to have his meal there.

RAKHAL (to M): "Please take your meal here. He is asking you to."

Sri Ramakrishna was seated on his bed. He looked like a five-year-old boy. Just then the crazy woman climbed the stairs and stood near the door.

M (in a low voice, to Sashi): "Ask her to salute him and go away. Don't make any fuss."

Sashi took her downstairs.

It was the first day of the Bengali year. Many women devotees arrived. They saluted Sri Ramakrishna and the Holy Mother. Among them were the wives of Balaram and Manomohan, and the brāhmani of Bāgh-bāzār. Several of them had brought their children along. Some of the women offered flowers at the Master's feet. Two young girls, nine or ten years of age, sang a few songs.

It was afternoon. M and a few other devotees were seated near the Master. Narendra came in. He looked, as the Master used to say, like an unsheathed sword.

Narendra sat down near the Master and within his hearing expressed his utter annoyance with women. He told the devotees what an obstacle women were in the path of God-realization.

Sri Ramakrishna made no response. He listened to Narendra.

Narendra said again: "I want peace. I do not care even for God."

Sri Ramakrishna looked at him intently without uttering a word. Now and then Narendra chanted, "Brahman is Truth, Knowledge, the Infinite."

Friday, April 16, 1886

The moon was shining brilliantly, flooding the garden paths, the trees, and the water of the lake with its white rays. Girish, M, Latu, and a few other devotees were seated on the steps leading to the lake. The house stood to the west of the lake. A lamp burnt in the Master's room on the second floor. Sri Ramakrishna was sitting on his bed. There were several devotees in the room. That evening Narendra, Kali, and Tarak had gone to Dakshineswar. They intended to spend the night in the Panchavati, meditating on God.

Girish, Latu, and M went to Sri Ramakrishna's room. Sashi and one or two devotees had been attending on the Master. Baburam, Niranjan, and Rakhal also entered the room. It was a large room. Some medicines and a few other accessories were kept near the bed. One entered the room by a door at the north end.

Since Sri Ramakrishna had to be tended all night, the devotees stayed awake by turns. The devotee who tended him fixed Sri Ramakrishna's mosquito net and then either lay on a mat on the floor or spent the night sitting up. Since Sri Ramakrishna got very little sleep on account of his illness, his attendant, too, slept very little.

That evening Sri Ramakrishna was somewhat better. The devotees saluted the Master and sat down on the floor. The Master asked M to bring the lamp near him. He greeted Girish cordially.

MASTER (to Girish): "Are you quite well? (To Latu) Prepare a smoke for him and give him a betel-leaf."

A few minutes afterwards he asked Latu to give Girish some refreshments. Latu said that they had been sent for.

Sri Ramakrishna was sitting up. A devotee offered him some garlands of flowers. Sri Ramakrishna put them around his neck one by one. The devotees looked at him wonderingly. He took two garlands from his neck and gave them to Girish.

Every now and then Sri Ramakrishna asked whether the refreshments had been brought.

M was fanning the Master. On the bed was a sandal-wood fan, the offering of a devotee. The Master gave it to M, who continued to fan him with it. He also gave M two garlands.

M had lost a son aged seven or eight about a year and a half before. The child had seen the Master many a time. Latu was telling Sri Ramakrishna about M.

LATU: "M wept bitterly last night at the sight of some books that had belonged to his dead child. His wife is almost mad with grief. She sometimes treats her other children violently. She makes scenes at home because he spends the night here now and then."

Sri Ramakrishna seemed worried to hear of this.

GIRISH: "It is nothing to be wondered at. Even after receiving the instruction of the Bhagavad Gītā, Arjuna fainted from grief at the death of his son Abhimanyu."

Girish was given the refreshments on a tray. Sri Ramakrishna took a grain and Girish accepted the rest as prasād. He sat in front of the Master and began to eat. He needed water to drink. There was an earthen jug in the southeast corner of the room. It was the month of April and the day was hot. Sri Ramakrishna said, "There is some nice water here."

The Master was so ill that he had not enough strength even to stand up. And what did the disciples see to their utter amazement? They saw him leave the bed, completely naked, and move toward the jug! He himself was going to pour the water into a tumbler. The devotees were almost frozen with fear. The Master filled the tumbler. He poured a drop or two into his hands to see whether it was cool. He found that it was not very cool; but since nothing better could be found, he reluctantly gave it to Girish.

Girish was eating the sweets. The devotees were sitting about, and M was fanning Sri Ramakrishna.

GIRISH (to the Master): "Deben Babu has decided to renounce the world."

On account of his illness Sri Ramakrishna could hardly talk. Touching his lips with his finger, he asked Girish, by signs, "Who will feed his wife and children?"

GIRISH: "I don't know."

The other devotees remained silent. Girish began talking again while he ate the refreshments.

GIRISH: "Sir, which is wiser—to renounce the world regretfully, or to call on God, leading a householder's life?"

MASTER (*to M*): "Haven't you read the Gītā? One truly realizes God if one performs one's worldly duties in a detached spirit, if one lives in the world after realizing that everything is illusory.

"Those who regretfully renounce the world belong to an inferior class.

"Do you know what a householder jnāni is like? He is like a person living in a glass house. He can see both inside and outside."

Again there was silence in the room.

MASTER (*to M*): "The refreshments are hot and good."

M (*to Girish*): "Yes, they were bought from Fagu's shop. The place is famous."

MASTER (*smiling*): "Yes, famous."

GIRISH: "They are really nice.

(*To the Master*) "Sir, my mind is now on a very lofty plane. Why does it come down again?"

MASTER: "That always happens when one leads a worldly life. Sometimes the householder's mind goes up; sometimes it goes down. Sometimes he feels a great deal of devotion; sometimes he feels less. This happens because he lives in the midst of 'woman' and 'gold.' Sometimes a householder contemplates God or chants His name, and sometimes he diverts his mind to 'woman' and 'gold.' He is like an ordinary fly, which now sits on a sweetmeat and now on filth or rotting sores.

"But it is quite different with sannyāsis. They are able to fix their minds on God alone, completely withdrawing them from 'woman' and 'gold.' They can enjoy the Bliss of God alone. A man of true renunciation cannot enjoy anything but God. He leaves a place where people talk of worldly things; he listens only to spiritual talk. A man of true renunciation never speaks about anything but God. The bees light only on flowers, in order to sip honey; they do not enjoy anything else."

Girish went to the small terrace to rinse his hands.

MASTER (to M): "A man needs God's grace to fix his whole mind on Him. Well, Girish has eaten a great many sweets. Tell him not to eat anything else tonight."

Girish returned to the room and sat in front of the Master. He was chewing a betel-leaf.

MASTER (to Girish): "Rakhal has now understood what is good and what is bad, what is real and what is unreal. He lives with his family, no doubt, but he knows what it means. He has a wife. And a son has been born to him. But he has realized that all these are illusory and impermanent. Rakhal will never be attached to the world.

"He is like a mudfish. The fish lives in the mud, but there is not the slightest trace of mud on its body."

GIRISH: "Sir, I don't understand all this. You can make everyone pure and unattached if you want to. You can make everyone good, whether he is a worldly man or a sannyāsi. The Malaya breeze, I believe, turns all trees into sandal-wood."

MASTER: "Not unless there is substance in them. There are a few trees, the cotton-tree for instance, which are not turned into sandal-wood."

GIRISH: "I don't care."

MASTER: "But this is the law."

GIRISH: "But everything about you is outside the law."

The devotees were listening to this conversation in great amazement. Every now and then the fan in M's hand stopped moving.

MASTER: "Yes, that may be true. When the river

of bhakti overflows, the land all around is flooded with water to the depth of a pole.

(*To M*) "When one develops love of God, one needs nothing else."

M: "Yes, sir."

The conversation turned to the crazy woman who regarded Sri Ramakrishna as her lover. The devotees called her "Pāgli"[3] and tried to keep her away from the Master.

MASTER (*to Girish and the others*): "Pāgli cherishes the attitude of madhur toward me. One day she came to Dakshineswar. Suddenly she burst out crying. 'Why are you crying?' I asked her. And she said, 'Oh, my head is aching!' (*All laugh.*) Another day I was eating when she came to Dakshineswar. She suddenly said, 'Won't you be kind to me?' I had no idea of what was passing through her mind, and went on eating. Then she said, 'Why did you push me away mentally?' I asked her, 'What is your attitude?' She said that she regarded me as her sweetheart. 'Ah!' I said. 'But I look on all women as manifestations of the Divine Mother. All women are mothers to me.' Thereupon she said, 'I don't know all that.' Then I called Ramlal and said to him: 'Ramlal, listen to her! What is she talking about —this "pushing away mentally"?' Even now she keeps up that attitude."

GIRISH: "Blessed indeed is Pāgli! Maybe she is crazy. Maybe she is beaten by the devotees. But she meditates on you twenty-four hours a day. No matter how she meditates on you, no harm can ever touch her.

"Sir, how can I ever express my own feelings about it? Just think what I was before, and what I have become now by meditating on you! Formerly I was

---

[3] Bengali word for "crazy woman."

indolent; now that indolence has turned into resignation to God. Formerly I was a sinner; now I have become humble. What else can I say?"

The devotees remained silent. Rakhal expressed his sympathy for Pāgli. He said: "We all feel sorry for her. She causes so much annoyance, and for that she suffers too."

NIRANJAN (to Rakhal): "You feel that way for her because you have a wife at home. But we could kill her."

RAKHAL (sharply): "Such bragging! How dare you utter such words before him [meaning Sri Ramakrishna]?"

MASTER (to Girish): " 'Woman' and 'gold' alone constitute the world. Many people regard money as their very lifeblood. But however much you may love money, one day, perhaps, every bit of it will slip through your fingers.

"They alone make good use of their money who spend it for the worship of God or in the service of holy men and devotees. Their money bears fruit.

"I cannot eat anything offered by physicians. I mean those who traffic in human suffering. To me their money is blood and pus."

Sri Ramakrishna mentioned two physicians in this connexion.

GIRISH: "Dr. Rajendra Dutta is a generous person. He doesn't accept a penny from anybody. He gives away money in charity."

Saturday, April 17, 1886

It was the night of the full moon. For some time Narendra had been going to Dakshineswar daily. He

spent a great deal of time in the Panchavati in prayer
and contemplation. This day he returned from Dakshineswar in the evening. Tarak and Kali were with
him.

It was eight o'clock in the evening. Moonlight and
the south wind added to the charm of the garden house.
Many of the devotees were meditating in the room
downstairs. Referring to them, Narendra said to M,
"They are shedding their upādhis one by one."

A few minutes later M came into Sri Ramakrishna's
room and sat down on the floor. The Master asked him
to wash his towel and the spittoon. M washed them
in the reservoir.

Next morning Sri Ramakrishna sent for M. After
taking his bath in the Ganges and saluting the Master,
he had gone to the roof. Sri Ramakrishna asked M to
bring his grief-stricken wife to the garden house, where
she could have her meal.

The Master said to M, by a sign: "Ask her to come.
Let her stay here a couple of days. She may bring the
baby."

M: "Yes, sir. It would be fine if she developed intense love of God."

Sri Ramakrishna again answered by signs: "Oh, grief
pushes out devotion. And he was such a big boy.

"Krishnakishore had two sons. They were of the
same age as Bhavanath, and each had two university
degrees. They both died. And Krishnakishore, jnāni
that he was, could not at first control himself. How
lucky I am that I have none!

"Why doesn't Kishori come?"

A DEVOTEE: "He comes to the Ganges every day
for his bath."

MASTER: "But why doesn't he come here?"

DEVOTEE: "I shall ask him to come, sir."

MASTER: "Why doesn't Harish come?"

Two young girls aged nine and ten, who belonged to M's family, sang several songs about the Divine Mother for the Master. They had sung for him when he had visited M's house at Śyāmpukur. The Master was very much pleased with their songs. After they had finished, they were sent for by the devotees to sing for them downstairs.

MASTER (to M): "Don't teach the girls any more songs. It is different if they sing spontaneously. But they will lose their modesty by singing before anyone and everyone. It is very necessary for women to be modest."

Flowers and sandal-paste were placed before the Master in a flower basket. He sat on his bed and worshipped himself with these offerings. Sometimes he placed flowers and sandal-paste on his head, sometimes on his throat, sometimes on his heart, and sometimes on his navel.

Manomohan of Konnagar came in and took a seat after saluting the Master. Sri Ramakrishna was still busy with the worship of his inner Self. He put a garland of flowers on his own neck. After a while he seemed to be pleased with Manomohan and gave him some flowers. M, too, received a flower.

It was about nine o'clock in the morning. The Master and M were talking. Sashi was also in the room.

MASTER (to M): "What were Narendra and Sashi talking about? What did they discuss?"

M (to Sashi): "What were you talking about?"

SASHI: "Was it Niranjan who told you about it?"

MASTER: "What were you discussing? I heard 'God,' 'Being,' 'Non-being,' and so forth."

SASHI (smiling): "Shall I call Narendra?"

MASTER: "Yes."

Narendra came in and took a seat.

MASTER (to M): "Ask him something. (To Narendra) Tell us what you were talking about."

NARENDRA: "I have indigestion. What's there to tell you about?"

MASTER: "You will get over your indigestion."

M (smiling): "Tell us about the experience of Buddha."

NARENDRA: "Have I become a Buddha, that you want me to talk about him?"

M: "What does Buddha say about the existence of God?"

NARENDRA: "How can you say that God exists? It is you who have created this universe. Don't you know what Berkeley says about it?"

M: "Yes, I do. According to him, esse is percipi.[4] The world exists as long as the sense-organs perceive it."

MASTER: "Nangtā used to say, 'The world exists in mind alone and disappears in mind alone.' But as long as 'I-consciousness' exists, one should assume the servant-and-master relationship with God."

NARENDRA (to M): "How can you prove by reasoning that God exists? But if you depend on faith, then you must accept the relationship of servant and Master. And if you accept that—and you can't help it—then you must also say that God is kind.

"You think only of the suffering in the world—why

[4] The existence of external objects depends on their being perceived.

do you forget that God has also given you so much happiness? How kind He is to us! He has granted us three very great things: human birth, the yearning to know God, and the companionship of a great soul."

All were silent.

MASTER (*to Narendra*): "I feel very clearly that there is Someone within me."

Narendra went downstairs. He was singing to himself:

> Lord, Thou hast lifted all my sorrow
> With the vision of Thy face,
> And the magic of Thy beauty
> Has bewitched my mind;
> Beholding Thee, the seven worlds
> Forget their never-ending woe;
> What shall I say, then, of myself,
> A poor and lowly soul? . . .

Narendra had a little indigestion. He said to M: "If one follows the path of bhakti, then the mind comes down a little to the body. Otherwise, who am I? Neither man nor God. I have neither pleasure nor pain."

It was about nine o'clock in the evening. Surendra and a few other devotees entered Sri Ramakrishna's room and offered him garlands of flowers. Baburam, Latu, and M were also in the room.

Sri Ramakrishna put Surendra's garland on his own neck. All sat quietly. Suddenly the Master made a sign to Surendra to come near him. When the disciple came near the bed, Sri Ramakrishna took the garland from his neck and put it around Surendra's. Surendra saluted the Master. Sri Ramakrishna asked him, by a sign, to rub his feet. Surendra gave them a gentle massage.

12

THE MASTER'S LOVE FOR HIS DEVOTEES

Wednesday, April 21, 1886

M AND NARENDRA were strolling in the garden of the house at Cossipore. Narendra was very much worried because he had not yet been able to solve his family's financial difficulties.

NARENDRA: "I don't care for the job at the Vidyāsāgar School. I have been thinking of going to Gayā. I have been told that a zemindar there needs the services of a manager for his estate. There is no such thing as God."

M (*smiling*): "You may say that now, but later on you will talk differently. Scepticism is a stage in the path of God-realization. One must pass through stages like this and go much farther; only thus can one realize God. That is what the Master says."

NARENDRA: "Has anybody seen God as I see that tree?"

M: "Yes, our Master has seen God that way."

NARENDRA: "It may be a hallucination."

M: "Whatever a person experiences in a particular state is real for him in that state. Suppose you are dreaming that you have gone to a garden. As long as the dream lasts, the garden is real for you. But you think of it as unreal when your mind undergoes a change, as, for instance, when you awake. When your mind attains the state in which one sees God, you will know God to be real."

NARENDRA: "I want truth. The other day I had a great argument with Sri Ramakrishna himself."

M (*smiling*): "What happened?"

NARENDRA: "He said to me, 'Some people call me God.' I replied, 'Let a thousand people call you God, but I shall certainly not call you God as long as I do not know it to be true.' He said, 'Whatever many people say is indeed truth; that is dharma.' Thereupon I replied, 'Let others proclaim a thing as truth, but I shall certainly not listen to them unless I myself realize it as truth.'"

M (*smiling*): "Your attitude is like that of Western savants—Copernicus and Berkeley, for instance. The whole world said it was the sun that moved, but Copernicus did not care. Everybody said the external world was real, but Berkeley paid no heed."

NARENDRA: "Can you give me a History of Philosophy?"

M: "By whom? Lewis?"

NARENDRA: "No, Überweg. I must read a German author."

M: "You just said, 'Has anybody seen God as I see that tree?' Suppose God comes to you as a man and says, 'I am God.' Will you believe it then? You certainly remember the story of Lazarus. After his death, Lazarus said to Abraham, 'Let me go back to the earth and tell my friends and relatives that hell and the after-life exist.' Abraham replied: 'Do you think they will believe you? They will say it is a charlatan who is telling them these things.' The Master says that God cannot be known by reasoning. By faith alone does one attain everything—knowledge and super-

knowledge. By faith alone can one see God and become intimate with Him."

It was about three o'clock in the afternoon. Sri Ramakrishna was in bed. Ramlal, who had come from
Dakshineswar, was massaging his feet. Gopal of Sinthi
and M were in the room.

Sri Ramakrishna asked M to shut the windows and
massage his feet. At the Master's request Purna had
come to the Cossipore garden in a hired carriage. M
was to pay the carriage hire. Sri Ramakrishna made a
sign to Gopal, asking whether he had obtained the
money from M. Gopal answered in the affirmative.

At nine o'clock in the evening Surendra, Ram, and
the others were about to return to Calcutta. It was the
sultry month of April and Sri Ramakrishna's room became very hot during the day; so Surendra had brought
some straw screens to keep the room cool.

SURENDRA: "Why, nobody has hung up these straw
screens. People here pay no attention to anything."

A DEVOTEE (smiling): "The devotees here are now
in the state of Brahmajnāna. They feel, 'I am He.'
The world is unreal to them. When they come down
to a lower plane and regard God as the Master and
themselves as His servants, they will pay attention to
the service of Sri Ramakrishna." (All laugh.)

Thursday, April 22, 1886

In the evening Rakhal, Sashi, and M were strolling
in the garden at Cossipore.

M: "The Master is like a child—beyond the three
gunas."

SASHI AND RAKHAL: "He himself has said that."

RAKHAL: "He sits in a tower, as it were, from which

he gets all information and sees everything; but others cannot go there and reach him."

M: "He said, 'In such a state of mind one sees God constantly.' In him there is not the slightest trace of worldliness. His mind is like dry fuel, which catches fire quickly."

SASHI: "The other day he described different kinds of intelligence to Charu. The right intelligence is that through which one attains God; but the intelligence that enables one to become a deputy magistrate or a lawyer, or to acquire a house, is a mean intelligence."

M: "Ah, what wonderful words!"

SASHI: "Kali said to the Master: 'What's the good of having joy? The Bhils are joyous. Savages are always singing and dancing in a frenzy of delight.' "

RAKHAL: "He [meaning the Master] replied to Kali: 'What do you mean? Can the Bliss of Brahman be the same as worldly pleasures? Ordinary men are satisfied with worldly pleasures. One cannot enjoy the Bliss of Brahman unless one completely rids oneself of attachment to worldly things. There is the joy of money and sense experience, and there is the Bliss of God-realization. Can the two ever be the same? The rishis enjoyed the Bliss of Brahman.' "

M: "You see, Kali nowadays meditates on Buddha; that is why he speaks of a state beyond Bliss."

RAKHAL: "Yes, Kali told the Master about Buddha. Sri Ramakrishna said to him: 'Buddha is an Incarnation of God. How can you compare him to anybody else? As he is great, so is his teaching great.' Kali said to him: 'Everything, indeed, is the manifestation of God's power. Both worldly pleasure and the Bliss of God are the manifestation of that power.' "

M: "What did the Master say to that?"

RAKHAL: "He said: 'How can that be? Is the power to beget a child the same as the power through which one realizes God?'"

Sri Ramakrishna was sitting in his room on the second floor. Narendra, Rakhal, Sashi, Surendra, M, Bhavanath, and other devotees were present. Dr. Mahendra Sarkar and Dr. Rajendra Dutta were also there to examine him. His condition was growing worse.

The house rent was between sixty and sixty-five rupees. Surendra bore most of the expenses and had rented the house in his name. The other householder devotees contributed financial help according to their power. A cook and a maid had been engaged to look after the members of the household.

MASTER (to Dr. Sarkar and the others): "The expenses are mounting."

DR. SARKAR (pointing to the devotees): "But they are ready to bear them. They do not hesitate to spend money. (To Sri Ramakrishna) Now, you see, gold is necessary."

MASTER (to Narendra): "Why don't you answer?"

Narendra remained silent. Dr. Sarkar resumed the conversation.

DR. SARKAR: "Gold is necessary, and also woman."

RAJENDRA: "Yes, his [meaning Sri Ramakrishna's] wife has been cooking his meals."

DR. SARKAR (to the Master): "Do you see?"

MASTER (smiling): "Yes—but very troublesome!"

DR. SARKAR: "If there were no troubles, then all would become paramahamsas."

MASTER: "If a woman touches me I fall ill. That part of my body aches as if stung by a horned fish."

DR. SARKAR: "I believe that. But how can you get along without woman?"

MASTER: "My hand gets all twisted up if I hold money in it; my breathing stops. But there is no harm in spending money to lead a spiritual life in the world —if one spends it, for instance, in the worship of God and the service of holy men and devotees.

"A man forgets God if he is entangled in the world of māyā through a woman. It is the Mother of the Universe who has assumed the form of māyā, the form of woman. One who knows this rightly does not feel like leading the life of māyā in the world. But he who truly realizes that all women are manifestations of the Divine Mother may lead a spiritual life in the world. Without realizing God one cannot truly know what a woman is."

A few minutes later the physicians took their leave. Sri Ramakrishna and M were engaged in conversation. The Master was telling M how he felt about woman.

MASTER (to M): "They say I cannot get along without 'woman' and 'gold.' They don't understand the state of my mind.

"If I touch a woman my hand becomes numb; it aches. If in a friendly spirit I approach a woman and begin to talk to her, I feel as if a barrier had been placed between us. It is impossible for me to cross that barrier.

"If a woman enters my room when I am alone, at once I become like a child and regard her as my mother."

As M listened to these words, he became speechless with wonder at Sri Ramakrishna's exalted state of mind. Bhavanath and Narendra were sitting at a distance, talking together. Bhavanath had married and was

trying to find a job; so he could not visit Sri Ramakrishna frequently at Cossipore. He had said to M:
"I understand that Vidyāsāgar wants to start a new
school. I have to earn my livelihood. Will it be possible for me to secure a job in that school?" The Master was much worried about Bhavanath's being entangled in worldly life. Bhavanath was twenty-three
or twenty-four years old.

MASTER (to Narendra): "Give him a lot of courage."

Narendra and Bhavanath smiled. Sri Ramakrishna
said to Bhavanath, by signs: "Be a great hero. Don't
forget yourself when you see her weeping behind her
veil. Oh, women cry so much—even when they blow
their noses! (Narendra, Bhavanath, and M laugh.)

"Keep your mind firm on God. He who is a hero
lives with a woman but does not indulge in physical
pleasures. Talk to your wife only about God."

A few minutes later Sri Ramakrishna said to Bhavanath, by a sign, "Take your meal here today."

BHAVANATH: "Yes, sir. I am quite all right. Don't
worry about me."

Surendra came in and took a seat. The devotees offered garlands of flowers to the Master every evening.
Sri Ramakrishna put these garlands around his neck.
Surendra sat quietly in the room. Sri Ramakrishna was
in a very happy mood and gave him two garlands.
Surendra saluted the Master and put them around his
neck.

All sat in silence and looked at Sri Ramakrishna.
Surendra saluted the Master again and stood up. He
was about to leave. He asked Bhavanath to hang the
straw screens over the windows.

Hirananda came in with two of his friends. He was
a native of Sindh, about twenty-two hundred miles

from Calcutta. After finishing his college education in Calcutta in 1883, he had returned to Sindh and taken charge of editing two papers, the *Sindh Times* and the *Sind Sudhār*. While studying in Calcutta he had often visited Keshab Chandra Sen and had come to know him intimately. He had met Sri Ramakrishna at the Kāli temple at Dakshineswar and had spent an occasional night there with the Master. Hearing of Sri Ramakrishna's illness, he now came to Calcutta from Sindh to see him. The Master himself had been very eager to see Hirananda.

Sri Ramakrishna pointed to Hirananda and said to M, by signs: "A very fine boy. Do you know him?"

M: "Yes, sir."

MASTER (*to Hirananda and M*): "Please talk a little. I want to hear you both."

When M remained silent, Sri Ramakrishna asked him: "Is Narendra here? Call him."

Narendra entered the room and sat near the Master.

MASTER (*to Narendra and Hirananda*): "I want to hear you two talk."

Hirananda was silent for a few moments and then after great hesitation began the conversation.

HIRANANDA (*to Narendra*): "Why does a devotee of God suffer?"

His words were sweet as nectar. Everyone in the room could feel that his heart was filled with love.

NARENDRA: "The plan of the universe is devilish. I could have created a better world."

HIRANANDA: "Can one feel happiness without misery?"

NARENDRA: "I am not making a plan for a universe, but simply giving my opinion of the present plan.

"But all these problems are solved if we have faith

only in one thing, and that is pantheism. All doubts disappear if one believes that everything is God. God alone is responsible for all that happens."

HIRANANDA: "Very easy to say that."

Narendra sang Śankara's Six Stanzas on Nirvāna:

Om. I am neither mind, intelligence, ego, nor chitta,
Neither the ears nor the tongue, nor the senses of smell
   and sight;
Neither ākāśa nor air, nor fire nor water nor earth:
I am Eternal Bliss and Awareness—I am Śiva, I am
   Śiva.

I am neither the prāna nor the five vital breaths,
Neither the body's seven elements[1] nor its five sheaths,
Nor hands nor feet nor tongue, nor other organ of
   action:
I am Eternal Bliss and Awareness—I am Śiva, I am
   Śiva.

Neither greed nor delusion, loathing nor liking, have I;
Nothing of pride or ego, of dharma or liberation;
Neither desire of the mind nor object for its desiring:
I am Eternal Bliss and Awareness—I am Śiva, I am
   Śiva.

Nothing of pleasure and pain, of virtue and vice, do I
   know,
Of mantra or sacred place, of Vedas or sacrifice;
Neither am I the eater, the food, nor the act of eating:
I am Eternal Bliss and Awareness—I am Śiva, I am
   Śiva.

Death or fear have I none, nor any distinction of caste;
Neither father nor mother, nor even a birth, have I;

[1] I.e. water, blood, flesh, fat, bone, marrow, and semen.

Neither friend nor comrade, neither disciple nor guru:
I am Eternal Bliss and Awareness—I am Śiva, I am
  Śiva.

I have no form or fancy: the All-pervading am I;
Everywhere I exist, and yet am beyond the senses;
Neither salvation am I, nor anything to be known:
I am Eternal Bliss and Awareness—I am Śiva, I am
  Śiva.

HIRANANDA: "Good!"

SRI RAMAKRISHNA (*to Hirananda, by a sign*): "Give
him an answer."

HIRANANDA: "It is all the same, whether you look
at a room from a corner or look at it from the middle.
It is the same God-Consciousness, whether one says, 'O
God, I am Thy servant,' or, 'I am He.' One may
enter a room by several doors."

All sat in silence. Hirananda said to Narendra,
"Please sing some more." Narendra sang the Five
Stanzas on the Kaupin:[2]

Roaming ever in the grove of Vedānta,
Ever pleased with his beggar's morsel,
Wandering onward, his heart free from sorrow,
Blest indeed is the wearer of the loincloth.

Sitting at the foot of a tree for shelter,
Eating from his hands his meagre portion,
Wrapped in a garment fine or ugly,
Blest indeed is the wearer of the loincloth.

Satisfied fully by the Bliss within him,
Curbing wholly the cravings of his senses,

[2] The loincloth of the sannyāsi; it is an emblem of renunciation.

Contemplating always the Absolute Brahman,
Blest indeed is the wearer of the loincloth.

As Sri Ramakrishna heard the line, "Contemplating always the Absolute Brahman," he said in a very low voice, "Ah!" Then, by a sign, he said to the devotees, "That is the characteristic of a yogi."

Narendra finished the hymn:

Witnessing the changes of mind and body,
Naught but the Self within him beholding,
Heedless of outer, of inner, of middle,
Blest indeed is the wearer of the loincloth.

Chanting Brahman, the word of redemption,
Meditating only on "I am Brahman,"
Living on alms and wandering freely,
Blest indeed is the wearer of the loincloth.

Again Narendra sang:

Meditate on Him, the Perfect, the Embodiment of Bliss;
Meditate on Him, the Formless, the Root of the universe,
The Hearer behind the ear, the Thinker behind the mind,
The Speaker behind the tongue, Himself beyond all words:
He is the Life of life, the Ultimate, the Adorable.

MASTER (to Narendra): "And that one—'All that exists art Thou.'"

Narendra sang:

I have joined my heart to Thee: all that exists art Thou;

Thee only have I found, for Thou art all that exists.
O Lord, Beloved of my heart, Thou art the Home of all;
Where, indeed, is the heart in which Thou dost not
    dwell?
Thou hast entered every heart: all that exists art Thou.

Whether sage or fool, whether Hindu or Mussalmān,
Thou makest him as Thou wilt: all that exists art Thou.
Thy presence is everywhere, whether in heaven or in
    Kaabā;
Before Thee all must bow, for Thou art all that exists.

From earth below to the highest heaven, from heaven
    to deepest earth,
I see Thee wherever I look: all that exists art Thou.
Pondering, I have understood, I have seen beyond a
    doubt;
I find not a single thing that may be compared to Thee.
To Jāfar[3] it has been revealed that Thou art all that
    exists.

As the Master listened to the line "Thou hast entered
every heart," he said by a sign: "God dwells in everybody's heart. He is the Inner Guide."

As Narendra sang the line "I see Thee wherever
I look: all that exists art Thou," Hirananda said to
him: "Yes, 'All that exists art Thou.' Now you say:
'Thou! Thou! Not I, but Thou!'"

NARENDRA: "Give me a one and I'll give you a
million. Thou art I; I am Thou. Nothing exists but I."

Narendra recited a few verses from the Ashtāvakra
Samhitā. The room again became silent.

MASTER (to Hirananda, pointing to Narendra): "He
seems to be walking with an unsheathed sword in his
hand. (To M, pointing to Hirananda) How calm! Like

[3] The author of the song.

a cobra, quiet before the charmer, with its hood spread."

Sri Ramakrishna fell into an inward mood. Hirananda and M were seated near him. There was complete silence in the room. The Master's body was being racked with indescribable pain. The devotees could not bear the sight of this illness; but somehow the Master made them forget his suffering. He sat there, his face beaming as if there were no trace of illness in his throat.

The devotees had placed flowers and garlands before him as their loving offerings. He picked up a flower and touched with it first his head, then his throat, heart, and navel. To the devotees he appeared a child playing with flowers.

Sri Ramakrishna used to tell the devotees that his divine visions and moods were accompanied by the rising of a spiritual current inside his body.

Now he talked to M.

MASTER: "I don't remember when the current went up. Now I am in the mood of a child. That is why I am playing this way with the flowers. Do you know what I see now? I see my body as a frame made of bamboo strips and covered with a cloth. The frame moves. And it moves because someone dwelling inside moves it.

"Again, I see the body to be like a pumpkin with the seeds scooped out. Inside this body there is no trace of passion or worldly attachment. It is all very clean inside, and—"

It became very painful for Sri Ramakrishna to talk further. He felt very weak. M quickly guessed what the Master wanted to tell the devotees, and said, "And you are seeing God inside yourself."

MASTER: "Both inside and outside. The indivisible

Satchidānanda—I see It both inside and outside. It has merely assumed this sheath [meaning his body] for a support and exists both inside and outside. I clearly perceive this."

M and Hirananda listened intently to these words about his exalted state of God-Consciousness. A few moments later Sri Ramakrishna looked at them and resumed the conversation.

MASTER: "You all seem to me to be my kinsmen. I do not look on any of you as a stranger.

"I see you all as so many sheaths,[4] and the heads are moving.

"I notice that when my mind is united with God the suffering of the body is left aside.

"Now I perceive only this: the Indivisible Satchid-ānanda is covered with skin, and this sore in the throat is on one side of it."

The Master again fell silent. A few minutes later he said: "The attributes of matter are superimposed on Spirit, and the attributes of Spirit are superimposed on matter. Therefore when the body is ill a man says, 'I am ill.'"

Hirananda wanted to understand what the Master had just said; so M told him, "When hot water scalds the hand, people say that the water scalds; but the truth is that it is the heat that scalds."

HIRANANDA (to the Master): "Please tell us why a devotee of God suffers."

MASTER: "It is the body that suffers."

Sri´ Ramakrishna seemed about to say something more. Hirananda and M eagerly awaited his words.

Sri Ramakrishna said, "Do you understand?"

M said to Hirananda, in a whisper: "The body

---

[4] Referring to their bodies.

suffers for the purpose of teaching men. His life is like a book of reference. In spite of so much physical suffering, his mind is one hundred per cent united with God."

HIRANANDA: "Yes, it is like Christ's crucifixion. But still the mystery remains—why should he, of all people, suffer like this?"

M: "The Master says it is the will of the Divine Mother. This is how She is sporting through his body."

The two devotees were talking in whispers. Sri Ramakrishna asked Hirananda, by a sign, what M was talking about. Since Hirananda could not understand the sign, Sri Ramakrishna repeated it.

HIRANANDA: "He says that your illness is for the teaching of men."

MASTER: "But that's only his guess.

(To M and Hirananda) "My mood is changing. I think that I should not say to everyone, 'May your spiritual consciousness be awakened.' People are so sinful in the Kaliyuga; if I awaken their spiritual consciousness I shall have to accept the burden of their sins."

M (to Hirananda): "He will not awaken people's spiritual consciousness except at the right time. When a person is ready, he will awaken his spiritual consciousness."

Friday, April 23, 1886

It was Good Friday. Hirananda had taken his mid-day meal at the Cossipore garden house. About one o'clock in the afternoon he was stroking Sri Rama-krishna's feet. M sat near by. Latu and one or two other devotees were going in and out of the room.

It was the Master's earnest desire that Hirananda should stay for some time at the Cossipore garden house.

While massaging the Master's feet, Hirananda conversed with him. He spoke in a very sweet voice, as if trying to console a child.

HIRANANDA: "Why should you worry so much? You can enjoy peace of mind if you have faith in the physician. You are a child."

MASTER (to M): "How can I have faith in the doctor? Dr. Sarkar said that I would not recover."

HIRANANDA: "But why should you worry so much about that? What is to happen must happen."

M (to Hirananda, aside): "He is not worrying about himself. The preservation of his body is for the welfare of the devotees."

It was a sultry day and the room became very hot at noontime. The straw screens had been hung over the windows. Hirananda adjusted them. The Master looked at him.

MASTER (to Hirananda): "Please don't forget to send the pajamas."

Hirananda had told Sri Ramakrishna that he would feel more comfortable if he wore the pajamas used in Sindh. Sri Ramakrishna was reminding him of them.

Hirananda had not eaten well. The rice had not been well cooked. The Master felt very sorry about it and asked him again and again if he would like to have some refreshments. On account of his illness he could hardly talk; but still he repeated the question. He said to Latu, "Did you too eat that rice?"

Sri Ramakrishna could hardly keep the cloth on his body. He was almost always naked, like a child. Hirananda had brought with him one or two of his

Brāhmo friends. Therefore every now and then the Master pulled the cloth to his waist.

MASTER (*to Hirananda*): "Will you take me for an uncivilized person if I don't cover my body with my cloth?"

HIRANANDA: "What difference does that make with you? You are but a child."

MASTER (*pointing to a Brāhmo devotee*): "But he doesn't feel that way."

Hirananda was about to take his leave. In a very few days he was going to start for Sindh.

MASTER (*to Hirananda*): "Suppose you don't go to Sindh."

HIRANANDA (*smiling*): "But there is nobody there to do my work. I have my duties."

MASTER: "How much do you earn?"

HIRANANDA (*smiling*): "My work doesn't bring me a large salary."

MASTER: "Still, how much?"

Hirananda laughed.

MASTER: "Why don't you live here?"

Hirananda did not reply.

MASTER: "Suppose you give up the job."

Hirananda said nothing. He was ready to take his leave.

MASTER: "When will you see me again?"

HIRANANDA: "I shall leave for Sindh the day after tomorrow. I shall see you that morning."

Hirananda left.

M was seated by the Master's side.

MASTER (*to M*): "He is a fine young man, isn't he?"

M: "Yes, sir. He has a very sweet nature."

MASTER: "He said that Sindh is twenty-two hundred

miles from Calcutta; and he has come all that way to see me."

M: "True, sir. That would be impossible without real love."

MASTER: "He wants very much to take me to Sindh."

M: "The journey is very painful. It takes four or five days by train."

MASTER: "He has three university degrees."

M: "Yes, sir."

Sri Ramakrishna was tired. He wanted to take a little rest. He asked M to open the shutters of the windows and spread the straw mat over his bed. M was fanning him. Sri Ramakrishna became drowsy.

After a short nap Sri Ramakrishna said to M, "Did I sleep?"

M: "A little."

It was afternoon. Many devotees were sitting in the Master's room. Narendra, Sarat, Sashi, Latu, Nityagopal, Girish, Ram, M, and Suresh were present.

Kedar came in. This was his first visit to the Master for some time. While staying in Dāccā, in connexion with his official duties, he had heard of Sri Ramakrishna's illness. On entering Sri Ramakrishna's room he took the dust of the Master's feet on his head and then joyously gave it to the others. The devotees accepted it with bowed heads. All sat without uttering a word. Sri Ramakrishna seemed about to go into an ecstatic mood. Now and then he breathed heavily as if trying to suppress his emotion.

The Master drew Kedar's attention to Narendra and said: "He has renounced everything. (*To the devotees*) Kedar once said to Narendra, 'You may reason and argue now, but in the end you will roll on the ground, chanting Hari's name.'"

Surendra was seated behind the other devotees. The
Master looked at him with a smile and said to Kedar,
"Ah, how sweet his nature is!" Kedar understood the
Master's hint and went toward Surendra.

Surendra was very sensitive. Some of the devotees
had been collecting funds from the householder
devotees to meet the expenses of the Cossipore garden
house. Surendra felt piqued at this. He had been bearing most of the expenses himself.

SURENDRA (to Kedar): "How can I sit near all these
holy people? A few days ago some of them [referring
to Narendra] put on the ochre robe of the sannyāsi
and went on a pilgrimage to Buddha-Gayā. They
wanted to see bigger sādhus there."

Sri Ramakrishna was trying to console Surendra.
He said: "You are right. They are mere children.
They don't know what is good."

SURENDRA (to Kedar): "Doesn't our gurudeva⁵ know
our inner feelings? He does not care for money. It is
our inner attitude that pleases him."

Sri Ramakrishna with a nod of his head approved
Surendra's words.

The devotees had brought various food offerings for
the Master and placed them in front of him. Sri
Ramakrishna put a grain on his tongue and gave the
plate to Surendra. He asked Surendra to distribute the
prasād to the devotees. Surendra went downstairs
with the offerings.

MASTER (to Kedar): "You had better go downstairs and explain it all to Surendra. See that they
don't get into any hot arguments."

M was fanning Sri Ramakrishna. The Master said

⁵ Referring to Sri Ramakrishna.

to him, "Won't you eat anything?" He sent M
downstairs.

It was about dusk. Girish and M were strolling
near the small reservoir in the garden.

GIRISH: "I understand that you are writing something about the Master.[6] Is it true?"

M: "Who told you that?"

GIRISH: "I have heard about it. Will you give it to
me?"

M: "No, I won't part with it unless I feel it is
right to do so. I am writing it for myself, not for
others."

GIRISH: "What do you mean?"

M: "You may get it when I die."

It was evening. A lamp was lighted in the Master's
room. Amrita Basu, a Brāhmo devotee, came in. Sri
Ramakrishna had expressed his eagerness to see him.
M and a few other devotees were there. A garland of
jasmine lay in front of the Master on a plantain leaf.
There was perfect silence in the room. A great yogi
seemed to be silently communing with God. Every
now and then the Master lifted the garland a little, as
if he wanted to put it around his neck.

AMRITA (tenderly): "Shall I put it around your
neck?"

Sri Ramakrishna accepted the garland. He had a long
conversation with Amrita. When the latter was about
to take his leave, the Master said, "Come again."

[6] After Sri Ramakrishna's death M published his notes
of conversations with the Master in five volumes. *The
Gospel of Sri Ramakrishna* is an English translation of
these books from the original Bengali. The present book
is abridged from *The Gospel of Sri Ramakrishna.*

AMRITA: "Yes, sir. I should like to come very much. But I live at a great distance; so I cannot always come."

MASTER: "Do come, and take the carriage hire from here."

The devotees were amazed at the Master's love for Amrita.

The next day M came to the garden house accompanied by his wife and a son. The boy was seven years old. It was at the Master's request that he brought his wife, who was almost mad with grief owing to the death of one of her sons.

That day the Master several times allowed M's wife the privilege of waiting on him. Her welfare seemed to occupy his attention a great deal. In the evening the Holy Mother came to the Master's room to feed him. M's wife accompanied her with a lamp. The Master tenderly asked her many questions about her household. He requested her to come again to the garden house and spend a few days with the Holy Mother, not forgetting to ask her to bring her baby daughter. When the Master had finished his meal M's wife removed the plates. He chatted with her a few minutes.

About nine o'clock in the evening Sri Ramakrishna was seated in his room with the devotees. He had a garland of flowers around his neck. He told M that he had requested his wife to spend a few days at the garden house with the Holy Mother. His kindness touched M's heart.

M was fanning him. The Master took the garland from his neck and said something to himself. Then in a very benign mood he gave the garland to M.

⇝ 13 ⇜

AFTER THE PASSING AWAY

Sᴿɪ Rᴀᴍᴀᴋʀɪsʜɴᴀ passed away on Sunday, August 15, 1886, plunging his devotees and disciples into a sea of grief. They were like men in a shipwreck. But a strong bond of love held them together and they found comfort and courage in one another's company. They could not enjoy the friendship of worldly people and would talk only of their Master. "Shall we not behold him again?"—this was the theme of their thought and the dream of their sleep. Alone, they wept for him; walking in the streets of Calcutta, they were engrossed in the thought of him. The Master had once said to M, "It becomes difficult for me to give up the body when I realize that after my death you will wander about weeping for me." Some of them thought: "He is no longer in this world. How surprising that we still enjoy living! We could give up our bodies if we liked, but still we do not." Time and again Sri Ramakrishna had told them that God reveals Himself to His devotees if they yearn for Him and call on Him with whole-souled devotion. He had assured them that God listens to the prayer of a sincere heart.

The young unmarried disciples of the Master, who belonged to his inner circle, had attended on him day and night at the Cossipore garden house. After his passing away most of them returned to their families

against their own wills. They had not yet formally
renounced the world. For a short while they kept their
family names. But Sri Ramakrishna had made them
renounce the world mentally. He himself had initiated
several of them into the monastic life, giving them the
ochre cloths of sannyāsis.

Two or three of the Master's attendants had no place
to live. To them the large-hearted Surendra said:
"Brothers, where will you wander about? Let us rent
a house. You will live there and make it our Master's
shrine; and we householders shall come there for
consolation. How can we pass all our days and nights
with our wives and children in the world? I used to
spend a little money for the Master at Cossipore. I
shall gladly give it now for your expenses." Accordingly
he rented a house for them at Barānagore, in the
suburbs of Calcutta, and this place gradually
transformed into a math, or monastery.

For the first few months Surendra contributed thirty
rupees a month. As the other members joined the
monastery, one by one, he doubled his contribution,
which he later increased to a hundred rupees. The
monthly rent for the house was eleven rupees. The
cook received six rupees a month. The rest was spent
on food.

The younger Gopal brought the Master's bed and
other articles of daily use from the garden house at
Cossipore. The brāhmin who had been the cook at
Cossipore was engaged for the new monastery. The first
permanent member was the elder Gopal. Sarat spent
the nights there. In the beginning Sarat, Sashi,
Baburam, Niranjan, and Kali used to visit the
monastery every now and then, according to their
convenience. Tarak, who had gone to Vrindāvan follow-

ing the Master's death, returned to Calcutta after a few months and soon became a permanent member of the monastery. Rakhal, Jogin, Latu, and Kali were living at Vrindāvan with the Holy Mother when the monastery was started. Kali returned to Calcutta within a month, Rakhal a few months later, and Jogin and Latu after a year. The householder devotees frequently visited the monastic brothers and spent hours with them in meditation and study.

After a short time Narendra, Rakhal, Niranjan, Sarat, Sashi, Baburam, Jogin, Tarak, Kali, and Latu renounced the world for good. Sarada Prasanna and Subodh joined them some time later. Gangadhar, who was very much attached to Narendra, visited the math regularly. It was he who taught the brothers the hymn sung at the evening service in the Śiva temple at Benares. He had gone to Tibet to practise austerity; now, having returned, he lived at the monastery. Hari, at first only a visitor at the monastery, soon embraced the monastic life and thus completed the list of the Master's sannyāsi disciples.[1]

Surendra was indeed a blessed soul. It was he who laid the foundation of the great Order later associated with Sri Ramakrishna's name. His devotion and sacrifice enabled those earnest young men to renounce the world for the realization of God. Through him Sri Ramakrishna made it possible for them to live in the world as embodiments of his teaching: the renunciation of "woman" and "gold" and the realization of God.

The brothers lived at the math like orphan boys. Sometimes they would not have the money to pay their house rent; sometimes they would have no food

[1] The monastic names of the Master's disciples who renounced the world soon after his death were as follows:

in the monastery. Surendra would come and settle all these things. He was the big brother of the monks. Later on, when they thought of his genuine love, the members of this first math shed tears of gratitude.

The new monastery became known among the Master's devotees as the Barānagore Math. Narendra, Rakhal, and the other young disciples were filled with intense renunciation. One day Rakhal's father came to the math and asked Rakhal to return home. "Why do you take the trouble to come here?" Rakhal said to him. "I am very happy here. Please pray to God that you may forget me and that I may forget you too." The young disciples said to each other: "We shall never return to the worldly life. The Master enjoined

Narendra	Swami	Vivekananda
Rakhal	Swami	Brahmananda
Jogin	Swami	Jogananda
Niranjan	Swami	Niranjanananda
Latu	Swami	Adbhutananda
Baburam	Swami	Premananda
Tarak	Swami	Shivananda
Hari	Swami	Turiyananda
Sarat	Swami	Saradananda
Sashi	Swami	Ramakrishnananda
Kali	Swami	Abhedananda
Gangadhar	Swami	Akhandananda
Gopal (elder)	Swami	Advaitananda
Sarada Prasanna	Swami	Trigunatitananda
Subodh	Swami	Subodhananda

Tulasi, a young man of Bāghbāzār, had visited the Master a few times both in Calcutta and in Dakshineswar, and received his blessings. Now he began to frequent the monastery and soon became one of its members. Formally initiated into the spiritual life by Swami Vivekananda, Tulasi also renounced the world and took the name of Swami Nirmalananda.

upon us the renunciation of 'woman' and 'gold.' How can we go back to our families?"

Sashi had taken charge of the daily worship in the math. The Master's relics had been brought from Balaram's house and Sri Ramakrishna was worshipped daily in the worship hall. Narendra supervised the household. He was the leader of the monastery. He would often tell his brother disciples that the selfless actions enjoined in the Gita were worship, japa, meditation, and so on, and not worldly duties. The brothers at the math depended on him for their spiritual inspiration. He said to them, "We must practise sādhanā; otherwise we shall not be able to realize God."

He and his brother disciples, filled with an ascetic spirit, devoted themselves day and night to the practice of spiritual discipline. Their one goal in life was the realization of God. They followed to their hearts' content the injunctions prescribed in the Vedas, Purānas, and Tantras for an austere life. They spent their time in japa and meditation and study of the scriptures. Whenever they would fail to experience the Divine Presence, they would feel as if they were on the rack. They practised austerity, sometimes alone under trees, sometimes in a cremation ground, sometimes on the bank of the Ganges. Again, sometimes they spent the entire day in the meditation room of the monastery in japa and contemplation; sometimes they gathered to sing and dance in a rapture of delight. All of them, and Narendra particularly, were consumed with the desire to see God. Now and then they would say to each other, "Should we not starve ourselves to death to see God?"

Monday, February 21, 1887

Narendra, Rakhal, Niranjan, Sarat, Sashi, Kali, Baburam, Tarak, and Sarada Prasanna were living in the monastery. All day the members had been fasting in observance of the Śivarātri.[2] Sarat, Kali, Niranjan, and Sarada were planning to go to Puri the following Saturday, on a pilgrimage to the sacred Jagannāth. Jogin and Latu were at Vrindāvan and had not yet seen the new place.

Narendra had gone to Calcutta that morning to look after a lawsuit in which his family had been involved since his father's death. At nine o'clock in the morning M arrived at the math. Tarak saw him and began to sing in praise of Śiva, Rakhal joining him. They danced as they sang. Narendra had recently composed the song.

Sashi finished the morning worship in the shrine. Sarat then sang about Śiva to the accompaniment of the tānpurā.

Narendra had just arrived from Calcutta. He had not yet taken his bath. Kali asked him, "How about the lawsuit?" "Why should you bother about it?" Narendra replied sharply.

Narendra took his bath in the Ganges and returned to the monastery. He carried his wet cloth and towel in his hand. Sarada prostrated himself before Narendra. He too had been fasting on account of the Śivarātri. He was going to the Ganges for his bath. Narendra

2 The night of Śiva. On this day the devotees fast, spending the whole night in meditation, prayer, and other spiritual exercises.

entered the worship room and saluted the picture of
Sri Ramakrishna, who was daily worshipped there as
the Deity. For a few minutes he was absorbed in
meditation.

Arrangements were being made to worship Śiva in
the evening. Leaves of the bel-tree were gathered
for the worship. Bel-wood was chopped for the homa.

In the evening Sashi, who was in charge of the
worship at the monastery, burnt incense before the
pictures of the various gods and goddesses.

The worship of Śiva was to take place under the
bel-tree in the monastery compound. The Deity was to
be worshipped four times, during the four watches of
the night. The brothers assembled under the bel-tree.
Bhupati and M were present. One of the young
members of the math was in charge of the worship.
Kali was reading from the Gitā. Now and then he
argued with Narendra.

KALI: "I alone am everything. I create, preserve,
and destroy."

NARENDRA: "How is it possible for me to create?
Another power creates through me. Our various actions
—even our thoughts—are caused by that power."

M (to himself): "The Master used to say: 'As long
as a man feels that it is he who meditates, he is under
the jurisdiction of the Ādyāśakti, the Primal Power.
Śakti must be acknowledged.'"

Kali reflected in silence a few moments and then
said: "The actions you are talking about are illusory.
There is not even any such thing as thought. The
very idea of these things makes me laugh."

NARENDRA: "The 'I' that is implied in 'I am He'
is not this ego. It is that which remains after one
eliminates mind, body, and so on."

After completing the recital of the Gitā, Kali chanted: "Śāntih! Śāntih! Śāntih!"

Narendra and the other devotees stood up and circled round and round the tree, singing and dancing. Now and then they chanted in chorus: "Śiva Guru! Śiva Guru!"

It was midnight, the fourteenth day of the dark fortnight of the moon. Pitch darkness filled all the quarters. Men, birds, and animals were all hushed into silence. The young sannyāsis were clad in gerruā robes. The words "Śiva Guru," chanted in their full-throated voices, rose into the infinite sky like the rumblings of rain clouds and disappeared in the Indivisible Satchidānanda.

The worship was over. The sun, about to rise, was painting the eastern horizon crimson. In this sacred twilight, the conjunction of night and day, the holy Brāhmamuhurta, the young worshippers finished their baths in the Ganges.

In the morning the devotees went to the shrine room, prostrated themselves before the Deity, and gradually assembled in the big hall. Narendra was clad in a new ochre cloth. The bright orange colour of his apparel blended with the celestial lustre of his face and body, every pore of which radiated a divine light. His countenance was filled with fiery brilliance and yet touched with the tenderness of love. He appeared to all as a bubble that had risen up in the Ocean of Absolute Existence and Bliss and assumed a human body to help in the propagation of his Master's message. All eyes were fixed on him. Narendra was then just twenty-four years old, the very age at which the great Chaitanya had renounced the world.

Balaram had sent fruit and sweets to the monastery

for the devotees' breakfast. Rakhal, Narendra, and a few others partook of the refreshments. After eating one or two morsels some of them cried out, "Blessed indeed is Balaram!" All laughed.

Narendra now began to joke like a boy. He was imitating Sri Ramakrishna. He put a sweet into his mouth and stood still, as if in samādhi. His eyes remained unblinking. A devotee stepped forward and pretended to hold him up by the hand lest he should drop to the ground. Narendra closed his eyes. A few minutes later, with the sweetmeat still in his mouth, he opened his eyes and drawled out, "I—am—all—right." All laughed loudly.

Refreshments were now given to everyone. M looked on at this wonderful mart of happiness. The devotees shouted joyfully, "Jai Gurumahārāj!"[3]

Monday, March 25, 1887

M arrived at the Barānagore Math to visit his brother disciples. Devendra accompanied him. M had been coming to the monastery very frequently and now and then had spent a day or two. The previous week he had spent three days at the math. He was very eager to observe the spirit of intense renunciation of these young men.

It was evening. M intended to spend the night in the monastery. Sashi lighted the lamp in the worship room and chanted the name of God. Next he burnt incense before all the pictures of gods and goddesses in the various rooms. The evening service began. Sashi conducted the worship. The members of the math, with M and Devendra, stood with folded hands and sang the hymn of the ārati.

[3] Victory to the Guru!

When the worship was over, Narendra and M became engaged in conversation. Narendra was recalling his various meetings with Sri Ramakrishna.

NARENDRA: "One day, during one of my early visits, the Master in an ecstatic mood said to me, 'You have come!' 'How amazing!' I said to myself. 'It is as if he had known me a long time.' Then he said to me, 'Do you ever see light?' I replied: 'Yes, sir. Before I fall asleep I feel something like a light revolving near my forehead.' "

M: "Do you see it even now?"

NARENDRA: "I used to see it frequently. In Jadu Mallick's garden house the Master one day touched me and muttered something to himself. I became unconscious. The effect of the touch lingered with me a month, like an intoxication.

"When he heard that a proposal had been made about my marriage, he wept, holding the feet of the image of Kāli. With tears in his eyes he prayed to the Divine Mother: 'O Mother, please upset the whole thing! Don't let Narendra be drowned.'

"After my father's death my mother and my brothers were starving. When the Master met Annada Guha one day, he said to him: 'Narendra's father has died. His family is in a state of great privation. It would be good if his friends helped him with money.'

"After Annada had left I scolded him. I said, 'Why did you say all those things to him?' Thus rebuked, he wept and said, 'Alas! for your sake I could beg from door to door.'

"He tamed us by his love. Don't you think so?"

M: "There is not the slightest doubt about it. His love was utterly unselfish."

NARENDRA: "One day when I was alone with him

he said something to me. Nobody else was present. Please don't repeat it to anyone here."

M: "No, I shall not. What did he say?"

NARENDRA: "He said: 'It is not possible for me to exercise occult powers; but I shall do so through you. What do you say?' 'No,' I replied, 'you can't do that.'

"I used to laugh at his words. You must have heard all these things from him. I told him that his visions of God were all hallucinations of his mind.

"He said to me: 'I used to climb to the roof of the kuthi and cry: "O devotees, where are you all? Come to me, O devotees! I am about to die. I shall certainly die if I do not see you." And the Divine Mother told me, "The devotees will come." You see, everything is turning out to be true.'

"What else could I say? I kept quiet.

"One day he shut the door of his room and said to Devendra Babu and Girish Babu, referring to me, 'He will not keep his body if he is told who he is.' "

M: "Yes, we have heard that. Many a time he repeated the same thing to us, too. Once you came to know about your true Self in nirvikalpa samādhi at the Cossipore garden house. Isn't that true?"

NARENDRA: "Yes. In that experience I felt that I had no body. I could see only my face. The Master was in the upstairs room. I had that experience downstairs. I was weeping. I said, 'What has happened to me?' The elder Gopal went to the Master's room and said, 'Narendra is crying.'

"When I saw the Master he said to me: 'Now you have known. But I am going to keep the key with me.'

"I said to him, 'What is it that happened to me?'

"Turning to the devotees, he said: 'He will not

keep his body if he knows who he is. But I have put a veil over his eyes.'

"One day he said to me, 'You can see Krishna in your heart if you want.' I replied, 'I don't believe in Krishna or any such nonsense!' (*Both M and Narendra laugh.*)

"I have noticed a peculiar thing. Some men, objects, or places make me feel as if I had seen them before, in a previous birth. They appear familiar to me. One day I went to Sarat's house in Calcutta, on Amherst Street. Immediately I said to Sarat: 'This house seems familiar to me. It seems to me that I have known the rooms, the passages, and the rest of the house for many, many days.'

"I used to follow my own whims in everything I did. The Master never interfered. You know that I became a member of the Sādhāran Brāhmo Samāj."

M: "Yes, I know that."

NARENDRA: "The Master knew that women attended the meetings of the Brāhmo Samāj. A man cannot meditate with women sitting in front of him; therefore he criticized the meditation of the Brāhmo Samāj. But he didn't object to my going there. But one day he said to me, 'Don't tell Rakhal about your being a member of the Brāhmo Samāj, or he too will feel like becoming one.'"

M: "You have greater strength of mind. That is why the Master didn't prevent your going to the Samāj."

NARENDRA: "I have attained my present state of mind as a result of much suffering and pain. You have not passed through any such suffering. I now realize that without trials and tribulations one cannot resign oneself to God and depend on Him absolutely.

"Well, X— is so modest and humble! He is totally self-effacing. Can you tell me how I can develop humility?"

M: "Speaking about your ego, the Master said, 'Whose ego is it?' "

NARENDRA: "What did he mean?"

M: "The Master meant that it was God alone who kept this ego in you so that He might accomplish many things through you."

The conversation turned to other devotees.

NARENDRA: "The Master said about Vijay Goswámi, 'He is knocking at the door.' "

M: "That is to say, he has not yet entered the room. At Syámpukur Vijay said to the Master, 'I saw you at Dáccá in this tangible form, in this very body.' You were there too."

NARENDRA: "Devendra Babu and Ram Babu want to renounce the world. They are trying hard. Ram Babu told me privately that he would give up the world after two years."

M: "After two years? After making provision for his children?"

NARENDRA: "Besides, he will rent his present house and buy a small house. Other relatives will arrange his daughter's marriage."

Friday, April 8, 1887

About eight o'clock in the morning two devotees, one a householder and the other a monk, were conversing in a room in the Baránagore monastery, when M came in. The devotees were of the same age— twenty-four or twenty-five years old. M intended to spend three days at the monastery. He went to the shrine and saluted the Deity. After visiting Narendra, Rakhal, and the other brothers, he at last came into the room where the two devotees were engaged in conversation. The householder devotee wanted to renounce the world. The monk was trying to persuade him not to do so.

MONK: "Why don't you finish the few duties you have in the world? Very soon they will be left behind.

"A man was told that he would go to hell. He asked a friend, 'What is hell like?' Thereupon the friend began to draw a picture of hell on the ground with a piece of chalk. No sooner had the picture been drawn than the man rolled over it and said, 'Now I have gone through hell!' "

HOUSEHOLDER: "I don't relish worldly life. Ah, how happy you are here!"

MONK: "Why don't you renounce the world if you want to? Why do you talk about it so much? But I repeat, why don't you enjoy the fun once for all?"

Sashi finished the regular worship. About eleven the brothers of the math returned from the Ganges after taking their baths. They put on clean cloths, went to the shrine, saluted the Deity, and meditated a little while.

After the food was offered to the Deity they had their meal. M ate with them.

It was evening. Incense was burnt before the pictures of gods and goddesses and the worship was performed. Rakhal, Sashi, the elder Gopal, and Harish were seated in the big hall. M also was there. Rakhal warned one of the brothers to be careful about the food to be offered to the Master in the shrine.

RAKHAL (to Sashi and the others): "One day I ate

part of his [meaning the Master's] refreshments before he took them. At this he said: 'I cannot look at you. How could you do such a thing?' I burst into tears."

THE ELDER GOPAL: "One day at Cossipore I breathed hard on his food. At this he said, 'Take that food away.' "

M and Narendra were pacing the verandah and recalling old times.

NARENDRA: "I did not believe in anything."

M: "You mean the forms of God?"

NARENDRA: "At first I did not accept most of what the Master said. One day he asked me, 'Then why do you come here?' I replied, 'I come here to see you, not to listen to you.' "

M: "What did he say to that?"

NARENDRA: "He was very much pleased."

Saturday, April 9, 1887

The members of the math were resting a little after their meal. Narendra and M sat under a tree in the garden to the west of the monastery. It was a solitary place and no one else was present. Narendra was recounting to M his various experiences with Sri Ramakrishna. Narendra was about twenty-four years old, and M thirty-two.

M: "You must remember vividly your first visit to him."

NARENDRA: "That day I sang two songs."

Narendra sang them for M:

Let us go back once more, O mind, to our own abode.
Here in this foreign land of earth
Why should we wander aimlessly in strangers' guise?
These living beings all about, and the five elements,
Are strangers to you, every one; none is your own.

Why do you so forget yourself,
In love with strangers, O my mind?
Why do you so forget your own?

Ascend the path of Truth, O mind. Unflagging, climb,
With love as the lamp to light your way.
As your provisions for the journey, bring with you
The virtues, heedfully concealed; for, like two high-
    waymen,
Greed and delusion lie in wait to seize your wealth.
And keep beside you constantly,
As guards to shelter you from harm,
Tranquillity and self-control.

Companionship with holy men will be for you
A welcome rest-house by the road;
There rest awhile your weary limbs, asking your way,
If ever you should be in doubt, of him who watches
    there.
Should anything along the path arouse your fear,
Loudly invoke the name of the Lord;
For He is ruler of that road,
And even Death must bow to Him.

And again:

> O Lord, must all my days be spent
> Utterly in vain?
> Down the path of hope
> I gaze with longing, day and night.
>
> Thou art the Lord of all the worlds,
> And I but a beggar here;
> How can I ask of Thee
> To come and dwell within my heart?
>
> My heart's humble cottage door
> Is standing open wide;
> But once be gracious, Lord,
> And enter there and quench its thirst.

M: "What did he say after listening to your songs?"

NARENDRA: "He went into samādhi. He said to Ram Babu: 'Who is this boy? How well he sings!' He asked me to come again."

M: "Where did you see him next?"

NARENDRA: "At Rajmohan's house. The third visit was at Dakshineswar again. During that visit he went into samādhi and began to praise me as if I were God. He said to me, 'O Nārāyana, you have assumed this body for my sake.' But please don't tell this to anybody else."

M: "What else did he say?"

NARENDRA: "He said: 'You have assumed this body for my sake. I asked the Divine Mother, "Mother, unless I enjoy the company of some genuine devotees completely free from 'woman' and 'gold,' how shall I live on earth?"' Then he said to me, 'You came to me at night, woke me up, and said, "Here I am!"' But I did not know anything of this. I was sound asleep in our Calcutta house."

M: "In other words, you may be both present and absent at the same time. It is like God, who is both formless and endowed with form."

NARENDRA: "But you must not tell this to anyone else. At Cossipore he transmitted his power to me."

M: "Didn't it happen when you used to meditate before a lighted fire under a tree at the Cossipore garden house?"

NARENDRA: "Yes. One day, while meditating, I asked Kali to hold my hand. Kali said to me, 'When I touched your body I felt something like an electric shock coming to my body.'

"But you must not tell this to anybody here. Give me your promise."

M: "There is a special purpose in his transmission of power to you. He will accomplish much work through you. One day the Master wrote on a piece of paper, 'Naren will teach people.'"

NARENDRA: "But I said to him, 'I won't do any such thing.' Thereupon he said, 'Your very bones will do it.' He has given me charge of Sarat. Sarat is now yearning for God; the Kundalini is awakened in him. The Master used to call me Nārāyana."

M: "Yes, I know he did."

NARENDRA: "At Cossipore he said: 'Now the key is in my hands. He will give up his body when he knows who he is.'"

M: "Didn't he say it when you were in nirvikalpa samādhi?"

NARENDRA: "Yes. At the time it seemed to me I had no body. I felt only my face.

"I was studying law at home to prepare for the examinations. Suddenly I said to myself, 'What am I doing?'"

M: "Didn't it happen when the Master was at Cossipore?"

NARENDRA: "Yes. Like an insane person I ran out of our house. He asked me, 'What do you want?' I replied, 'I want to remain immersed in samādhi.' He said: 'What a small mind you have! Go beyond samādhi! Samādhi is a very trifling thing.'"

M: "Yes, he used to say that vijnāna is the stage after jnāna. It is like going up and down the stairs after reaching the roof. What other things did he say about you?"

NARENDRA: "Once I said to him, 'The forms of God and things like that, which you see in your visions, are all hallucinations.' He had so much faith in my words that he went to the Divine Mother in the temple and told Her what I had said to him. He asked Her, 'Are these hallucinations, then?' Afterwards he said to me, 'Mother told me that all these are real.'

"Perhaps you remember that he said to me, 'When you sing, He who dwells here (*touching his heart*), like a snake, hisses as it were and then, spreading His hood, quietly holds Himself steady and listens to your music.'

"He has no doubt said many things about me; but what have I realized?"

M: "You have become the guardian of these young men. Yours is the entire responsibility. You have to bring up the brothers of the monastery."

NARENDRA: "Whatever spiritual disciplines we are practising here are in obedience to the Master's command. But it is strange that Ram Babu criticizes us for our spiritual practices. He says: 'We have seen him.[4] What need have we of any such practices?' "

M: "Let people act according to their faith."

NARENDRA: "But the Master asked us to practise sādhanā."

Narendra was again telling M about the Master's love for him.

NARENDRA: "How many times he prayed to the Divine Mother for my sake! After my father's death, when I had no food at home and my mother and sisters and brothers were starving too, the Master prayed to the Divine Mother to give me money."

M: "Yes, I know. You once told me about it."

NARENDRA: "But I didn't get any money. The Master told me what the Divine Mother had said to him: 'He will get simple food and clothes.'

[4] Sri Ramakrishna.

"He loved me so much! But whenever an impure idea crept into my mind he at once knew about it. While going around with Annada, sometimes I found myself in the company of evil people. On those occasions the Master could not eat any food from my hands. He could raise his hand a little, but he could not bring it to his mouth. On one such occasion, while he was ill, he brought his hand very close to his mouth but it did not go in. He said to me, 'You are not yet ready.'

"Now and then I feel great scepticism. At Baburam's house it seemed to me that nothing existed—as if there were no such thing as God."

M: "The Master used to say that he too had passed through that mood."

Both M and Narendra remained silent. Then M said: "You are all indeed blessed! You think of the Master day and night."

NARENDRA: "But how little! We don't yet feel like giving up the body because we haven't realized God."

It was night. Niranjan had just returned from Puri. The members of the math, and M, greeted him with great joy. Niranjan was telling them his experiences. He was then about twenty-five years old.

The evening worship was over. Some of the brothers were meditating. But many of them assembled in the big hall around Niranjan. They were talking. After nine o'clock Sashi offered food to the Deity.

The members of the math finished their supper, which consisted of home-made bread, some vegetables, and a little hard molasses.

Saturday, May 7, 1887

It was the full-moon day of the month of Vaiśākh. Narendra and M were seated on a couch in M's study in Calcutta. They were talking. Just before Narendra's arrival M had been studying *The Merchant of Venice, Comus,* and Blackie's *Self-culture,* which he taught at school.

Narendra and the other brothers of the monastery were full of yearning for God-realization. A fire of intense renunciation raged in their hearts.

NARENDRA: "I don't care for anything. You see, I am now talking with you, but I feel like getting up this minute and running away."

Narendra sat in silence a few minutes. Then he said, "I shall fast to death for the realization of God."

M: "That is good. One can do anything for God."

NARENDRA: "But suppose I cannot control my hunger."

M: "Then eat something and begin over again."

Narendra remained silent a few minutes.

NARENDRA: "It seems there is no God. I pray so much, but there is no reply—none whatsoever.

"How many visions I have seen! How many mantras shining in letters of gold! How many visions of the Goddess Kālī! How many other divine forms! But still I have no peace.

"Will you kindly give me six pice?"

Narendra asked for the money to pay his carriage hire to the Barānagore Math. Just then Satkari arrived in a carriage. Of the same age as Narendra, he dearly loved the members of the monastery. He lived near the math and worked in Calcutta. The carriage was his own. Narendra returned the money to M and said

that he would go with Satkari in his carriage. He asked
M to give them some refreshments.

M accompanied the two friends to the Barānagore
Math. He wanted to see how the brothers spent their
time and practised sādhanā. He wanted to see how
Sri Ramakrishna, the Master, was reflected in the
hearts of the disciples. Niranjan was not at the math.
He had gone home to visit his mother, the only relative
he had in the world. Baburam, Sarat, and Kali had
gone to Puri. They intended to spend a few days
there.

Narendra was in charge of the members of the
monastery. Prasanna[5] had been practising austere
sādhanā for the past few days. Once Narendra had
told him of his desire to fast to death for the realization
of God. During Narendra's absence in Calcutta,
Prasanna had left the monastery for an unknown destination. When Narendra heard about it, he said to the
brothers, "Why did Rājā[6] allow him to go?" But
Rakhal had not been in the monastery at the time,
having gone to the Dakshineswar temple for a stroll.

NARENDRA: "Just let Rājā come back to the
monastery! I shall scold him. Why did he allow Prasanna to go away? (To Harish) I am sure you were
lecturing him then, standing with your feet apart.
Couldn't you prevent his going away?"

Harish replied in a very low voice, "Brother Tarak
asked him not to go, but still he went away."

[5] Sarada Prasanna, one of the Master's young disciples,
was addressed as Prasanna by Sri Ramakrishna and his
disciples.

[6] Rakhal was addressed as "Rājā" by all the brothers.
"Rakhal-Rāj," the "King of the cowherd boys," is one of
the names of Sri Krishna, and Sri Ramakrishna often spoke
of Rakhal as one of the intimate companions of Krishna.

NARENDRA (*to M*): "You see what a lot of trouble I am in! Here, too, I am involved in a world of māyā. Who knows where this boy has gone?"

Rakhal returned from Dakshineswar. Narendra told him about Prasanna's going away from the monastery. Prasanna had left a letter for Narendra. This was the substance of the letter: "I am going to Vrindāvan on foot. It is very risky for me to live here. Here my mind is undergoing a change. Formerly I used to dream about my parents and other relatives. Then I dreamt of woman, the embodiment of māyā. I have suffered twice; I had to go back to my relatives at home. Therefore I am going far away from them. The Master once told me, 'Your people at home are apt to do anything; never trust them.'"

Rakhal said: "These are the reasons for his going away. Once he remarked: 'Narendra often goes home to look after his mother, brothers, and sisters; he supervises the family's lawsuit. I am afraid that I too may feel like going home, following his example.'"

Narendra remained silent.

Rakhal was talking to them about making pilgrimages. He said: "We have achieved nothing by staying here. The Master always exhorted us to realize God. Have we succeeded?"

Rakhal lay down. The other devotees were either lying down or sitting.

RAKHAL: "Let us go to the Narmadā."

NARENDRA: "What will you achieve by wandering about? Can one ever attain jnāna, that you are talking about it so much?"

A DEVOTEE: "Then why have you renounced the world?"

NARENDRA: "Must we go on begetting children

because we have not realized God? What are you talking about?"

Narendra went out, returning after a few minutes. Rakhal was still lying down.

A member of the monastery who was also lying down said teasingly, feigning great suffering on account of his separation from God: "Ah! Please get me a knife. I have no more use for this life. I can't stand this pain any more!"

NARENDRA (*feigning seriousness*): "It is there. Stretch out your hand and take it."

Everybody laughed.

The conversation again turned to Prasanna.

NARENDRA: "Even here we are involved in māyā. Why have we become sannyāsis, I wonder?"

It was dusk. Sashi burnt incense before the picture of Sri Ramakrishna in the worship room and then before the pictures of gods and goddesses in the other rooms.

The evening worship began. The members of the math and the other devotees stood with folded hands near the door of the shrine and witnessed the ārati. Then they all sang in chorus a hymn to Śiva, to the accompaniment of bell and gong.

It was eleven o'clock at night when their supper was over. The brothers prepared a bed for M, and all went to sleep.

At midnight M was wide awake. He said to himself: "Everything is as it was before. The same Ayodhyā[7] —only Rāma is not there." M silently left his bed. It was the full-moon night of Vaiśākh, the thrice-blessed day of the Buddhists, associated with Buddha's birth,

---

[7] The modern Oudh, in the United Provinces. It was the capital of Rāma's kingdom.

attaining of nirvāna, and passing away. M was walking alone on the bank of the Ganges, meditating on the Master.

It was Sunday. M had arrived the day before and was planning to stay till Wednesday. The householder devotees generally visited the monastery on Sundays.

The *Yogavāśishtha* was being studied and explained. M had heard a little about the teachings of this book from Sri Ramakrishna. It taught the absolute identity of Brahman and the soul, and the unreality of the world. The Master had forbidden him and the other householder devotees to practise spiritual discipline following the method of Advaita Vedānta, since the attitude of the oneness of the soul and God is harmful for one still identified with the body. For such a devotee, the Master used to say, it was better to look on God as the Lord and himself as His servant.

The conversation turned to the *Yogavāśishtha*.

M: "Well, how is Brahmajnāna described in the *Yogavāśishtha?*"

RAKHAL: "Hunger, thirst, pain, pleasure, and so on, are all māyā. The annihilation of the mind is the only means to the realization of Brahman."

M: "What remains after the annihilation of the mind is Brahman. Is that not true?"

RAKHAL: "Yes."

M: "Sri Ramakrishna used to say that. Nangtā taught him that way."

Narendra and the other devotees were going to the Ganges to bathe. M accompanied them. The sun was very hot; so M took his umbrella. Sarat, a devotee from Barānagore, was going with them to take his bath. He often visited the monastery.

M (to Sarat): "It is very hot."

NARENDRA: "Is that your excuse for taking the umbrella?"

M laughed.

The members of the monastery were clad in gerruā.

M (to Narendra): "It is really very hot. One is liable to get a sunstroke."

NARENDRA: "I see that your body is the obstacle in your path of renunciation. Isn't that so? I am talking of you, Devendra Babu—"

M laughed and said to himself, "Is it merely the body?"

After bathing, the devotees returned to the monastery. They washed their feet and entered the worship room. Saluting the Deity, they offered flowers.

There was a big plot of wooded land to the west of the monastery compound. M was seated alone under a tree, when suddenly Prasanna appeared. It was about three o'clock in the afternoon.

M: "Where have you been all these days? Everyone has been so worried about you. Have you seen the brothers? When did you arrive?"

PRASANNA: "Just now. Yes, I have seen them."

M: "You left a note saying that you were going to Vrindāvan. We were terribly worried about you. How far did you go?"

PRASANNA: "Only as far as Konnagar."[8]

Both of them laughed.

M: "Sit down. Tell me all about it. Where did you stop first?"

[8] A small town only a few miles from Barānagore, on the other side of the Ganges.

PRASANNA: "At the Dakshineswar temple garden. I spent the night there."

M (*smiling*): "What is Hazra's present mood?"

PRASANNA: "Hazra asked me, 'What do you think of me?'"

Both laughed.

M (*smiling*): "What did you say?"

PRASANNA: "I said nothing."

M: "Then?"

PRASANNA: "Then he asked me whether I had brought tobacco for him."

Both laughed.

PRASANNA: "He wanted me to wait on him." (*Laughter.*)

M: "Where did you go next?"

PRASANNA: "By degrees I got to Konnagar. I spent the night in the open. I intended to proceed farther and asked some gentlemen whether I could procure enough money there for a railway ticket to the up-country."

M: "What did they say?"

PRASANNA: "They said, 'You may get a rupee or so; but who will give you the whole fare?'"

Both laughed.

M: "What did you take with you?"

PRASANNA: "Oh, one or two pieces of cloth and a picture of the Master. I didn't show the picture to anybody."

Sashi's father came to the math. He wanted to take his son home. During Sri Ramakrishna's illness Sashi had nursed the Master for nine months with unswerving zeal. He had won a scholarship in the final High School examination for his academic ability and had studied up to the B.A., but he had not appeared at the examination. His father, a poor brāhmin, was a devout Hindu and spent much of his time in spiritual practice. Sashi was his eldest son. His parents had hoped that, after completing his education, he would earn money and remove the family's financial difficulties. But Sashi had renounced the world for the realization of God. Whenever he thought of his father and mother he felt great anguish of heart. Many a time he said to his friends, with tears in his eyes: "I am at a loss as to my duty. Alas, I could not serve my parents; I could not be of any use to them. What great hope they placed in me! On account of our poverty my mother did not have any jewelry. I cherished the desire to buy some for her. But now all my hopes are frustrated; it is impossible for me to return home. My Master asked me to renounce 'woman' and 'gold.' I simply cannot return home."

After Sri Ramakrishna's passing away Sashi's father had hoped that his son would come back to his family. The boy had spent a few days at home, but immediately after the establishment of the new monastery he had begun to frequent it and in a few days had decided to live there as one of the members. Every now and then his father came to the monastery to persuade him to come home; but he had not succeeded.

This day, on learning that his father had come, Sashi fled the monastery by another door. He did not want to meet him.

Sashi's father knew M. They paced the upper verandah together and talked.

SASHI'S FATHER: "Who is in charge of this place? Narendra alone is the cause of all the mischief. For a while all these young men returned home and devoted themselves to their studies."

M: "There is no one in charge here. They are all equals. What can Narendra do? Can a man renounce home against his own will? Have we householders, for instance, been able to give up our homes altogether?"

SASHI'S FATHER: "You are doing the right thing. You are serving both the world and God. Can't one practise religion after your method? That is exactly what we want Sashi to do. Let him live at home and come here too. You have no idea how much his mother weeps for him."

M became sad and said nothing.

SASHI'S FATHER: "And if you speak of searching for holy men, I know where to find a good one. Let Sashi go to him."

Rakhal and M were walking on the verandah to the east of Kali's room.

RAKHAL (earnestly): "M, let us practise sādhanā! We have renounced home for good. When someone says, 'You have not realized God by renouncing home; then why all this fuss?,' Narendra gives a good retort. He says, 'Because we could not attain God, must we beget children?' Ah! Every now and then Narendra says nice things. You had better ask him."

M: "What you say is right. I see that you too have become restless for God."

RAKHAL: "M, how can I describe the state of my mind? Today at noontime I felt great yearning for the Narmadā. M, please practise sādhanā; otherwise you will not succeed.

"Many people think that it is enough not to look

at the face of a woman. But what will you gain merely by turning your eyes to the ground at the sight of a woman? Narendra put it very well last night, when he said: 'Woman exists for a man as long as he has lust. Free from lust, he sees no difference between man and woman.'"

M: "How true it is! Children do not see the difference between man and woman."

RAKHAL: "Therefore I say that we must practise spiritual discipline. How can one attain Knowledge without going beyond māyā?

"Let's go to the big hall. Some gentlemen have come from Barānagore. Narendra is talking with them. Let's go and listen to him."

M did not enter the room. As he was pacing outside he overheard some of the conversation.

NARENDRA: "There is no fixed time or place for the sandhyā and other devotions."

GENTLEMAN: "Sir, can one realize God through spiritual practice alone?"

NARENDRA: "Realization depends on God's grace; without it mere worship and prayer do not help at all. Therefore one should take refuge in Him."

GENTLEMAN: "May we come now and then and disturb you?"

NARENDRA: "Please come whenever you like. We take our baths in the Ganges at your ghāt."

GENTLEMAN: "I don't mind that. But please see that others don't use it."

NARENDRA: "We shall not use your ghāt, if that is what you mean."

GENTLEMAN: "No, I don't mean exactly that. But if you see other people using it, then you had better not go."

It was dusk. The evening worship was over. They assembled in the big hall. M, too, was seated there. Prasanna was reading from the *Guru Gītā*.

Narendra sang:

I salute the Eternal Teacher, the embodiment of the
    Bliss of Brahman,
The essence of knowledge and liberation, the giver of
    Supreme Joy;
Who is all-pervading, like the ākāśa, and is the goal of
    Vedānta's teachings;
Who is One, eternal, stainless, pure, and is the con-
    stant Witness of all things;
Who dwells beyond all moods, transcending the three
    gunas.

As Narendra sang in his melodious voice, the minds of the devotees became steady, like a candle flame in a windless place.

Rakhal was seated in Kali's room. Prasanna sat near him. M, too, was there.

Rakhal had renounced the world, leaving behind his wife and child. A fire of intense renunciation burnt day and night in his heart. He was thinking seriously of going away, by himself, to the bank of the Narmadā or some other holy place. Still, he was trying to per- suade Prasanna not to run away from the monastery.

RAKHAL (*to Prasanna*): "Where do you want to go? Here you are in the company of holy men. Wouldn't it be foolish to go away from them? Where will you find another like Narendra?"

PRASANNA: "My parents live in Calcutta. I am afraid of being drawn by their love. That is why I want to flee to a distant place."

RAKHAL: "Can our parents love us as intensely as

Gurumahārāj [meaning Sri Ramakrishna] did? What have we done for him, to deserve all this love? Why was he so eager for the welfare of our body, mind, and soul? What have we done for him, to deserve all this?"

M (to himself): "Ah! Rakhal is right. Therefore a person like Sri Ramakrishna is described as the 'Ocean of Mercy without any reason.'"

PRASANNA (to Rakhal): "Don't you yourself feel like running away from here?"

RAKHAL: "Yes, now and then I have a fancy to spend a few days on the bank of the Narmadā. I say to myself, 'Let me go to a place like that and practise sādhanā in a garden.' But I hesitate to live in a garden that belongs to worldly people."

Tarak and Prasanna were talking in the big hall. Tarak had lost his mother. His father, like Rakhal's father, had married a second time. Tarak himself had married but had lost his wife. Now the monastery was his home. He too was trying to persuade Prasanna to live there.

PRASANNA: "I have neither knowledge nor love of God. What have I in the world for a support?"

TARAK: "It is no doubt difficult to attain knowledge; but how can you say you have no love?"

PRASANNA: "I have not yet wept for God. How can I say I have love? What have I realized in all these days?"

TARAK: "But you have seen the Master. And why do you say that you have no knowledge?"

PRASANNA: "What sort of knowledge are you talking about? Knowledge of what? Certainly of God. But I am not even sure of God's existence."

TARAK: "Yes, that's true. According to the jnāni, there is no God."

M (to himself): "Ah! The Master used to say that those who seek God pass through the state that Prasanna is now experiencing. In that state sometimes one doubts the very existence of God. I understand that Tarak is now reading Buddhist philosophy. That is why he says that according to the jnāni God does not exist. But Sri Ramakrishna used to say that the jnāni and the bhakta will ultimately arrive at the same destination."

Narendra and Prasanna were talking in the meditation room. Rakhal, Harish, and the younger Gopal were seated in another part of the room. After a while the elder Gopal came in.

Narendra was reading from the Gitā and explaining the verses to Prasanna:

The Lord dwells in the hearts of all beings, O Arjuna, and by His māyā causes them to revolve as though mounted on a machine. Take refuge in Him with all your soul, O Bhārata. By His grace you will gain Supreme Peace and the Everlasting Abode. . . . Abandon all dharmas and come to Me alone for shelter. I will deliver you from all sins; do not grieve.

NARENDRA: "Did you notice what Krishna said? 'Mounted on a machine.' The Lord, by His māyā, causes all beings to revolve as though mounted on a machine. To seek to know God? You are but a worm among worms—and you to know God? Just reflect a moment: what is a man? It is said that each one of the myriads of stars that shine overhead represents a solar system. This earth of ours is a part of only one solar system, and even that is too big for us. Like an

insect man crawls on this earth, which, compared to
the sun, is only a tiny ball."

Narendra sang:

We are born, O Lord, in the dust of earth,
And our eyes are blinded by the dust;
With dust we toy like children at play:
O give us assurance, Thou Help of the weak!

Wilt Thou cast us out of Thy lap, O Lord,
For a single mistake? Wilt Thou turn away
And abandon us to our helplessness?
Oh, then we shall never be able to rise,
But shall lie for ever dazed and undone.

Mere babes are we, Father, with childish minds;
At every step we stumble and fall.
Why, then, must Thou show us Thy terrible face?
Why, Lord, must we ever behold Thy frown?

Small are we: oh, do not be angry with us,
But tenderly speak to us when we do wrong;
For though Thou dost raise us a hundred times,
A hundred times we shall fall again.
What else can one do with a helpless mind?

Then he said to Prasanna: "Surrender yourself at
His feet. Resign yourself completely to His will.

"Don't you remember Sri Ramakrishna's words? God
is the hill of sugar and you are but an ant. One grain
is enough to fill your stomach, and you think of bringing home the entire hill! That is why I scolded Kali,
saying: 'You fool! Do you want to measure God with
your tape and foot-rule?'

"God is the Ocean of Mercy. Be His slave and take
refuge in Him. He will show compassion. Pray to
Him: 'Protect me always with Thy compassionate face.
Lead me from the unreal to the Real, from darkness

to Light, from death to Immortality. Reveal Thyself to me and protect me always with Thy compassionate face.' "

PRASANNA: "What kind of spiritual discipline should one practise?"

NARENDRA: "Repeat His name."

PRASANNA: "Now you are saying that there is a God. Again, it is you who say that according to Chārvāka and many other thinkers the world was self-created."

NARENDRA: "Haven't you studied chemistry? Who combines the different elements? It is a human hand that combines hydrogen, oxygen, and electricity to prepare water. Everybody admits the existence of an intelligent force—a Force that is the essence of knowledge and that guides all these phenomena."

PRASANNA: "How are we to know that God is kind?"

NARENDRA: "The Vedas say, 'That which is Thy compassionate face.' John Stuart Mill stated the same thing. He said, 'How much kindness must He have —He who has implanted kindness in the hearts of men!' The Master used to say: 'Faith is the one essential thing. God exists. He is very near us. Through faith alone does one see Him.' "

PRASANNA: "Sometimes you say that God does not exist, and now you are saying all these things! You are not consistent. You keep changing your opinions."

All laughed.

NARENDRA: "All right! I shall never change what I have just said. As long as one has desires and cravings, so long one doubts God's existence. A man cherishes some desire or other. Perhaps he has the desire to study or pass the university examination or become a scholar, and so forth and so on."

Narendra sang again, in a voice choked with emotion:

Hail to Thee, our God and Lord; hail, Giver of every
   blessing;
Hail, Thou giver of good!
O Redeemer from fear, from danger and suffering,
Upholder of the worlds,
Hail, Lord! Victory to Thee!

Unfathomable and infinite, immeasurable, beyond com-
   pare,
O God, none equals Thee.
Lord of the Universe, O All-pervading Truth,
Thou, the supreme Ātman,
Hail, Lord! Victory to Thee!

O Thou All-compassionate One, adored by the whole
   universe,
I bow before Thy feet.
Thou art the only refuge in life and death, O Lord;
Before Thy feet I bow.
Hail, Lord! Victory to Thee!

This is our only prayer, O Lord: what other boon can
   we implore?
Thus do we pray to Thee:
Grant us wisdom here, and in the life hereafter
Reveal to us Thy face.
Hail, Lord! Victory to Thee!

Again Narendra sang, describing how very near God
is to us—as near as the musk to the deer—and exhort-
ing his brother disciples to drink deep from the cup
of Divine Bliss:

Drinking the bliss of Hari from the cup of prema,
Sādhu, be intoxicated!
Childhood you spent in crying, and youth in women's
   control;

Now, in your old age, full of phlegm and wind,
You wait for the funeral couch
To bear you to the cremation ground.

Within the musk-deer's navel the fragrant musk is
    found;
But how can one make it understand?
Without the proper teacher to guide him on his way,
Man, too, is blindly roaming through the world,
Deluded as the foolish deer
That wanders on from wood to wood.

M heard all this from the verandah.

Narendra got up. As he left the room he remarked,
"My brain is heated by talking to these youngsters."

He met M on the verandah and said, "Please, let us
have a drink of water."

One of the members of the math said to Narendra,
"Why, then, do you say that God does not exist?"

Narendra laughed.

Monday, May 9, 1887

The next morning M was sitting alone under a tree
in the garden. He said to himself: "Sri Ramakrishna
has made the brothers of the monastery renounce lust
and greed. Ah, how eager they are to realize God! This
place has become a veritable Paradise, and the brothers
living here are embodiments of Nārāyana. It is not
many days since the Master passed away; that is why
all the ideas and ideals he stood for are there, almost
intact. The Master has made these brothers renounce
their homes. Why has he kept a few in the world? Is
there no way of liberation for them?"

From a room upstairs Narendra saw M sitting alone
under the tree. He came down.

NARENDRA: "You may speak of leading a detached

life in the world, and all that, but you will not attain anything unless you renounce 'woman' and 'gold.' Vain is the life of a person who does not take delight in the teachings of Vedānta and drink the Nectar of Divine Bliss. No liberation is possible for a man unless he puts on the loincloth of a sannyāsi. The world must be renounced. Why should a man be entangled in worldliness? Why should he be ensnared by māyā? What is man's real nature? He is the blessed Śiva, the Embodiment of Bliss and Spirit."

Narendra recited a hymn, the Eight Stanzas on the glory of Krishna. M remained spellbound as he listened to the hymn. He said to himself: "How intense Narendra's dispassion is! This is how he has infused the spirit of dispassion into the hearts of the other brothers of the monastery. Their very presence awakens in the hearts of the Master's householder devotees the desire for renunciation of 'woman' and 'gold.' Ah, how blessed are these all-renouncing brothers! Why has the Master kept us few in the world? Will he show us a way? Will he give us the spirit of renunciation or will he delude us with worldliness?"

After the meal all were resting. The elder Gopal was copying some songs. Niranjan was on a visit to his mother. Sarat, Baburam, and Kali were in Puri.

Narendra, with one or two brothers, left for Calcutta. He had to see to his lawsuit. He intended to return in the evening; the brothers could not bear his absence.

In the afternoon Rabindra arrived, looking like a mad person. He was barefoot and had only half of his black-bordered cloth round his waist. His eyeballs were rolling like a madman's. All asked him anxiously what was the matter.

"Let me recover my breath!" he said. "I shall tell you everything presently. I am certainly not going back home; I shall stay at this very place with you all. She is certainly a traitor! Let me tell you something, friends. For her sake I gave up my habit of drinking, which I had indulged in for five years. I have not taken a drop for the last eight months. And she is a traitor!"

The brothers of the math said: "Be calm, please! How did you come?"

RABINDRA: "I have come barefoot all the way from Calcutta."

The brothers wanted to know where he had lost the other half of his cloth.

RABINDRA: "When I was leaving her place she began to pull at my cloth. That is how half of it was torn off."

The brothers asked him to bathe in the Ganges and cool off; then they would hear his story.

Rabindra belonged to a respectable family of Calcutta. He was twenty or twenty-two years old. He had first met Sri Ramakrishna at the Dakshineswar temple and had received his special blessing. On one occasion he had spent three nights with the Master. His disposition was very sweet and tender, and the Master had loved him dearly. Once he had said to Rabindra: "You will have to wait some time; you have to go through a few more experiences. Nothing can be done now. You see, the police can't do much just when the robbers attack a house. When the plundering is almost over, the police make their arrests."

Rabindra had many virtues. He was devoted to God and to service of the poor. He had many spiritual qualities. But he had walked into the snare of a prostitute. Then, suddenly, he discovered that the

woman was unfaithful to him. Therefore he had come
to the math in this dishevelled state, resolved not to
go back to the world.

A devotee accompanied Rabindra to the Ganges. It
was his inmost desire that Rabindra's spiritual consciousness should be awakened in the company of these
holy men. When Rabindra finished his bath, the devotee took him to the adjacent cremation ground, showed
him the corpses lying about, and said: "The brothers
of the math come here every now and then to meditate
on God. It is a good place for meditation. Here one
sees clearly that the world is impermanent."

Rabindra sat down in the cremation ground to meditate. But he could not meditate long; his mind was
restless.

Rabindra and the devotee returned to the math.
They went to the worship room to salute the Deity.
The devotee said to him, "The brothers of the math
meditate in this room."

Rabindra sat there to meditate, but could not meditate long there either.

DEVOTEE: "How do you feel? Is your mind very
restless? Is that why you have got up from your seat?
Perhaps you could not concentrate well."

RABINDRA: "I am sure I shall not go back to the
world. But the mind is restless."

M and Rabindra were talking. No one else was
present. M was telling him stories from the life of
Buddha. At that time the members of the math regularly read the lives of Buddha and Chaitanya. M said
to Rabindra that Buddha's spiritual consciousness was
first awakened by hearing a song of some heavenly
maidens.

M sang the song:

We moan for rest, alas! but rest can never find;
We know not whence we come, nor where we float
   away.
Time and again we tread this round of smiles and tears;
In vain we pine to know whither our pathway leads,
And why we play this empty play. . . .

That night Narendra, Tarak, and Harish returned
from Calcutta. They said, "Oh, what a big meal we
had!" They had been entertained by a devotee in
Calcutta.

The members of the monastery assembled in the
big hall. Narendra heard Rabindra's story. He sang
by way of giving instruction to him:

> O man, abandon your delusion!
> Cast aside your wicked counsels!
> Know the Lord and free yourself
> From earthly grief and pain!
> For a few days' pleasure only,
> You have quite forgotten Him
> Who is the Comrade of your soul.
> Alas, what mockery!

A few minutes later the brothers went to Kali's
room. Girish Ghosh had just sent two of his new
books to the monastery: the *Life of Buddha* and the
Life of Chaitanya.

Since the founding of the new math Sashi had
devoted himself heart and soul to the worship and
service of the Master. All were amazed at his devotion.
Just as he had tended Sri Ramakrishna's physical body
during his illness, so now, with the same unswerving
zeal, he worshipped the Master in the shrine room.

A member of the monastery was reading aloud from
the lives of Buddha and Chaitanya. He was a little

sarcastic while reading Chaitanya's life. Narendra snatched the book from his hand and said, "That is how you spoil a good thing!"

Narendra read the chapter describing how Chaitanya bestowed his love upon all, from the brāhmin to the pariah.

A BROTHER: "I say that one person cannot give love to another person."

NARENDRA: "But the Master gave it to me."

BROTHER: "Well, are you sure you have it?"

NARENDRA: "What can you understand about love? You belong to the servant class. All of you must serve me and massage my feet. Don't flatter yourselves by thinking you have understood everything. Now go and prepare a smoke for me."

All laughed.

THE BROTHER: "I surely will not."

M (to himself): "Sri Ramakrishna has transmitted mettle to all the brothers of the math. It is no monopoly of Narendra's. Is it possible to renounce 'woman' and 'gold' without this inner fire?"

May 10, 1887

It was Tuesday, a very auspicious day for the worship of the Divine Mother. Arrangements were being made for Her special worship at the monastery.

M was going to the Ganges to take his bath. Rabindra was walking alone on the roof. He heard Narendra singing the Six Stanzas on Nirvāna:

Death or fear have I none, nor any distinction of caste;
Neither father nor mother, nor even a birth, have I;
Neither friend nor comrade, neither disciple nor guru:
I am Eternal Bliss and Awareness—I am Śiva, I am
Śiva.

I have no form or fancy: the All-pervading am I;
Everywhere I exist, and yet and beyond the senses;
Neither salvation am I, nor anything to be known:
I am Eternal Bliss and Awareness—I am Śiva, I am
Śiva.

Rabindra went to the Ganges to take his bath. Presently he returned to the monastery clad in his wet cloth.

Narendra said to M in a whisper: "He has bathed in the Ganges. It would be good to initiate him now into sannyās."

Both Narendra and M smiled.

Prasanna asked Rabindra to change his wet cloth and gave him a dry gerruā cloth. Narendra said to M, "Now he is going to put on the garb of renunciation."

M (with a smile): "What kind of renunciation?"

NARENDRA: "Why, the renunciation of 'woman' and 'gold.'"

Rabindra put on the ochre cloth and entered Kali's room to meditate.

Appendices

APPENDIX A

Sri Chaitanya

Chaitanya, the great apostle of Vaishnavism in Bengal, was born at Navadvip, or Nadiā, in A.D. 1485. At that time Nadiā was famous as an educational centre, especially for its school of logic. Its Sanskrit academies drew students from all parts of India.

Chaitanya's father, Jagannāth Miśra, was a brāhmin who had come to Nadiā from Sylhet, in Assam, to complete his education. He had married Sachi Devi, the daughter of a well-known pundit, and had settled down to the life of a Hindu householder. He had ten children: eight daughters, all of whom died in infancy, and two sons, the elder named Viśwarupa and the younger, Viśvambhara, afterwards known as Chaitanya. Viśwarupa's mind was infected by the religious atmosphere of Nadiā and at the age of sixteen, on the night before he was to have been married, he took the vows of monastic life and, with pilgrim-staff and begging-bowl in hand, left the world on his spiritual quest.

Now Viśvambhara, or Nimāi, as he was affectionately called on account of his having been born in a shed under a neem tree, remained the sole comfort of his parents. When he was five years old, he should have gone to school like the other lads of his age; but because of his mother's objection he stayed at home. Sachi Devi was haunted by the fear that her only remaining child might follow his brother's example.

Nimāi was full of fun and life. He loved to tease the pious and learned brāhmins with his boyish pranks and upset all the sedate and orderly traditions of the place. He joined with other boys in robbing orchards and in other innocent mischief. He teased little girls and often disturbed elderly brāhmins at their devotions by running away with their sacred images or by hiding their clothes when they were bathing. He shocked his brāhmin parents by a total disregard of caste prejudices, touching unclean refuse and other things which were pollution to the twice-born. When reproved by his mother, he would say: "You do not send me to school. I am ignorant. How can I know what is clean or unclean? In my eyes nothing is pure or impure. All things are alike to me." His answer revealed the mind of a true sannyāsi, which is above the caste rules and restrictions.

At the age of six Nimāi was sent, at the insistence of Jagannāth's neighbours, to one of the Sanskrit academies and placed under a pundit named Gangādās. Thus he entered upon the first stage of a brāhmin's life, that of brahmacharya. The boy was precocious and in a very short time was engaged in disputes with pundits about the intricacies of Sanskrit grammar and logic; but he still retained all the vivacity of boyhood and delighted in poking fun at the grave and reverent scholars of Nadiā.

At the age of twenty Nimāi had acquired so great a reputation that he established an academy of his own, on the bank of the Ganges, to which many pupils came, attracted by his wit and his brilliant dialectics. Up to this time he was outwardly occupied with the development of his intellect. No one detected his inner religious fervour, which subsequently raised him to the exalted position of a prophet. He shared in the scepticism of the dons of Nadiā and imbibed all their intellectual pride. In several intellectual bouts he defeated famous scholars of his day, representing Benares and other seats of learning, who had come to Nadiā to win the customary "letters of victory" with which the vanquished acknowledged the superior skill of their antagonists in logic, grammar, rhetoric, and similar subjects.

In a short time Nimāi married and settled down as a householder, thus entering upon the second stage of a brāhmin's life. His father died about this time. Soon afterwards he went to eastern Bengal and Assam, whence his father's family had come. His learned discussions with the pundits there enhanced his scholastic reputation. On his return he was grieved to find that his wife had died of snake-bite. To console his mother he married again; but soon he started off, with her reluctant consent, on a pilgrimage to Gayā, to offer the customary oblations of food and drink for the solace of his father's spirit.

This visit to Gayā was the turning-point of his life. The place itself was hallowed by the sacred memories of Hinduism and Buddhism. And it was here that he came under the influence of a venerable Vaishnava guru, Iśvara Puri, and was initiated by him into the mysteries of the bhakti cult, which worshipped Sri Krishna as its Ideal Deity. Before the image of Vishnu in the great temple he fell into a trance, and he did not come back to full consciousness of the world until he was taken to his school at Nadiā by his companions. His whole spiritual outlook was changed. He was no longer the proud pundit, conscious of his intellectual superiority, whose chief delight was to confound an opponent by argument. Now he began to spend hours in chanting the name and glories of Krishna and discoursing on divine love. The arrogant scholar became the humblest of the humble. Tears wet his cheeks as he spoke of Krishna and His love.

"Be like a tree," Chaitanya would often say to his companions. "The tree gives shade even to him who cuts off its boughs. It asks no water of anyone, though it be withering for want of it. It bears alike rain and storm and the burning rays of the sun, and yet continues to give fragrant flowers and delicious fruits. Patiently serve others even as a tree, and let this be your motto."

To set an example of humility, he, an aristocratic brāhmin, would go down to the river and help the old and infirm to carry their burdens or wash their clothes; and when anyone, out of respect for his brāhminhood, hesitated to accept his services, he would say: "Do not, I pray you, prevent me. When I serve you I serve God. These little deeds are holiness for me."

Once, during one of his pilgrimages, he joined a crowd collected round a brāhmin in a temple, who, with tears pouring down his face, was reciting the Gītā with intense rapture, heedless of the ridicule and laughter that greeted the numerous mistakes in intonation and grammar that he was making. Deeply touched, Nimāi said to him, "Tell me, sir, what deep meaning do you find in these words, to inspire you to such rapture?" The brāhmin replied: "Sir, I am very ignorant and do not know the meaning of the words. But as I read the Gītā, I see Krishna, dark and beautiful, sitting in Arjuna's chariot, teaching divine truth. This makes me weep for sheer delight." Chaitanya embraced him and said, "You are truly worthy to read the Gītā, for you have understood the essence of its meaning."

His pride of scholarship completely disappeared. Instead of following the complicated rituals of orthodox Hinduism, he organized kirtan parties of singers and dancers, which, headed by himself and his chief disciple, Nityānanda, assembled in temples or courtyards of houses and went in procession through the streets, chanting the praise of Hari and His love for mankind.

The brāhmin aristocracy of Nadiā, though untouched by the emotional fervour of the young reformer's religious teaching, was greatly disturbed by the excitement it caused and especially by the presence of low-caste people in the religious processions he organized. His open defiance of caste rules disgusted the brāhmins. Finding their protests and threats of spiritual penalties futile, they appealed to the Mussalmān authorities. But the judge, who was a Mussalmān by faith, was impressed with Chaitanya's face, lit up in divine ecstasy, and with the spiritual fervour of his companions. Instead of punishing them, he sent them away with his blessings. There were many Mussalmāns among Chaitanya's followers.

Now Chaitanya decided to take the vows of monastic life. It was very difficult for him to obtain his mother's permission. But with the utmost tenderness he clasped her feet and consoled her by promising to live wherever she might bid him and obey her wishes always, as he had done before. It was agreed between them that he should make Puri his headquarters, so that his mother could easily get news of him and sometimes see him at Nadiā. Soon after his initiation into sannyās, he started on a pilgrimage to Vrindāvan, associated with Krishna's early life. There he experienced repeated ecstasies.

The last eighteen years of his life Chaitanya spent at Puri, near the temple of Jagannāth, preaching the cult of bhakti, the principal tenets of which were kindness to living beings, love for God's name, and service to the devotees of God. He kindled a great flame of passionate devotion in the hearts of his followers. A wave of religious fervour swept over Bengal and Orissa, especially intensifying the spiritual life of the common people. He was soon recognized by his intimate disciples as an Incarnation of God.

Chaitanya took special delight in the beauties of nature. He would be profoundly moved by a glorious sunset, a noble river, or a grove of aśoka trees laden with flowers. His power over wild beasts and all the denizens of the forest is said to have been marvellous.

Though worshipped by thousands of people, among whom were many aristocrats of the land, he himself, like all great Indian teachers, lived an extremely ascetic life and sternly reproved any form of self-indulgence on the part of those who wished to become his intimate disciples.

His life in Puri was mostly spent in a state of God-intoxication. Rapturous discourses, deep contemplation, transcendental moods in which he tasted the divine love, were daily occurrences. Once, in a state of self-forgetfulness, he fell into the ocean while singing Hari's name and was dragged out, still in an unconscious state, in the nets of some fishermen. Soon his bodily strength became exhausted because of the ardour of his religious zeal. He passed away in 1533, at the age of forty-eight, leaving his great work in charge of the order of Vaishnava monks, or Goswāmis, which he founded.

APPENDIX B

Tantra[1]

Tantra is an important system of Hindu religious philosophy, and its close affinity to the Vedas is apparent. The Tantra scriptures themselves contain references to its Vedic origin. In its subsequent development, however, Tantra shows a more pronounced influence of the Upanishads, as well as of Yoga and the Purānas. The ritualistic worship of modern Hinduism has been greatly coloured by Tantra, and this fact is particularly noticeable in Bengal, Kashmir, Gujarat, and Malabar.

Reality, according to Tantra, is Chit, or Pure Consciousness, which is identical with Sat, or Pure Being, and Ānanda, or Pure Bliss. Thus both Vedānta and Tantra show a general agreement about the nature of Reality, with, however, an important difference which will be presently stated. Though transcending words and thought, this Being-Consciousness-Bliss, or Satchidānanda, becomes restricted through māyā, and Its transcendent nature is then expressed in terms of forms and categories.

According to the Vedas, Satchidānanda, or Brahman, is in Its true nature Pure Spirit; and māyā, which is inherent in It, functions only on the relative plane at the time of the creation, preservation, and destruction

[1] This Appendix is based mainly on an article published under the title of "Tantra as a Way of Realization" by Pramathanath Mukhopadhyaya in *The Cultural Heritage of India*, Vol. II, Sri Ramakrishna Centenary Committee, Belur Math, Calcutta, 1937.

of the universe; neither is the creation ultimately real, nor are created beings, for true knowledge reveals only an undifferentiated Consciousness. According to Tantra, on the other hand, Satchidānanda is called Śiva-Śakti, the hyphenated word suggesting that Śiva, or the Absolute, and Śakti, or Its creative power, are eternally conjoined like a word and its meaning: the one cannot be thought of without the other. A conception of Pure Consciousness or Being which denies Śakti, or the power to become, is, according to Tantra, only half of the truth. Satchidānanda is essentially endowed with the power of self-evolution and self-involution. Therefore perfect experience is the experience of the whole—that is to say, of Consciousness as Being and Consciousness as power to become. It is only in the relative world that Śiva and Śakti are thought of as separate entities. Furthermore, Tantra affirms that both the world process and the jiva, or individual soul, are real, and not merely illusory superimpositions upon Brahman. In declaring that the jiva finally becomes one with Reality, Tantra differs from Qualified Nondualism and pure Dualism.

Māyā, according to Tantra, veils Reality and polarizes It into what is conscious and what is unconscious, what is existent and what is non-existent, what is pleasant and what is unpleasant. Through polarization, the Infinite becomes finite, the Undifferentiated differentiated, the Immeasurable measured. For the same reason, non-dual Reality becomes evolved—and this becoming is real and not merely apparent as in Vedānta —into a multiplicity of correlated "centres" or entities of diverse nature, acting and reacting upon one another in various ways. Some of the centres, such as human beings, evolve the power of feeling, cognition, and will, while others lack such power, there being various degrees of power or lack of power. Some centres, again, are knowers, and some, objects of knowledge; some, enjoyers, and some objects of enjoyment. The various determining conditions which constitute and maintain a centre, for instance a jiva, also limit or restrict it, accounting for its actions and reactions. These determinants are the "fetters" (pāśa) which weave the whole fabric of the jiva's phenomenal life. By them it is bound and made to act like an "animal" (paśu).

Though Reality evolves, by Its own inscrutable power, into a multiplicity of centres animate and inanimate, yet in Its true nature It always remains pure Consciousness, Being, and Bliss. In the state of evolution, Reality does not cease to be Itself, though neither the act nor the fact of evolution is denied by Tantra.

Thus a finite centre in any position in the process of evolution never ceases to be a "point" of Pure Reality through which the Infinite opens Itself and through which It can be reached. When a jiva faces this point it is none other than Reality, and when it faces the veil of māyā it is finite, conditioned, and bound by fetters. Thus in every jiva-centre there are elements of both individuality and infinitude, phenomenality and reality. One direction of the functioning of māyā, called the "outgoing current," creates the jiva-centre with its fetters; a reversal of this direction, called the "return current," reveals the Infinite. Tantra (especially its disciplines prescribed in the "left-hand" path, to be explained later) shows the way to change the outgoing current into the return current, transforming what operates as a bond for the jiva into a "releaser" or "liberator." As Tantra says: "One must rise by that by which one falls"; "the very poison that kills becomes the elixir of life when used by the wise." The various impulses and desires associated with the outgoing current form, as it were, the net of the phenomenal world in which the jiva has been caught. Some of these impulses appear to be cardinal or primary knots in this net. The only question is how to transform these cardinal impulses for material enjoyment (bhoga) into spiritual experiences (yoga); how to bring about the sublimation of desires. If this can be done, what now binds will be reversed in its working, and the finite jiva will realize its identity with Infinite Reality.

The jiva, caught in the outgoing current, perceives duality and cherishes the notions of pleasure and pain, acceptance and rejection, body and soul, spirit and matter, and so on. But if the non-duality of Śiva-Śakti alone exists, as asserted by Tantra, all these distinctions must be relative. Thus the distinction between man and woman, the desire for each other which is one of the cardinal desires, and the physical union between them all belong to the relative plane, where a perennial conflict between the flesh and the Spirit is assumed, and where a jiva acts like an animal bound by the fetters of common convention. The distinction is a valid one and may even be valuable as long as the jiva remains on the relative plane. The observance of moral or social conventions, however desirable on that plane, does not make the jiva other than an animal. In order that the jiva may know that it is really Śiva (the Absolute), it must resolve every kind of duality and realize the fact that whatever exists and functions on the physical or moral level is Śiva-Śakti, the ever inseparable Reality and its Power. When one realizes that the whole process of creation, preservation, and destruction is but the manifestation of the lilā, or sportive pleasure, of Siva-Śakti, one does not see anything carnal or gross in the universe; for such a person everything becomes an expression of Śiva-Śakti. The special technique of the Tāntric discipline is to transform the outgoing current of diversification into the return current of gradual integration, to gather separation, polarity, and even opposition into identification, harmony, and peace.

The two currents, however, do not operate singly,

one excluding the other; they are concurrent, though the emphasis, which oscillates, is now laid on one and now on the other. Thus in all affirmations of duality and difference, the affirmation of non-duality and identity is immanent, and one sees unities, equalities, and similarities, and not a mere chaos of colliding particles, even when the outgoing current functions in the creation and preservation of the universe. Our ordinary experience, too, shows system, though this system reveals to us limited and conditioned identities. In brief, though differentiation is the prevailing feature of the outgoing current, identity is either implicit in it or conditionally visible.

Let us take the example of a man and woman. Subject to certain limits and conditions, the two in a way may be equated; the difference between them is patent but can be eliminated. Emphasis on the difference, however, constitutes the fetters of man and woman, as is seen in common experience. These fetters will disappear when their real identity and not their pragmatic equality is realized. Hence the question is how to affirm or rather reaffirm an identity which is veiled.

The method of Non-dualistic Vedānta is to negate all limiting adjuncts, which it calls unreal, until one sees nothing but Brahman, or pure and undifferentiated Consciousness, in the man and woman. In order to reach the affirmation of oneness, every vestige of duality must be rigorously discarded; in other words, Vedānta asks the aspirants to renounce the world of names and forms. But this is more easily said than done, for such renunciation can be practised by only a few.

Tantra, whose technique is different, prescribes the discipline of sublimation. Physical man and woman, floating along the outgoing current of the cosmic process, are, no doubt, different from each other, but by means of the return current they can be sublimated into cosmic principles and realized as the one whole, that is, Śiva-Śakti. In reversing the outgoing current, the aspirant has to "bring together" the complements or poles so as to realize their identity; thus the physical union of man and woman is sublimated into the creative union of Śiva-Śakti. The left-hand path of Tantra under certain very stringent conditions prescribes to the aspirant, or sādhaka, belonging to the "heroic" type to be described later, spiritual disciplines of ritualistic readjustment with woman, and shows how to sublimate the so-called "carnal" act gradually until the experience of the supreme non-dual Śiva-Śakti with its perfect bliss is attained. The technique is to make the very same carnal desire which constitutes the strongest fetter of the animal man an "opening" or channel for the experience of Satchidānanda. If the right track is followed and all the conditions are fulfilled, the aspirant succeeds in his endeavour.

The Tāntric method of sublimation consists of three steps: purification, elevation, and reaffirmation of identity on the plane of Pure Consciousness. First, the aspirant must rid himself of the dross of grossness by reversing the outgoing current into the return current. According to Tantra, in the process of evolution, the pure cosmic principles (tattvas) at a certain stage cross the line and pass into impure principles, the latter constituting the realm of nature, which is like a "coiled" curve, in which the jiva is held a prisoner and where it wanders, caught in a net of natural determinism from which there is no escape unless the coiled curve can be made to uncoil itself and open a channel for its release and ascent into the realm of the pure cosmic principles. Until this is done the jiva remains afloat on the outgoing current, moves with it, and cherishes desires which are gross or carnal. Whether yielding pleasure or pain, these desires fasten the chain upon it with additional links. Its hope lies in uncoiling the coil of nature that has closed upon it.

This is called in the technical language of Tantra the "awakening" of the Kundalini, or coiled-up serpent power, by which one moves from the plane of impure principles to that of pure principles. The head of this coiled serpent is turned downward; it must be turned upward. This change of the direction of the serpent power, which after evolving the jiva remains involved in it, is called purification. The next step is called elevation: the order in which the cosmic principles move along the outgoing current must be reversed with the starting of the return current. Ascent is to be made in the order that is the reverse to that in which the descent was made. The aspirant must raise himself from the grosser and more impure elements to the subtler and the purer ones until he attains to the realization of Śiva-Śakti. The last step is the reaffirmation in consciousness of his identity with Śiva-Śakti. This is the general framework of the method of sublimation into which can be fitted all the methods of sublimation followed by the Dualistic, Non-dualistic, and other systems of thought.

The spiritual awakening of a sādhaka is described in Tantra by means of the symbol of the awakening and rising of the Kundalini power. What is this Kundalini? Properly understood, it is not something mystical or esoteric, peculiar to Tantra, but the basis of the spiritual experiences described by all religious faiths. Every genuine spiritual experience, such as the seeing of light or a vision, or communion with the Deity, is only a manifestation of the ascent of the Kundalini. Let us try to understand the Kundalini with the help of an illustration from physical science. There are two kinds of energy in a particle of matter: potential and kinetic, the sum total of which is a constant. The kinetic energy, which is only a fraction of the total energy, is responsible for the movement or action of the particle. There exists a particular ratio between the kinetic and the total energy; when this ratio is changed by inter-molecular action, the nature of the particle changes: one element is transformed into another. According to Tantra, the Kundalini, in the form of cosmic energy, is present in everything, even in a particle of matter. Only a fraction of it, like the kinetic energy, is operative, while an un-measured residuum is left, like the potential energy, "coiled up" and untapped at the "base root." It is a vast magazine of power, of which the operative energy, like the kinetic energy of the particle, is only a fraction. In the jiva-centre, also, there are this potential energy of the Kundalini, which is the storehouse of the energy of the body (physical, subtle, and causal), and also the active energy of the Kundalini, which accounts for the action and movement of the jiva. The coiled-up Kundalini is the central pivot upon which the whole complex apparatus of the body and mind moves and turns. A specific ratio between the active and total energies of the Kundalini determines the present condition and behaviour of the bodily apparatus. A change in the ratio is necessary to effect a change in its present working efficiency by transforming the grosser bodily elements into finer. A transformation, dynamization, and sublimation of the physical, mental, and vital apparatus is only possible through what is called the rousing of the Kundalini and its reorientation from "downward facing" to "upward facing." By the former the physical body has been made a "coiled curve," limited in character, restricted in functions and pos-sibilities. By the force of the latter it breaks its fetters and transcends its limitations. This is the general principle. But there are different forms of spiritual disciplines by which this magazine of latent power can be acted upon. Faith and love act as a most power-ful lever to raise the coiled-up Kundalini; so also the disciplines of rājayoga and jnānayoga. The repetition of the Lord's name or a holy mantra, and even music, help in this process. Tantra recognizes all this. The student of Tantra should bear in mind the psychological aspect of the process of the rise of the Kundalini, which is more of an unfoldment, expansion, and elevation of consciousness than a mechanical accession to an increased and higher power. The aim of waking the Kundalini is not the acquisition of greater power for the purpose of performing miraculous feats or the enjoyment of material pleasures; it is the realization of Satchidānanda.

The passage of the awakened Kundalini lies through the Sushumnā, which is described as the central nerve in the nervous system. A kind of hollow canal, the Sushumnā passes through the spinal column connecting the base centre (chakra) at the bottom of the spine with the centre at the cerebrum. Tantra speaks of six centres[2] through which the Sushumnā passes; these centres are so many spheres or planes, described in Tantra as different-coloured lotuses with varying numbers of petals. In the ordinary worldly person these centres are closed, and the lotuses droop down like buds. As the Kundalini rises through the Sushumnā canal and touches the centres, these buds turn upward as fully opened flowers and the aspirant obtains spiritual experiences. The goal of spiritual practice is to make the Kundalini rise from those centres which are lower and more gross to those which are higher and more conscious. During this upward journey of the Kundalini, the jiva is not quite released from the relative state till it reaches the sixth centre or plane, which is the "opening" for the experience of Reality. At this sixth centre (the two-petalled white lotus located at the junction of the eyebrows) the jiva sheds its ego and burns the seed of duality, and its higher self rises from the ashes of its lower self. It now dies physically, as it were, in order to be able to live in Pure Consciousness. The sixth centre is the key by which the power

[2] See Glossary under Kundalini.

in the thousand-petalled lotus in the cerebrum, which is like the limitless ocean, is switched on to the little reservoir which is the individual self, filling the latter and making it overflow and cease to be the little reservoir. Finally the Kundalini rises to the lotus at the cerebrum and becomes united with Śiva, or the Absolute; and the aspirant realizes, in the transcendental consciousness, his union with Śiva-Śakti.

Tantra discusses the qualifications of the teacher and the student, and also the mantras or sacred words, the diagrams, deities, rituals, and mental dispositions important in the practice of its disciplines.

A qualified teacher, or guru, must be a man of good birth and unsullied character. Compassionate and serene, he should be versed in the Tāntric and other scriptures, repeat regularly God's holy name, and offer oblations in the sacrificial fire. Furthermore, he should possess a pleasing disposition and the power to fulfil his disciples' wishes. The help of a guru is indispensable for a student of Tantra. Vital changes take place in him as the Kundalini ascends and the impure elements of his body and mind become pure. In the practice of spiritual disciplines, the aspirant passes through a series of crises and needs outside help. It is true that the Divine Mother, who is none other than the Kundalini itself, bestows this help in the form of grace whenever a real crisis comes, but a human medium is necessary. The guru is an adept in the Tāntric practices, has experimented with its disciplines, and has verified their result for himself. The disciple does not look upon his guru as a human being, but as the embodiment of God. As the physician of the soul, the guru occupies a position of extreme responsibility, guides the disciple in difficult practices, and looks after his welfare in every respect.

Like the teacher, the disciple should come of a good family and possess a blameless character and guileless nature. Keen-minded, versed in the scriptures, and kind-hearted, he should have faith in the life after death, perform his duties toward his parents, and be free from pride of lineage, scholarship, or wealth. Furthermore, he should shun the company of non-believers and be ready to serve the teacher in all humility. The three types of aspirants will be described later.

A responsible teacher should not be in a hurry to accept a disciple, nor should an aspirant accept as his teacher a person to whom he is not attracted. The mode of initiation or instruction varies, depending upon the competence of the teacher and the qualifications of the student. An ordinary initiation is given by means of elaborate rituals. But these become secondary in the higher type of initiation, through which the disciple very soon becomes blessed with deep spiritual experiences.

Mantras play a most important part in the Tāntric discipline, just as do sacrifices and hymns in the disciplines of the Vedas and the Purānas respectively. The word *mantra* means, literally, "that which, when reflected upon, gives liberation." The mantra is the sound-equivalent of the deity, that is to say, Chit or Consciousness; the external image is the material form of the mantra. The sound-vibration is the very first manifestation of Chit and nearest to It. It is really intermediate between Pure Consciousness and the physical object, being neither absolutely immaterial like the former nor dense like the latter. Tantra regards vibration and illumination as two parallel manifestations of the same cosmic energy or Śakti, and teaches that as such they can both lead to the realization of Chit. It is the vibration created by utterance of the mantra that enables the aspirant to realize Chit, which otherwise eludes the grasp of even an intelligent person. Thus mantras are not mere words, but are forms of concentrated thought of exceeding potency; they are revealed to the seers in the hour of their illumination. The aspirant finds that a mantra and the deity with which it is associated are identical, the deity being the illumination embodied in the mantra. To the ignorant, the vibration created by the mantra is only a physical phenomenon, and the mantra itself nothing but a sound, but to the adept it is both illuminative and creative. Illumination is hidden in the mantra, like an oak tree in an acorn. As soon as this illumination is expressed, the mantra becomes endowed with a wonderful power and reveals the cosmic energy latent in it. Tantra believes that mantras have not been created by human brains, but are eternally existent, and that through their repetition the aspirant attains to perfection.

Mystical diagrams called "yantras" are used in the Tantric rituals. A yantra is a diagrammatic equivalent of the deity, just as a mantra is its sound-equivalent. It is not like the schematic sketch of a molecule, used by the chemist, but is a true representation, as revealed to the adept, of the basic power which evolves and maintains an object of worship. When the yantra is given real potency, the deity is there. In the Tāntric ritual the yantra is the real object of worship, the image being its more tangible representation. There is a fundamental relationship between the mantra and the yantra.

The image of the deity through which one communes with Ultimate Reality is also an embodiment of Consciousness and not just a figure of wood or stone. If the worship is properly performed, then the image, the mantra, the yantra, and the various other accessories of worship all become changed into forms and expressions of Consciousness, as in the Christian communion the wine and bread turn into the blood and flesh of Christ.

To the uninitiated, the mantras and the yantras employed in Tāntric worship may appear as meaningless jargon and magical diagrams. The same is true, as far as the uninformed are concerned, of all the cumbrous formulas, equations, and notations used by the chemist and the physicist. For example, $E = mc^2$ makes no more sense to the ignorant than a mantra, for instance Om or Hring. Yet the formula of Einstein has been the means of releasing the energy, of unbelievable potency, locked in the atom. The same is true of the mystical formulas used in Tantra; they are really shorthand statements of certain basic experiences. The same faithful exactitude in the ritual is demanded of the student of Tantra, and the same degree of proficiency in the understanding of mantras and yantras, as is required of the student in the physical sciences. A popular version of the Kundalini or other principles of Tantra may be given, just as one may be given of the Relativity Theory or the Quantum Mechanics; but the actual proofs lie, in the one case as in the other, in delicate experiments which are unfortunately beyond the reach and comprehension of the average individual. Tantra claims that mantras are efficacious, that the diagrams used in the worship are potent, that the deities, or devatās, are conscious entities, that supernatural powers are attained, and that the earnest aspirant experiences the rise of the Kundalini through the different spinal centres and finally realizes his identity with Satchidānanda.

Let us briefly consider a Tāntric ritual as observed in the worship. The aim of Tantra is to guide aspirants to realize both the supreme end of liberation and the secondary ends of wealth, sense-pleasure, and righteousness, according to their inner evolution and desires. It therefore lays down an endless variety of rituals suited to different times, places, and individual competencies. Usually a Tāntric ritual consists in the assigning of the different parts of the body to different deities, the purifying of the elements of the body, breath-control, meditation, imparting of life to the image, and mental and physical worship. These are all calculated to transform the worshipper, the worshipped, the accessories, and the act of worship into consciousness, which they all are in essence. As the culmination of the ritual, the aspirant realizes his oneness with all. Harmony on the physical and mental planes is necessary for success in worship; this is created in the gross physical elements by means of prescribed postures, in the vital breaths by means of breath-control, in the cerebrum by the correct utterance of mantras, and in the mental states by meditation. Ablution (snāna) purifies the physical body, and this purification is followed by an inner satisfaction (tarpana). By means of appropriate meditative rituals the gross, subtle, and causal bodies are freed of their respective taints (bhutasuddhi). The purpose of meditation (dhyāna) is to enable the worshipper to feel his oneness with the deity. This meditation on oneness, the central feature of the Tāntric worship, is quite different from that of dualistic religions, which maintain a distinction between the deity and its devotee. "Only by becoming divine can one worship the divine." The last part of the ritual consists of a sacrifice (homa) in which the devotee completely surrenders himself to the deity, merges in him, and loses his identity in him. At this stage there is no more distinction between the worshipper and the worshipped, the finite and the infinite, the individual and the Absolute.

It is claimed that Tantra is a kind of experimental science and that the realization promised by it is an experimentally verified fact. Theories and speculations are tentative only; the motto of Tantra is: "Live by what you can actually prove and verify." Nothing need be accepted on the basis of such a statement as "Thus saith the Lord." But initially it is required of the sādhaka, as in all the sciences, to follow the guidance of a teacher who has tried the experiment before him and seen the result for himself.

Several paths have been prescribed by Tantra for the awakening of the Kundalini; one of these is called

the Vāmāchāra or "left-hand" path, which, partly
on account of ignorance of the principles involved and
partly on account of its abuse by irresponsible persons,
has made the whole science of Tantra suspect. The
ritual of this path is, like other genuine spiritual practices, based upon the principle of the "return current,"
which seeks to reverse the process that creates the bonds
of the animal man. The five ingredients used by followers of this path are cereals, fish, meat, wine, and
sexual union. These, however, have different connota-
tions for different classes of aspirants. The underlying
principle of Vāmāchāra is to emphasize the fact that
a man makes progress in spiritual life not by cowardly
and falsely shunning that which makes him fall, but by
seizing upon it and sublimating it so as to make it a
means of liberation. For a certain type of aspirant,
called "heroic," the actual drinking of wine and practice of sexual union are prescribed, and the teacher
carefully points out that the joy and stimulation arising
from these are to be utilized for the uplift of the mind
from the physical plane. For instance, the aspirant is
asked to offer wine at first to the deity and then to par-
take of it as a sacramental offering. The same is the case
with cereals, fish, and meat. The pleasure resulting
from their enjoyment is gradually sublimated. Sexual
union, the disciple is taught, is something sacred, whose
purpose is the creation of new life, and it should therefore not be resorted to in an irresponsible manner.
Tantra never countenances sexual excess or irregularity
for the purpose of the gratification of carnal desire. To
break chastity, it says, is to lose or shorten life. Furthermore, sexual union has a deeper spiritual significance
in that it reveals behind duality a unity which is present in all phenomenal experiences. Even on the physical
plane, a couple becomes united in joy, but the unity
of Śiva-Śakti and the bliss derived from it are experienced only by liberated souls. Woman, associated with
the Tāntric practices in order to help man in his path

of renunciation, is an object of veneration to all schools of Tantra. She is regarded as the embodiment of Śakti, or the power that projects and pervades the universe. To insult a woman is a grievous sin. The aspirant learns from the teacher how to use the aforesaid five "ingredients" for his spiritual awakening. By the power of the mantra, the rituals, meditation, prayer, sincerity, and the grace of the guru and the Divine Mother, the disciple gradually acquires a nature by which everything he does in his ordinary life becomes an act of worship, and he develops an understanding which makes him realize what Śankarāchārya meant when he wrote in one of his hymns to the primordial Śakti: "O Lady Supreme, may all the functions of my mind be Thy remembrance, may all my words be Thy praise; may all my acts be an obeisance to Thee!"

Tantra divides sādhakas, or spiritual aspirants, into three groups according to their mental disposition: animal, heroic, and divine. The man with animal disposition (paśu) moves along the outgoing current and earns merit and demerit from his worldly activities. He has not yet raised himself above the common round of convention, nor has he cut the three knots of "hate, fear, and shame." Swayed by his passions, he is a slave of six hostile impulses: lust, greed, pride, anger, delusion, and envy. He is not allowed even to touch the five ingredients of the left-hand ritual.

The student competent for the hazardous ritual with the five ingredients already described is called a hero (vira). He has the inner strength to "play with fire" and to burn his worldly bonds with it. Established in complete self-control, he does not forget himself even in the most trying and tempting circumstances. He is a man of fearless disposition, inspiring terror in those who cherish animal propensities. Pure in motive, gentle in speech, strong in body, resourceful, courageous, intelligent, adventurous, and humble, he cherishes only what is good.

The sādhaka of divine (divya) disposition has risen above all the bonds of desire and has no desire left to sublimate. One of the Tāntric scriptures describes such an aspirant as sparing in speech, beloved of all, introspective, steady, sagacious, and solicitous about others' welfare. He never swerves from the path of truth and can do no evil. Good in every way, he is regarded as the embodiment of Śiva. In his worship he does not need physical aids for rousing his spiritual emotions; the meditative mood is spontaneous with him. He is always in ecstasy, enjoying "inner woman and wine." For the five ingredients used by a hero he substitutes consciousness (chit), bliss (ānanda), and exaltation (bhāva).

Tantra claims that its disciplines have a universal application; it admits the validity of the rituals of the Vedas, the discrimination and renunciation of the Upanishads, the purifying disciplines of rājayoga, and the passionate love for the Deity described in the Purānas. It exhorts the sādhaka to exercise will and self-effort, practise self-surrender, and long for divine grace. Tantra promises its devotees not only enjoyment of worldly happiness but also liberation, and acknowledges that the power of the Kundalini can be aroused by the sincere pursuit of the spiritual disciplines recommended by all the great religions of the world.

Glossary
and Index

GLOSSARY

āchārya Religious teacher.

adharma Unrighteousness; the opposite of dharma.

Adhyātma Rāmāyana A book dealing with the life of Rāma and harmonizing the ideals of jnāna and bhakti.

Advaita Non-duality; a school of Vedānta philosophy, teaching the oneness of God, soul, and universe, whose chief exponent was Śankarāchārya.

Advaita Goswāmi An intimate companion of Sri Chaitanya.

Adyāśakti The Primal Energy; an epithet of the Divine Mother.

ahamkāra Ego or "I-consciousness." *See* inner organs.

ajnāna A term of Vedānta philosophy meaning ignorance, individual or cosmic. According to Non-dualistic Vedānta it is responsible for the perception of multiplicity in the relative world, and also for man's bondage and suffering.

ākāśa Ether or space; the first of the five elements evolved from Brahman. It is the subtlest form of matter, into which all the elements are ultimately resolved. *See* five elements.

akshara Unchanging; also a name of Brahman.

Anāhata Śabda Another name for Om.

Ānanda Bliss.

ānandamayakośa The sheath of bliss. *See* kośa.

Ānandamayi (*Lit.*, Full of Bliss) An epithet of the Divine Mother.

ānnā A small Indian coin, one sixteenth of a rupee.

annamayakośa The gross physical sheath. *See* kośa.

ārati Worship of the Deity accompanied by the waving of lights.

Arjuna A hero of the *Mahābhārata* and the friend of Krishna. *See* Pāndavas.

artha Wealth, one of the four ends of human pursuit. *See* four fruits.

Ashtāvakra Samhitā A standard book on Advaita Vedānta.

aśvattha The peepal-tree.

Ātman The Self or Soul; denotes also the Supreme Soul, which, according to Advaita Vedānta, is one with the individual soul.

Aum Same as Om.

Avatār Incarnation of God.

avidyā A term of Vedānta philosophy meaning ignorance, cosmic or individual. *See* ajnāna.

avidyāmāyā Māyā, or illusion causing duality, has two aspects, namely, avidyāmāyā and vidyāmāyā. Avidyā-māyā, or the "māyā of ignorance," consisting of anger, passion, and so on, entangles one in worldliness. Vidyā-māyā, or the "māyā of knowledge," consisting of kindness, purity, unselfishness, and so on, leads one to liberation. Both belong to the relative world. *See* māyā.

Ayodhyā The capital of Rāma's kingdom in northern India; the modern Oudh.

babu Well-to-do gentleman; also equivalent to Mr. or Esq.

Balāi A pet name of Balarāma, Krishna's elder brother.

Balarāma Sri Krishna's elder brother.

bathing-ghat *See* ghat.

bel A tree whose leaves are sacred to Śiva; also the fruit of the same tree.

Bhagavad Gitā A well-known Hindu scripture, comprising eighteen chapters of the *Mahābhārata*.

Bhagavān (*Lit.*, One endowed with the six attributes, viz. infinite treasures, strength, glory, splendour, knowledge, and renunciation) An epithet of the Godhead; also the Personal God of the devotee.

Bhāgavata A sacred book of the Hindus, especially of the Vaishnavas, dealing with the life of Sri Krishna.

bhakta A follower of the path of bhakti, divine love; a worshipper of the Personal God.

bhakti Love of God; single-minded devotion to one's Chosen Ideal.

bhaktiyoga The path of devotion, followed by dualistic worshippers.

Bhārata A name of Arjuna.

Bhaskarananda A saint contemporary with Sri Ramakrishna.

bhāva Existence; feeling; emotion; ecstasy; samādhi; also
denotes any one of the five attitudes that a dualistic
worshipper assumes toward God. The first of these
attitudes is that of peace; assuming the other four, the
devotee regards God as the Master, Child, Friend, or
Beloved.

bhāvamukha An exalted state of spiritual experience,
in which the aspirant keeps his mind on the borderline
between the Absolute and the Relative. From this position he can contemplate the ineffable and attributeless
Brahman and also participate in the activities of the
relative world, seeing in it the manifestation of God
alone.

Bhavatārini (Lit., the Saviour of the Universe) A name
of the Divine Mother.

Bhil A savage tribe of India.

Bhishma One of the great heroes of the war of
Kurukshetra, described in the Mahābhārata.

bhoga Enjoyment.

Bibhishana A brother of Rāvana, the monster-king of
Ceylon, whom he succeeded; but, unlike him, a faithful
devotee of Rāma.

Bodha Consciousness; Absolute Knowledge.

Bodh-Gayā A place near Gayā, where Buddha attained
illumination.

Brahma The name by which the Brāhmos invoke God.

Brahmā The Creator God; the First Person of the
Hindu Trinity, the other two being Vishnu and Śiva.

brahmachāri A religious student devoted to the practice
of spiritual discipline; a celibate belonging to the first
stage of life. See four stages of life.

brahmacharya The first of the four stages of life: the
life of an unmarried student. See four stages of life.

Brahmajñāna The Knowledge of Brahman.

Brahmajñāni A knower of Brahman. Sri Ramakrishna
used the term "modern Brahmajñānis" to denote the
members of the Brāhmo Samāj.

Brahmamayi (Lit., the Embodiment of Brahman) A
name of the Divine Mother.

Brahman   The Absolute; the Supreme Reality of Vedānta philosophy.

Brahmānda   (*Lit.*, the egg of Brahmā) The universe.

Brāhmani (*Lit.*, brāhmin woman) The brāhmin woman who taught Sri Ramakrishna the Vaishnava and Tantra disciplines, also known as the Bhairavi Brāhmani.

brāhmin   A member of the priestly caste, the highest caste in Hindu society.

Brāhmo   Member of the Brāhmo Samāj.

Brāhmo Samāj   A theistic organization of India, founded by Rājā Rammohan Roy.

Braja   Same as Vrindāvan.

Buddha   (*Lit.*, one who is enlightened) The founder of Buddhism.

buddhi   The determinative faculty of the mind, which makes decisions; sometimes translated as "intellect." *See* inner organs.

Captain   Colonel Viswanath Upadhyaya of Nepal, the Resident of the Nepalese Government in Calcutta, and a devotee of Sri Ramakrishna. The Master addressed Viswanath as "Captain."

causal body   One of the three bodies or seats of the soul, the other two being the gross body and the subtle body. It is identical with deep sleep.

Chaitanya   Spiritual Consciousness; also the name of a prophet born in 1485 A.D., who lived at Navadvip, Bengal, and emphasized the path of divine love for the realization of God; he is also known as Gaurānga, Gaur, Gorā, or Nimāi. *See* Appendix A, p. 567.

Chaitanyadeva   Same as Chaitanya.

chakra   Any one of the six centres, or lotuses, in the Sushumnā, through which the Kundalini rises. *See* Kundalini.

chāmara   A fan made of a yak tail, used in the temple service.

Chandi   A sacred book of the Hindus, in which the Divine Mother is described as the Ultimate Reality.

chāndni   An open portico; the word is used in the text to denote the open portico at the Dakshineswar temple, with steps leading to the Ganges.

chātak A species of bird.

Chidākāśa The Ākāśa, or Space, of Chit, Absolute Consciousness; the All-pervading Spirit.

Chit Consciousness.

chitta The mind-stuff. *See* inner organs.

Chosen Ideal *See* Ishta.

conch-shell A trumpet used in the temple service.

dāl Lentils; also a soup made from lentils.

darśanas The six systems of orthodox Hindu philosophy, namely, the Sāmkhya of Kapila, the Yoga of Patanjali, the Vaiśeshika of Kanāda, the Nyāya of Gautama, the Purva Mimāmsā of Jaimini, and the Vedānta or Uttara Mimāmsā of Vyāsa.

Daśaratha The father of Rāma.

dāsya One of the five attitudes assumed by the dualistic worshipper toward his Chosen Ideal: the attitude of a servant toward his master.

dayā Compassion.

Dayananda The founder of the Ārya Samāj (1824-1883 A.D.).

deva (*Lit.*, shining one) A god.

Devendra(nath) Tagore A religious leader of Sri Ramakrishna's time; father of Rabindranath Tagore.

devotee The word is generally used in the text to denote one devoted to God, a worshipper of the Personal God, or a follower of the path of love. A devotee of Sri Ramakrishna is one who is devoted to Sri Ramakrishna and follows his teachings. The word "disciple," when used in connexion with the Master, refers to one who had been initiated into spiritual life by Sri Ramakrishna and who regarded Sri Ramakrishna as his guru.

dharma Righteousness, one of the four ends of human pursuit; generally translated as "religion," it signifies rather the inner principle of religion. *See* four fruits. The word is also loosely used to mean "duty."

Dhruva A saint in Hindu mythology.

Dolayātrā The Hindu spring festival associated with Sri Krishna.

Drona One of the great military teachers in the *Mahābhārata*.

Durgā A name of the Divine Mother.

Durgā Pujā The worship of Durgā; the name of a popular Hindu religious festival.

Duryodhana One of the heroes of the *Mahābhārata,* the chief rival of the Pāndava brothers.

Dvaita The philosophy of Dualism.

ego of Knowledge (of Devotion) The ego purified and illumined by the Knowledge (or Love) of God. Some souls, after realizing their oneness with Brahman in samādhi, come down to the plane of relative consciousness. In this state they retain a very faint feeling of ego so that they may teach spiritual knowledge to others. This ego, called by Sri Ramakrishna the "ego of Knowledge," does not altogether efface their knowledge of oneness with Brahman even in the relative state of consciousness. The bhakta, the lover of God, coming down to the relative plane after having attained samādhi, retains the "I-consciousness" by which he feels himself to be a lover, a child, or a servant of God. Sri Ramakrishna called this the "devotee ego," the "child ego," or the "servant ego."

eight fetters Namely, hatred, shame, lineage, pride of good conduct, fear, secretiveness, caste, and grief.

eight siddhis or occult powers A person endowed with these eight powers can make himself as small as an atom, as huge as a mountain, as heavy as the earth, as light as air; he can reach anything he likes, rule everything he wants, conquer everything, and fulfil all desires.

"Englishman" A term often used by Sri Ramakrishna in referring to men educated in English schools or influenced by European ideas.

ether Ākāśa or all-pervading space.

fakir Beggar; often a religious mendicant.

five elements Namely, ether (ākāśa), air (vāyu), fire (agni), water (ap), and earth (kshiti).

five organs of action The hands, the feet, the organ of speech, and the organs of generation and evacuation.

five sheaths *See* kośa.

five vital breaths or prānas Namely, prāna, apāna, samāna, vyāna, and udāna. These five names denote the five functions of the vital force, such as breathing, digesting, evacuating, etc.

four fruits The four ends of human pursuit, namely, dharma (righteousness), artha (wealth), kāma (fulfilment of desire), and moksha (liberation).

four stages of life Namely, brahmacharya (life of unmarried student), gārhasthya (life of married householder), vānaprastha (life of retired householder), and sannyās (life of monk).

Gangā The Ganges.

Gangāsāgar The mouth of the Ganges at the Bay of Bengal, considered a sacred place by the Hindus.

garden house A rich man's country house set in a garden.

Gaur Short for Gaurānga.

Gaurānga A name of Sri Chaitanya.

Gauri (Lit., of fair complexion) A name of the Divine Mother; also the name of a pundit devoted to Sri Ramakrishna.

Gayā A sacred place in northern India.

Gāyatri A sacred verse of the Vedas recited daily by Hindus of the three upper castes after they have been invested with the sacred thread; also the presiding deity of the Gāyatri.

gerruā (Lit., ochre) The ochre cloth of a monk.

ghāt Bathing place on a lake or river.

Gitā Same as the Bhagavad Gitā.

golakdhām A game in which the player tries to get to "heaven" by passing through different planes; on each false step he falls into a particular "hell."

Gopāla The Baby Krishna.

gopis The milkmaids of Vrindāvan, companions and devotees of Sri Krishna.

Gorā A name of Sri Chaitanya.

goswāmi Vaishnava priest.

Govardhan A hill near Vrindāvan, which Sri Krishna lifted with His finger to protect the villagers from a deluge of rain.

Govinda(ji) A name of Sri Krishna.

guna   According to Sāmkhya philosophy, Prakriti (Nature or matter) consists of three gunas (usually translated as "qualities") known as sattva, rajas, and tamas. Tamas stands for inertia or dullness; rajas, for activity or restlessness; sattva, for balance or righteousness.

guru(deva)   Spiritual teacher.

Gurumahārāj   A respectful way of referring to the guru.

Haladhari   A priest in the temple garden at Dakshineswar and a cousin of Sri Ramakrishna.

Hāldārpukur   A small lake at Kāmārpukur.

Hanumān   The great monkey devotee of Rāma, mentioned in the *Rāmāyana*.

Hārdwār   A sacred place on the bank of the Ganges at the foot of the Himālayas.

Hari   God; a name of Vishnu, the Ideal Deity of the Vaishnavas.

Hari Om   Sacred words by which God is often invoked.

hathayoga   A school of yoga that aims chiefly at physical health and well-being.

hathayogi   A student of hathayoga.

Hazra   A devotee who lived at the Dakshineswar temple garden and was of a perverse disposition.

"hero"   A religious aspirant described in the Tantra, who is permitted sexual intercourse under certain conditions.

hide-and-seek   The Indian game of hide-and-seek, in which the leader, known as the "granny," bandages the eyes of the players and hides herself. The players are supposed to find her. If any player can touch her, the bandage is removed from his eyes and he is released from the game.

Holy Mother   The name by which Sri Ramakrishna's wife was known among his devotees.

homa   A Vedic sacrifice in which oblations are offered into a fire.

Hriday   Sri Ramakrishna's nephew, who served as his attendant during the period of his spiritual discipline. He was expelled from the temple garden at Dakshineswar on account of an action which displeased the temple authorities.

Hrishikesh A village on the Ganges at the foot of the Himālayas, where sādhus practise austerities.

hubble-bubble A water-pipe for smoking.

Ida A nerve in the spinal column. *See* Sushumnā.

inner organs The four inner organs of perception, namely, manas (mind), buddhi (determinative faculty), chitta (mind-stuff), and ahamkāra ("I-consciousness").

Ishan A name of Śiva; also the name of a devotee of Sri Ramakrishna.

Ishta(deva) The Chosen Ideal, Spiritual Ideal, or Ideal Deity of the devotee.

Iśvara The Personal God.

Iśvarakoti A perfected soul born with a special spiritual message for humanity. "An Incarnation of God or one born with some of the characteristics of an Incarnation is called an Iśvarakoti." (Sri Ramakrishna)

jada samādhi Communion with God in which the aspirant appears lifeless, like an inert object.

Jagannāth The Lord of the Universe; a name of Vishnu.

jal The Bengali word for water.

Jamunā The sacred river Jumnā, a tributary of the Ganges.

Janaka, King One of the ideal kings in Hindu mythology and the father of Sitā. Sri Ramakrishna often described him as the ideal householder, who combined yoga with enjoyment of the world.

japa Repetition of God's name.

jilipi A kind of sweetmeat.

jiva The embodied soul; a living being; an ordinary man.

jivanmukta One liberated from māyā while living in the body.

jivātmā The embodied soul.

jnāna Knowledge of God arrived at through reasoning and discrimination; also denotes the process of reasoning by which the Ultimate Truth is attained. The word is generally used to denote the knowledge by which one is aware of one's identity with Brahman.

jnānayoga The path of knowledge, consisting of discrimination, renunciation, and other disciplines.

jnāni One who follows the path of knowledge and discrimination to realize God; generally used to denote
a Non-dualist; wise person.

Kailās A peak of the Himālayas, regarded as the sacred
abode of Śiva.

Kāli A name of the Divine Mother; the presiding Deity
of the Dakshineswar temple. She is often referred to
and addressed by Sri Ramakrishna as the Ādyāśakti, the
Primal Energy.

Kālighāt A section of northern Calcutta, where is situated
the famous temple of Kāli.

Kāliyadaman Ghāt A bathing place on the Jamunā at
Vrindāvan, where Sri Krishna subdued the snake
Kāliya.

Kaliyuga One of the four yugas or cycles. See yuga.

Kalpataru The Wish-fulfilling Tree; refers to God.

Kalpa-tree Same as Kalpataru.

kāma Fulfilment of desire, one of the four ends of human
pursuit. See four fruits.

Kamalākānta A mystic poet of Bengal.

kamandalu The water-bowl of a monk.

Kāmārpukur Sri Ramakrishna's birthplace.

kāminikānchan (Lit., "woman" and "gold") A term used
by Sri Ramakrishna to refer to lust and greed.

Kānāi A pet name of the youthful Sri Krishna.

Kānchi A holy place in southern India.

Kapila A great sage in Hindu mythology, the reputed
author of the Sāmkhya philosophy.

karma Action in general; duty; ritualistic worship.

karmayoga (Lit., union with God through action) The
path by which the aspirant seeks to realize God through
work without attachment; also the ritualistic worship
prescribed in the scriptures for realizing God.

Kartābhajā A minor Vaishnava sect which teaches that
men and women should live together in the relationship
of love and gradually idealize their love by looking on
each other as divine.

Kāśi Benares.

kathak A professional reciter of stories from the Purāna
in an assembly.

kavirāj Native physician of India.

kāyastha One of the subsidiary castes in Bengal.

Keshab (Chandra Sen) The celebrated Brāhmo leader (1838-1884 A.D.).

kirtan Devotional music, often accompanied by dancing.

kośa (Lit., sheath or covering) The following are the five kośas as described in the Vedānta philosophy: (1) the annamayakośa, or gross physical sheath, made of and sustained by food; (2) the prānamayakośa, or vital sheath, consisting of the five prānas or vital breaths; (3) the manomayakośa, or mental sheath; (4) the vijnānamayakośa, or sheath of intelligence; and (5) the ānandamayakośa, or sheath of bliss. These five sheaths cover the Soul, which is the innermost reality of the jiva and is untouched by the characteristics of the sheaths.

Krishna An Incarnation of God whose life is given in the Bhāgavata and the Mahābhārata.

kshara Changeable.

kshatriya A member of the second or warrior caste in Hindu society.

Kundalini (Lit., the Serpent Power) It is the spiritual energy lying dormant in all individuals. According to the Tantra there are six centres in the body, designated as Mulādhāra, Svādhisthāna, Manipura, Anāhata, Viśuddha, and Ājnā. These are the dynamic centres where the spiritual energy becomes vitalized and finds special expression with appropriate spiritual perception and mystic vision. These centres, placed in the Sushumnā, form the ascending steps by which the Kundalini, or spiritual energy, passes from the foot of the spine to the cerebrum. When an easy pathway is formed along the Sushumnā through these centres, and the Kundalini encounters no resistance in its movements upward and downward, then there is the Shatchakrabheda, which means, literally, the penetrating of the six chakras, or mystic centres. The Mulādhāra chakra, situated between the base of the sexual organ and the anus, is regarded as the seat of the Kundalini. The centres are metaphorically described as lotuses. The Mulādhāra is said to be a four-petalled lotus of a red colour. The Svādhisthāna chakra, situated at the base of the sexual organ, is a six-petalled vermilion lotus. The Manipura, situated in the region of the navel, contains ten petals and is bluish, like a rain-cloud. The Anāhata, placed in the region of the heart, is a twelve-petalled scarlet lotus. The Viśuddha, at the lower end of the throat, has sixteen petals and is smoky purple. The Ājnā, situated in the space between the eyebrows, is a two-petalled white lotus. In the cerebrum there is the Sahasrāra, the thousand-petalled lotus, the abode of Śiva, which is as white as the silvery full moon, as bright as lightning, and as mild and serene as moonlight. This is the highest goal, and here the awakened spiritual energy manifests itself in its full glory and splendour.

kuthi The bungalow in the Dakshineswar temple garden, where the proprietors and their guests stayed while visiting Dakshineswar.

Lakshmi The Consort of Vishnu and Goddess of Fortune.
lilā The divine play; the Relative. The creation is often explained by the Vaishnavas as the lilā of God, a conception that introduces elements of spontaneity and freedom into the universe. As a philosophical term, the Lilā (the Relative) is the correlative of the Nitya (the Absolute).
lotus Each of the six centres along the Sushumnā is called a lotus, since they have a form like that of a lotus blossom. See Kundalini.
luchi A thin bread made of flour and fried in butter.

M Mahendranath Gupta, one of Sri Ramakrishna's foremost householder disciples and the recorder of *The Gospel of Sri Ramakrishna*.
Madan A Bengali mystic and writer of songs.
Mādhava A name of Sri Krishna.
madhur One of the five attitudes cherished by the Vaishnava worshipper toward his Ideal Deity, Krishna: the attitude of a wife toward her husband or of a woman toward her paramour.
Mahābhārata A famous Hindu epic.
mahābhāva The most intense ecstatic love of God.

Mahākārana   (*Lit.*, the Great Cause) The Transcendental Reality.

Mahāmāyā   The Great Illusionist; a name of Kāli, the Divine Mother.

Mahānirvāna   The great Nirvāna or samādhi.

Mahānirvāna Tantra   A standard book on Tantra philosophy.

Maharshi   (*Lit.*, a great rishi or seer of truth) An epithet often applied to Devendranath Tagore, the father of the poet Rabindranath.

Mahāshtami   The second day of the worship of Durgā, the Divine Mother.

mahātmā   A high-souled person.

Mahāvir   (*Lit.*, great hero) A name of Hanumān, the monkey devotee of Rāma.

māhut   Elephant-driver.

Maidān   A great open park in Calcutta.

Malaya breeze   The fragrant breeze that blows from the Malaya (Western Ghāt) Mountains.

manas   Mind. See inner organs.

Manikarnikā Ghāt   The famous cremation ground in Benares.

Manipura   The third centre in the Sushumnā. See Kundalini.

manomayakośa   The mental sheath. See kośa.

mantra   Holy Sanskrit text; also the sacred formula used in japa.

Manu   The celebrated lawgiver of ancient India, who is supposed to be the author of the *Manusamhitā* or *Code of Manu*.

Manusamhitā   A book on Hindu law by Manu.

math   Monastery.

Mathur Babu   The son-in-law of Rāni Rasmani, and a great devotee of Sri Ramakrishna, whom he provided with all the necessities of life at the temple garden.

māyā   A term of Vedānta philosophy denoting ignorance obscuring the vision of God; the Cosmic Illusion on account of which the One appears as many, the Absolute as the Relative; it is also used to denote attachment.

"māyā of ignorance"   See avidyāmāyā.

"māyā of knowledge"   See avidyāmāyā.

māyāvādi A follower of the māyā theory of the Vedānta philosophy, according to which the world of names and forms is illusory, like a dream.

mlechchha A non-Hindu, a barbarian. This is a term of reproach applied by orthodox Hindus to foreigners, who do not conform to the established usages of Hindu religion and society. The word corresponds to the "heathen" of the Christians and the "kafir" of the Mussalmāns.

moksha Liberation or final emancipation, one of the four ends of human pursuit. *See* four fruits.

mridanga An earthen drum used in devotional music.

mukti Liberation from the bondage of the world, which is the goal of spiritual practice.

Mulādhāra The first and lowest centre in the Sushumnā. *See* Kundalini.

Mussalmān A follower of Mohammed.

nahabat Music tower.

Nānak The founder of the Śikh religion and the first of the ten Gurus of the Śikhs. He was born in the Punjab in 1469 A.D. and died in 1538.

Nangtā (*Lit.,* the Naked One) By this name Sri Ramakrishna referred to Totapuri, the sannyāsi who initiated him into monastic life and who went about naked.

Nārada A great sage and lover of God in Hindu mythology.

Naralīlā God manifesting Himself as man.

Nārāyana A name of Vishnu.

Naren Same as Narendranath.

Narendra(nath) A disciple of Sri Ramakrishna, subsequently world-famous as Swami Vivekananda.

Narmadā A river in central India flowing into the Arabian Sea.

nātmandir A spacious hall supported by pillars in front of a temple, meant for devotional music, religious assemblies, and the like.

Navadvip A town in Bengal which was the birthplace of Sri Chaitanya.

Navavidhān (*Lit.,* the New Dispensation) The name of

the Brāhmo Samāj organized by Keshab Chandra Sen after his disagreement with some of the members of the Brāhmo Samāj.

neem A tree with bitter leaves.

"Neti, neti" (*Lit.*, "Not this, not this") The negative process of discrimination, advocated by the followers of Non-dualistic Vedānta.

New Dispensation *See* Navavidhān.

ni The seventh note in the Indian musical scale.

Nimāi A familiar name of Sri Chaitanya.

Niranjan One of the intimate disciples of Sri Rama-krishna.

Nirguna Brahman (*Lit.*, Brahman without attributes) A term used to describe the Absolute.

Nirvāna Final absorption in Brahman, or the All-per-vading Reality, by the annihilation of the individual ego.

nirvikalpa samādhi The highest state of samādhi, in which the aspirant realizes his total oneness with Brahman.

Nitāi A pet name of Nityānanda.

Nitya The Absolute.

Nityānanda (*Lit.*, Eternal Bliss) The name of a beloved disciple and companion of Sri Chaitanya.

nityasiddha (*Lit.*, eternally perfect) A term used by Sri Ramakrishna to describe some of his young disciples endowed with great spiritual power.

Nyāya Indian Logic, one of the six systems of orthodox Hindu philosophy, founded by Gautama.

ochre cloth The garment of ochre colour used by Vedāntic sannyāsis.

Olcott, Col. One of the well-known leaders of the Theo-sophical Society.

Om The most sacred word of the Vedas; also written as Aum. It is a symbol of God and of Brahman.

Padmalochan A great pundit of Bengal, who recognized the true significance of Sri Ramakrishna's spiritual experiences.

pāgli Mad woman.

Panchavati A grove of five sacred trees planted by Sri

Ramakrishna in the temple garden at Dakshineswar for his practice of spiritual discipline.

Pāndava(s)   The five sons of Pāndu: King Yudhisthira, Arjuna, Bhima, Nakula, and Sahadeva. They are some of the chief heroes of the *Mahābhārata*.

pāni   Water.

paramahamsa   One belonging to the highest order of sannyāsis.

Paramahamsa(deva)   A name for Sri Ramakrishna.

Paramātman   The Supreme Soul.

Pārvati   Daughter of King Himālaya; the Consort of Śiva, She is regarded as an Incarnation of the Divine Mother; one of Her names is Umā.

Pātanjala   One of the six systems of orthodox Hindu philosophy, also known as Yoga philosophy.

Pāvhāri Bābā   An ascetic and yogi of great distinction who was a contemporary of Sri Ramakrishna.

Phalgu   A river in northern India which flows under a surface of sand.

Pingalā   A nerve in the spinal column. *See* Sushumnā.

Prabhās   A holy place in Kathiawar, in western India, where Sri Krishna gave up His body.

Prahlāda   A great devotee of Vishnu, whose life is described in the Purāna. While a boy, he was tortured for his piety by his father, the demon King Hiranyakaśipu. The Lord, in His Incarnation as Man-lion, slew the father.

Prakriti   Primordial Nature; the material substratum of the creation, consisting of sattva, rajas, and tamas.

prāna   The vital breath that sustains life in a physical body. *See* five vital breaths.

prānamayakośa   The vital sheath, consisting of the five prānas. *See* kośa.

prasād   Food or drink that has been offered to the Deity; also the leavings of a meal partaken by a holy man. It is regarded as possessing spiritual merit.

prema   Ecstatic love of the most intense kind.

premā-bhakti   Ecstatic love of God.

pujā   Ritualistic worship.

Purāna(s)   Books of Hindu mythology.

Puri Situated in Orissa; it is one of the four principal holy places of India, the other three being Dwārakā, Kedārnāth, and Rāmeśwar; also one of the ten denominations of monks belonging to the school of Śankara.

Purusha (*Lit.*, a man) A term of the Sāmkhya philosophy, denoting the individual conscious principle; the universe evolves from the union of Prakriti and Purusha. The word also denotes the soul and the Absolute.

Qualified Non-dualism A school of Vedānta founded by Rāmānuja, according to which the soul and Nature are the modes of Brahman, and the individual soul is a part of Brahman.

Rādhā Sri Krishna's most intimate companion among the gopis of Vrindāvan.

Rādhākānta (*Lit.*, the Consort of Rādhā) A name of Sri Krishna.

Rādhikā Same as Rādhā.

rāga-bhakti Supreme love, making one attached only to God.

Raghuvir A name of Rāma; the Family Deity of Sri Ramakrishna.

Rājā (*Lit.*, king) A title of honour.

Rājarājeśvari (*Lit.*, the Empress of kings) A name of the Divine Mother.

rajas The principle of activity or restlessness. *See* guna.

rājasic Pertaining to, or possessed of, rajas.

Rāma(chandra) The hero of the *Rāmāyana*, regarded by the Hindus as a Divine Incarnation.

Rāmānuja A famous saint and philosopher of southern India, the founder of the school of Qualified Non-dualism (1017-1137 A.D.).

Rāmāyana A famous Hindu epic.

Rāmeśwar Situated at the southernmost extremity of India and considered one of its four principal holy places, the other three being Dwārakā, Kedārnāth, and Puri.

Ramlal A nephew of Sri Ramakrishna, and a priest in the Kāli temple at Dakshineswar.

Rāmlīlā A Hindu religious festival depicting Rāma's

life, which is observed annually by the Hindus of northern India.

Rāmprasād A Bengali mystic and writer of songs about the Divine Mother.

Rāni (*Lit.*, queen) A title of honour conferred on a woman.

Rasmani, Rāni A wealthy woman of the śudra caste, the foundress of the Kāli temple at Dakshineswar.

Rāvana The monster-king of Ceylon, who forcibly abducted Sitā, the wife of Rāma.

rishi A seer of truth; the name is also applied to the pure souls to whom were revealed the words of the Vedas.

rudrāksha Beads made from rudrāksha pits, used in making rosaries.

sā, re, gā, mā, pā, dhā, ni The notes of the Indian musical scale, corresponding to do, re, mi, fa, sol, la, si.

sādhaka An aspirant devoted to the practice of spiritual discipline.

sādhanā Spiritual discipline.

Sādhāran Brāhmo Samāj A branch of the Brāhmo Samāj.

sādhu Holy man; a term generally used with reference to a monk.

Saguna Brahman Brahman with attributes; the Absolute conceived as the Creator, Preserver, and Destroyer of the universe; also the Personal God according to Vedānta.

Sahasrāra The thousand-petalled lotus in the cerebrum. *See* Kundalini.

Śaiva A worshipper of Śiva.

sakhya One of the five attitudes cherished by the dualistic worshipper toward his Chosen Ideal: the attitude of one friend toward another.

Śākta A worshipper of Śakti, the Divine Mother, according to the Tantra philosophy.

Śakti Power, generally the Creative Power of Brahman; a name of the Divine Mother.

samādhi Ecstasy, trance, communion with God.

Sāmkhya One of the six systems of orthodox Hindu philosophy; founded by Kapila.

Sanātana Dharma (*Lit.*, the Eternal Religion) Refers to Hinduism, formulated by the rishis of the Vedas.

sandesh A Bengali sweetmeat made of cheese and sugar.

sandhyā Devotions or ritualistic worship performed by caste Hindus every day at stated periods.

Śankara A name of Śiva; also short for Śankarāchārya, the great Vedāntist philosopher.

Śankarāchārya One of the greatest philosophers of India, an exponent of Advaita Vedānta (788-820 A.D.).

sannyās The monastic life, the last of the four stages of life. *See* four stages of life.

sannyāsi A Hindu monk.

śanta One of the five attitudes cherished by the dualistic worshipper toward his Chosen Ideal. It is the attitude of peace and serenity, in contrast with the other attitudes of love, which create discontent and unrest in the minds of devotees on account of their separation from God. Many Vaishnavas do not recognize the attitude of śanta, since it is not characterized by an intense love of God.

Śāntih Peace.

Sarada Devi The name of Sri Ramakrishna's wife, also known as the Holy Mother.

Sarasvati The goddess of learning and music.

sāri A woman's wearing-cloth.

Sat Reality, Being.

Satchidānanda (*Lit.*, Existence-Knowledge-Bliss Absolute) A name of Brahman, the Ultimate Reality.

sattva The principle of balance or righteousness. *See* guna.

sāttvic Pertaining to, or possessed of, sattva.

Śikhs A religious and martial sect of the Punjab.

Śitā The wife of Rāma.

Śiva The Destroyer God; the Third Person of the Hindu Trinity, the other two being Brahmā and Vishnu.

six passions Namely, lust, anger, avarice, delusion, pride, and envy.

six systems *See* darśanas.

"Soham" (*Lit.*, "I am He") One of the sacred formulas of the Non-dualistic Vedāntist.

Sonthāls A savage tribe of central India.

śrāddha   A religious ceremony in which food and drink
   are offered to deceased relatives.
Sri   The word is often used as an honorific prefix to the
   names of deities and eminent persons; or celebrated works
   generally of a sacred character; also used as an auspicious sign at the commencement of letters, manu-
   scripts, etc.
Sridāma   A devotee and companion of Sri Krishna.
Subhadrā   The sister of Sri Krishna.
subtle body   One of the three bodies or seats of the soul.
   At death the subtle body accompanies the soul in its
   transmigration; during the dream state the soul identifies
   itself with the subtle body. See causal body.
śudra   A member of the fourth or labouring caste in
   Hindu society.
Śuka(deva)   The narrator of the Bhāgavata and son of
   Vyāsa, regarded as one of India's ideal monks.
Sumeru   The sacred Mount Meru of Hindu mythology,
   around which all the planets are said to revolve.
Sushumnā   Sushumnā, Idā, and Pingala are the three
   prominent nādis, or nerves, among the innumerable
   nerves in the nervous system. Of these, again, the
   Sushumnā is the most important, being the point of
   harmony of the other two and lying, as it does, between
   them. The Idā is on the left side, and the Pingalā on
   the right. The Sushumnā, through which the awakened
   spiritual energy rises, is described as the Brahmavart-
   man, or Pathway to Brahman. The Idā and Pingalā are
   outside the spine; the Sushumnā is situated within the
   spinal column and extends from the base of the spine
   to the brain. See Kundalini.
Svādhisthāna   The second centre in the Sushumnā. See
   Kundalini.
Swami   (Lit., lord) A title of the monks belonging to
   the Vedānta school.
swastyayana   A religious rite performed to secure welfare
   or avert a calamity.
Śyāmā   (Lit., the Dark One) A name of Kāli, the Divine
   Mother.

Tagore   An aristocratic brāhmin family of Bengal.

tamāla   A tree with dark blue leaves, a favourite tree of Sri Krishna.

tamas   The principle of inertia or dullness. *See* guna.

tāmasic   Pertaining to, or possessed of, tamas.

tānpurā   A stringed musical instrument.

Tantra   A system of religious philosophy in which the Divine Mother, or Power, is the Ultimate Reality; also the scriptures dealing with this philosophy.

Tantric   A follower of Tantra; also, pertaining to Tantra.

tapasyā   Religious austerity.

tarpan   A ceremony in which a libation of water is made to dead relatives.

Totapuri   The sannyāsi who initiated Sri Ramakrishna into monastic life.

Trailanga Swami   A holy man who lived in Benares and was a contemporary of Sri Ramakrishna.

tulsi   A plant sacred to Vishnu.

Tulsi(dās)   A great devotee of Rāma and the writer of a life of Rāma.

Turiya   (*Lit.*, the fourth)   A name of the Transcendental Brahman, which both transcends and pervades the three states of waking, dream, and deep sleep.

Uddhava   The name of a follower of Sri Krishna.

upādhi   A term of Vedānta philosophy denoting a limitation imposed upon the Self or upon Brahman through ignorance.

Upanishad(s)   The well-known scriptures of the Hindus.

vaidhi-bhakti   Devotion to God associated with rites and ceremonies prescribed in the scriptures.

Vaikuntha   The heaven of the Vaishnavas.

Vaiśākh   The first month of the Hindu calendar, falling in the summer season.

Vaishnava   (*Lit.*, follower of Vishnu)   A member of the well-known dualistic sect of that name, generally the followers of Sri Chaitanya in Bengal and of Rāmānuja and Madhva in south India.

vaiśya   A member of the third or merchant caste in Hindu society.

Vālmiki   The author of the *Rāmāyana*.

Varuna The presiding deity of the ocean in Hindu mythology.

Vasus A class of celestial beings.

vātsalya One of the five attitudes cherished by the dualistic worshipper toward his Chosen Ideal: the attitude of a mother toward her child.

Vedānta (*Lit.*, the conclusion or the essence of the Vedas) A system of philosophy ascribed to Vyāsa, discussed mainly in the Upanishads, the Bhagavad Gītā, and the *Brahma Sutras*.

Vedāntist A follower of Vedānta.

Veda(s) The most sacred scriptures of the Hindus.

Videha (*Lit.*, detached from the body) An epithet given to King Janaka on account of the spirit of detachment he showed toward the world.

vidyā Knowledge leading to liberation, i.e. to the Ultimate Reality.

vidyāmāyā The "māyā of knowledge." *See* avidyāmāyā.

Vidyāsāgar, Iswar Chandra A great educator and philanthropist of Bengal.

Vijayā day The last day of the worship of Durgā, when the image is immersed in water.

vijnāna Special Knowledge of the Absolute, by which one affirms the universe and sees it as the manifestation of Brahman.

vijnānamayakośa The sheath of intelligence. *See* kośa.

vijnāni One endowed with vijnāna.

vilwa Same as bel.

vinā A stringed musical instrument.

Virāt The first manifestation of Brahman in Hindu cosmology; the Spirit in the form of the universe; the All-pervading Spirit.

Viśālākshi (*Lit.*, the Large-eyed One) A name of the Divine Mother; also the name of a stream near Kāmārpukur.

Vishnu The Preserver God; the Second Person of the Hindu Trinity, the other two being Brahmā and Śiva; the Personal God of the Vaishnavas.

Viśishtādvaita The philosophy of Qualified Non-dualism.

Viswanath *See* Captain.

viveka Discrimination.

Vivekachudāmani   A treatise on Vedānta by Śankara.

Vrindāvan   A town on the bank of the Jamunā river associated with Sri Krishna's childhood.

Vyāsa   The compiler of the Vedas and father of Śukadeva.

"Woman" and "gold"   *See* footnote p. 128.

Yaśodā   Sri Krishna's foster-mother.

yoga   Union of the individual soul and the Universal Soul; also the method by which to realize this union.

Yogavāśishtha   The name of a well-known book on Vedānta.

yogi   One who practises yoga.

yogini   Woman yogi.

Yogopanishad   The name of an Upanishad.

Yudhisthira, King   One of the principal heroes of the *Mahābhārata,* known for his truthfulness, righteousness, and piety. *See* Pāndavas.

yuga   A cycle or world period. According to Hindu mythology, the duration of the world is divided into four yugas, namely, Satya, Tretā, Dwāpara, and Kali. In the first, also known as the Golden Age, there is a great preponderance of virtue among men, but with each succeeding yuga virtue diminishes and vice increases. In the Kaliyuga there is a minimum of virtue and a great excess of vice. The world is said to be now passing through the Kaliyuga.

zemindar   Landlord.

INDEX